THE PRESENT LAW OF
ABUSE OF LEGAL PROCEDURE

THE PRESENT LAW OF
ABUSE OF LEGAL PROCEDURE

BY

PERCY HENRY WINFIELD, LL.D.

OF ST JOHN'S COLLEGE, CAMBRIDGE, AND THE INNER TEMPLE,
BARRISTER-AT-LAW; LECTURER IN LAW AT ST JOHN'S
AND TRINITY COLLEGES, CAMBRIDGE

CAMBRIDGE
AT THE UNIVERSITY PRESS
1921

CAMBRIDGE UNIVERSITY PRESS
Cambridge, New York, Melbourne, Madrid, Cape Town,
Singapore, São Paulo, Delhi, Mexico City

Cambridge University Press
The Edinburgh Building, Cambridge CB2 8RU, UK

Published in the United States of America by Cambridge University Press, New York

www.cambridge.org
Information on this title: www.cambridge.org/9781107639393

© Cambridge University Press 1921

This publication is in copyright. Subject to statutory exception
and to the provisions of relevant collective licensing agreements,
no reproduction of any part may take place without the written
permission of Cambridge University Press.

First published 1921
First paperback edition 2013

A catalogue record for this publication is available from the British Library

ISBN 978-1-107-63939-3 Paperback

Cambridge University Press has no responsibility for the persistence or
accuracy of URLs for external or third-party internet websites referred to in
this publication, and does not guarantee that any content on such websites is,
or will remain, accurate or appropriate.

PREFACE

THIS book is supplementary to the author's *History of Conspiracy and Abuse of Legal Procedure* published this year by the Cambridge University Press in the series entitled *Cambridge Studies in English Legal History*. As was pointed out in the Preface to that book, the scope of the series made it necessary to split into two books what was originally intended to be one volume. In general, the line of cleavage between the history and the present law was tolerably well-marked, but in Embracery, Misconduct of Jurors, and Frivolous Arrests, it was so blurred as to make separation impracticable. The present law relating to these topics will therefore be found in Chapters VII and VIII of the *History of Conspiracy and Abuse of Legal Procedure*.

The law relating to Perjury is so easily accessible in the textbooks on Criminal Law, and Contempt of Court has been so thoroughly explored by Mr Oswald, that the inclusion of them in this book would have added nothing to it except bulk.

The time will come when the law reformer will lay his hand upon abuse of legal procedure, and the author would respectfully suggest that a little extension of the law of Conspiracy would suffice to cover all the ground occupied by Embracery, Common Barratry, and (at least on their criminal side) Maintenance and Champerty. Indeed, it would be merely harking back to the original idea of Conspiracy, which at its birth was implicated almost exclusively with abuse of legal procedure; and it would also be in keeping with the modern tendency to widen the law of Conspiracy. Reform would thus take the line of least resistance with respect both to the past and to the present, and the happy despatch would be given to some cataleptic parts of the law, whose very names are unfamiliar to many practitioners.

PREFACE

The author gladly repeats from the Preface of his earlier book the expression of his sincere gratitude to his friend, Professor Hazeltine, for his continuous help and encouragement; and to the past and present editors of the *Law Quarterly Review*—Sir Frederick Pollock and Mr A. E. Randall—for their kindness in allowing parts of this book (when the war interrupted its completion) to be published in the *Review*. The care and courtesy of the staff of the Cambridge University Press have also been greatly appreciated.

P. H. W.

10 *August* 1921.

CONTENTS

	PAGES
PREFACE	v—vi
INDEX OF STATUTES	x—xi
INDEX OF CASES	xii—xix
INDEX OF YEAR BOOKS	xx

CHAP.

I MAINTENANCE AND CHAMPERTY AS TORTS 1–93

PRELIMINARY	1–2
ARRANGEMENT OF CHAPTER	2
PERSONAL DISABILITIES	3–4
LOCALITY OF WRONG	4
PROCEEDINGS CAPABLE OF INTERFERENCE	4–10
WHAT IS INTERFERENCE?	10–21
DEFENCES	21–84
(1) Professional legal assistance.	22–28
(2) Kinship	28–31
(3) Contingent and reversionary interests	31–34
(4) Master and servant	34–39
(5) Assistance to poor.	40–41
(6) Compulsion by law	41–42
(7) Friendship and courtesy	42–44
(8) Assignment of choses in action	44–69
(9) Interest of other kinds	69–84
REMEDIES	84–90
BURDEN OF PROOF	90–93

viii CONTENTS

CHAP.   PAGES

II MAINTENANCE AND CHAMPERTY AS
AFFECTING CONTRACTS 94–111

ARRANGEMENT OF CHAPTER 94

PERSONS 94–106

PLACE 106–107

PROCEEDINGS CAPABLE OF INTERFERENCE . . 107

WHAT IS INTERFERENCE? 107–109

DEFENCES 109–111

REMEDIES 111

BURDEN OF PROOF 111

III MAINTENANCE AND CHAMPERTY AS
CRIMES 112–116

IV AGREEMENTS AFFECTING LEGAL PRO-
CEDURE OTHERWISE THAN BY WAY OF
MAINTENANCE OR CHAMPERTY . . 117–157

ARRANGEMENT OF CHAPTER 117

AGREEMENTS IN RESTRAINT OF CRIMINAL PRO-
CEDURE 117–140

AGREEMENTS IN RESTRAINT OF CIVIL PROCEDURE . 140–145

AGREEMENTS GROUNDING CRIMINAL LIABILITY . 146–157

V CRIMINAL CONSPIRACY TO ABUSE PRO-
CEDURE 158–173

COMBINATION 158–165

FALSITY AND MALICE 165–170

PURPOSE OF COMBINATION 170–173

VI MALICIOUS PROSECUTION 174–204

WHAT IS A PROSECUTION? 174–181

FAVOURABLE ENDING OF PROSECUTION . . . 181–187

CONTENTS

CHAP.   PAGES

VI (*cont.*)

 Lack of reasonable and probable cause . . 187–196

 Malice 196–197

 Scope of action as to persons 197–199

 Scope of action as to matter 199–204

VII ABUSE OF PROCEDURE BY JUDICIAL OFFICERS 205–228

 Arrangement of chapter 205

 Judicial officers in general 205–216

  Civil remedies 205–212
  Criminal remedies 212–215
  Other remedies 215

 Justices of peace 216–227

  Civil remedies 216–224
  Criminal remedies 224–226
  Other remedies 226

 Bribery 227–228

 Extortion 228

VIII PREVENTIVE PROCEEDINGS 229–243

 Arrangement of chapter 229

 Criminal procedure 229–236

 Civil procedure 236–238

 Summary interference of court . . . 238–243

 Writ of prohibition 243

GENERAL INDEX 244–256

a 5

INDEX OF STATUTES

3 Ed. I. c 25 (maintenance and champerty), 6, 94, 112
—— c. 26 (extortion), 42, 89, 95, 96, 112
—— c. 28 (maintenance and champerty), 95, 112
—— c. 29 (deceit), 116
12 Ed. I. c. 4 (Statutum Walliae), 146
13 Ed. I. c. 49 (maintenance and champerty), 14, 30, 95, 96, 112
21 Ed. I (?) (Statutum de Conspiratoribus), 6, 112
28 Ed. I. c. 11 (maintenance and champerty), 6, 22, 25, 27, 28, 30, 31, 32, 42, 83, 84, 89, 111, 112, 113
25 Ed. III. st. 5, c. 2 (treason), 159
1 Rich. II. c. 4 (maintenance and champerty), 7, 90, 112, 116
—— c. 7 (maintenance), 34
—— c. 9 (maintenance), 16
12 Rich. II. c. 2 (bribery), 227
5 Hen. IV. c. 14 (fines), 138
1 Hen. V. c. 3 (forgery), 153
23 Hen. VI. c. 9 (sheriffs), 139
3 Hen. VII. c. 14 (King's household), 159
4 Hen. VII. c. 12 (Justices of Peace), 224
32 Hen. VIII. c. 9 (maintenance and champerty), 16, 33, 89, 111, 112, 116
5 & 6 Ed. VI. c. 16 (bribery), 227
13 Eliz. c. 5 (fraudulent conveyances), 56
18 Eliz. c. 5 (informers), 157
27 Eliz. c. 10 (informers), 157
29 Eliz. c. 6 (forfeiture), 49
3 Jac. I. c. 7 (attornies), 24
7 Jac. I. c. 5 (Justices of Peace), 217
16 Car. I. c. 10 (habeas corpus), 215
31 Car. II. c. 2 (habeas corpus), 216
7 & 8 Will. III. c. 3 (treason), 186
4 & 5 Anne c. 3 (attornment), 32
4 Geo. I. c. 11 (stolen goods), 148, 149
6 Geo. I. c. 23 (stolen goods), 148
3 Geo. II. c. 25 (juries), 26
25 Geo. II. c. 36 (dog stealing), 150
10 Geo. III. c. 16 (Parliamentary elections), 7

43 Geo. III. c. 141 (judges), 218
56 Geo. III. c. 138 (pillory), 157
60 Geo. III. & 1 Geo. IV. c. 4 (copy of indictment), 186
3 Geo. IV. c. 46 (levy of fines), 139–140
6 Geo. IV. c. 50 (juries), 26
7 & 8 Geo. IV. c. 29 (stolen goods), 148, 149
9 Geo. IV. c. 55 (stolen goods), 149
3 & 4 Will. IV. c. 42 (arbitration), 155
6 & 7 Will. IV. c. 71 (tithes), 74
8 & 9 Vict. c. 18 (lands clauses), 55
—— c. 47 (dog stealing), 150
11 & 12 Vict. c. 43 (summary jurisdiction), 157
—— c. 44 (Justices of Peace), 216–224
14 & 15 Vict. c. 100 (criminal procedure), 230
20 & 21 Vict. c. 85 (divorce), 144
22 & 23 Vict. c. 17 (vexatious indictments), 229–236, 237–238
24 & 25 Vict. c. 95 (criminal statutes repeal), 148, 149, 150
24 & 25 Vict. c. 96 (larceny), 148, 149, 150, 156
26 & 27 Vict. c. 125 (statute law revision), 157
29 & 30 Vict. c. 19 (Parliamentary oaths), 70
30 & 31 Vict. c. 35 (Criminal Law Amendment), 232, 234, 235
30 & 31 Vict. c. 142 (County Courts), 239
31 & 32 Vict. c. 125 (Parliamentary elections), 8, 143
32 & 33 Vict. c. 62 (debtors), 72, 177, 203, 231
32 & 33 Vict. c. 71 (bankruptcy), 67
33 & 34 Vict. c. 28 (solicitors), 100–103
—— c. 65 (larceny advertisements), 150
—— c. 78 (tramways), 180
34 & 35 Vict. c. 48 (Justices of Peace), 227
36 & 37 Vict. c. 66 (choses in action), 50, 54
—— (jurisdiction), 238

INDEX OF STATUTES xi

38 & 39 Vict. c 55 (Public Health), 179
38 & 39 Vict. c. 77 (removal of judges), 215
39 & 40 Vict. c. 36 (sheriffs,etc.),72,203
42 & 43 Vict. c. 22 (prosecution of offenders), 154
———— c. 59 (repeal of acts), 157
———— c. 75 (Parliamentary elections), 8
44 & 45 Vict. c. 41 (Conveyancing Act), 33 .
———— c. 44 (solicitors), 103
———— c. 60 (libels), 231
48 & 49 Vict. c. 69 (Criminal Law Amendment), 203, 231
50 & 51 Vict. c. 28 (merchandise marks), 231
———— c. 55 (sheriffs), 89, 95, 139
———— c. 71 (Coroners), 213
51 & 52 Vict. c. 43 (County Courts), 215, 239
52 & 53 Vict. c. 49 (arbitration), 142, 155, 156
56 & 57 Vict. c. 61 (public authorities), 216, 218, 221, 227
57 & 58 Vict. c. 56 (statute law revision), 221

59 & 60 Vict. c. 51 (vexatious actions), 236–238
60 & 61 Vict. c. 65 (land transfer), 89
6 Ed. VII. c. 34 (corruption), 231
———— c. 47 (trade disputes), 37, 76, 241
7 Ed. VII. c. 23 (criminal appeal), 156
8 Ed. VII. c. 15 (costs in criminal cases), 235
———— c. 45 (incest), 231
———— c. 48 (newspapers), 150
———— c. 67 (children), 231
1 & 2 Geo. V. c. 6 (perjury), 230
———— c. 55 (national insurance), 79
4 & 5 Geo. V. c. 58 (imprisonment), 147, 157, 173, 227, 228
———— c. 59 (bankruptcy), 67, 177, 194, 231
5 Geo. V. c. 34 (defence of realm), 231
5 & 6 Geo. V. c. 90 (indictments), 167, 186, 235
6 & 7 Geo. V. c. 50 (larceny), 148, 149
7 Geo. V. c. 4 (grand juries), 235–236

INDEX OF CASES

Abrath v. N.E.R. Co., 188, 192, 195, 196, 197
Ackerley v. Parkinson, 207, 209
Adams v.London&c.BuildersLd.,102
Alabaster v. Harness, 15, 20, 22, 31, 33, 43, 70, 78, 86, 101, 110
Allardice v. Boswell, 207
Alfin v. Hewlett, 111
Allen v. Flood, 197
Amerideth's Case, 74, 116
Anderson v. Gorrie, 205, 207, 219
Anderson v. Radcliffe, 2, 17, 26, 27, 57, 97, 99–100
Angell v. Oodeen, 106
Angerstein, In re, 141
Anonymous (3 Ed. VI), 169, 170
— (28–29 Eliz.), 51
— (39 & 40 Eliz.), 67
— (10 Jac. I), 189
— (21 Car. II), 221
— (26 Car. II), 182
— (30 Car. II), 191, 196
— (7 Will. III), 49
— (2 Anne), 189
Archbishop of Canterbury v. Hudson, 7
Arundell v. Tregono, 198
Ashby v. White, 85
Asher v. Whitlock, 17
Ashford v. Price, 101
Ashley's Case, 161, 162
A.-G. of Duchy of Lancaster v. L. & N.W.R. Co., 240
Attorneys' & Solicitors' Act, 1870. In re, 97, 98, 101
Atwood v. Monger, 184, 189
Austin v. Dowling, 175

Bainbrigge v. Moss, 99, 108
Baker v. Hall & Lumley, 163
Baker v. Townsend (or Townshend), 133, 134, 156
Ball v. Warwick, 107
Barnes v. Constantine, 26, 181
Barratt v. Kearns, 209
Barrow v. Grey, 51
Barton v. Bricknell, 223
Basébé v. Matthews, 184, 185
Beeley v. Wingfield, 132, 133, 134
Bell v. Fox, 182

Bell v. Smith, 54
Bellers v. Russell, 31
Berdan v. Greenwood, 242
Bessell v. Wilson, 223
Best v. Aier, 182
Bilke v. Havelock, 140
Blachford v. Dod, 193
Blackman v. Trunkett, 198
Blake v. Albion Life Assurance Society, 239
Blanchard v. Lilly, 156
Bloomfield v. Blake, 172
Bloxam v. Metrop. R. Co., 78
Boaler, In re, 237
Boaler v. Holder, 184
Bottomley v. Brougham, 206, 209
Boucher v. Wiseman, 139
Bourne, Ex p., 200
Box v. Taylor, 190
Bradlaugh v. Newdegate, 2, 5, 11, 14, 18, 22, 31, 36, 37, 39, 40, 41, 52, 70, 79, 86, 87, 88, 89
Bradley v. Carr, 209, 212
Bradshaw v. Waterlow & Sons, Ld., 193, 194, 196
Breay v. Royal British Nurses Association, 78
Brett v. Close, 144
Breverton's Case, 49
British &c. Association Ld. v. Foster, 243
British Cash &c. Ld. v. Lamson & Co. Ld., 2, 3, 18, 21, 22, 75–76, 85, 90, 113
Brittain v. Kinnaird, 220
Broad v. Ham, 192, 193
Brook v. Hook, 124
Brook v. King, 118
Brooking v. Maudslay, 242
Brooks v. Blain, 194
Broun v. Kennedy, 17, 28, 105
Brown v. Chapman, 200, 201
Brown v. Hawkes, 197
Browne, Ex p., 200
Browne v. Stradling, 176, 177
Brownlow's Case, 7
Bulwer v. Smith, 199
Bunbury v. Fuller, 220
Burke v. Greene, 16, 31, 60
Burley v. Bethune, 218, 219

INDEX OF CASES

Burnand *v.* Rodocanachi, 68
Burstall *v.* Beyfus, 241
Bushell's Case, 210
Busst *v.* Gibbons, 193
Byne *v.* Moore, 179
Bynoe *v.* Bank of England, 185

Caldecott, *Ex p.*, 121, 125, 141
Calder *v.* Halkett, 210
Cambrian Mining Co., *In re*, 64
Cannon *v.* Rands, 120
Cannon's Case, 30, 31
Carratt *v.* Morley, 211
Carrington *v.* Harway, 69
Castellain *v.* Preston, 68
Castrique *v.* Behrens, 202
Caudle *v.* Seymour, 222, 225
Cave *v.* Mountain, 218, 220
Chaffers, *In re*, 236
Chambers *v.* Robinson, 184
Chambers *v.* Taylor, 188, 191
Chapman *v.* Pickersgill, 201
Chatterton *v.* Secretary of State for India, 238
Chowne *v.* Baylis, 122
Christie, *In re*, 200
Churchill *v.* Siggers, 185, 203
Clare *v.* Joseph, 102
Claridge *v.* Hoare, 122, 126
Clark *v.* Woods, 222
Clarke *v.* Postan, 176
Clements *v.* Ohrly, 176
Clift, *In re*, 106
Clissold *v.* Cratchley, 202
Clubb *v.* Hutson, 135
Cockburn *v.* Edwards, 103
Cockell *v.* Taylor, 56
Cohen *v.* Mitchell, 68
Cohen *v.* Morgan, 176
Cole *v.* Booker, 40, 41
Collingrove, The, 199
Collins *v.* Blantern, 121, 129, 130, 133, 143, 153
Colquhoun, *Ex p.*, 106
Comfort *v.* Betts, 53
Comyn *v.* Sabine, 212
Consolidated Exploration Co. *v.* Musgrave, 72, 137
Constantine *v.* Barnes, 25, 26
Cooke *v.* Cooke, 141
Coppock *v.* Bower, 143
Cornford *v.* Carlton Bank, 199
Cotterell *v.* Jones, 41
Cotton *v.* James, 201
County Hotel & Wine Co. Ld. *v.* L. & N.W.R. Co., 55
Cox *v.* English &c. Bank, Ld., 188
Coxon *v.* Gorst, 240, 241
Cracknall *v.* Janson, 239

Crepps *v.* Durden, 222
Critchell *v.* L. & S.W.R. Co., 239
Cromwell (Lord) & Townsend's Case, 39, 115
Cullen *v.* Morris, 210
Cullom *v.* Sherman, 49

Damont, Ruddock and Sherman's Case, 181
Danby *v.* Beardsley, 174, 175
Danzey *v.* Metrop. Bk of England & Wales, 101
Davies, *In re*, 200
Davies *v.* London &c. Insurance Co., 127
Davis *v.* Billing, 243
Davis *v.* Capper, 222
Davis *v.* Freethy, 57, 98
Davis *v.* Hardy, 193
Davis *v.* Holding, 141
Davis *v.* Noak, 176
Davy *v.* Garrett, 242
Daw *v.* Swaine, 202
Dawkins *v.* Rokeby, 198, 207, 210
Dawson *v.* G.N. & City R. Co., 55, 63, 66
Dawson *v.* Vasandeau, 176
De Hoghton *v.* Money, 63, 64, 108
Deeringe & Bettingham's Case, 5
Defries *v.* Milne, 63, 66, 67
Delagal *v.* Highley, 194
Delisser *v.* Towne, 196
Deney *v.* Ridgy, 182
Dew *v.* Parsons, 140
Dewar *v.* Elliott, 126
Dickinson *v.* Burrell, 65–66
Dobson *v.* Groves, 156
Dogatte *v.* Lawry, 188–189
Drage *v.* Ibberson, 130
Dubois *v.* Keats, 177
Dunch *v.* Bannester, 73–74, 116
Dunch & Doyley's Case, 73
Dymock's Case, 7
Dyson *v.* A.-G., 240, 241
Dyve *v.* Manyngham, 139

E. S—, *In re*, 9
Eager *v.* Dyott, 176
Earle *v.* Hopwood, 97, 98
Earle's Shipbuilding &c. Co. *v.* Atlantic Transport Co., 57
Edgcombe *v.* Rodd, 131, 134
Edwards *v.* Aberayron &c. Insurance Society, 142
Edwards *v.* Ferris, 222
Egerton *v.* Brownlow, 117, 144–145
Elborough *v.* Ayres, 37
Elliott *v.* Richardson, 78, 141
Ellis *v.* Torrington, 55, 56, 57, 63, 66

xiv INDEX OF CASES

Elsee *v.* Smith, 176, 203
Elworthy *v.* Bird, 133

Fallowes *v.* Taylor, 130–131
Farley *v.* Danks, 201
Farmer *v.* Darling, 190
Farnham *v.* Milward & Co., 241
Fentiman, *Ex p.*, 225
Ferguson *v.* Earl of Kinnoull, 211
Filder *v.* L.B. & S.C.R. Co., 78
Finch *v.* Cokaine, 29
Findon *v.* Parker, 15, 18, 22, 32, 73, 74
Fischer *v.* Kamala Naicker, 14, 92
Fisher *v.* Apollinaris Co., 136
Fisher *v.* Bristow, 183, 199
Fitzjohn *v.* Mackinder, 178, 185
Fitzroy *v.* Cave, 36, 39, 52, 53, 54, 55, 60, 61, 62. 67
Fivaz *v.* Nicholls, 123
Fleming *v.* Dollar, 243
Flight *v.* Leman, 10, 11, 91, 92
Flower *v.* Sadler, 119, 120, 125, 127
Floyd *v.* Barker, 164, 168, 169, 170, 206, 212
Ford *v.* Radford, 57, 58, 59, 75
Forrest *v.* M.S. & L.R. Co., 78
Fraser *v.* Balfour, 199
Fray *v.* Blackburn, 207, 208
Freeman *v.* Arkell, 179
Fuller *v.* Cook, 188

Gallimore, *Ex p.*, 200
Gardner *v.* Jollye, 184
Garnett *v.* Ferrand, 206, 207, 209, 212
Garth *v.* Earnshaw, 133
Gelen *v.* Hall, 218
George *v.* Chambers, 222
Gibbs *v.* Pike, 204
Gifford's Case, 115
Gilding *v.* Eyre, 185
Gipps *v.* Hume, 144
Girlington *v.* Pitfield, 198
Glasgow Navigation Co. *v.* Iron Ore Co., 238
Glegg *v.* Bromley, 1, 56, 66, 68
Goddard *v.* Smith, 183
Goffin *v.* Donnelly, 210
Golding *v.* Crowle, 189
Golding *v.* Wharton Saltworks Co., 243
Goodall *v.* Lowndes, 137
Goodman *v.* Robinson, 69
Gostling, *Ex p.*, 233
Grant *v.* Thompson, 5, 6, 73, 79
Grassmoor Colliery Co. *v.* Workmen's Legal Friendly Society, 144
Gray *v.* Dight, 199

Green *v.* Hundred of Buccle-Churches, 211, 217, 221
Gregory *v.* Derby, 176
Greig *v.* National Amalgamated Union &c., 76, 78
Grell *v.* Levy, 104, 106–107
Grepe *v.* Loam, 239
Groenvelt *v.* Burwell, 186 206, 209
Guerrier, *Ex p.*, 125
Gundry *v.* Sainsbury, 102
Guy *v.* Churchill, 1, 57, 60, 74, 75

Haddrick *v.* Heslop, 193
Haggard *v.* Pélecier Frères, 210
Hall, *In re*, 106
Hall *v.* Dyson, 141
Hamilton *v.* Anderson, 207, 208
Hamond *v.* Howell, 208
Harding *v.* Cooper, 132
Harding *v.* Harding, 50
Hare *v.* L. & N.W.R. Co., 64
Harrington *v.* Long, 7, 14, 20, 60, 61
Harris *v.* Brisco, 5, 7, 15, 40, 92
Harris *v.* Warre, 176
Harrison *v.* National Provincial Bk of England, 195
Hartley *v.* Russell, 52, 60, 61
Harvey *v.* Bateman, 50
Harvey *v.* Morgan, 122
Haynes *v.* Rogers, 182
Heap *v.* Marris, 242
Heath *v.* Heape, 197
Hercot *v.* Underhill, 191
Hermann *v.* Jeuchner, 137
Hewlett *v.* Cruchley, 196
Hickman *v.* Kent &c. Sheepbreeders Association, 31, 36, 40, 79, 85
Hicks *v.* Faulkner, 193, 194, 197
Hill *v.* Sands, 27
Hilliar *v.* Dade, 193
Hills *v.* Mitson, 141
Hilton *v.* Woods, 16, 97, 98
Hocking *v.* Matthews, 199
Hoggart's Settlement, *In re*, 98
Holden *v.* Thompson, 8, 18, 26, 40, 75
Holroyd *v.* Breare, 209
Hope *v.* Evered, 203
Hope *v.* Hope, 144, 145
Hope *v.* International Financial Society, 142
Hord *v.* Cordery, 182
Horn *v.* Foster, 46
Hornbee's Case, 49
Horton *v.* Sayer, 142
Howard *v.* Bell, 74
Howard's (Lord) Case, 74
Hubbuck *v.* Wilkinson, 241
Hughes *v.* Statham, 96

INDEX OF CASES

Hull, *In re*, 215
Humphreys *v.* Polak, 241
Humphreys *v.* Welling, 141
Hunt *v.* Lines, 184
Hunter *v.* Daniel, 14, 60, 77
Huntley *v.* Simson, 194
Hurlestone *v.* Glaseour, 162, 163
Hutley *v.* Hutley, 11, 31, 59
Huxley *v.* Wootton, 238

James *v.* Kerr, 1, 2, 18, 103
James *v.* Phelps, 194
Jekyll *v.* Moore, 207
Jennings *v.* Johnson, 101, 102
Jerom *v.* Knight, 181, 182
Johnson, *Ex p.*, 200
Johnson *v.* Emerson, 195, 200
Johnson *v.* Ogilby, 126, 128, 129, 130
Johnstone *v.* Sutton, 196, 197
Jones' Case (31 Eliz.), 118
Jones, *In re* (1870), 27, 102
Jones, *In re* (1902), 237
Jones *v.* Brinley, 109
Jones *v.* German, 203
Jones *v.* Gwynn, 184, 189, 190, 196
Jones *v.* Linton, 103
Jones *v.* Merionethshire &c. Society, 119, 120, 121, 124, 127
Jones *v.* Reade, 102
Jones *v.* Roberts, 103
Jones *v.* Tripp, 103
Jordan *v.* Lewis, 186

Kaufmann *v.* Gerson, 145
Kearley *v.* Thomson, 141
Keir *v.* Leeman, 127, 130, 131, 132, 133, 135, 136
Kemp, *Ex p.*, 200
Kemp *v.* Neville, 209
Kendall *v.* Wilkinson, 216, 218
Kendillon *v.* Maltby, 207
Kennedy *v.* Broun, 104
Kennedy *v.* Hilliard, 210
Kenney *v.* Browne, 26
Keogh *v.* McGrath, 66
Kinnaird *v.* Field, 239
Kirby *v.* Simpson, 218
Kirk *v.* Strickwood, 132
Kirwan *v.* Goodman, 143
Kitchinman's Case, 189
Knight *v.* Bowyer, 61, 99
Knight *v.* Jermin, 182, 188, 191, 198
Knowlden *v.* R., 232
Knowles *v.* Roberts, 242
Kunwar Ram Lal *v.* Nil Kanth, 4

Lambert *v.* Taylor, 49
Lampet's Case, 45

Lamson *v.* Paragon Supply Co., Ld., 128
Lane *v.* Mallory, 51
Lane *v.* Santeloe, 218
Law *v.* Llewellyn, 208, 219, 222
Lawrence *v.* Norreys, 238
Le Brasseur & Oakley, *In re*, 106
Lea *v.* Charrington, 203
Leach *v.* Penton, 27
Leary *v.* Patrick, 223
Lechmere Charlton's Case, 28
Lee *v.* Page, 142
Legatt *v.* Tollervey, 186
Leigh *v.* Webb, 176
Lincoln's (Lord of) Case, 26
Linford *v.* Fitzroy, 218, 221
Lister *v.* Perryman, 188, 193
Livingston *v.* Ralli, 141
Livingstone *v.* Westminster Corporation, 220
Lound *v.* Grimwade, 122
Love's Case, 144
Lovet *v.* Fawkner, 181
Lumb *v.* Beaumont, 242

McCarthy *v.* Kennedy, 15, 40
McClatchie *v.* Haslam, 127
McDonald *v.* Rooke, 193
McKenzie *v.* British Linen Co., 124
McVittie *v.* Marsden, 223
Magnay *v.* Burt, 203
Manders *v.* Williams, 34
Mankleton *v.* Allen, 196, 198
Manning *v.* Fitzherbert, 189
Mapleback, *In re*, 121, 125, 141
Margate Pier Co. *v.* Hannam, 222
Marham *v.* Pescod, 182, 188
Marsh *v.* Vauhan, 181
Marshalsea, Case of the, 211
Mason *v.* Watkins, 119
Master *v.* Miller, 22, 31, 44, 47, 51, 69, 70
Masters, *In re*, 27, 97
May, *In re*, 106
May *v.* Lane, 54
Mayor of London *v.* Cox, 211
Mears *v.* L. & S.W.R. Co., 34
Mellor *v.* Baddeley, 185
Meredith's Case, 74
Metcalfe *v.* Hodgson, 209
Metropolitan Bank *v.* Pooley, 3, 114, 200, 238, 240
Miller, *In re*, 239
Millington *v.* Loring, 239
Mills *v.* Mills, 181
Mirams *v.* "Our Dogs" Publishing Co., 150
Mitchell *v.* Jenkins, 197
Mitchell's Case, 28

xvi INDEX OF CASES

Mittens v. Foreman, 177
Moor v. Row, 105
Moore v. Lawson, 240
Moore v. Rock, 189
Moore v. Usher, 10
Moravia v. Sloper, 211
Morgan, In re, 243
Morgan v. Higgins, 103
Morgan v. Hughes, 182, 183, 198
Morris v. Badger, 50
Morris v. Chapman, 96
Morrison v. Kelly, 185, 186, 187
Mouldsdale v. Birchall, 51
Mowse v. Weaver, 6, 17, 25, 30, 32, 39
Mudge v. Penge Urban Council, 242
Munster v. Lamb, 210
Muriell v. Tracy, 181, 189
Musgrove v. Newell, 191, 195
Mutrie v. Binney, 242

Nerot v. Wallace, 140
Neville v. London Express News-paper, Ld., 3, 6, 8, 11, 12, 15, 18, 22, 31, 36, 39, 40, 70, 71, 79–84, 85–89, 90, 91–93, 110, 113, 114, 116
Newsam v. Carr, 194
Noon's Case, 48
Norman v. Cole, 122
Norman v. Matthews, 238, 239
Norton v. Simmes, 139
Norton v. Syms, 139
Nottingham Corporation, In re, 72
Nyn v. Taylor, 181, 196, 198

Ogilvie v. West Australian &c. Cor-poration, Ld., 124
Oliver v. Bakewell, 74
Onely v. Earl of Kent, 23
Oram v. Hutt, 3, 15, 19, 37, 70, 78–79, 81, 82, 85, 92, 109–110, 114
Osbaldiston v. Simpson, 126, 137
Owen v. Lavery, 200

Pain v. Rochester, 188, 191
Palke v. Dunnyng, 181, 191
Pandit Gaya Parshad Tewari v. Sardar Bhagat Singh, 176
Panton v. Williams, 188
Paris v. Levy, 219, 222
Paris Skating Rink Co., In re, 63
Parker v. Langley, 183
Pater, Ex p., 28
Payn v. Porter, 179, 182, 189
Peacock v. Bell, 209, 211
Pearson v. Humes, 100
Pease v. Chaytor, 223
Pechell v. Watson, 41, 86, 91

Pedro v. Barrett, 184
Penrice v. Parker, 105
Penros' Case, 17, 105
Penson v. Hickbed, 50
Performing Rights Society, Ld. v. Thompson, 76
Person v. Hickled, 50
Persse v. Persse, 8, 9
Phillips v. Nayler, 195
Phipps, Ex p., 200
Pierson v. Hughes, 30, 100, 101, 103
Pilkington v. Green, 137
Pince v. Beattie, 97
Pitcher v. Rigby, 103
Pittman v. Prudential Deposit Bk, Ld., 97
Pollard v. Evans, 181, 182
Pool v. Bousfield, 143
Poulterers' Case, 160, 161, 162, 166
Powell v. Knowler, 59
Prevost v. Wood, 144
Price v. Crofts, 181
Price v. Phillips, 241
Prickett v. Greatrex, 222
Primrose v. Waterston, 212
Prince v. Haworth, 145
Prosser v. Edmonds, 63, 65–67

Quartz Hill Gold Mining Co. v. Eyre, 200, 201, 202
Quinn v. Leathem, 197

R. v. —, 40
— Allen, 48
— Armstrong, 171
— Badger, 226
— Bardell, 155
— Bather, 234
— Bayley, 239
— Beckley, 231
— Bell, 232
— Bennett, 232
— Best, 157, 163, 166, 171, 173
— Bishop of Norwich, 227
— Blakemore, 156
— Bloomsbury Income Tax Com-missioners, 220
— Bolton, 220
— Borron, 225
— Bradlaugh, 234
— Brangan, 186
— Bray, 231
— Brooke, 226
— Brown, 234
— Burgess, 147
— Burton, 230
— Clarke, 235
— Constable, 225
— Coombs, 130

INDEX OF CASES

xvii

R. v. Coyne, 233
— Crabbe, 235
— Crisp, 157
— Davie, 226
— Dexter, 232
— Dobson, 156
— Drinkwater, 149
— Eayres, 234
— Eyres, 226
— Falkland (Lord), 130
— Fielding, 218
— Fuidge, 232
— Gotley, 157
— Grimes, 171
— Hamp, 171
— Hann, 226
— Hardey, 155
— Harris, 235
— Herne, 158
— Holland, 226
— Hollingberry, 167
— Humphreys, 116
— Jackson, 225
— Jacobs, 164, 167
— Justices of Great Yarmouth, 220
— King, 149
— Kinnersley, 158, 164
— Kopelewitch, 234
— Ledbitter, 149
— Lord Mayor of London, Ex p. Gostling, 233
— McDaniel, 164–165
— Marsh, 213
— Marshall, 213
— Mather, 226
— Mawbey, 170, 171
— Metz, 232
— Moate, 156
— Murray, 167, 173
— Nichols, 159
— Nicholls, 159
— Nunneley, 220
— O'Donnell, 149
— Palmer, 218, 225
— Parish of Aickles, 51
— Pascoe, 149
— Phelps, 226
— Porter, 137, 172
— Rant, 130
— Roderick, 171
— Rogers, 232
— Roxburgh, 155
— Sainsbury, 226
— Scorey, 213
— Seaford Justices, 226
— Seton, 226
— Shrewsbury Justices, 226
— Skinner, 225

R. v. Slater, 158
— Southerton, 157
— Sprägg, 160, 164
— Steventon, 171
— Steward, 227
— Stone, 147
— Stukely, 213
— Taylor, 170
— Tibbits, 165, 172
— Twine, 49
— Tymberley, 170
— Vreones, 171
— Webster, 226
— Wendman, 49
— Williams, 226
— Young, 218, 224
Radnor v. Reeve, 209
Raja Rai Bhagwat Dayal Singh v. Debi Dayal Sahu, 4
Ram Coomar Coondoo v. Chunder Canto Mookerjee, 4
Ramshay, Ex p., 215
Randegger v. Holmes, 142
Rassam v. Budge, 242
Ratt v. Parkinson, 223
Ravenga v. Macintosh, 195
Rawlings v. Coal Consumers' Association, 121
Rayson v. South London Tramways Co., 180
Redway v. McAndrew, 199, 202
Reed v. Taylor, 196
Rees v. De Bernardy, 58, 108, 109
Reichel v. Magrath, 238
Republic of Peru v. Peruvian Guano Co., 240, 241, 242
Reynell v. Sprye, 62
Reynolds v. Kennedy, 185
Richmond v. Branson, 241
Roberts (Doe d.) v. Roberts, 173
Robson v. Spearman, 222
Rochester v. Solm, 166
Rogers v. Oxford &c. R. Co., 78
Roy v. Duke of Beaufort, 129
Royal Aquarium Society, Ld. v. Parkinson, 209, 210–211
Rubery v. Grant, 239

Salaman v. Secretary of State for India, 238
Sanderson v. Glass, 103
Saulkell's Case, 27, 90
Saunders v. Edwards, 182
Savile. v. Roberts, 181, 191
Savill Bros. Ld. v. Langman, 1, 8, 108, 109
Scarlet's Case, 168
Scavage v. Tateham, 222
Scott v. Avery, 142

xviii INDEX OF CASES

Scott *v.* N.S.P.C.C., 3, 37, 81, 86, 87
Scott *v.* Stansfield, 206, 208, 209
Seaman *v.* Netherclift, 207, 210
Seear *v.* Lawson, 58, 66, 68
Sewell *v.* N.T.C., Ld., 175
Shackell *v.* Rosier, 62
Shapcott *v.* Rowe, 198
Sharp *v.* Carter, 77
Sherington *v.* Ward, 198
Shotbolt's Case, 181
Shrosbery *v.* Osmaston, 193
Simpson *v.* Lamb, 97, 98
Skapholme *v.* Hart, 27, 105
Skelton *v.* Baxter, 79
Skinner *v.* Gunton (*or* Gunter), 181, 182
Smith *v.* Andrews, 27
Smith *v.* British Insurance Co., 242
Smith *v.* Cranshaw, 181, 182
Smith *v.* Selwyn, 128, 241
Smith *v.* Sydney, 185
Smith *v.* Tonstall, 204
Smith (W. H.) & Son *v.* Clinton, 62, 144
Smithson *v.* Symson, 184
Solicitor, *In re a*, (1909), 106
— (1911), 106
— (1912), 101
— (1913), 101
South *v.* Marsh, 48
South Hetton Coal Co. *v.* Haswell Coal Co., 241
Sprye *v.* Porter, 11, 59
Stafford's Case, 7
Stanley *v.* Jones, 59, 69
Stepney *v.* Wolfe, 77, 115
Stevens *v.* Bagwell, 8, 63
Stevens *v.* Midland Counties R. Co., 196, 197
Steward *v.* Gromett, 185
Stokes *v.* Grant, 243
Stone *v.* Yea, 18, 74
Stowball *v.* Ansell, 197
Strange *v.* Brennan, 97
Street *v.* Rigby, 141
Subley *v.* Mott, 181
Sugars *v.* Brinkworth, 137
Sutton *v.* Johnstone, 185, 190, 198, 207
Sydenham *v.* Keilaway, 160

Taaffe *v.* Downes, 208
Tailor & Towlin's Case, 166, 169
Tailour's (Clement) Case, 36
Tattersall *v.* Groote, 141
Taylor's Case, 182
Thomas *v.* Churton, 207, 209
Thomas *v.* Lloyd, 97
Thompson *v.* Charnock, 141

Thornhill *v.* Evans, 105
Throgmorton's Case, 198
Thrower *v.* Whetstone, 139
Thursby *v.* Warren, 23
Thurston *v.* Ummons, 20, 41
Timberley & Childe, 160, 170
Tinsley *v.* Nassau, 208
Tisdale *v.* Bedington, 7
Tisdall *v.* Bevington, 7
Trevor *v.* Wall, 211
Trevor's Case, 228
Trussell *v.* Monslowe, 100
Tullis *v.* Jacson, 142
Tunno *v.* Morris, 208
Turner *v.* Ambler, 193
Turner *v.* Burnaby, 42, 115
Turner *v.* Tennant, 102
Twiss *v.* Noblett, 63
Tyson *v.* Jackson, 52, 55, 98

Uppington *v.* Bullen, 98
Upton *v.* Basset, 16

Vacher & Sons, Ld. *v.* London Society of Compositors, 241
Vanderbergh *v.* Blake, 184, 189, 199, 201
Varrel *v.* Wilson, 188, 191
Vexatious Actions Act, *In re* (*In re* Jones), 237

Wale *v.* Hill, 188, 191, 196
Walker *v.* Bradford Old Bank, 50
Wallace *v.* Hardacre, 119, 127
Wallis *v.* Duke of Portland, 7, 8, 81
Walmesley *v.* Booth, 103
Walter D. Wallet, The, 199
Wanlace & Philipson's Case, 73
Ward, *In re*, 215
Ward *v.* Lloyd, 119, 121, 126, 127
Ward *v.* Stevenson, 222
Wason, *Ex p.*, 233
Waterer *v.* Freeman, 202
Watson *v.* Rodwell, 243
Weal *v.* Wells, 191
Webb *v.* Welles, 191
Wedgerfield *v.* De Bernardy, 59
Weldon *v.* Maples, Teesdale & Co., 243
Wells *v.* Wells, 106
West *v.* Smallwood, 218
Weston *v.* Beeman, 177
Weston *v.* Fournier, 218
Weston *v.* Sneyd, 221
Whitmore *v.* Farley, 121, 123, 137
Whitworth *v.* Darbishire, 243
Whitworth *v.* Hall, 200
Whorewood *v.* Corderoy, 182
Wicks *v.* Fentham, 184

INDEX OF CASES

Wiffen v. Bailey &c. Council, 179, 180, 202
Wild v. Hobson, 75
Wild v. Simpson, 97, 98
Wilkins v. Gill, 150
Williams v. Banks, 193
Williams v. Bayley, 120, 122, 125, 126, 127, 152
Williams v. Pigott, 103
Williams v. Protheroe, 14, 22, 34, 57
Williamson v. Henley, 62
Willins v. Fletcher, 184
Willis v. Howe, 239
Willis v. Maclachlan, 212
Wilson v. Short, 66
Wilson v. Strugnell, 137
Winch v. Keeley, 51

Windham v. Clere, 198
Windhill Local Board v. Vint, 122, 131, 135, 136
Wine v. Ware, 182
Wolverhampton & Staffs. Banking Co., Ex p., 141
Wood v. Downes, 26, 96, 98
Wood v. Griffith, 56
Woods v. Lyttleton, 241
Worthington v. Garstone, 24, 26
Wright v. Black, 182
Wright v. Prescot Urban Council, 241
Wright's Case, 163
Wyatt v. Palmer, 201, 241

Yeatman, Ex p., 99
York v. Allen, 49

INDEX OF YEAR BOOKS

M. 4 Ed. II; 13
M. 17   —   545; 31
T. ǂ 6 Ed. III, 33; 27, 28, 43
   15   —   4; 20
H. 21   —   10; 13
H. 22   —   pl. 4; 166, 170
H. 30   —   3; 12
P. 32   —   13–14
H. 42   —   6; 138
P. 42   —   14; 159
M. 42   —   24; 138
M. 47   —   9; 6, 81, 84
22 Lib. Ass. pl. 77; 167
27   —   12; 168, 169, 170
27   —   18; 212
27   —   34; 159
27   —   44; 159
27   —   73; 168
28   —   12; 158
30   —   15; 12
30   —   21; 168
42   —   5; 146
47   —   5; 6, 81, 84
50   —   1; 47
50   —   3; 13, 14
M. 19 Rich. II; 12
H. 3 Hen. IV, 8; 47
M. 7   —   30; 80–81
H. 13   —   16; 17, 18, 20, 25
M. 8 Hen. V, 8; 18
T. 3 Hen. VI, 53; 39, 84
M. 8   —   9–10; 34
H. 9   —   60; 206, 217
H. 9   —   64; 30, 32, 34, 40, 54
M. 11   —   10; 25
T. 11   —   11; 39
T. 11   —   39; 18, 32, 114
P. 11   —   41; 20–21, 33, 34
P. 11   —   42; 39
   14   —   6; 71
   14   —   13; 18
M. 19   —   31; 38, 39
M. 19   —   36; 153
P. 19   —   62; 48
H. 19   —   64; 1
   21   —   5; 40
M. 21   —   15; 19, 22, 29, 35, 36, 38, 42, 85
M. 21   —   40; 18
M. 22   —   5; 5, 19, 20, 36, 85, 114
M. 22   —   24; 35
M. 22   —   35; 18, 34, 40, 42, 43
P. 28   —   6; 18, 21, 41
T. 28   —   7; 19, 36, 85

T. 28 Hen. VI, 12; 19, 27, 36
T. 28   —   15; 19
T. 31   —   8; 19
T. 31   —   9; 35
H. 32   —   24; 18, 20, 27, 38, 44, 71, 72
H. 34   —   23; 26
H. 34   —   25; 30, 38, 71
H. 34   —   26; 27
H. 34   —   30; 35, 44, 45, 77
H. 34   —   35; 18
T. 35   —   25
   36   —   1; 139
   36   —   12; 18
   37   —   13; 45, 49
P. 37   —   25; 18
M. 39   —   5; 18, 30, 38, 39
   39   —   19; 18, 32, 34
M. 39   —   26; 49
P. 2 Ed. IV, 2; 77
M. 5   —   8; 47, 49
M. 6   —   2; 32
M. 6   —   5; 31
P. 7   —   5; 139
M. 7   —   15; 18
M. 8   —   13; 14, 16, 17
P. 9   —   3; 217
M. 9   —   32; 43
M. 10   —   19; 10
M. 12   —   4; 43
M. 12   —   5; 146
M. 17   —   5; 42
P. 18   —   1; 42
P. 18   —   2; 18, 42, 73
M. 18   —   12; 71
P. 18   —   14; 18
H. 18   —   28; 118–119
M. 19   —   3; 29, 32, 34, 38, 39, 43, 44, 114
M. 19   —   15; 19
P. 21   —   31; 30
M. 21   —   67; 27
P. 22   —   11; 22
2 Rich. III, 9; 183
M. 2 Hen. VII, 8; 47
M. 5   —   13; 11, 19, 85
P. 5   —   20; 25
M. 9   —   7; 22
M. 9   —   18; 11, 13, 15, 77, 84, 114–115
M. 14   —   2; 29
H. 15   —   2; 1, 43, 77
T. 18   —   25, 44
M. 20   —   11; 21
H. 21   —   19; 48
M. 21   —   40; 19, 35

CHAPTER I

MAINTENANCE AND CHAMPERTY AS TORTS

PRELIMINARY

§ 1. Whatever may be the historical accuracy of the view that champerty is a species of maintenance[1], there is no doubt that it is now firmly rooted in our law. It is noted as long ago as Hil. 9 Hen. VI, f. 64 that the Court said that every champerty is maintenance, and that the party shall have a writ of maintenance thereof as well as a writ of champerty; and MARTIN J. said in this case:‑

> And I have taken it to be law that maintenance is when a man maintains to have part or all of the very thing which is [the subject of] the action; or to have other thing to maintain the same plaint; or if a man has nothing to meddle or no real excuse for meddling but of his evil wish,—in all these cases he is a maintainer.

Again, in Hil. 15 Hen. VII, f. 2[2], it was held that every champerty implies in itself maintenance, but not e converso[3]. Within the last generation this view has been judicially affirmed[4], and an exposition of the law which ignores it must necessarily contain a good deal of repetition. It is not proposed to treat these wrongs under separate headings, but to deal with them jointly in their relation to the law of torts, crimes, and contracts respectively. As a preliminary, definition may be attempted.

According to *Termes de la Ley*,

> maintenance is where any man gives or delivers to another that is plaintiff or defendant in any action àny sum of money or other thing, to maintain his plea, or takes great pains for him when he hath nothing therewith to do.

---

[1] *Hist. of Abuse of Legal Procedure*, p. 140.
[2] Br. *Abr. Champ.* 6 to same effect.   [3] So too 2 Inst. 208.
[4] *Per* KAY J. in *James* v. *Kerr* (1889), 40 Ch. Div. at p. 456; CHITTY J. in *Guy* v. *Churchill* (1888), 40 Ch. Div. at p. 488; LINDLEY M.R. in *Savill Bros. Ld.* v. *Langman* (1898), 79 L.T. at p. 47; PARKER J. in *Glegg* v. *Bromley* [1912] 3 K.B., at p. 490; LORD FINLAY L.C. in *Neville* v. *London Express Newspaper, Ld.* [1919] A.C. at pp. 382, 386.

W. L. P.

2   ARRANGEMENT OF CHAPTER

LORD COLERIDGE C.J. in *Bradlaugh* v. *Newdegate* (1883) considered this "perhaps the fullest and completest" of all the definitions[1], and it commended itself to the Bench both before and after that decision[2], and though attempts to define maintenance at all at the present day have been deprecated as likely to be either unsuccessful or useless, there is no solid reason against adopting this one[3].

Champerty may be defined as "the unlawful maintenance of a suit in consideration of some bargain to have part of the thing in dispute, or some profit out of it"[4]. It is immaterial whether the champertous agreement be verbal or written[5].

ARRANGEMENT OF CHAPTER

§ 2. The scope of the actions for maintenance and champerty as torts will be treated as follows:

(1) *As to persons.*

(2) *As to place.*

(3) *Legal proceedings with which unlawful interference is possible.*

(4) *What is such interference?*

(5) *Defences which can be pleaded.*

(6) *Remedies.*

(7) *The burden of proof.*

---

[1] 11 Q.B.D. at p. 5.

[2] *Anderson* v. *Radcliffe* (1858), 3 E.B. and E. 806; *per* WILLIAMS J. at p. 825. *James* v. *Kerr* (1889), 40 Ch. Div. 449; *per* KAY J. at p. 458. There is some doubt whether "action" is not too narrow; *post* § 5.

[3] FLETCHER MOULTON L.J. in *British Cash, etc. Ld.* v. *Lamson and Co. Ld.* [1908] 1 K.B. 1006, at pp. 1013–1014. The learned Lord Justice expressed the opinion that the law had radically changed since the old definitions had been made, and that this change renders any adaptation of them useless. Circumstances have unquestionably changed in the sense that great men do not commit maintenance, and that very few people commit it at all, and the law has changed in the sense that exceptions to maintenance have widened, but it is submitted that this does not affect the above definition. Bl. IV. 134 is to the same effect, and Addison (*Law of Torts*, ed. 8, p. 30) adopts it. BRAY J. in *Scott* v. *N.S.P.C.C.* (1909), 25 T.L.R. at p. 790. VISCOUNT HALDANE in *Neville* v. *London Express Newspaper, Ld.* [1919] A.C. at p. 390; LORD ATKINSON, *ibid.* 402.

[4] 1 Hawk, P.C. ch. 84, sect. 1. F.N.B. 172 A is materially the same. So is Bl. IV. 135. Addison (*op. cit.* p. 31) makes insolvency of the plaintiff essential. Authority is lacking for this.

[5] F.N.B. 172 L. 1 Hawk, P.C. ch. 84, sect. 5.

PERSONAL DISABILITIES

PERSONAL DISABILITIES

§ 3. Questions of personal capacity or disability in suing or defending an action of maintenance or champerty need not detain us long. They are subject to the rules that prevail in the law of torts generally, and are accessible in any of the text-books[1].

In one case only has any special point arisen as to the particular torts with which we are dealing. Doubts have been raised as to whether a corporation is liable to the action of maintenance. These originated in recent times with a *dictum* of EARL SELBORNE L.C. in *Metropolitan Bank* v. *Pooley*[2] that a corporation in liquidation as distinct from the individual liquidator is incapable of committing maintenance. This was rather unwarrantably regarded in some quarters as laying down the law that an action of maintenance is not available against a corporation. The point was raised in *British Cash, etc.* v. *Lamson & Co., Ld.*[3], but proved to be unnecessary to the decision, and COZENS-HARDY M.R. preserved an open mind upon it[4]. In *Scott* v. *N.S.P.C.C.*[5], the defendants were a corporation, and put forward no defence on that ground[6]. *Neville* v. *London Express Newspaper, Ld.*[7] probably settled that a limited company may be liable for maintenance. VISCOUNT READING C.J. held that if EARL SELBORNE'S *dictum* in *Metropolitan Bank* v. *Pooley* meant that the appellant company could not be prosecuted for maintenance, no question could be raised as to its accuracy, but if it meant that a civil action could not be brought against a limited company which by its servants had been guilty of maintenance, it did not now represent the law. But he was of opinion that the *dictum* did not affect the decision in *Neville* v. *London Express Newspaper, Ld.* because it was

[1] Pollock, *Law of Torts*, ch. III, sect. I. Addison, *Law of Torts*, ch. IV. Clerk and Lindsell, *Law of Torts*, ch. II. A bankrupt cannot sue for maintenance, because the cause of action passes to the trustee in bankruptcy, and such an action may be summarily dismissed as frivolous and vexatious. *Metropolitan Bank* v. *Pooley* (1885), L.R. 10 A.C. 210.
[2] (1885), L.R. 10 A.C. 210, 217–218.   [3] [1908] 1 K.B. 1006.
[4] *Ibid.* at p. 1012. Cf. BUCKLEY L.J., at p. 1021.
[5] (1909), 25 T.L.R. 789 (at *nisi prius*).
[6] Cf. LORD PARKER in *Oram* v. *Hutt* [1914] 1 Ch. at p. 103; but his opinion is on maintenance as a crime.
[7] [1917] 1 K.B. 402.

4 LOCALITY OF WRONG

concerned with a company in liquidation, and EARL SELBORNE had relied on the limited authority possessed by the liquidator as justifying the view which he expressed.

It is quite clear that a limited company may be held liable for the acts of its servants which it authorizes, if the servant has improperly carried out the authority which the company could and did give[1].

The Court of Appeal[2] ordered a new trial on the ground of the perversity of the jury's verdict in the court below. They said nothing as to the liability of the company to be sued, but it is unlikely that they would have sent a case for re-trial if they had held the view that the action could not be brought in any circumstances against a corporation; and when the case reached the House of Lords, the point was raised neither in argument nor in any of the judgments, though the order of the Court of Appeal with respect to maintenance was discharged and judgment was entered for the defendant company on other grounds[3].

LOCALITY OF WRONG

§ 4. The Judicial Committee of the Privy Council has held that the English laws of maintenance and champerty are not of force as specific laws in India. The reason for this decision was that these laws were originally designed to meet offences committed chiefly by high officers of state, that they had fallen into comparative desuetude in England at the time at which India was acquired by the Crown, and that their application there would be inappropriate[4].

LEGAL PROCEEDINGS WITH WHICH UNLAWFUL INTERFERENCE IS POSSIBLE

§ 5. Maintenance and champerty are committed when there is improper interference with another man's suit or plea. What then does "suit" signify? It is said that it does not include a

---

[1] [1917] 1 K.B. 402. [2] [1917] 2 K.B. 564.
[3] [1919] A.C. 368.
[4] *Ram Coomar Coondoo* v. *Chunder Canto Mookerjee* (1876), L.R. 2 A.C. (P.C.) 186, 208–209. 4 Ind. App. 23. The Court reviewed the history of the subject at pp. 208–209 in the first-mentioned report. *Kunwar Ram Lal* v. *Nil Kanth* [1893] L.R. 20 Ind. App. 112. *Raja Rai Bhagwat Dayal Singh* v. *Debi Dayal Sahu* [1908] L.R. 35 Ind. App. 48.

PROCEEDINGS CAPABLE OF MAINTENANCE 5

criminal prosecution[1], and it was resolved by the whole Court in an anonymous Star Chamber case that if a man assist a plaintiff in that Court, it is not maintenance because it is to the advantage of the King; but that if he assist an informer in another court in an information on a penal law, this is maintenance for which he would be punishable in the Court of Star Chamber[2]; and it appears to have been decided in the same Court in *Deeringe and Bettingham's Case* that it is lawful for any man to disburse money in the prosecution of any cause for the King, such as an indictment or information in the Exchequer or Star Chamber[3]. The Court may possibly have been laying down in both these cases a principle of exemption from criminal liability only, of one who maintains a criminal prosecution. On the other hand, in *Bradlaugh* v. *Newdegate* (1883), LORD COLERIDGE C.J. said that the doctrine of maintenance is not confined to civil actions, and that the common interest which all subjects have in seeing that the law of the land is respected was not sufficient to justify the defendant in supporting a penal action brought by a common informer against the plaintiff[4]; but his actual decision related only to a penal action, and his *dictum* was dismissed as such in the only recent decision on the question,—*Grant* v. *Thompson*[5]. In this case, it was held that the doctrine of maintenance is confined to civil actions and does not apply to criminal prosecutions, partly because the latter ought to be untrammelled, partly because the action for malicious prosecution is a sufficient remedy for unjust prosecution. Neither ground seems to be entirely convincing. Admitting the undoubted principle that prosecutors ought not to be hindered, the Court appears to have ignored

[1] Russ. (ed. 7), I. 588 and Arch. (ed. 24), 1194 cite *Harris* v. *Brisco* (1886), 17 Q.B.D. 504, which is no authority on this point. Arch. also refers to 1 Hawk. P.C. ch. 83, 84, and Roscoe, *Crim. Evid.* (ed. 13) where there is nothing to the purpose.

[2] (Mich. 6 Jac. 1), Godbolt, 159.

[3] Hudson, *Treatise on Court of Star Chamber*, p. 90. No further reference is given. Mich. 22 Hen, VI, f. 5 is inconclusive; it is there stated that NEWTON J. thought that if one labour to indict me by reason of which I am indicted, I shall have a writ of maintenance against him, for the statute is general which does not allow any one to maintain; but PASTON J. held the contrary view. The statute mentioned was probably 28 Ed. I. c. 11.

[4] 11 Q.B.D. 1, at p. 13.   [5] (1895), 72 L.T. 264.

6 PROCEEDINGS CAPABLE OF MAINTENANCE

the qualification that this is not and never has been an absolute rule, and that abuse of procedure by a cruel and unjust indictment is still possible. And if maintenance is to be confined to civil proceedings, it ought to be made clear that its extension to criminal proceedings would be a mere duplication of the action for malicious prosecution. In fact, there are marked differences between the actions. The burden of proof is lighter in maintenance, and it is applicable where either party to the litigation has been helped. *Grant* v. *Thompson* appears, however, to represent the law[1].

As to civil actions, there is no doubt that it is maintenance or champerty to interfere officiously with them, whatever their nature. The derivation of champerty (*campi partitio*) might appear to limit it to real actions, but there is plenty of authority to show that a broader view prevailed from very early times. The earliest statutes—3 Ed. I. c. 25 and 28 Ed. I. c. 11—speak of the offence as including actions for the recovery of any sort of property[2], and the definition in Statutum de Conspiratoribus uses the general term *placita*. Kirketon J. in Mich. 47 Ed. III, f. 9[3], said: "and also a man shall have an action of champerty for maintenance in writ of debt to have part of the goods wherein they are received, as well as for maintenance in a plea of land to have part of that when it is recovered," and to this counsel assented[4].

It is scarcely questionable at the present day that "suit" includes an action in the Chancery Division. It was the better opinion more than a century ago that the purchase of land while a suit in equity concerning it depended was champertous[5], and in *Mowse* v. *Weaver*[6] (44 and 45 Eliz.), the two Chief Justices held in the Court of Star Chamber that if a bill had been exhibited in the Exchequer Chamber for the recovery of land, and the defendant had thereafter sold the land to another,

[1] Opinions approving it occur in *Neville* v. *London Express Newspaper, Ld.* [1919] A.C. 368, 394, 404.
[2] Coke, 2 Inst. 562. 28 Ed. I. c. 11, "extends to all actions, personal, real and mixed."
[3] Also in 47 Lib. Ass. pl. 5, and Fitz. *Abr. Champ.* 4. The writ was based on 28 Ed. I. c. 11.
[4] So too 1 Hawk, P.C. ch. 84, sect. 6, in speaking of 3 Ed. I. c. 25.
[5] 1 Hawk, P.C. ch. 84, sect. 16.　　　　　　[6] Moore, 655.

PROCEEDINGS CAPABLE OF MAINTENANCE 7

this would be champerty punishable by the ancient statutes[1]. Yet it is said to have been resolved by all the judges of England in a later Star Chamber case that if a man purchases land of B pending a suit for it in Chancery by A against B, this is not champerty, though the purchaser knows of the suit[2]. These cases deal with champerty rather as a crime than as a tort, but it is submitted that here there is no sound ground for distinguishing between the two, or for holding with respect to both at the present day that a corrupt bargain as to Chancery proceedings would not be wrongful. Indeed, in *Harris* v. *Brisco* (1886), a plaintiff in an action for redemption of a mortgage had been assisted by Brisco, and though in the circumstances this was held not to be maintenance, there was no hint that Brisco got judgment in his favour because maintenance of a suit in equity is not wrongful[3]. But it is not maintenance to take an assignment of an interest in a suit for debt while the suit is pending[4].

"Suit," it seems, also includes a proceeding in an ecclesiastical court. It is true that in *Tisdale* v. *Bedington* (39 and 40 Eliz.)[5], it was moved that an action of maintenance upon 1 Rich. II. c. 4 did not lie for maintaining a suit in a spiritual court because that statute applied only to suits in Common Law Courts, and the whole Court were of that opinion; but the Lord Chancellor in *Wallis* v. *Duke of Portland* (1797)[6] combated the idea that maintenance could not be committed in Courts Christian.

A further inference from the last-mentioned case is that an election petition under the Grenville Act[7] was a legal proceeding

[1] It will be recollected that the Exch. Ch. was divided into a Court of Equity and a Court of Common Law. Bl. III. 44.

[2] *Brownlow's Case* cited without further reference in Vin. *Abr. Maint.* (B) (2). His account of it can be eked out by *R.* v. *Hill* (8 Car. I), Godbolt, 450. In *Archbishop of Canterbury* v. *Hudson* (5 Car. I), Het. 164, the same point was raised but the case went off upon another issue. Hudson (p. 91) states that it was held by LORD EGERTON in *Dymock's Case* and *Stafford's Case* (3 Jac. I) that it is not champerty to buy land in Chancery pending the suit, or any action of trespass at Common Law, for such suits may still be kept on foot to prevent the owner selling.

[3] 17 Q.B.D. 504. [4] *Harrington* v. *Long* (1883), 2 Myl. and K. 590.

[5] Cro. Eliz. 594; also *sub nom. Tisdall* v. *Bevington*, Het. 68.

[6] 3 Ves. 494, at p. 502. Affirmed by H. L. Brown's *Parl. Cases*, App. I. 161.

[7] 10 Geo. III. c. 16.

8 PROCEEDINGS CAPABLE OF MAINTENANCE

for the purposes of the law of maintenance. At any rate, the Lord Chancellor allowed a demurrer to a bill for discovery brought by Wallis, an attorney, who had maintained such an election petition, on the ground (among others) that the discovery would disclose maintenance[1]. There is not the least reason for doubting that similar interference with an election petition at the present day would be equally objectionable. Indeed, the case is much stronger; for, while the procedure under the Grenville Act had very little real resemblance to a judicial proceeding, the method of trial substituted for it by 31 & 32 Vict. c. 125 (amended by 42 & 43 Vict. c. 75) is a genuine species of litigation[2].

Officious meddling with litigation in a prize court would also appear to be maintenance. In *Stevens* v. *Bagwell* (1808), the case, it is true, related to champerty as affecting contract, but the Master of the Rolls cited *Wallis* v. *Duke of Portland*[3] to shew that this offence is not confined to Common Law Courts[4].

Magistrates' licensing sessions are not courts, but merely statutory meetings of properly constituted persons. Proceedings before them are not litigious in character, and therefore interference in such proceedings cannot be champerty[5].

The instigation of proceedings in lunacy is not maintenance. This results from *Persse* v. *Persse*[6], where a father covenanted to settle for the benefit of his eldest son estates in which the father had an expectant interest as heir-at-law to an imbecile. Part of the consideration for the covenant was an undertaking by the son to sue out a commission of lunacy for the protection of the imbecile and his property and of the father's interest, and to take other necessary proceedings at his own expense in the father's name. The agreement was carried out by the son and he sought specific performance of the father's covenant when the imbecile died later, and his estates accrued to the

---

[1] *Ante* p. 7 *n* 6.

[2] Cf. LORD PHILLIMORE in *Neville* v. *London Express Newspaper, Ld.* [1919] A.C. at pp. 432–433.

[3] *Ubi sup.*   [4] 15 Ves. 139.

[5] *Savill Bros. Ld.* v. *Langman* (1898), 79 L.T. 44. *Qu.* whether proceedings involving the custody of children are within the law of maintenance? PHILLIMORE J. in *Holden* v. *Thompson* [1907] 2 K.B. at p. 493.

[6] (1840), 7 Cl. & F. 279.

PROCEEDINGS CAPABLE OF MAINTENANCE 9

father. The House of Lords pronounced in favour of the covenant, holding that it was not void or illegal for champerty or maintenance, or as against public policy, or as being a fraud on the jurisdiction in lunacy. LORD COTTENHAM L.C. held that "there was no suit to be maintained, and no property in litigation to be divided[1]." It is not clear whether Lord Cottenham meant that there was no suit in the sense that proceedings for a commission in lunacy are not judicial proceedings at all, or in the sense that, though such proceedings are judicial, there was no contract to interfere in them on the evidence before them. Upon either construction the reasoning is not easy to follow; for the inquiry under the commission whether or no a particular person be a lunatic is on the law side of the Court of Chancery[2], and thus appears to be a legal proceeding, or a "suit" with which meddling is possible; and that there was such meddling in the particular circumstances seems obvious from the fact that the proceedings were, in everything but name, the acts, not of the father who had a legal interest in them but, of the son whose interest independently of the agreement was much more remote.

Whatever be its interpretation, Lord Cottenham's judgment is reinforced by the policy of the law which encourages the institution of proceedings in lunacy in order to protect the person and property of the lunatic, and this would be impeded if all agreements relative to the costs of the proceedings, or to the ultimate division of the property were held void. He points this out in another part of his judgment which demolishes the argument that the contract was illegal as against public policy and as a fraud upon the great seal in the matter of lunacy[3]. A later decision recognizes the desirability of freedom in commencing lunacy proceedings, but at the same time indicates its limits[4]. A petitioner in lunacy had begun the proceedings not on his own initiative, but by the inducement of a solicitor who, after the inquiry, undertook to indemnify him against

[1] (1840), 7 Cl. & F. at p. 316. So too the report in West's Cases in H.L. at p. 138.
[2] Bl. *Comm.* III. 427. [3] At p. 316.
[4] *In re E. S—* (a supposed lunatic) (1876), 4 Ch. Div. 301. *Persse* v. *Persse* was not cited.

10 WHAT CONSTITUTES INTERFERENCE

costs. The alleged lunatic was proved to be of sound mind. The Court of Appeal unanimously deprived the petitioner of costs. No question of maintenance or champerty was raised, but the case shews that the Courts are not likely to allow the interests of the lunatic to be prejudiced[1], or their own jurisdiction to be abused by one who makes or abets a speculative petition, even though the law of maintenance be inapplicable.

Proceedings for divorce by private Act of Parliament are not an action or suit *quâ* the law of maintenance, and therefore that law was held not to be infringed where the mother of an illegitimate daughter placed £500 in the hands of the daughter's husband to enable him to procure such an Act[2]. This cannot of course be taken as any authority on maintenance of a divorce suit in the Probate, Divorce and Admiralty Division of the High Court[3].

According to an old case, a suit does not commence in the sense that it is capable of maintenance till the writ is returned, for till then it is not of record[4]; nor, on the other hand, does interference cease to be unlawful merely because it takes place after judgment, for it may hinder the party interfered with from suing an appeal[5]. But, as will be seen in the next section, the particular stage which a legal proceeding has reached—indeed, the fact that it has not even begun—is perhaps not material in order to affect the maintainer with liability[6].

WHAT CONSTITUTES INTERFERENCE?

§ 6. A mere agreement to maintain is doubtless unlawful within the domain of contract, and criminal under the statutes which will be discussed later[7]; but it is hard to say whether it is also tortious. The question resolves itself into two others:

(*a*) Is an agreement to maintain to be regarded as maintenance if no suit subsequently begins? *Flight* v. *Leman*

---

[1] The lunatic often needs protection against the very persons who have the strongest interest in taking legal action in connection with him. JAMES L.J. in 4 Ch. Div. at p. 304. Cf. Bl. *Comm.* I. 305.

[2] *Moore* v. *Usher* (1835), 7 Sim. 383, 384.

[3] *Qu.* whether the plea of "kinship" would have been available on similar facts before the Court at the present day? *Post* pp. 28 sqq.

[4] Mich. 10 Ed. IV, f. 19. So too Br. *Abr. Maint.* 36.

[5] I Hawk. P.C. ch. 83, sect. II.

[6] *Post* p. 17. [7] *Post* ch. III.

WHAT CONSTITUTES INTERFERENCE 11

indicates that it is not. There, a declaration in case alleged that the defendant unlawfully and maliciously procured T to prosecute an action on the case against the plaintiff in which the plaintiff secured a verdict. A Court of four judges unanimously held that no cause of action appeared because the declaration did not shew maintenance, as the action appeared not to have commenced, nor was want of reasonable and probable cause alleged[1]. But LORD COLERIDGE C.J. in *Bradlaugh* v. *Newdegate* (1883)[2] thought the distinction between instigation of a suit and support of a suit already commenced a narrow one, and LORD ATKINSON, in *Neville* v. *London Express Newspaper, Ld.*[3] considered that, as a consequence of *Hutley* v. *Hutley*[4] and *Sprye* v. *Porter*[5], it is no longer law. It should be noted, however, that these were opinions and not decisions of Lord Coleridge and Lord Atkinson, and that *Hutley* v. *Hutley* and *Sprye* v. *Porter* were cases on contract, not tort. On the other hand, the Court in *Flight* v. *Leman* based its judgment on a parallel between malicious prosecution and maintenance drawn by the Attorney-General in argument[6]. This comparison was hastily adopted, is entirely unsupported by historical evidence, and was denied in *Neville* v. *London Express Newspaper, Ld.* by LORD FINLAY L.C.[7], and LORD ATKINSON[8].

(*b*) Is an agreement to maintain tortious, if a suit be subsequently commenced, but the person who promised help give none? According to the older law, no. This appears from Hil. 9 Hen. VII, f. 18, where the whole Court said that if a man does not maintain in the action which ensues, the aggrieved party shall not have an action of maintenance, because he is not damaged by the previous agreement[9]. If this be law now—

[1] (1843), 4 Q.B. 883.
[2] 11 Q.B.D. at p. 8. [3] [1919] A.C. at p. 404.
[4] (1873), L.R. 8 Q.B. 112. [5] (1856), 7 E. and B. 58, 81.
[6] PATTESON J. and COLERIDGE J. thought the two actions strictly analogous. 4 Q.B. at pp. 888–889.
[7] [1919] A.C. at p. 385.
[8] *Ibid.* p. 404. Cf. LORD SHAW OF DUNFERMLINE at p. 418.
[9] Mich. 5 Hen. VII, f. 13 is apparently inconsistent with this. There, Serjeant Keble argued that if one takes money for maintenance, and does nothing, this is not punishable; "quod fuit negatum per omnes justiciarios exceptis duobus." But possibly the opinion was confined to maintenance as a crime (but see 1 Hawk. P.C. ch. 83, sect. 7), and the case itself was on an indictment for the gift and receipt of liveries.

12   WHAT CONSTITUTES INTERFERENCE

and it is by no means certain that it is[1]—it is submitted that the reason for it is open to criticism as a *petitio principii*. The Court assumed that the injured party suffered no damage. But it is clear that if A agrees to maintain B in an action between B and C, and A does nothing in pursuance of his agreement, C may yet suffer heavy loss. For B may prosecute the action relying on A's promised support, may lose it, and may be totally unable to pay costs incurred in its defence by C, who *ex hypothesi* has no remedy against A.

The answers to the questions which have been attempted in the preceding sub-sections are sufficiently inconclusive, and unfortunately similar doubts meet us when we try to solve analogous questions with regard to a champertous agreement.

If the suit ensues, even though the person who agreed to share in its spoils gives no aid, is he still liable? If, on the other hand, no action is prosecuted, is the act tortious independently of considering its fate in the law of crime or as a contract? The old authorities do not help us much in ascertaining what the law is, and are the more difficult to follow owing to the indeterminate boundary in them between civil and criminal cases. In a case on champerty in Hil. 30 Ed. III, f. 3, it was alleged that the defendant purchased the lands pending a *praecipe quod reddat* returnable on St Martin's Eve. The defendant pleaded that before that date he had bought a term of years in the lands. The plaintiff replied that the defendant did not deny that he had purchased the lands since the issue of the writ. All that he did plead was that he had purchased them before the return to the writ. In the end, the plaintiff was driven to disclose the date of the writ in the *praecipe*, and there the report ends. In Mich. 19 Rich. II[2], it was said by the whole Court that if I bargain for any land before the writ be purchased and the writ be brought against the tenant of the land, and then he deliver seisin, writ of champerty does not lie, because it shall be understood that the bargain is not made for such consideration[3],

[1] Cf. LORD ATKINSON in *Neville* v. *London Express Newspaper, Ld.* [1919] A.C. at p. 404.   [2] Bellewe.

[3] F.N.B. 172 D regards this as inconsistent with 30 Lib. Ass. pl. 15, but that seems to have been a criminal case, the purchase is not said to have been in good faith, and in neither the report nor the abridgments is any decision reported.

WHAT CONSTITUTES INTERFERENCE   13

which is no more than saying that if the purchase be in good faith it is not tortious. Nor is Br. *Abr. Champ.* 3 inconsistent with this. There the effect of an agreement made before the action is brought is queried, and Brooke thinks that it would be champerty[1]. In Hil. 9 Hen. VII, f. 18, the whole Court denied counsel's proposition that if *A* promises to maintain *B* in consideration of *B*'s enfeoffing him of half the land in dispute, and *B* accordingly conveys the lands to *A*, but no action ensues this is maintenance[2]. And the Court seemed to take no account of the fact that the purchase was, in the circumstances put, made in bad faith.

Before attempting to deduce any results from these *dicta*, we must consider more fully the attitude of the law to the motive of the defendant who engaged in the agreement. At first it seems to have wavered. According to Hil. 21 Ed. III, f. 10, where the King sued a writ of champerty against two, it was said that if, pending a real action, a stranger purchases the land of the tenant in fee for good consideration, and not to maintain the plea, this is not champerty, though by intendment the stranger for his interest will aid the tenant in his plea. No decision is reported here, and 50 Lib. Ass. pl. 3, where all the serjeants took the view that he who purchases in good faith pending the writ is a champertor, "for it is against statute, and also by intendment he wishes to maintain to escape his own loss," is equally inconclusive, quite apart from the fact that the case was not on champerty. Thus the same reasoning was applied in different cases to prove exactly opposite results. The contradictory statements in them may possibly relate to criminal champerty, but the early reports are just as baffling in their formulation of the law generally. For in Mich. 4 Ed. II a purchase of tenements which were the subject of litigation was said not to be champerty if the purchaser could aver that he did not take them in return for maintaining the plea[3], and Fitzherbert took this to be the rule in his time[4]. But in Pasch.

---

[1] Cf. 32 Hen. VIII. c. 9.

[2] The opinion was *obiter*, as the writ of champerty in this case was sued for interference in a writ of formedon upon which an action had in fact ensued.

[3] Fitz. *Abr. Champ.* 12. S. S. vol. XXVI. p. 135 translates the passage.

[4] F.N.B. 172 F.

14   WHAT CONSTITUTES INTERFERENCE

32 Ed. III, all the serjeants denied an assertion of NOTTON J. that if the purpose of the purchase pending the suit were not maintenance this would not be champerty, the ground being the same as that in 50 Lib. Ass. pl. 3[1], and in Henry VI's reign there are hints that some judges took this view[2]. To modern lawyers it may seem odd that there was ever any doubt whether purchase in good faith pending the suit should have been lawful, but the state of society under Edward III, Richard II, and the Lancastrian kings quite justified the presumption that a purchase was made with an evil motive, and there is no need to limit these cases, as Coke was inclined to do, to royal officers mentioned in 13 Ed. I. c. 49[3], though there can be no doubt that they were the worst offenders, and that their mere appearance in a proceeding might easily pollute the course of justice. By Coke's time, the sting had been drawn from champerty and maintenance by the Star Chamber, and he could write with truth that "if any other person [than such officers] purchase *bonâ fide* depending the suit, he is not in danger of champerty[4]." It is very improbable that the Courts of our own time would decide otherwise[5].

The question to what extent motive is relevant in maintenance generally was considered by LORD COLERIDGE C.J. in *Bradlaugh* v. *Newdegate* (1883)[6]. He quoted and adopted for the purposes of his decision an *obiter dictum* of the Judicial Committee of the Privy Council in *Fischer* v. *Kamala Naicker* (1860)[7] that maintenance "must be something against good policy and justice, something tending to promote unnecessary litigation, something that *in a legal sense is immoral*, and to the constitution of which a bad motive *in the same sense* is necessary." LORD COLERIDGE took legally immoral to mean "a motive which impels to an illegal act." Construed by the context of the quoted

---

[1] Fitz. *Abr. Champ.* 6. Not in printed Y.BB.
[2] *Per* DANBY C.J.C.P., in Mich. 8 Ed. IV, f. 13. And see Br. *Abr. Champ.* 10 and Fitz. *Abr. Champ.* 3.
[3] 2 Inst. 484.   [4] *Ibid.*
[5] *Harrington* v. *Long* (1833), 2 Myl. and K. 590. *Williams* v. *Protheroe* (1829), 3 Y. & J. 129. 2 M. & P. 779; BEST L.C.J., at p. 135 in first mentioned report, and at p. 786 in second. *Hunter* v. *Daniel* (1845), 4 Hare, 420; V.C. at p. 430.
[6] 11 Q.B.D. at pp. 9–10.   [7] 8 Moo. Ind. App. 170, 187.

WHAT CONSTITUTES INTERFERENCE 15

passage, this appears to mean "something against good policy and justice," or "tending to promote unnecessary litigation." If that be so, the position of a defendant to an action of maintenance appears to be this. If his motive were based on some legally recognized excuse for maintenance, it is blameless. But the legally recognized excuses for maintenance are not capable of exact enumeration. The Courts may possibly admit others, besides those falling under definite heads like assistance to the poor. So that the defendant's motive in these other possible cases depends for its goodness or badness, on whether the Courts think that his act is "against good policy," etc. Pushed to its limits, this means that a man can only be sure that his motive is good by finding out whether his act is one of the legally recognized exceptions from the law of maintenance, or by correctly guessing whether the Court will hold it to be such an exception in the case in which he is concerned. Assuming it to be such an exception, it appears that his belief in its existence, though based on insufficient grounds, does not vitiate his defence[1].

If innocent purchase while the suit depends be not tortious, much less is one made before the suit begins. But how if the agreement were made before commencement of the action with deliberate intent to assist in it and to share the proceeds, and the action either does not take place, or takes place, but the party lends no assistance in it? In the first event, it is conceived that his agreement is not tortious[2], in the second that he should be liable, though mediaeval authority is the other way[3].

Akin to this is the question whether a person, whose sole title to property is a champertous agreement or conveyance, acts lawfully in maintaining an action between two other persons which may possibly affect his title.

---

[1] *Harris* v. *Brisco* (1886), 17 Q.B.D. 504. LORD ABINGER C.B. and ROLFE B., in *Findon* v. *Parker* (1843), 11 M. & W. at p. 679. HAWKINS J., in *Alabaster* v. *Harness* [1894] 2 Q.B. at p. 905. LOPES L.J. in same case on appeal [1895] 1 Q.B. at p. 345. LORD SUMNER in *Oram* v. *Hutt* [1914] 1 Ch. at p. 107. DARLING J. in *McCarthy* v. *Kennedy* (*Times* newspaper, 8th Mch, 1905). VISCOUNT READING C.J. in *Neville* v. *London Express Newspaper, Ld.* [1917] 1 K.B. 402. LORD FINLAY L.C. in same case on appeal to H.L. [1919] A.C. at p. 387; LORD ATKINSON, *ibid.* at pp. 398–399.
[2] Hil. 9 Hen. VII, f. 18; *ante* p. 13.   [3] *Ante* p. 12.

16   WHAT CONSTITUTES INTERFERENCE

The judges disagreed on this point in Mich. 8 Ed. IV, f. 13. *A* had champertously enfeoffed *W.W.* pending an action by *D* against *A*. *A* made default in this action, and *D* recovered judgment, and entered the lands. *T*, the ousted tenant sued an action of deceit (apparently against *A*) and *W.W.* maintained this action. His only plea to a writ of maintenance sued against him by *D* was his interest derived from his title to the lands. CATESBY J. thought that the plea was good, as *W.W.* would have recovered the land if *T* had succeeded in the action for deceit. DANBY C.J.C.P., opposed this on the ground that *W.W.*'s title had an illegal origin. CHOKE J. admitted that the feoffment subjected *W.W.* to a penalty but nevertheless regarded it as valid[1] and as conferring an interest sufficient to justify *W.W.*'s maintenance[2].

We need not pause to discuss whether the later statute, 32 Hen. VIII. c. 9, would have covered such a case. It is enough to suggest that, at the present day, the defendant's conduct would be regarded as unlawful maintenance. At least, this is a reasonable deduction from *Hilton* v. *Woods*[3], where the plaintiff had agreed to give a solicitor part of the profits arising from the successful prosecution of a suit to establish his right to certain coal mines, upon being indemnified against the costs of the proceedings. It was held that the contract amounted to champerty and maintenance, but that the plaintiff was not disqualified from suing, since his title was vested in him before he entered into the illegal contract. The inference is that if he had not had a vested title, he could not have sued[4]. Much less could any other party to the champertous contract have lawfully maintained him.

If the champertor have acquired possession of the land under

---

[1] 1 Rich. II. c. 9, which was then in force, enacts that such feoffments 'shall be holden for none and of no value." But perhaps they were good as between feoffor and feoffee. Co. Litt. 368 *b*, 369 *a*.

[2] All the judges agreed that it was immaterial whether the land had been sold or given to *W.W.*

[3] (1867), L.R. 4 Eq. 432.

[4] Cf. *Upton* v. *Basset* (37 and 38 Eliz. C.B.) where BEAUMONT J. said *obiter* that feoffment upon maintenance or champerty is not void against the feoffor but against him who hath the right. *Burke* v. *Greene* (1814), 2 Ball & Beatty, 517.

WHAT CONSTITUTES INTERFERENCE 17

the champertous gift or agreement, the question arises whether this be not a sufficient interest in an action between A and B as to the land to justify the champertor's maintenance of A or B. Possession it will be recollected, even though legally defective in origin, "is good against all the world except the person who can shew a good title"[1].

For the purposes of maintenance, a suit may be regarded as still pending even after judgment is given in so far as the meddling tends to discourage the losing party from suing an appeal[2], but a *bonâ fide* transfer of the subject of litigation after the action is over, where there is no preceding agreement, would not now be champerty. The point may have been doubtful in earlier times. Penros, who was created a judge in Ireland in 1385, received whilst he was at the bar, as a fee, the land which he had professionally assisted the plaintiff to recover, and pleaded this as a defence to a writ of champerty. Whether he did so successfully does not appear, but Br. *Abr. Champ.* 3 apparently takes his case as the basis of the rule we have stated above[3], and Coke's opinion—which, whatever its merits, was probably representative of contemporary legal ideas—was that if his defence were held good, it must have been because the conveyance to him had been made after judgment[4], and the law thus stated is consistent with a *dictum* of DANBY C.J.C.P. in Mich. 8 Ed. IV, f. 13.

It has been contended quite recently that if assistance be given to a defendant, this is not maintenance, which (it was argued) is limited to aiding a plaintiff. The Court of Appeal found it unnecessary to decide the point, but one of its members described it

---

[1] *Asher* v. *Whitlock* (1865), L.R. 1 Q.B. 1, 5. Pollock and Wright, *Possession in the Common Law*, Pt II, ch. III, sect. 17.

[2] 1 Hawk. P. C. ch. 83, sect. 11.

[3] HANKFORD J., in Hil. 13 Hen. IV, f. 16 referred to *Penros' Case*, but rather in connection with the relation of counsel to client.

[4] 2 Inst. 564. Hawkins (1 P. C. ch. 84, sect. 20) follows Coke, and adds a warning as to the danger of meddling with gifts of this kind, owing to the strong presumption of champerty raised by them. Quite apart from champerty, such a gift may be void for undue influence; *Broun* v. *Kennedy* (1864), 33 L.J. (N.S.), Ch. 342; *post* p. 27. The presumption is not likely to be raised now. See *Anderson* v. *Radcliffe* (1858), 3 E.B. & E. 806. In spite of *Mowse* v. *Weaver*, Moore 655, and Hudson, it is not likely that a conveyance pending an appeal would now be criminal champerty.

W. L. P.

18   WHAT CONSTITUTES INTERFERENCE

as "a bold contention"[1]. It certainly was. The Year Books give no hint of it, and have many cases which imply the contrary[2], and in Mich. 7 Ed. IV, f. 15 it was said that, though the plaintiff recover against a defendant in an action, yet he can have action of maintenance against every one who maintains on behalf of the defendant[3]. Coke knew nothing of any such limitation, and the definitions in *Termes de la Ley* and Hawkins[4] expressly include assistance of a defendant. Moreover, cases occur in the 19th and 20th centuries where, whatever may have been the result, no question was raised as to the applicability of the law of maintenance in such circumstances[5]; and LORD ABINGER C.B., in *Findon* v. *Parker* (1843), said:

The law of maintenance, as I understand it upon the modern constructions is confined to cases where a man improperly, and for the purpose of stirring up litigation and strife, encourages others, either to bring actions, or to make defences which they have no right to make[6].

LORD COLERIDGE C.J. in *Bradlaugh* v. *Newdegate* (1883) agreed with the entire judgment of Lord Abinger[7]. Finally, several of the noble and learned lords who decided *Neville* v. *London Express Newspaper, Ld.* were emphatic in their opinion that it was immaterial which party were assisted[8]. It may be added that there is no logical reason for raising the alleged distinction, for whether the person maintained be plaintiff or defendant, the grievance to the other party is the same.

---

[1] *British Cash, etc. Ld.* v. *Lamson & Co. Ld.* [1908] 1 K.B. 1006. BUCKLEY L.J., at p. 1021. Counsel cited (at p. 1009) Stephen, *Dig. Cr. Law,* Art. 156 in support of their contention. I cannot find the learned author's proof of his statement there. In any event, it refers to the criminal law on maintenance.

[2] Hil. 13 Hen. IV, f. 16; Mich. 8 Hen. V, f. 8; Trin. 11 Hen. VI, f. 39; 14 Hen. VI, f. 13; Mich. 22 Hen. VI, f. 35; *ibid.* f. 24; Pasch. 28 Hen. VI, f. 6; Hil. 32 Hen. VI, f. 24; Hil. 34 Hen. VI, f. 35; 36 Hen. VI, f. 12; Pasch. 37 Hen. VI, f. 25; 39 Hen. VI, ff. 5 and 19; Pasch. 18 Ed. IV, f. 14; *ibid.* f. 2; Mich. 21 Hen. VII, f. 40.

[3] Br. *Abr. Maint.* 35 states this as if it were a decision.

[4] 1 P.C. ch. 83, sect. 3.

[5] E.g. *Stone* v. *Yea* (1822), Jac. 426. *James* v. *Kerr* (1888), 40 Ch. Div. 449. *Holden* v. *Thompson* [1907] 1 K.B. 489.

[6] 11 M. & W. 675, at p. 682.   [7] 11 Q.B.D. at p. 12.

[8] [1919] A.C. 368. LORD ATKINSON at p. 395. LORD PHILLIMORE at p. 428. LORD FINLAY L.C. by implication at pp. 394-395.

WHAT CONSTITUTES INTERFERENCE   19

The definition which we have adopted from *Termes de la Ley*[1] is general enough to include in improper assistance the gift or delivery of any property or the rendering of any considerable service, and this fairly represents the law now. In Mich. 22 Hen. VI, f. 5, the whole Court were of opinion that an Abbot had committed maintenance in giving 40s. to *W.E.* to labour the jurors impannelled in an appeal of mayhem, though it was not alleged that *W.E.* had distributed any of the money[2]; and according to Fitz. *Abr. Maint.* 11, if *A* gives money to *B* to distribute for a suit between *C* and *D*, and *B* does not distribute it, yet *A* is punishable in an action of maintenance, and if *B* had distributed it, both would have been punishable[3]. In Trin. 28 Hen. VI, f. 12[4]—the case of Clement Tailour—the defendant had delivered £5 of his own money to two other persons for distribution among the inhabitants of the county in their discretion in order to maintain the plea between his servant and Clement, and it was not alleged that any distribution had taken place. Prisot C.J.C.P. held that the mere delivery of the money constituted the maintenance, and it was so adjudged; and a majority of the Court expressed the same opinion in Mich. 5 Hen. VII, f. 13[5].

Giving money, or bearing the whole or part of the expense of a suit is the most natural way of committing the wrong[6], but saving another expenses which he might incur, or even trying to do so, is probably maintenance[7]. And a loan of money to the litigant has been adjudged to be as objectionable as a payment out and out[8]. Certain forms of interference which

[1] *Ante* p. 1.
[2] The earlier part of the report is in Mich. 21 Hen. VI, f. 15, and the facts of the case are also referred to in Trin. 28 Hen. VI, f. 7.
[3] Fitzherbert cites Trin. 28 Hen. VI, f. 7 where this appears in the argument of counsel; and Trin. 29 Hen. VI, which is missing from the Year Book. Jenk. 101 quotes all these passages for the same statement and also Mich. 21 Hen. VII, f. 40.
[4] A variant report is in Trin. 31 Hen. VI, f. 8. See also Trin. 28 Hen. VI, f. 7.
[5] Though the payment was made once for all, that was sufficient to justify the "adhuc manutenet" of the old writ of maintenance.
[6] 1 Hawk. P.C. ch. 83, sect. 4.   [7] *Ibid.* sect. 5.
[8] Mich. 19 Ed. IV, f. 15. It is immaterial at what stage of the maintained action the money is paid or promised. *Per* Lord Sumner in *Oram* v. *Hutt* [1914] 1 Ch. at p. 106.

2—2

20   WHAT CONSTITUTES INTERFERENCE

were easily possible when maintenance was prevalent are unlikely to occur at the present day. It was said that if a man of great power in the country came before the jury and stated openly that he wished to spend £20 for a certain party or to labour the jury, it would be maintenance though he gave nothing nor laboured the jury[1]. But improper meddling of a less trenchant kind might still occur, and should on principle be regarded as wrongful. On the other hand, mere friendly advice as to the proper method of recovering a debt is not maintenance[2]. Traces of extreme views are to be found in the older law, but the circumstances of the period explain them, and they cannot now be accepted. Thus, it was said to have been adjudged that where a man who had nothing to do with a suit came to the bar of the Court to see [visit] the matter for the other party without saying anything, yet the judges awarded him imprisonment[3]. Previous agreement between the maintainer and the person maintained is not essential. Thus, an action upon the case has been held to lie against one who commenced a suit against another in the name, and without the privity, of A to whom that other was indebted[4]. This might be taken as a belated distinction between maintenance and conspiracy, but the law did not make it consciously, and maintenance in early times was a species of conspiracy which very soon earned special attention by the legislature.

As already stated, the mere taking an assignment of an interest of a debt which is in litigation is not maintenance[5]. Nor probably is the officious giving of evidence. Certainly, in Pasch. 11 Hen. VI, f. 41, CHEYNE C.J.K.B. said that if an ancient

[1] *Per* NEWTON J., in Mich. 22 Hen. VI, f. 5. Cf. Y.B. 15 Ed. III (*Rolls Series*), 4. In an assize of novel disseisin a panel was challenged because it was arrayed by the device of Simon de Swanland, a "meinteinour," and on proof of this an *alias summoneas* was awarded.

[2] 1 Hawk. P.C., ch. 83, sect. 11. Cf. HAWKINS J., in *Alabaster* v. *Harness* [1894] 2 Q.B. at p. 900.

[3] *Per* Littleton *arguendo* in Hil. 32 Hen. VI, f. 24. PRISOT C.J.C.P., remarked appropriately, "C'est fort ley," and pointed out that unless he spoke the judges could not know why he came to the bar. The pendulum sometimes swung the other way. THIRNING C.J.C.P., was of opinion in Hil. 13 Hen. IV, f. 16 that "speaking of great words" to jurors was not maintenance. The context indicates that the "great words" were threats.

[4] *Thurston* v. *Ummons* (15 Car. I) March 47.

[5] *Harrington* v. *Long* (1833), 2 Myl. & K. 590. *Ante* 14.

DEFENCES: 21

man of the county who has the best knowledge of the right and title comes with the defendant to declare his right in that matter, this is maintenance[1], and in Pasch. 28 Hen. VI, f. 6, FORTESCUE C.J.K.B. distinguished between a person praying to be examined by the Court and thereon being requested to say what he knows—which is justifiable maintenance—and volunteering information—which is punishable; and he applied the same distinction to information given to jurors, and the Court admitted this[2]. But the harsh view which these cases represent—that a witness must have a *subpoena* or must suppress the truth—was reprobated long ago[3], and "to-day it is looked upon as part of the duty of citizens to be ready and willing to assist the administration of justice by giving evidence when they can do so usefully"[4]. If evidence be relevant, the motive with which it is given is immaterial.

Other facts which constitute maintenance and champerty are necessarily incident to a discussion of defences to an action for either, and these we now proceed to consider.

DEFENCES TO CHAMPERTY AND MAINTENANCE

§ 7. Maintenance is officious meddling in a suit. But what is "officious"? The vagueness of this term has probably saved maintenance from total disappearance from modern law. Most of the mediaeval litigation on the topic centred on its meaning[5], and judicial feeling with respect to it has undergone a revulsion. In Henry VI's reign, it looks as if the law presumed that anybody committed maintenance who helped a litigant in any way. In our own times, this is no longer so, and decisions of the last century have so enlarged the limited exceptions of the old law that a plaintiff in an action of maintenance has much less prospect of success[6].

---

[1] The opinion was *obiter*.

[2] So too 1 Hawk. P.C. ch. 83, sect. 6, and REDE J., in Mich. 20 Hen. VII, f. 11.

[3] *Per* BULLER J., in *Master* v. *Miller* (1791), 4 T.R. at p. 340.

[4] *Per* FLETCHER MOULTON L.J., in *British Cash, etc. Ld.* v. *Lamson & Co. Ld.* [1908] 1 K.B. at p. 1013.

[5] Cf. FLETCHER MOULTON L.J., *ubi sup.*—"it is far easier to say what is not maintenance than to say what is maintenance."

[6] See *dicta* in the following passages as to the changed view of the law:

22 DEFENCES:

No general principle underlies the various defences which we have to discuss. It has been suggested that they are reducible to the rule that the defendant is not liable unless it be shewn that he knew that he was doing wrong, but this only leads to a barren discussion of what "wrong" means, and has not commended itself to the Court of Appeal[1]. Nor can it be said that the assistance must always be based on a community of interest with the litigant or in the subject matter of the litigation, for if it be given merely for charitable purposes, that is a good defence. But if there be no logical principle for the exceptions, we have it on good authority that they are probably not exhaustive[2], and though this makes the law uncertain, it frees us from some of the old decisions which changed circumstances have made inapplicable, and at the same time makes the law adaptable to our own times.

(1) PROFESSIONAL LEGAL ASSISTANCE

In Br. *Abr. Maint.* 4 (Mich. 21 Hen. VI, f. 15) there is an opinion of the Court that a counsellor of the law, attorney, solicitor, officers for process and pleas *et hujusmodi*, can take money lawfully, and in Pasch. 22 Ed. IV, f. 11, GENNEY J. said that a man of law may maintain[3]. It may be taken that immunity of this kind was well recognized long before this[4], and the limits of it can best be considered under headings appropriate to each branch of the profession:

BULLER J., in *Master* v. *Miller* (1791), 4 T.R. at p. 340. BEST L.C.J., in *Williams* v. *Protheroe* (1829), 3 Y. & J. at p. 135, and 2 M. & P. at p. 786. LORD ABINGER C.B. in *Findon* v. *Parker* (1843), 11 M. & W. at pp. 679, 682. LORD COLERIDGE C.J., in *Bradlaugh* v. *Newdegate* (1883), 11 Q.B.D. at p. 14. COZENS-HARDY M.R. in *British Cash, etc. Ld.* v. *Lamson & Co. Ld.* [1908] 1 K.B. at p. 1012. Viscount Haldane in *Neville* v. *London Express Newspaper, Ld.* [1919] A.C. at p. 389; LORD SHAW OF DUNFERMLINE, *ibid.* 414.

[1] See RIGBY L.J.'s criticism of it in *Alabaster* v. *Harness* [1895] 1 Q.B. at p. 345. The learned L.J. felt himself unable to reduce the exceptions to any simple rule, and thought that justification for maintenance must either be a common interest recognized by the law, or the case must fall under some specific exception recognized by the law.

[2] *Per* FLETCHER MOULTON L.J., in *British Cash. etc. Co. Ld.* v. *Lamson & Co. Ld.* [1908] 1 K.B. at p. 1013.

[3] So too Yaxley *arguendo* in Mich. 9 Hen. VII, f. 7.

[4] 28 Ed. I. c. 11 is more appropriate to criminal maintenance, but there can be little doubt that its exception of pleaders and learned men was general. See also P. and M. I. 211–217.

PROFESSIONAL LEGAL ASSISTANCE 23

(a) *Attornies*. The history of the law is not entirely intelligible here without a sketch of the history of attornies themselves. It will be recollected that prior to the Judicature Act, 1873, a "solicitor" was, strictly speaking, a legal practitioner who was employed to conduct suits in Chancery, the older word "attorney-at-law" being restricted to one who practised in the Common Law Courts. Originally, the solicitor was inferior to the attorney, and this continued till the 17th century[1]. Solicitors had at first no defined legal position, and they seem to have escaped the penalties of maintenance by their inferiority of social position, since they were but a species of servant to the person for whom they acted, and the servant might maintain his master[2]. Thus, in *Thursby* v. *Warren* (5 Car. I), all the Court conceived that a solicitor of an inferior rank who solicits causes for his clients may take recompense, but that if a person of superior rank should do it, it would be maintenance[3]; and in *Onely* v. *Earl of Kent* (18 Eliz.)[4], DYER C.J.C.P. appeared to see nothing objectionable in allowing one who does not seem to have been an attorney to recover his fees[5]. The usage of allowing these solicitors in Chancery probably arose through the Common Law Courts allowing their attornies to practise in Courts to which they were not admitted, and in the Court of Chancery itself an impetus was given to the increase of this unprofessional class by the absurd limitation of their professional brethren to six Clerks. By 1596, their office was so overworked that the under-clerks of each were formally recognized, though restricted in numbers. Under these again were deputies, and all were eager for fees.

To expedite proceedings with such an understaffed professional Clerks' office, extensive bribery was necessary, and a class of men sprang up whose business it was "to conduct, expedite, and solicit causes[6]." These "solicitors," without proper qualification or standing, nevertheless were on the same

---

[1] Poley, *Law Affecting Solicitors*, p. 1.
[2] Cf. Hudson, pp. 94–95.
[3] Cro. Car. 159.   [4] Dyer, 355 *b*.
[5] See E. B. V. Christian, *Short History of Solicitors*, ch. III. and pp. 45, 73; Jenks, *Short History of English Law*, 203–209; P. and M. I. 212–214.
[6] Christian, p. 73.

24 DEFENCES:

footing in the conduct of a suit as attornies. In the Star Chamber, precisely similar causes led to the same result. The attornies of that Court were at first two in number, and Hudson thought that their increase to four was excessive.

"But in our own age," he adds, "there are stepped up a new sort of people called solicitors, unknown to the records of the law, who like the grasshoppers of Egypt, devour the whole land; and these I dare say (being authorized by the opinion of the most reverend and learned lord chancellor that ever was before him) were express maintainers, and could not justify their maintenance upon any action brought"[1].

The inadequate numbers of the official attornies and their technical ineptitude naturally made the public prefer somebody who could do what they paid him to do. Hence solicitors flourished in spite of professional jealousy, and their fees were recoverable. In *Worthington* v. *Garstone* (22 & 23 Eliz.)[2], the plaintiff who had been promised £100 by the defendant for soliciting and prosecuting an action between defendant and X, got a verdict for £75 in an action upon the case against the defendant, the Court agreeing that it was lawful to be a solicitor, if not for maintenance, and provided money were not laid out with that object.

Solicitors were a sufficiently considerable body of men by 1605 to make their regulation by 3 Jac. I. c. 7 advisable. There they are mentioned together with "attornies" and "servants." The latter term no doubt included the amateur solicitor, and the solicitor who followed the law as a calling. All three classes were severely penalised by that Act if they deliberately delayed a suit, and this is not surprising when a solicitor is said to have thrashed his clerk because he had managed to secure an order of the Court which expedited the client's business. It is clear too from Hudson that the mode in which they conducted legal business left much to be desired. By Charles II's time, their numbers had generated some *esprit de corps*, though even then the profession was too often the refuge of the profligate and incompetent. The other branch of the legal profession had by this time attained to an honourable standard, and the day was

---

[1] Hudson, pp. 94–95.   [2] Hob. 67.

PROFESSIONAL LEGAL ASSISTANCE 25

long past when counsellors "did sit in Paul's upon stools against the pillars and walls to get clients"[1]; and there had been a technical and moral improvement in the profession as a whole comparable to that in medicine when surgery ceased to be in the hands of the blacksmith, the weaver, the barber.

In the history of our law there is nothing to shew that an attorney, or a solicitor (when his position had become assured) in exercising his profession committed maintenance even when the severest view was taken of that offence. 28 Ed. I. c. 11 (Art. sup. Cart.) excepted from its penal provisions the taking counsel of pleaders, or of learned men in the law for a man's fee[2]. It is implied as early as Hil. 13 Hen. IV, f. 16 that an attorney may maintain, and in *Mowse* v. *Weaver* (44 and 45 Eliz.), the two Chief Justices, and EGERTON C.S. said in the Star Chamber that

no man can justify maintenance in soliciting suits except he be servant to the party for whom he solicits, or of his fee learned in the law, or son, or brother, or has a particular interest in right or in reversion or remainder of the land[3].

---

[1] Christian, p.45 citing "Description of England" in Holinshed's *Chronicle*.

[2] See Coke's commentary on this, 2 Inst. 562.

[3] Moore, 655. It is needless to labour the point at the present day, but for historical purposes the following may be added: Mich. 11 Hen. VI, f. 10; the defendant to a writ of maintenance pleaded that a long time before the action which he was alleged to have maintained he had been retained as a general attorney to collect the debts and sue the debtors of the person maintained, and as such sued the plaintiff for debt; MARTYN J. said, "If he be a man of law with a matter it will excuse him of maintenance for this cause." So too, in Trin. 35 Hen. VI (not in Y.B., but in Fitz. *Abr. Maint.* 21) it was held by the whole Court that an attorney may give of his own monies to a serjeant or apprentice for his client, and this is not maintenance. Again, FROWYK C.J.C.P., in Trin. 18 Hen. VII (Keilwey, 50) said of a plea that the defendant was an attorney that it was good, for as he was attorney by authority of his master, it was lawful for him to do everything to his master's advantage; but if he did it without his master's command, an action was maintainable against him. "And if I deliver money to an attorney to sue an action for me, this is justifiable maintenance, as well for the messenger as for my attorney, but without my authority it is maintenance as well in him who pays as in the attorney." See too Keble *arguendo* in Pasch. 5 Hen. VII, f. 20; and 2 Inst. 564. Vin. *Abr. Maint.* (E), (5) cites without further reference *Constantine* v. *Barnes* (37 Eliz.), Yelv. 46, for the statement that retainer of a general attorney to prosecute all a client's causes is maintenance if the attorney sues in his name. I cannot find support of this in the references available, and it is inconsistent with 1 Hawk. P.C. ch. 83, sect. 28 (which need not here be confined to criminal law) and with Mich. 11 Hen. VI, f. 10 (*supra*).

26 DEFENCES:

There is dubious authority for the proposition that the attorney would be liable if he acted in a Court to which he was not admitted[1], but the reason given for this—that otherwise a man might make such warrant of attorney to any great man— has long ceased to be of probable occurrence, and there is weighty opinion against the alleged rule[2]. At the present day the point is of little importance, since a solicitor who practised in a Court to which he is not admitted would incur penalties of another sort[3].

If attornies and solicitors are not, as such, liable to the penalties of maintenance, it by no means follows that they are privileged any more than other people if their assistance be improper. MOYLE J. in Hil. 34 Hen. VI, f. 23 said that it is maintenance in an attorney if he or another person learned in the law proffer money to the inquest, and in *Turner* v. *Burnaby* (12 Will. III)[4], where two attornies at the tavern agreed each to name 24 jurors to the sheriff, out of whom he should return 24 to try the issue, the Court were of opinion that if the sheriff should return a jury at the denomination of any person he would commit a misdemeanour, and it might be maintenance in him at whose request it was done, but here, it being by consent of the attornies on either side, *consensus tollit errorem*[5]. One of the objects of the statutes relating to maintenance and champerty was to stop speculations in suits by attornies[6], and consistently with this an agreement by an attorney to indemnify a party against all costs of a suit on being allowed to retain one half of the proceeds has been held to be maintenance and cham-

---

[1] Vin. *op. cit.* (4) again quotes *Constantine* v. *Barnes* where it was said that it was the *Lord of Lincoln's Case* in the Star Chamber, where he was censured for it. There is no such reference in *Barnes* v. *Constantine*, Yelv. 46, nor in Cro. Eliz. Viner gives no other.

[2] 1 Hawk. P.C. ch. 23, sect. 28.

[3] Poley, 508.   [4] 12 Mod. 564.

[5] 3 Geo. II. c. 25 (repealed by 6 Geo. IV. c. 50, sect. 52) prescribed more efficient methods for the nomination, summoning and return of the jury. Other cases which shew that misbehaviour on the part of a solicitor may be maintenance or champerty are *Worthington* v. *Garstone* (*ante* 24). *Wood* v. *Downes* (1811), 18 Ves. 120, 126. *Holden* v. *Thompson* [1907] 2 K.B. 489. 76 L.J.K.B. 889.

[6] See ERLE C.J., in *Anderson* v. *Radcliffe* (1858), 3 E.B. & E. at p. 818. *Kenney* v. *Browne* (1796). 3 Ridge. P.C. 462, 498–502.

PROFESSIONAL LEGAL ASSISTANCE 27

perty[1]; and even a simple indemnity against all the costs of a suit seems to be objectionable, though it does not amount to these torts[2].

On the other hand, a loan by a solicitor to his client is unexceptionable[3], and he may well take an assignment of the subject matter of a pending suit by way of security for costs already due[4]. But of this more will be said in discussing contracts[5].

(β) *Counsel.* There is no need to expend energy in demonstrating that a counsel commits no wrong in properly assisting his client. This appears from the exception in 28 Ed. I. c. 11 (Art. sup. Cart.)[6]. The point was never thought worth argument, and the Year Books and later reports imply or express his immunity from maintenance[7]. But just like an attorney he loses this immunity if his interference is improper, as by giving money to maintain, or by threatening a juror[8]. It is not champerty if without any preceding agreement he takes a transfer of the

[1] *In re Masters* (1835). 1 H. & W. 348. 4 Dowl. P.C. 18. Cf. *Box* v. *Barnaby*, Hob. 117: "if an attorney follow a cause to be paid in gross, when it is recovered, that is champerty."

[2] *In re Jones* (1870), L.R. 6 Ch. 497. (The solicitor was ordered to pay the defendants the costs of the suit when it was dismissed against them. Nothing was said of champerty or maintenance. The principle would appear to be that the act approaches to speculation in a suit, and this is equally applicable to a promise by the attorney that he will never ask for repayment of the expenses which he incurs on his client's behalf. 1 Hawk. P.C. ch. 83, sect. 28). *Leach* v. *Penton* (Mich. Ja. B) cited without further reference in Vin. *Abr. Maint.* (E) (6) queries the point. *Ibid.* (M) (12) cites *Smith* v. *Andrews* (1649), Style, 183, for the rule that if an attorney prosecute his client's cause without fees, this is not maintenance. But that was mere argument of counsel citing *Hill* v. *Sands* (16 Car. I) to which no further reference is given. See too 1 Hawk. P.C. *ubi supra.*

[3] 1 Hawk. P.C. ch. 83, sect. 28.

[4] *Anderson* v. *Radcliffe* (1858), 3 E.B. & E. 806.   [5] *Post* p. 96.

[6] *Ante* p. 25; and see Coke's interpretation of the Statute, 2 Inst. 562.

[7] HERLE C.J.C.P. in Trin. 6 Ed. III, f. 33 (a man may have the aid of the learned). DANBY J., in Hil. 32 Hen. VI, f. 24, conceded that a Serjeant's duty is to supervise his client's affairs. The Court in Br. *Abr. Maint.* 14 (a counsellor can lawfully take money). CHOKE J., in Mich. 21 Ed. IV, f. 67, implies that counsel in considering the sufficiency of an indictment laid before them might get information elsewhere, and there is also an implication of their immunity. PRISOT C.J.C.P., in Trin. 28 Hen. VI, f. 12 and in Hil. 34 Hen. VI, f. 26. *Saulkell's Case* (3 Car. I), Het. 78. See too 1 Hawk. P.C. ch. 83, sect. 7.

[8] 1 Hawk. P.C. *ubi sup.* Hudson, 93. *Skapholme* v. *Hart* (1680), Finch, 477.

28　　　　　　　　DEFENCES:

thing sued for after the suit is over[1], but at the present day he will do well to consider these and the like bargains from the point of view of the independent rule that they may be objectionable on the ground of undue influence rather than with regard to the question whether they are champerty or maintenance[2]. He is, it may be added, liable to punishment for contempt of court for conduct in his professional capacity which merits it[3].

(2) KINSHIP

The principle that kinship of some sort was a defence to maintenance was recognized in the old law, but with little certainty as to its basis, and still less as to its limits. In the almost total absence of recent authority on the topic, it is something very like guess-work to say what line the Courts of our own time would take with respect to it. It is submitted that they are more likely to probe matters further than to rest content with the inference that mere kinship negatives officiousness in supporting a litigant, or, to put the matter in another way, that they would perhaps treat kinship as but one ingredient in forming a defence which would ultimately fall under that of "interest,"—of which more hereafter.

According to Coke's commentary, 28 Ed. I. c. 11 (Art. sup. Cart.) excepts from its provisions the taking counsel of parents[4]. We proceed to discuss the old authorities for what they are worth, but they are scarcely more than scraps and fragments.

In Trin. 6 Ed. III, f. 33, HERLE C.J.C.P. was of opinion that the ordinances against champerty did not forbid a man to have the aid of his parents[5], and he said that every law supposes that the son must aid his father, and therefore in this case it was not maintenance where the defendants to the writ of champerty were J. de R., E. de R., who was father of J. de R., and P.I. who was father-in-law of J. de R. In the original

---

[1] *Ante* p. 15.

[2] *Broun* v. *Kennedy* (1864), 33 L.J. (N.S.), Ch. 342. *Post* 105.

[3] *Lechmere Charlton's Case* (1836), 2 My. & Cr. 316. *Ex parte Pater* (1864), 9 Cox C.C. 544. That he is liable for similar misconduct in his private capacity merely goes to shew that he is on the same footing there as any layman. *Mitchell's Case* (1741), 2 Atk. 173.

[4] 2 Inst. 562.　　[5] Br. *Abr. Champ.* 11 has "amies" instead of "parents."

KINSHIP 29

action P. de S. had sued a writ of entry against E. de R., and J. de R. purchased all the land except two acres. The relationship between E. de R. and J. de R. was pleaded on their behalf, and HERLE's statement of the law was given upon this. Later it was said that E. de R. had given the lands to J. de R. in frank-marriage with P.I.'s daughter. If this were done before P. de S. sued E. de R., it puts a different complexion on the case, for it gives J. de R. a substantial and morally clean interest in the case independently of his kinship.

About a century and a half later, though the defendant to a writ of maintenance said that he was the son-in-law of him whom he was alleged to have maintained, yet he could not justify maintenance for this cause, for a distinction was taken between maintenance in a real action and in any other action. In a real action he could have justified if the land could have come to him in any manner, since it was lawful for those who got lands by remainder, reversion or descent to aid the tenant[1]. Here then, the mere defence of kinship could have been successful in case of interference in a real action only in so far as it showed an interest in the subject of the suit. This is more satisfactory than the view that kinship *per se* is a defence, and it had been well put in argument in Mich. 21 Hen. VI, f. 15[2], and is borne out by an *obiter dictum* of REDE J. in Mich. 14 Hen. VII, f. 2[3], and by *Finch* v. *Cokaine* (30 & 31 Eliz.)[4], where all the Court held that a lease by father to son with a view to bringing "ejectione firme" was not against the form of 28 Ed. I. c. 11, on the grounds both of natural duty and the immediate possibility of inheritance which the son has; and in this case it was said to have been adjudged in the same year that a lease by a brother to a half brother with the same object was against the statute because there was no immediate possibility of inheritance

---

[1] Mich. 19 Ed. IV, f. 3. So too 1 Hawk. P.C. ch. 83, sect. 4.

[2] Ascue argued that if I, heir to my father, give money to a counsellor to counsel my father in a suit this is not maintenance; to which Markham retorted that this was for the interest and right the son had in the land.

[3] "If one has married my cousin who can inherit my land, it is lawful for him to maintain and aid me in any action against me: but if his wife who is my cousin dies, so that no issue of him remains alive, if he shall aid me in my suit, that is maintenance in him."

[4] Sav. 95.

30 DEFENCES:

between them[1]. "But query," adds the reporter, "if they were brothers of the whole blood, or if it was between father and son who was not heir apparent?" But there are *dicta* which apparently adopt the idea that mere relationship is a good plea. Thus, MOYLE J. in Hil. 34 Hen. VI, f. 25, where the question was whether a master could maintain his servant, said without qualification that a father can interfere for his children and *vice versa*, and much more can a master interfere for the servant, for whereas the father need not find food, drink or necessaries for his sons, the master must do so for his servant. In *Mowse v. Weaver*, there is an *obiter dictum* which we have already quoted to the effect that a son and brother (*inter alios*) are capable of justifying maintenance[2]. Coke, in commenting on 13 Ed. I. c. 49, says that a child cannot enfeoff his father or the father the child without being amenable to the statute, but that both may do it upon the other statutes relating to champerty[3]. Hawkins writes that no conveyance or promise thereof relating to lands in suit made by father to son, or by ancestor to heir apparent, is within 28 Ed. I. c. 11, since it only gives them the greater encouragement to do what by nature they are bound to do[4]. As to brothers, it was said in Pasch. 21 Ed. IV, f. 31 that a brother can maintain because it is lawful for every "cosin" to the party to come to the bar with him[5], and the opinion in *Mowse v. Weaver*[6] was to the like effect. Similar flotsam can be gathered from the reports as to remote relations[7], and it was

[1] Coke when A.-G. charged Lord Sheffield for standing in Court to hear his brother's case as a maintainer; but it was held an unjust cause in other respects as well. Hudson, 90. At p. 89, he says that in *Cannon's Case* (no further reference) it was adjudged that a curator of an orphan's goods in a Court Christian may sue in Chancery for those goods. Here again the gist of the exemption is not merely standing *in loco parentis*, but having an interest in the protected person's property or in its preservation.

[2] 44 and 45 Eliz. Moore, 655; *ante* 25.

[3] 2 Inst. 484. *Ibid.* 563.   [4] 1 P.C. ch. 84, sect. 19.

[5] Catesby. He was made judge of C.P. in 21 Ed. IV, Nov. 20, 1481. MOYLE J., had said the same thing of the cousin in Hil. 34 Hen. VI, f. 25 and MARKHAM J., of both brother and cousin in Mich. 39 Hen. VI, f. 5. Cf. VAUGHAN C.J., in *Pierson v. Hughes* (24 Car. II), Freeman, 71, 81.

[6] *Ante* 25.

[7] Hil. 9 Hen. VI, f. 64: "A man can maintain his blood and one who is of his alliance." (*Per* MARTIN J., or according to Br. *Abr. Maint.* 3, MARTIN J. and BABINGTON C.J.C.P.). Mich. 22 Hen. VI, f. 35 (NEWTON C.J.C.P., as to kinsmen). According to Hudson (p. 90), who queries the decision, LEE

CONTINGENT INTERESTS 31

even argued that because a man was a godfather he could lawfully maintain his godson[1]. Quite apart, however, from their inconclusiveness as to the law then existing, they are of little use at the present day[2]. The real principle, it is suggested, is that stated at the beginning of this sub-section. It would, for example, be a good defence to an action on champerty to shew that the defendant had identified himself with a party in the original action, if he were heir to that party, and the fact that the party maintained had no legal title is perhaps immaterial[3].

(3) CONTINGENT AND REVERSIONARY INTERESTS

The question whether a person, who has a future interest (apart from kinship) in the subject of the litigation, can maintain lawfully must next be discussed. Several of the cases to which we shall refer were rather on criminal than civil liability, but there is little doubt that they need not be limited to the former in the modern law of maintenance and champerty. In Mich. 17 Ed. II, f. 545, it was held on a writ of champerty prosecuted at the King's suit under 28 Ed. I. c. 11 that the purchase of a reversion is not champerty; and in the same year[4], counsel put it that if one entered as heir to his father, and then leased the tenements to termors for life, who rendered the lands to

C.J. held in *Cannon's Case* that the nephew could not disburse money for the uncle. Mich. 6 Ed. IV, f. 5 is indecisive as to the brother-in-law.

[1] Townshend in Mich. 6 Ed. IV, f. 5.

[2] Cf. the Irish cases, *Burke* v. *Greene* (1814), 2 Ball & Beatty, 517; *Bellers* v. *Russell* (1809), 1 Ball & Beatty, 96.

[3] RIGBY L.J., in *Alabaster* v. *Harness* [1895] 1 Q.B. at p. 346, stated that this had been specifically decided. Nor is this inconsistent with *Hutley* v. *Hutley* (*post* 59) where the maintainer, it is true, had an interest as heir-at-law in the property to be recovered, but had no interest except a distant relationship with the party maintained. The defence of kinship was noticed in *Neville* v. *London Express Newspaper, Ld.* [1919] A.C. 368 by LORD FINLAY L.C. at p. 387, VISCOUNT HALDANE at p. 389, and LORD SHAW OF DUNFERMLINE at p. 414. LORD COLERIDGE C.J., in *Bradlaugh* v. *Newdegate* (1883), 11 Q.B.D. 1 at p. 11, in referring to BULLER J.'s judgment in *Master* v. *Miller* (1791), 4 T.R. 340, said that his instances there shewed that common interest included (*inter alios*) heir, brother, son-in-law, and brother-in-law; but he seemed to regard their relationship as a medium to a justifiable interest rather than as a justification *per se*. And this applies to the other instances mentioned—fellow commoner, landlord defending the tenant in a tithe suit, the rich man for charity, the master for the servant and *vice versa*. Cf. *Hickman* v. *Kent Sheepbreeders Association* (1920), 36 T.L.R. 528, 532.

[4] Fitz. *Abr. Champ.* 14 (not in printed Y.B.).

32 DEFENCES:

him pending the writ [sued in connection with the land], it is not champerty, and to this all the judges agreed. The lessor may lawfully maintain his termor without a surrender by the termor; *a fortiori* he may do so after such a surrender[1], and the result of the reports is in favour of this deduction. Thus STRANGEWAYS J. in Hil. 9 Hen. VI, f. 64 admitted the argument that if I grant the reversion of my tenant for life to *B*, without the tenant's attornment, and then the tenant is impleaded and *B*[2] maintain him, this is maintenance, for the grant of the reversion is void; but he added that if I grant to *B* a term of years contingent on my tenant for life, *X*, predeceasing me, and then my tenant is impleaded, *B* can lawfully maintain, and yet he has nothing[3]. The opinion that *B* cannot maintain in the first case was questionable for the tenant could be forced in equity to attorn to his new landlord[4]. But since the need for attornment has been abolished[5], the point is of no importance. In Trin. 11 Hen. VI, f. 39 it was held by BABINGTON and PASTON JJ. that a tenant can be maintained by his lord whether the latter's interest be legal or (as was the case here) equitable. Both MOYLE and DANBY JJ. were agreed in 39 Hen. VI, f. 19 that the lessor may legally maintain the termor, and MOYLE J. again in Mich. 6 Ed. IV, f. 2 said that a lessor may come and give evidence with the lessee in an action of trespass by the lessee, and none shall have maintenance against him[6], for though a judgment against the lessee cannot bind the lessor directly, yet it may prejudice his title[7]. All the Court in Mich. 19 Ed. IV, f. 3 were of opinion that a reversioner or remainderman could give money where the land was in demand to save their interest[8], and the Court in *Mowse* v. *Weaver* resolved the same[9].

---

[1] 1 Hawk. P.C. ch. 84, sect. 18.
[2] Correction for "E."
[3] PASTON J. also said that a lord can maintain his tenant.
[4] 1 Hawk. P.C. ch. 83, sect. 13.
[5] 4 & 5 Anne. c. 3.
[6] The reference in Vin. *Abr. Maint.* (G) 2 to another case 6 Ed. IV, 29 is untraceable.
[7] 1 Hawk. P.C. ch. 83, sect. 12.
[8] So too Br. *Abr. Maint.* 53.
[9] *Ante* 25. Cf. Coke, 2 Inst. 562 in commenting on the "prochein amyes" whose advice is excepted from 28 Ed. I. c. 11 (Art. sup. Cart.). 1 Hawk. P.C. ch. 83, sect. 21. ROLFE B., in *Findon* v. *Parker* (1843), 11 M. & W. at p. 684.

CONTINGENT INTERESTS 33

The *rationale* of the rule is put from another point of view by Hawkins. The lord, he says, is in many cases bound by the law to warrant the lands to his tenant, and even in cases where he is not so bound, the law ought to permit him to maintain[1]. As in our own times there is in nearly every conveyance of lands under the Conveyancing Act, 1881, one or more implied warranties, this reasoning is sound; and where a reversioner maintains his tenant it can be justified either on that ground, or because the reversioner may take steps to see that his own title is not prejudiced. Where, however, the conveyance is out-and-out of the transferor's whole interest, his justification of maintenance must be referred to liability on his warranty (if any) express or implied. A case of this sort occurs in Pasch. 11 Hen. VI, f. 41. *B* had granted a rent to *C* with a warranty. An assize of rent was brought against *C*, who prayed *B* to come with evidence of the rent. *B* came accordingly and set up these facts as a defence to a writ of maintenance. The Court shewed a difference of opinion, HALS J. regarding it as enough that, apart from any question of warranty, *B*'s possession of the evidences of title and *C*'s request entitled him to maintain. CHEYNE C.J.K.B. did not agree with this[2]. The matter was adjourned, but on the point of warranty there was no disagreement. The justification of the landlord on his tenant's behalf may be regarded as settled. LORD ESHER M.R. took this to be the case, and his opinion has the more weight because he was not disposed to give a wide range to defences to maintenance[3]. A surrender by a reversioner to the tenant pending a plea is not champerty[4]. Here it may be noted that 32 Hen. VIII. c. 9, sect. 4 makes it lawful for any person, who is in lawful possession by taking the yearly rents or profits of lands, tenements, or hereditaments, to get by any reasonable means the pretenced right or title of any other person.

According to the older authorities, a man commits champerty

---

[1] 1 P.C. ch. 83, sect. 21.
[2] Br. *Abr. Maint.* 51; "et fuit in maner agree que il est bon barre," though *B* was not vouched to warranty.
[3] *Alabaster* v. *Harness* [1895] 1 Q.B. 339, at pp. 342–3.
[4] F.N.B. 172 E. As to the position of an heir, see sub-sect. (2) *ante* p. 28; for that of a tenant assisting his lord, *post* p. 74.

W. L. P.

34   DEFENCES:

if he grant a rent out of land pending a suit for the land[1], but not if the rent be granted out of other lands[2]; and it is also champerty if a disseisee pending an action relating to the land grant part of it in return for a covenant to maintain[3]. Finally, there is no reason to suppose that, at the present day, a reversionary interest in personal property is in any respect different from that in real property as regards the rule that the reversioner has a good defence to maintenance or champerty, if he supports the possessor of the property in litigation. It was thought long ago that a bailor could support his bailee in an action of detinue for the bailor's charters brought against the bailee by a third person[4] and as the bailor now has sufficient property in the goods, where it is a simple bailment, to sue on his own account[5], he has sufficient interest to assist the bailee.

(4) MASTER AND SERVANT
As in the case of kinship, there is scarcely any modern authority on the question whether the relation of master and servant is a good defence to an action of maintenance against either.

That a master might lawfully maintain his servant seems never to have been questioned, though differences of opinion shew themselves on the limits within which he might do so. MARTIN J. asserted this in Hil. 9 Hen. VI, f. 64, NEWTON C.J.C.P. in Mich. 22 Hen. VI, f. 35, BRYAN C.J.C.P. in Mich. 19 Ed. IV, f. 3; and CHEYNE C.J.K.B. in Pasch. 11 Hen. VI, f. 41 gives as the reason that the master is bound to be with his servants and they with him. It is not reading too much into this *dictum* to say that it evidences the strong mutual obligations of master and servant in a feudal society. The early history of livery supports this[6], and we get from it an intelligible theory of the rule that the master might maintain his servant.

[1] F.N.B. Champ. 172 K. Coke, 2 Inst. 562. 1 Hawk. P.C. ch. 84, sect. 7.
[2] F.N.B. Champ. 172 L. 1 Hawk. P.C. ch. 84, sect. 7. As to arrears of rent, see *Williams* v. *Protheroe* (*post* 57).
[3] F.N.B. 172 G.
[4] *Per* MOYLE J. in 39 Hen. VI, f. 19.
[5] *Manders* v. *Williams* (1849), 4 Exch. 339. *Mears* v. *L. & S.W.R. Co.* (1862), 11 C.B. N.S. 850.
[6] Cf. Mich. 8 Hen. VI, ff. 9–10 and Br. *Abr. Act. sur le statute* 14 for a case on 1 Rich. II. c. 7. No decision is reported.

MASTER AND SERVANT 35

If he were not allowed to do so he would lose valuable property
—the service—through prolonged litigation. The servant was
not his property, but in that age when service was far more
within the domain of status than contract, he was quite near
enough to property to justify his employer in seeing to it that
he was not decoyed away, damaged by bodily force, or rendered
incapable of service by law-suits. To this effect is an opinion
of FINEUX C.J. noted in Mich. 21 Hen. VII, f. 40:

> If my servant be arrested for debt, or other thing in London, or
> in a certain privileged town, I can maintain my servant, and spend
> my own money to aid him, and this for the loss of his services:
> but if my servant be impleaded by *praecipe quod reddat de terre*,
> I cannot maintain him, for I have no loss of his service by this[1].

This was one qualification of the rule. It was only natural that
the possibility of livery and other abuses should make other qualifications necessary. Thus in Hil. 34 Hen. VI (f. 30), Robert Horn
sued a writ of maintenance against J.D. and P.H. for maintaining
a suit between Horn and F.S. It was argued that F.S. was
J.D.'s servant, and that as he could not speak English he had
prayed J.D. and P.H. to procure some apprentice in English
Law to be his counsel, and that they had acceded to his request.
MOYLE J. held that the master could interfere for the servant
because he was bound to find him food, drink, and necessaries;
but PRISOT C.J.C.P. and DANBY J. refused to go as far as
holding unreservedly that a master maintains his servant
innocently, and limitations had already been recognized in two
earlier cases of the same reign. In Mich. 21 Hen. VI, f. 15,
an Abbot was sued for maintaining his servant, Martin Prideaux,
in an appeal of mayhem brought by Martin against certain
persons. It was first of all pleaded that the Abbot had merely
procured the assistance of men learned in the law to aid Martin.
To this it was replied that the Abbot had given 6s. 8d. of his
own money to the lawyer. The Court held this replication bad,

---

[1] Jenkins (102) says that I may lay out the servant's wages in the *praecipe*,
but not my own money. Neither the report nor the abridgments of it support
this. Br. *Abr. Maint.* 52 does. That is an abridgment of Trin. 31 Hen. VI,
f. 9, the report of which case does not bear out the abridgment. The Table
of Matters appended to Y.B. 21–39, Hen. VI turns a mere argument of
Portington in Mich. 22 Hen. VI, f. 24 into the statement, "Home maintaine
pur son servant, maintenance gist vers maistre."

36 DEFENCES:

and NEWTON and PASTON J.J. said this was not maintenance, for a master may maintain his servant and bring his own counsel with him to give counsel for his servant, or pay an apprentice to give such counsel; *secus* if money be given for his servant to a juror to influence his verdict. It then transpired that the Abbot had done this, and it was held that his gift of 40s. to W.E. to bribe the jurors to give a verdict for Martin in the appeal of mayhem was maintenance[1]. The second case is that of Clement Tailour (Trin. 28 Hen. VI, f. 12). The defendant justified there because the plaintiff in the first action was his servant, and he prayed Serjeant Moyle to be the servant's counsel and Moyle acted as such. It was replied that the defendant had given £5 of his own to T.H. and J.F. to distribute among the inhabitants of the county to maintain the first action. PRISOT C.J.C.P. said that where the justification of service was possible it included the gift of money to men learned in the law to act as counsel of the servant; but that a man can never give money to jurors for their verdict. He referred to Mich. 21 Hen. VI, f. 15 just cited, and it was adjudged maintenance.

Such is the result of the Year Books. How, if at all, must the law be modified to meet present circumstances? Blackstone mechanically reproduces the rule that the master may maintain the servant[2], and within the last fifty years judicial *dicta*[3] and one decision[4] occur which recognize it, but discuss neither its principle nor its limits. In another case, it is implied that some valuable interest in the suit is needed as well[5]. The relation of master and servant has in large businesses lost almost entirely its personal relation, and has been considerably modified in this respect even where it is purely domestic. If we are still to

---

[1] See also Mich. 22 Hen. VI, f. 5 and Br. *Abr. Maint.* 14; Trin. 28 Hen. VI, f. 7. All are needed for an eclectic report.

[2] I. 429.

[3] *Elborough* v. *Ayres* (1870), L.R. 10 Eq. 367. *Fitzroy* v. *Cave* [1905] 2 K.B. at p. 371 (*per* COZENS-HARDY L.J.). *Neville* v. *London Express Newspaper, Ld.* [1919] A.C. at p. 389 (*per* VISCOUNT HALDANE) and p. 427 (*per* LORD PHILLIMORE).

[4] *Hickman* v. *Kent Sheepbreeders Association* (1920), 36 T.L.R. 528, 532–533. Affirmed by C.A. without reference to this defence, 37 T.L.R. 163.

[5] *Per* LORD COLERIDGE C.J., in *Bradlaugh* v. *Newdegate* (1883), 11 Q.B.D. at p. 11. Cf. *Hickman's Case* (*supra*).

MASTER AND SERVANT

accept the principle of the old books that possible loss of service is what justifies the master's interference, we must at the same time admit that modern economic conditions would probably lead the Courts, not to adopt blindly the rule that any employer can interfere on behalf of any of his servants but, to scrutinize the facts of each particular case in order to find out whether the principle underlying the rule is applicable. It is incredible that a limited company which employs a thousand servants should be justified merely on the ground of service in maintaining one of those servants in an action for breach of promise of marriage; or, to put a less extreme case, that a trade union (even allowing for the Trade Disputes Act, 1906) should have *carte blanche* to aid its officials in litigation in which employment constitutes the only community of interest between the union and the official assisted[1]. A similar view of the law was taken by BRAY J. in *Scott* v. *The National Society for the Prevention of Cruelty to Children*[2], where the defendant society had maintained an action for slander on behalf of one of its officials against a third person. The Society itself was not defamed. The learned judge admitted that interest in retaining the services of the servant was one of the grounds on which the defence of master and servant was founded, but held that the defence was inapplicable because the Society had interfered in the slander proceedings on the ground that it thought that its reputation was likely to be injured, and not because the official was its servant. On the other hand, there seems to be nothing objectionable in a master exerting himself to protect his domestic servant from a blackmailing action. There is nothing in *Elborough* v. *Ayres* (1870), and *Bradlaugh* v. *Newdegate* to which we have already referred[3] to shew that such distinctions would not be taken into account. In the former case, the secretary of a company was prosecuted by a shareholder for issuing a false balance sheet. The prosecution failed, and the secretary was maintained in an action for malicious prosecution (in which he recovered £50 damages) by a resolution of the directors

---

[1] *Oram* v. *Hutt* [1913] 1 Ch. 259; [1914] 1 Ch. 98, a case on contract (*post* p. 109), is not inconsistent with this view.

[2] (1909), 25 T.L.R. 789. A *nisi prius* case.   [3] *Ante* 36.

38   DEFENCES:

authorizing the secretary to instruct the company's solicitors to take such proceedings at the company's expense with reference to the prosecution as they might be advised. The Court refused, at the suit of the shareholder, to restrain taxation of costs and the subsequent proceedings in the action, and left the question of maintenance to be dealt with by a court of law. It had been admitted that the fact of maintenance, though known to both parties in the action would not have been a good plea. The VICE-CHANCELLOR[1] refused to express any opinion as to whether this were maintenance.

It is scarcely necessary to add that tampering with a jury on the servant's behalf or using other improper methods would be as objectionable now as it was in Henry VI's reign.

There is not much that is decisive in the old law on the converse question whether the servant may lawfully maintain his master. The tendency was to assume that he might. Such was the opinion of MOYLE J. in Hil. 34 Hen. VI, f. 25. In Mich. 39 Hen. VI, f. 5, the defendant pleaded that he had been retained by a litigant in the first action to ride with him to London, and that when he came there he aided his master in all his needs in the suit. MARKHAM J. held that the employment being special— merely to ride with the master to London—this was no defence, but that it would have been if the employment had been of a general character. For the rest, nothing is traceable in the Year Books but arguments of counsel or undecided cases[2]. Considering the scandalous prevalence of livery, one might expect that some emphatic expression of opinion would have appeared in the Year Books on service of this sort which would certainly be maintenance as well. But the servant who was kept for that purpose was not likely to be worth suing, and the statutory penalties against his employer were nominally more efficacious. At all events there is nothing in the judgment of MARKHAM J.

---

[1] L.R. (1870), 10 Eq. 367 at p. 373.

[2] Wangford in Hil. 32 Hen. VI, f. 24 argued that the servant could maintain; so too Colow in Mich. 19 Ed. IV, f. 3. Vavasour, another counsel in the same case said that this had been decided in Mich. 21 Hen. VI, f. 15 (ante 35); if so, it is not stated in the report. Mich. 19 Hen. VI, f. 31 sets out the defence of service to a writ of maintenance (Br. *Abr. Maint.* 13 is to the same effect), but no result is reported.

MASTER AND SERVANT 39

just quoted which is inconsistent with the view that an action for maintenance against such a servant would have been well founded. On the other hand, common sense would allow any master to expect a certain amount of assistance in litigation properly given by those in his employ.

After the Year Book period we have the scantiest authority as to such assistance. An opinion of some weight in the Star Chamber is that a servant may solicit suits on behalf of his master[1], and there is a paragraph in Hawkins which seems reasonable enough though the cases he cites are but slender support for a good deal of it[2]. It seems clear, he says, that a person generally retained by another as his servant to do all manner of services, and not for a particular occasion only[3] may justify riding about to speed his business[4], and going to counsel on his behalf, and shewing his evidences to the counsel or the jury[5], and standing by him at a trial between him and another[6]; but it is certain that he cannot lawfully lay out any of his own money to assist the master in the suit[7].

There is some indication that the defence would now be recognized[8], but its limits can only be hinted by gauging the extent to which circumstances have changed since Tudor times. Livery is dead and gone, and the personal tie between master and servant has been much loosened. It is submitted then that a servant may lawfully maintain his master in so far as such aid is incidental to his service, and that if he goes beyond this he must prove some interest or other defence which the law allows[9].

---

[1] *Mowse* v. *Weaver* (44 & 45 Eliz.), Moore, 655. The case is nominally a criminal one, but the opinion need not be limited to criminal law. Cf. *Lord Cromwell and Townsend's Case* (28 Eliz.), 2 Leon. 133.

[2] 1 P.C. ch. 83, sect. 24. See last note.

[3] Mich. 39 Hen. VI, f. 5 cited for this correctly; *ante* 38.

[4] Mich. 19 Ed. IV, f. 3 cited for this is only argument; *ante* 38, n. 2.

[5] Mich. 19 Hen. VI, f. 31 cited. No decision reported; *ante* 38, n. 2.

[6] Pasch, 11 Hen. VI, f. 42 cited. Does not go so far in particulars.

[7] Trin. 3 Hen. VI, f. 53 and Trin. 11 Hen. VI, f. 11 cited. The first does not support the statement, the second does.

[8] See *Fitzroy* v. *Cave* [1905] 2 K.B. at p. 371 (*per* COZENS-HARDY L.J.; but possibly the statement refers only to the master maintaining the servant). *Neville* v. *London Express Newspaper, Ld.* [1919] A.C. at p. 389 (*per* VISCOUNT HALDANE), p. 414 (*per* LORD SHAW OF DUNFERMLINE).

[9] This is practically the view of LORD COLERIDGE C.J. in *Bradlaugh* v. *Newdegate* (1883), 11 Q.B.D. 1 at p. 11.

40 DEFENCES

(5) ASSISTANCE TO THE POOR

The heading which we have adopted is preferable to "charity," as that phrase is occasionally used in the reports in the wider sense of friendly aid rather than the relief of poverty. Assistance of a litigant because of his poverty is unobjectionable in principle and is recognized by the Common Law. If it were not, the poor man in view of the expense of litigation in any civilized system of law would be compelled to endure many injuries sooner than spend time and money on the trial of an arguable case[1]. MARTIN J. in Hil. 9 Hen. VI, f. 64 said *obiter*, "I can give gold or silver to a man who is poor to maintain his plea, if he himself cannot for poverty, and it is not maintenance against the law." PASTON J. was of the same opinion in 21 Hen. VI, f. 5, and it was conceded by counsel in Mich. 22 Hen. VI, f. 35. Hawkins[2] and Blackstone[3] state it as a rule, but no decisive authority adopting it is discoverable before *Harris* v. *Brisco* (1886)[4]. There, the defendant to an action of maintenance had aided one, Nailer, in an action for the redemption of a mortgaged farm. The Court of Appeal gave a considered judgment for the defendant, holding that his assistance of Nailer in the belief that he was a poor man oppressed by a rich one was a good defence, and that it was not necessary that the defendant should have acted after full inquiry into the circumstances even though, if he had done so, he would have found that there was no reasonable or probable ground for the proceedings in which he had assisted. The Court expressly adopted the proposition that charity is a good defence as part of English law[5]. Later decisions and *dicta* are to the same effect[6].

[1] Cf. LORD COLERIDGE C.J. in *Bradlaugh* v. *Newdegate* (1883), 11 Q.B.D. 1 at p. 11.   [2] 1 P.C. ch. 83, sect. 26.

[3] 1. 429. *Obiter dictum* of C.J. in *R.* v. —— (1 and 2 Jac. II, B.R.). 3 Mod. 97, is to the same effect.

[4] 17 Q.B.D. 504.   [5] 17 Q.B.D. at p. 513.

[6] *Holden* v. *Thompson* [1907] 2 K.B. 489. The C.A. and H.L. recognized this defence *obiter* in *Neville* v. *London Express Newspaper, Ld.* [1917] 2 K.B. at p. 567; [1919] A.C. at pp. 387, 389, 398–399, 414, 427. See too, *Hickman* v. *Kent Sheepbreeders Association* (1920), 36 T.L.R. 528, 535. *Cole* v. *Booker* (1913), 29 T.L.R. 295. DARLING J., in *McCarthy* v. *Kennedy* [*Times* newspaper 8th March, 1905 (other instalments of report published March 3rd, 4th, 7th)]; it is submitted that the learned judge attached too loose a meaning to "charity," and that this perhaps accounts for the seemingly contradictory finding of the jury. According to his direction to them, the fact that the

COMPULSION BY THE LAW 41

It is, of course, quite possible to abuse this defence, and in that case, it is submitted, the action of maintenance would lie. In *Pechell* v. *Watson* (1841)[1], a declaration in case stated that the defendants maliciously and unlawfully had upheld and maintained X in an action between the present plaintiffs and X. The jury found a verdict against the defendants for the costs incurred by the plaintiffs in the original action. The person whom they had instigated in that action was a pauper. It was also held that it was for the defendants to plead that they were interested in the action, not for the plaintiff to allege that he was not. There is nothing inconsistent in *Cotterell* v. *Jones* (1851)[2] with *Pechell* v. *Watson*. All that was decided there was that an action upon the case would not lie against two persons for conspiring together maliciously and without reasonable and probable cause to commence, and actually commencing, an action against the plaintiff in the name of a third person, who, to the knowledge of the defendants was a pauper, without an allegation of legal damage resulting therefrom; and it was doubted whether such an action would lie with such an allegation. The action in any event was not one of maintenance but was for malicious prosecution, or rather for case in the nature of conspiracy which is the root of the modern action for malicious prosecution[3]. If an action of maintenance had been brought at the present day upon the same facts, and if proof had been given of damages—expenses laid out on the original action would be quite enough to ground these[4]—there can be no reasonable doubt that the plaintiff would have won his action.

(6) COMPULSION BY THE LAW

Witnesses have already been considered[5]. Jurors[6] are also excused on the ground of legal compulsion as was admitted by the Court in Pasch. 28 Hen. VI, f. 6, where long before the charitable motive is mixed with personal spite is immaterial. This is not consistent with *Pechell* v. *Watson* or *Cole* v. *Booker* (*ubi sup.*); in the latter case it was held that though charity may be indiscreet it must not—indeed cannot be—mercenary.   [1] 8 M. and W. 691.   [2] 11 C.B. 713.

[3] See the judgment of Jervis C.J. Cf. *Thurston* v. *Ummons* (15 Car. I), March, 47.

[4] *Bradlaugh* v. *Newdegate* (1883), 11 Q.B.D. 1 at p. 15. Cf. *post* pp. 86 sqq.

[5] *Ante*, p. 21.

[6] For offences of jurors generally, see *Hist. of Abuse of Legal Procedure*, ch. VII.

42 DEFENCES:

alleged maintenance the defendants had been made members of a commission to the Ordinary to inquire *de jure patronatus* and had found for one, Ingow, against whom the present plaintiff had sued a *quare impedit*. Again, all the Court held in Mich. 17 Ed. IV, f. 5 that a juror can exhort his companions to give a verdict for the plaintiff or defendant on the merits of the case, and this would not be maintenance. The justices held a similar plea good in Pasch. 18 Ed. IV, f. 1.

But a juror has no more excuse than any other person for acting corruptly within the province of his legal duties, or for outstepping its bounds altogether. If he give money—be it his own or another's—to corrupt his fellow jurors[1], or if after the verdict has been returned he require the judge to give judgment for the plaintiff[2] he presumes upon his office and is liable for maintenance.

The same principles apply to officials connected with the administration of the law. The older reports, if they yield nothing decisive, at any rate shew the drift of judicial opinion, which is reasonable enough to be applicable at the present day. Such persons can avail themselves of the defences open to laymen[3], and while fees payable *virtute officii* to such persons can be lawfully accepted[4], bribes cannot. Statutory penalties were inflicted upon officials guilty of misconduct of this kind[5]. It seems clear that if their acts constituted maintenance, they could not take refuge in their official character against a civil action for maintenance.

(7) FRIENDSHIP AND COURTESY

Advice given to a friend as to the best mode of conducting litigation is lawful[6]. So apparently is that given as a matter of courtesy to a stranger. These points do not seem to have been seriously questioned. Such difficulties as there are begin when attempts are made to draw the line between friendship and officiousness.

---

[1] Mich. 17 Ed. IV, f. 5.
[2] Pasch. 18 Ed. IV, f. 2. Conceded by LYTTLETON J.
[3] Mich. 22 Hen. VI, f. 35, *post* 43.
[4] *Per opinionem curiae*, Mich. 21 Hen. VI, f. 15. Br. *Abr. Maint.* 14.
[5] E.g. 3 Ed. I. c. 26. Cf. *Turner* v. *Burnaby* (12 W. III), 12 Mod. 564.
[6] 28 Ed. I. c. 11 (Art. sup. Cart.) allows counsel to be taken of next friends. Coke says that they must be so, not only in blood, but in estate. 2 Inst. 562.

FRIENDSHIP AND COURTESY 43

A sheriff was sued for maintenance in Mich. 22 Hen. VI, f. 35. His defence was that the person whom he was alleged to have maintained had prayed his advice in an action brought against him by the present plaintiff. The defendant advised him to go to London to appear before the judges, and purchased for him a *supersedeas*. The Court adjudged it to be no maintenance, for, if it were, no friend could counsel another; advice given to a husbandman at his request was no more maintenance than these facts were[1]. It can scarcely be doubted that a modern Court would take the same view, and HAWKINS J. hinted as much in *Alabaster* v. *Harness*[2].

Passing to the alleged limits of the defence, BRYAN C.J.C.P. in Mich. 19 Ed. IV, f. 3, put the case of one of a company of Lombards coming to London, and one of his company going with him to a man who knows the law, and advising him as to his ability. This, said BRYAN, could not be maintenance, but he added that the delivery of any money by his companion to the man of law would be; "and I understand this case has been judged in our books, that a man can go with a neighbour to inquire for a man knowing the law." In Hil. 15 Hen. VII, f. 2, in a writ of champerty the plaintiff counted that the defendant had maintained J.S. in a *subpoena* brought by J.S. against R.D. for debt, to have part thereof. The defendant said that J.S. was an alien, not in Burgundy, outside the allegiance of the King, that he did not know how to speak English or Latin, and that he came to the defendant because he knew how to speak his language, and asked him to introduce him to some man learned in the law. J.S. then promised that if he recovered against R.D. the defendant should be satisfied and paid of his duty. It appears from the abridgment of the case that there was a preceding debt owing from J.S. to the defendant[3]. This

---

[1] According to Br. *Abr. Champ.* 8, HERLE J. said that a man can have the aid of his friends. The report in Trin. 6 Ed. III, f. 33 has "parents" instead of "friends." In Mich. 9 Ed. IV, f. 32, CHOKE J. said *obiter* that a man may pay another to be of counsel with his brother or cousin. In Mich. 12 Ed. IV, f. 4, the plea was that the defendant had, on the request of his neighbour, informed him of a lawyer; but no result is reported.

[2] [1894] 2 Q.B. 897 at p. 900, citing 1 Hawk. P.C. ch. 83, sect. 11, that friendly advice as to the proper action to recover a debt is not maintenance.

[3] Br. *Abr. Champ.* 6 makes it the reason for the decision. The fact might be inferred from other parts of the report. Br. *Abr.* makes it certain.

44 DEFENCES:

very material addition makes the decision of the Court—that the plea was good—intelligible and consistent with BRYAN J.'s opinion in Mich. 19 Ed. IV, f. 3. It amounts to no more than a justification of the defendant's remuneration on the ground that it consisted in the assignment to him of a chose in action. Assignment of a debt had already been recognized in Mich. 34 Hen. VI, f. 30 as an exception from the law prohibiting maintenance. There was a direct conflict of judicial opinion in Hil. 32 Hen. VI, f. 24 as to whether a promise by a third person to the attorney of one of the parties in an action, that he would reward him well if he were diligent, were maintenance[1]. There is an opinion in Trin. 18 Hen. VII that it is maintenance if a third person deliver money, without my authority, to an attorney to sue an action for me[2]. According to Hawkins, saving another expenses in a suit on the ground of friendship or interest, or even trying to do so, is maintenance, but BULLER J. in *Master v. Miller* (1791), appears to imply that it is not[3]. In fact, such authority or lack of authority as there is, confronts us with the dilemma of drawing no deduction at all, or of drawing one that would be little more than a guess at the attitude of a modern court. On principle mere neighbourly advice is as unobjectionable now as it always has been. Assistance beyond this should as a matter of prudence, if not of legal duty, be avoided.

(8) ASSIGNMENT OF CHOSES IN ACTION

Hitherto we have treated maintenance and champerty as torts, postponing to a later heading their effect on contracts. In this section, however, the law of contract as well as that of torts will be taken into consideration, as the principles applicable in both systems are in general the same in this connection, and the context will indicate such differences as occur.

We are not concerned with choses in action apart from their relation to the law of champerty and maintenance, and must therefore attempt to keep the discussion within that somewhat narrow compass.

Choses in action were not originally assignable at Common

---

[1] PRISOT C.J.C.P. thought that there was no harm in the request. DANBY J., *contra.*

[2] *Per* FROWYK C.J.C.P., Keilwey, 50.

[3] 4 T.R. at p. 340.

ASSIGNMENT OF CHOSES IN ACTION   45

Law so as to enable the assignee to sue in his own name. The reason according to Coke's report of *Lampet's Case* was the great wisdom and policy of the sages and founders of our law, who have provided that no possibility, right, title, nor thing in action shall be granted or assigned to strangers, for that would be the occasion of multiplying of contentions and suits, of great oppression of the people, and chiefly of terre-tenants, and the subversion of the due and equal execution of justice[1].

So too, Jenkins states that "buying of debts is maintenance at Common Law, and punishable by indictment or informa-tion"[2]. This theory has been exploded. It has been pointed out that the Year Books do not support it, and that the true ground is the strictly personal view of contract adopted in their infancy by the two leading systems of law[3]. It may be added that Coke's theory is perilously close to an anachronism. It is true that maintenance and champerty were well known at an early stage of our law, but they were known almost exclusively as modes of corruption and oppression in the hands of the King's officers, and other great men. Maintenance of the sort that they usually committed was something much coarser than an attempt to assign or to receive a chose in action. To say of a chose in action that it could not be assigned in early times, because that would infringe the law of maintenance is to imply a development in the law of maintenance which it scarcely possessed till Henry VI's reign—the very period in which it was expressly held that it did not apply to assignment of a debt.

Mich. 34 Hen. VI, f. 30 is the first case in which the neat question was raised whether such assignment were maintenance[4].

---

[1] 10 Rep. 48 *a*. So too Co. Litt. 232 *b*, n. 1.

[2] "Eight Centuries of Reports," 3rd cent. Case IX. The quotation is apparently a note to 37 Hen. VI, f. 13, which occupies nearly four pages in the Y.B. and in which the word maintenance is not even mentioned. No other reference is given by Jenkins, and the conclusion is that he was in-fluenced by a current idea for which Coke was responsible.

[3] Pollock's *Law of Contract* (ed. 8), 229, and App. Note F. Cf. Mait. *Coll. Pap.* I. 382; Warren, *Choses in Action*, 31–32; Ames in *A–A Essays*, III. 580 sqq.

[4] In Hil. 9 Hen. VI, f. 64, Paston J. raised the point incidentally, but his dictum, "et issint c̄ fuit chose en accion et issint tout void" is far from implying that the assignment was objectionable on the ground of main-tenance. See Pollock, *Cont.* App. F, p. 748.

46   DEFENCES:

Robert Horn sued a writ of maintenance against Stephen Foster alleging that Stephen had maintained a plaint of debt on behalf of F's administrators against Robert Horn. For Stephen, it was alleged that Horn owed F £100 by an "obligacion," that F owed Foster £100, that F assigned his suit to Foster in full satisfaction of the debt, and delivered to him the "obligacion." Horn consented to this. F commanded Foster to sue Horn, in case of default, in F's name. F died. Foster delivered the "obligacion" to his attorney to sue on it in the administrators' name. The administrators agreed, the attorney sued, and this was the alleged maintenance. The opening words of Littleton's argument support the true view as to the reason for the former non-assignability of debts.

Sir, this is not a plea: for I conceive that no one can give nor grant a duty to another; for if one be in debt to me by a lease or by a simple contract, I cannot give nor grant this duty for any satisfaction.

Wangford, in reply, contended that a duty of a thing which is contract could be assigned for a satisfaction, though he admitted that a claim arising from something not a contract, e.g. trespass, could not be so assigned. PRISOT J.:

I think the same, for every one who has cause to meddle can well justify the maintenance; as if one be obliged to my use, and I have the obligation, it is lawful for me to meddle, and to sue this suit at my own cost, and in the name of another.

The King was an early exception to the rule against assignability of choses in action. In fact, much of the earlier reported litigation in connection with the topic was on this exception. Of fourteen cases in Brooke's *Abridgement* on *Choses in Action*, no less than eleven relate to it[1]. The reason for the exception, it has been suggested, was "the universal succession accruing to the Crown on forfeiture" in those times[2]. Choses in action

---

[1] Pleas 1, 2, 4, 5, 6, 7, 9, 10, 11, 12, 13.

[2] Pollock, *Cont.* (ed. 8), App. F, p. 748. Two other suggested influences on the formation of the exception are (i) the maxim that the King is the fountain of justice, and therefore cannot be guilty of maintenance or champerty; (ii) the King is above the law, and therefore the principles of the Common Law do not avail against him. *The Laws of England*, IV. § 845 n. The first of these proceeds on the assumption (which we believe to be inaccurate) that assignment of choses in action was forbidden at Common Law on the ground of maintenance. Of the second there is no historical trace.

ASSIGNMENT OF CHOSES IN ACTION 47

would fall under the property forfeited, and freedom of alienation by the Crown followed as a natural consequence[1] "for the
Courts did not feel themselves bold enough to tie up the
property of the Crown, or to prevent that from being transferred"[2]. At the risk of a slight digression, the ambit of the
Crown's powers in such assignment may be briefly noted. It
was held that they extended to wardships, as in Mich. 5 Ed. IV,
f. 8, where the Court rejected a plea to a writ of ravishment
of ward that the grant of the wardship by the King to the
plaintiff had taken place after the marriage of the ward which
constituted the wrong. He can probably also grant a rent or
right of re-entry. According to Brooke, it was said to be law
in a case of 32 Hen. VIII that the King can grant a chose in
action which is personal, e.g. debt and damages, or a "chose
mixt" such as wardship, but not a "chose reall," like an action
for land and things of that kind such as rights, entries, actions[3].
But according to a variant report of the same author the matter
was doubtful[4], and in any event the case appears to have been
on the construction of the statute for the dissolution of the
monasteries[5]. Moreover, there is an earlier judicial opinion
that the King can assign a rent, or a right of re-entry[6]. It is
said that the debt in order to be assignable by the Crown must
be due by deed[7], but there is very little foundation for the rule.
It seems to be traceable to 50 Lib. Ass. pl. 1, where CAVENDISH J.
put it that if a man were outlawed for felony and it were found
by office that a stranger was his debtor, the King should have
the debt for forfeiture, though it be a chose in action. Holt
and Hannemere, neither of whom was then on the bench, did
not question this, but qualified it by adding that the debt must
be due by deed, and not by contract, because otherwise the
debtor would be worse off against the assignee than against the
assignor; for whereas he could wage his law against an ordinary

[1] Hil. 3 Hen. IV, f. 8.
[2] *Per* BULLER J. in *Master* v. *Miller* (1791) at p. 340.
[3] *Abr. Pat.* 98, quoted with approval by GAWDY J. in 30 Eliz. 3 Leon. 198.
[4] *Abr. Chose in Action*, 14.   [5] 31 Hen. VIII. c. 13.
[6] HUSSEY [HUSE] C.J.K.B. in Mich. 2 Hen. VII, f. 8. Other references
commonly given to 11 Rep. 12, 3 Rep. 1, 1 Leon. 21, leave the matter
precisely where it was.
[7] Shep. *Abr. Chose in Action*, 338.

48 DEFENCES:

creditor, he could not against the King[1]. This is an intelligible reason why, on the law as it then stood, the King should not acquire that particular kind of debt by forfeiture, though we may note parenthetically that it is a procedural difficulty that has disappeared with the wager of law; but it was not even argued—much less decided—in this case that a debt due to the King otherwise than by deed could not be assigned by him. Nor is it clear how the argument that was in fact put forward can now prevail against the decision in *South* v. *Marsh* (32 Eliz.) where it was held that a debt merely evidenced by signed writing and not under seal was assignable to the Crown, because the note makes the debt a certainty, and therefore a true debt and assignable[2].

The case just cited also shews that an assignment to the King was just as much an exception to the Common Law rule prohibiting assignment of choses in action as an assignment by the King. It had already been conceded in Hil. 21 Hen. VII, f. 19 that an obligation could be granted to the King, though the grant was not by deed enrolled; and the more general proposition was agreed to by all the Barons of Exchequer in *Noon's Case* (31 Eliz.)[3], while two years earlier they were equally unanimous in holding that even if the debt were not naturally such, but only by circumstances (e.g. a debt upon a bond for the performance of covenants) yet it was assignable to the Crown. A statute still in force provides that no debt is to be assigned to the King by a debtor or accountant to the King except that already *bonâ fide* due to the debtor or accountant; and the statute avoids assignments which infringe it[4]. It has also been held that part of a debt cannot be assigned to the King[5].

It seems that the King can assign a recognizance[6]. If the King grant an annuity or charge his revenue, it must be said

---

[1] See too Br. *Abr. Chose in Action*, 9.
[2] 3 Leon. 234.
[3] 2 Leon. 67.
[4] 7 Jac. I. c. 15.
[5] *R.* v. *Allen* (undated), Owen, 2. No reason is given.
[6] The basis of this appears to be a note in 1 Dyer, 1 b. At any rate the authorities cited in Shep. *Abr. Chose in Action*, 338 and in Com. *Dig. Assignment* (D) and *Grant* (G) are reducible to it. In Com. *Dig. Assignment* (D) it is also stated that a recognizance in Chancery can be granted by the King. This is a repetition of 2 Rolle *Abr.* 198 whose ultimate authority is an argument of Hody in Pasch. 19 Hen. VI, f. 62 (at f. 64 a).

ASSIGNMENT OF CHOSES IN ACTION 49

out of whose hands the grant is to be received, for the King cannot charge his person[1]. And he cannot assign a claim to unliquidated damages because of their uncertainty[2]; but to this we must refer again in considering to what extent this is legally possible in the case of his subjects generally[3].

It has been held that the King's assignee cannot in turn assign, "for there cannot by law be any assignment made by a common person of this debt"[4], but it does not follow that such an assignment could not be made in Equity, nor is it reasonable that the King's assignee should at the present day be in a worse position than any other assignee[5].

The rule is well settled that the King's assignee can sue in his own name[6]. If he prefer to do so, he can sue in the King's name[7].

The doctrine that choses in action are now assignable made its way into modern law with a certain amount of ebb and flow. The familiar rule that they are assignable in Equity dates back to the latter part of the 17th century[8]. It was apparently not acceptable in the middle of the 15th century. In Hil. 37 Hen. VI, f. 13, several were indebted to *A*. *B* bought these debts of *A*, and entered into an obligation of £1000 to pay *A* £500 on a certain day. *B* sued *A* in Chancery to be discharged from his bond, because debts assigned to him could only be released by *A*, and could only be sued for in *A*'s name, being things in action, and so the bond was given without valuable consideration. The

---

[1] *Hornbee's Case* (1691), Freeman K.B. 331. *Anon* (7 Will. III), 1 Salk. 58.
[2] 5 Ed. IV, f. 8. Br. *Abr. Chose in Action*, 11. Note in 1 Dyer, 1 *b*.
[3] *Post* pp. 55 sqq.
[4] *R. v. Twine* (3 Jac. I), Cro. Jac. 179 (Decision of all the BB. of Exchequer).
[5] The limits on the royal right of assignment are collected in Shep. *Abr. Chose in Action*; Com. *Dig. Assignment* (D) and *Grant* (G), (1); Warren, *Choses in Action*, 34. *Laws of England*, IV. § 845. Older authorities cited are not always convincing. Thus it is said that the King cannot grant an obligation forfeited to him before seizure. This is traceable to *Cullom v. Sherman* (12 Jac. I), 1 Roll. 7 which is upon the construction of 28 Eliz. c. 8, and even so only contains an opinion of COKE C.J.K.B. that there was no forfeiture before seizure.
[6] Mich. 39 Hen. VI, f. 26 [said to be the common course of the Exchequer. Br. *Abr. Prerog.* 45 puts this in the mouth of Grenefield (counsel)]. *Breverton's Case* (Hil. 28 Hen. VIII), 1 Dyer, 30 *b*. *R. v. Wendman* (3 Jac. I), Cro. Jac. 82 (Exch. Ch.). *Lambert v. Taylor* (1825), 4 B. and C. 138.
[7] *York* v. *Allen* (36 Eliz.), Sav. 133 (Exch.).
[8] Jenks, *Short History of English Law*, 301-2.

W. L. P. 4

50 DEFENCES:

Chancellor, as the matter was doubtful in law, adjourned the parties to the Exchequer Chamber, and there it was well debated before him and the judges of both Benches. All the judges held that there was no duty vested in *B*, and that in conscience the obligation ought to be annulled, and annulled in the Chancery it accordingly was[1].

It was held in Elizabeth's reign that it was not maintenance to buy a bill of debt (in this case a foreign bill of exchange), "for it is usual among merchants to make exchange of money for bills of debt *et e contra*." GAWDY J. added that it was not maintenance to assign a debt with a letter of attorney to sue for it, unless it were assigned "to be recovered, and the party to have part of it"[2]. (The "party" is the assignor.) On the other hand, it is said not to be maintenance if a surety, after paying his debt, gets the obligee to promise him to sue the principal on the same bond and to pay the surety what he should recover[3].

At the present day, it is not essential to the validity of an assignment that consideration should be given for it, whether the assignment be under the Judicature Act, 1873, sect. 25 (6)[4] or whether it be equitable, provided in the latter case the donor has done everything required to be done by him in order to complete the transfer[5]. But the question of consideration in earlier times was complicated by the application of the law of maintenance to assignments. Thus, where the assignment was in satisfaction of a debt due from the assignor to the assignee, sale of the debt to the assignee was good[6]; so was gift of it to a stranger, but sale to a stranger was maintenance. This looks at first sight peculiar, but the idea seems to have been that, if the stranger paid for what he got, he would be more likely to undertake litigation to secure its benefit than if he

---

[1] Some of the facts have been taken from Jenkins, 108. All material parts of what is stated above are given in both reports.

[2] *Penson* v. *Hickbed.* Cro. Eliz. 170 and *sub nom. Person* v. *Hickled*, 155.

[3] Vin. *Abr. Maint.* (E) 19 n. cites *Morris* v. *Badger*, Palm. 189 (untraceable).

[4] *Harding* v. *Harding* (1886), 17 Q.B.D. 442. *Walker* v. *Bradford Old Bank* (1884), 12 Q.B.D. 511.

[5] *Harding* v. *Harding* (*supra*). Cf. Jenks. in *L.Q.R.* XVI. 241.

[6] See reference to Jenkins in next note, and *Harvey* v. *Bateman*, Noy 52.

ASSIGNMENT OF CHOSES IN ACTION 51

took it as a gift[1]. Other alleged limits on the right to assign have either disappeared in modern law, or rest upon authority which scarcely bears examination[2]. BULLER J.'s historical review of maintenance in *Master* v. *Miller* (1791)[3] sums up the progress of the law:

Courts of equity from the earliest times thought the doctrine [*sc.* of maintenance as applied to choses in action] too absurd for them to adopt; and therefore they always acted in direct contradiction to it[4]. And we shall soon see that courts of law also altered their language on the subject very much.

He referred to *R.* v. *Parish of Aickles* (13 Will. III), where the Court indicated that indirect effect might be given to assignment of an apprentice[5].

"So an assignment of a chose in action has always been held a good consideration for a promise....though the debt assigned was uncertain[6.]".... "But still it must be admitted that though the courts of law have gone the length of taking notice of assignments of choses in action....yet in many cases they have adhered to the formal objection that the action shall be brought in the name of the assignor. ....I see no use or convenience in preserving that shadow when the substance is gone[7]."

We have seen then that the law as to assignment of choses in action has developed almost untrammelled by attempts to

---

[1] See Jenkins' rendering of *Lane* v. *Mallory* (12 Jac. I). Also reported in Hob. 4; Cro. Jac. 342; and 1 Roll. 26. These other reports shew that the case was on *assumpsit*, not assignment of a chose in action, for no complete assignment had been made. Vin. *Abr. Maint.* (E) 27 n. refers to *Barrow* v. *Grey*, Cro. Jac. 552, for the statement that assignment of a debt or recognizance to a stranger is a void and illegal consideration. No such case is traceable in any volume of Croke.

[2] E.g. a mere agreement between counsel is reported in *Anon.* (28–29 Eliz.), Godbolt, 81, that if a bond be for performance of covenants in an indenture of lease, it may be assigned with the lease, because they are concomitants, and the assignee has an interest in the lease and may sue on the bond; but if the covenants be first broken and the lease be assigned, suit by the assignee on the bond is directly maintenance.

[3] 4 T.R. at p. 340.

[4] The equitable doctrine was not developed till the latter part of the 17th century. *Ante* 49.

[5] 12 Mod. 553.

[6] *Mouldsdale* v. *Birchall* (12 Geo. III), 2 Bl. Rep. 820.

[7] ASHURST J., in *Winch* v. *Keeley* (27 Geo. III), 1 T.R. 619, said that the expense caused by sending a plaintiff from one side of Westminster Hall to the other led the Common Law Courts to take no notice of this objection.

4—2

52   DEFENCES:

bring it within the law of champerty and maintenance. No one would now contend that the assignment is void as such because it savours of, or constitutes, either of these offences. But equally it ought not to be arguable that the assignment of a chose in action is outside the law of champerty and maintenance if it be made with the improper purpose of stirring up litigation.

The motive, therefore, with which the chose in action is assigned ought to be material, provided of course it is one which is assignable at all. The very definitions of maintenance and champerty express or imply this, and the reports to some extent illustrate it[1]. In *Hartley* v. *Russell* (1825)[2], a creditor, who had instituted proceedings at law and in equity against a debtor, agreed with the debtor to abandon these proceedings in consideration of the debtor giving him a lien on securities in the hands of another creditor, with authority to sue such other creditor, and agreeing to do his best to assist in adjusting his accounts with the holder of the securities, and in recovering his securities. It was held that this agreement was not champertous, but that it would have been if it had been stipulated that the creditor should maintain the proceedings instituted by the debtor against the holder of the securities in consideration of profits to be derived by the debtor from the suit. In *Tyson* v. *Jackson* (1861)[3], it was held not to be champerty or maintenance for a legatee too poor to sue for his legacy, or to employ an attorney for that purpose, to sell the legacy for less than it was worth to a buyer who purchased it in order to institute a suit for its payment. Motive was discussed by the Court of Appeal in *Fitzroy* v. *Cave*[4]. The plaintiff had taken from the defendant's creditors an absolute assignment of their debts in consideration of a covenant by him that if the plaintiff should recover the amount of the debts from the defendant, he would pay over to the creditors their respective debts or so much thereof as he might be able to realize after payment of the costs necessarily incurred by him. The plaintiff and defendant were co-directors of a company, and the plaintiff being dissatisfied with the conduct of the

---

[1] For a description of motive in maintenance see *Bradlaugh* v. *Newdegate* (1883), 11 Q.B.D. 1, at p. 11; and *ante* pp. 14–15.

[2] 2 Sim. and Stu. 244.

[3] 30 Beav. 384.   [4] [1905] 2 K.B. 364.

ASSIGNMENT OF CHOSES IN ACTION 53

defendant as a director admitted that he took the assignment with a view to procure an adjudication of bankruptcy against the defendant, and thus to ensure his removal from the directorate. In a considered judgment it was held that the plaintiff could recover the debts assigned, that the assignment was not invalid as savouring of maintenance or being otherwise against public policy, and that the decision of LAWRANCE J. must be reversed. COZENS-HARDY L.J. said:

I fail to see that we have anything to do with the motives which actuate the plaintiff, who is simply asserting a legal right consequential upon the possession of property which has been validly assigned to him (at p. 374).

MATTHEW L.J. agreed with COZENS-HARDY L.J.'s judgment. COLLINS M.R. used more guarded language:

if the transaction as described in the document was free from all taint of maintenance, the title of the assignee was absolute, and could not be impeached because he acted maliciously in contemplation of law in enforcing it (at p. 370).

It is useless to deny the authority of this decision[1], but, with all submission to its learned authors, it is difficult to agree with it. It may be conceded at once that the agreement was not maintenance according to the definition of that term, but nothing turned upon that, for it had been held long before that if an agreement savoured of maintenance or champerty that was enough, and the Court admitted as much in *Fitzroy* v. *Cave* itself[2]. It is true also that the Court held itself to be bound by *Comfort* v. *Betts*[3], a previous decision of the Court of Appeal, and appeared to think that it was indistinguishable from this case, except for presence of improper motive, which in *Fitzroy* v. *Cave* was held to be immaterial. But it is submitted that this is exactly what constituted a vital distinction. In *Comfort* v. *Betts*, a deed was executed by the defendant's creditors, reciting an agreement that their debts should be assigned to the plaintiff on the terms that he should proceed to recover the same, and should pay to them respectively, out of the aggregate sum

---

[1] It was followed (but not with express reference to the point under discussion) in *Defries* v. *Milne* [1913] 1 Ch. 98.

[2] At p. 371. Cf. *De Hoghton* v. *Money* (1866), L.R. 2 Ch. 164.

[3] [1891] 1 Q.B. 737.

54 DEFENCES:

recovered, such proportionate part thereof as should represent the individual debt due to them respectively, or such part thereof as might have been recovered; and the deed assigned the respective debts of the creditors to the plaintiff absolutely. All that was decided was that the deed was an absolute assignment within the Judicature Act, 1873, sect. 25 (6); and neither in argument nor in judgment was any point raised as to maintenance. It is difficult to see how any such point could have been raised. The plaintiff certainly had no direct interest in the suits which he proposed to bring, nor does it appear from the facts that he was entitled to receive a percentage or to make a deduction on what he did recover[1]. On the other hand, there is nothing to shew that he had any improper motive, or was doing anything beyond assisting creditors to get payment of debts of too trivial an amount to make it worth while to attempt their recovery in any other way. But the case was far otherwise in *Fitzroy* v. *Cave*, where the object of the assignee was to force the debtor into bankruptcy irrespective of whether he paid a farthing or twenty shillings in the pound, and solely to get rid of him as a co-director. If this were not an abuse of bankruptcy proceedings, what is?[2] The decision in *Fitzroy* v. *Cave* does not go further than holding that the motive of the assignee in getting an assignment of a chose in action under the Judicature Act, 1873, sect. 25 (6) is immaterial. But even if it be limited to this, it is hard to avoid the conclusion that the assumption of the Master of the Rolls that there was nothing savouring of maintenance was a begging of the question[3], and that the other two learned L.JJ. seem to have tacitly assumed that the Judicature Act affected the general principles of the law of maintenance[4].

[1] See collateral reports in 60 L.J.N.S. (Common Law), 656. 7 T.L.R. 475.
[2] This criticism of *Fitzroy* v. *Cave* is directed to the action of the Court in holding that motive was immaterial. Had they decided that it was material, but legal in the circumstances, they would apparently have taken the view of motive developed, pp. 14–15, *ante*. Cf. opinion of BAYLEY J. in *Bell* v. *Smith* (1826), 5 B. & C. at p. 194, that the assignment of a policy of marine insurance *pendente lite* merely to make the assignor a competent witness in the suit (which related to the policy) was a strong instance of maintenance or champerty.
[3] See counsel's argument in *Fitzroy* v. *Cave* [1905] 2 K.B. at p. 367.
[4] It apparently has not. *May* v. *Lane* (1894), 64 L.J.N.S. (Common Law), 236 (RIGBY L.J. at p. 238).

ASSIGNMENT OF CHOSES IN ACTION 55

The discussion of what are choses in action and whether all of them are assignable is appropriate to the consideration of choses in action generally, but incidentally these questions have touched the law of champerty and maintenance. Thus it has been held not to be champerty or maintenance if an impecunious legatee sell his legacy for less than its full value to a buyer who purchases it with a view to sue for payment of it[1]. So too, a claim to compensation under the Lands Clauses Consolidation Act, 1845, sect. 68, in respect of an interest in lands injuriously affected within the meaning of that section is capable of assignment; for it is to be regarded, not as a claim to damages for a wrongful act but, as a claim of a right to compensation for damage which might be done in the lawful exercise of statutory powers[2]. "An assignment of a mere right of litigation is bad....but an assignment of property is valid, even although that property may be incapable of being recovered without litigation"[3]. Consistently with this, an option given by a railway company to the lessee of a railway hotel of renting the refreshment rooms at the station has been regarded as property, and its assignment held not to be champertous, though it took place pending litigation[4].

A still more recent illustration is *Ellis* v. *Torrington*, the somewhat complicated facts of which may be thus paraphrased. *A*, the freeholder of a house, let it to *B*. *B* sub-let it to Torrington. Torrington sub-let it to Ellis. Ellis took an assignment of *A*'s freehold interest together with the benefit of the covenant in it to repair. Ellis also took from *B* (whose own interest had expired) an assignment of the benefit of *B*'s covenant for repair as against Torrington. It was contended that this last assignment was of a bare right of action for damages for breach of contract (the house having fallen into disrepair), that it offended the law of maintenance and champerty, and that it was therefore unenforceable. But the Court of Appeal unanimously held that it was enforceable, because Ellis was seeking to enforce a right

---

[1] *Tyson* v. *Jackson* (1861), 30 Beav. 384.
[2] *Dawson* v. *G. N. & City R. Co.* [1905] 1 K.B. 260.
[3] *Ibid.* at p. 271 (*per* STIRLING L.J. who delivered the judgment of the C.A.). Cf. COZENS-HARDY L.J. in *Fitzroy* v. *Cave* [1905] 2 K.B. at p. 371. *Hill* v. *Boyle* (1867), L.R. 4 Eq. 260.
[4] *County Hotel & Wine Co. Ld.* v. *L. & N.W.R. Co.* [1918] 2 K.B. 251.

56 DEFENCES:

incidental to property, and not a bare right of action. So far from multiplying actions, the assignment enabled Ellis to obtain by one action what would have required three actions had there been no assignment[1].

It follows that a mere assignment of the proceeds of litigation does not contravene the law of champerty and maintenance; that, if to this assignment there be added a stipulation that the assignee shall participate in the litigation contemplated, it is lawful if he have some legal interest (independent of that acquired by the assignment itself) in the property in dispute; but that where his interest is generated only by the assignment itself, such a stipulation would be improper.

The reports illustrate this statement of the law. In the recent case of *Glegg* v. *Bromley*, the plaintiff, a married woman was suing the defendant for slander. She was heavily indebted to her husband and by way of further security assigned to him all the interest or money to which she might become entitled under the action. She obtained a verdict for £200 damages, and her assignment was held not to be of a mere expectancy or cause of action, but of property, i.e. of the fruits of an action as and when recovered. Discussion centred rather on the application of 13 Eliz. c. 5, but the point of champerty and maintenance was also raised. All three judges in the Court of Appeal were unanimous that there was nothing in it[2]. PARKER J. pointed out that what was assigned was "not an existing chose in action, but future property identified by reference to an existing chose in action," that nothing passed in such future property till it came into existence, and that no question of maintenance could ever arise. It had long before been decided that mortgage of the subject of a suit *pendente lite*, in order to enable the mortgagor to carry on his claim, is not champertous[3]. The proceeds of a suit may also be purchased outright without committing maintenance[4], but a purchase *pendente lite* by an

---

[1] *Ellis* v. *Torrington* [1920] 1 K.B. 399. For brevity's sake, several of the underleases and assignments have been omitted from the facts.

[2] [1912] 3 K.B. 474. See VAUGHAN WILLIAMS L.J. at p. 484; FLETCHER MOULTON L.J. at p. 488; PARKER J. at pp. 489–491.

[3] *Cockell* v. *Taylor* (1851), 15 Beav. 103, 116. Cf. *Wood* v. *Griffith* (1818), 1 Sw. 43, at p. 55.   [4] *Harrington* v. *Long* (1833), 2 Myl. & K. 590.

ASSIGNMENT OF CHOSES IN ACTION   57

attorney is champerty or maintenance, because he might have the opportunity of imposing on his client from his superior knowledge of the value of the subject matter of the suit[1]; where he becomes attorney to his client only after purchase this reasoning does not apply, and the assignment to him is good[2]. On the other hand, a mortgage to the attorney *pendente lite* is unobjectionable[3]. In *Williams* v. *Protheroe* (1829), by articles of agreement between the vendor and purchaser of an estate, it was agreed that the purchaser bearing the expenses of certain suits commenced by the vendor against an occupier for bygone rent, should have the rent so to be recovered, and also any sum that could be recovered for dilapidations, and that the purchaser at his expense might use the vendor's name in any action which he might think fit to commence against the occupier for arrears of rent or dilapidations. This agreement was held not to be void as amounting to champerty. BEST L.C.J. pointed out that the vendor was said to be entitled to the bygone rents independently of the agreement, and

to say that the agreement respecting dilapidations is champerty, would be carrying the law of maintenance and champerty further than it was ever carried in times when that law was necessary for the then state of society[4].

In *Guy* v. *Churchill* (1888)[5], the plaintiffs, during the pendency of an action, became bankrupt, and K was appointed trustee in bankruptcy. K did not wish to undertake the risk of the action. He therefore assigned the right to sue it to F, a creditor in the bankruptcy, on condition that F should at his own expense continue the action free from K's control, and that K would, so far as the rules and practice of the Court would permit, give all the assistance in his power to F to carry on the action. Its proceeds after deducting actual disbursements not paid by the defendants (but not including F's solicitor and

---

[1] *Simpson* v. *Lamb* (1857), 7 E. & B. 84. LORD CAMPBELL in *Anderson* v. *Radcliffe* (1858), 3 E.B. & E. 806, at p. 816.

[2] *Davis* v. *Freethy* (1890), 24 Q.B.D. 519.

[3] *Anderson* v. *Radcliffe, ubi sup.*

[4] 3 Y. & J. at p. 135. Also reported in 2 M. & P. 779. Followed and applied by C.A. in *Ellis* v. *Torrington* [1920] 1 K.B. 399. See also *Earle's Shipbuilding, etc. Co.* v. *Atlantic Transport Co.* (1899), 43 Sol. J. 691.

[5] 40 Ch. Div. 481. Distinguished in *Ford* v. *Radford* (1920), 64 S.J. 571.

58 DEFENCES:

client costs) were to be divided into four parts, three of which were to go to *F*, and one to *K*. *F* obtained an order of course to carry on the action. The defendants moved to discharge it on the ground that the assignment was champertous. *F* was acting as trustee for himself and the other creditors including the plaintiffs' solicitors, who were also *F*'s solicitors. It was held that the fact that some of the creditors were to carry on the action at their own risk and expense, and were to take a larger share in the proceeds than they would otherwise have done did not bring the case within the law of champerty and maintenance, and that the transaction was permitted by the bankruptcy laws. CHITTY J. said that, apart from the bankruptcy law and the relation of the parties, the assignment would have been plainly void for champerty, and expressed an opinion, though certainly a qualified one, that the interest of the creditors in the action took the case out of the law against champerty and maintenance, apart from consideration of what the bankruptcy statutes allowed[1].

In *Rees* v. *De Bernardy*[2], it was held that a contract by a person to communicate information on the terms of getting a share of any property that may thereby be recovered by the recipient of the information is, if there be nothing more, not champerty. But a stipulation that the informant shall himself recover the property, or actively assist in its recovery, makes the contract against the policy of the law and void, even if the property is in the hands of a trustee or of the Court and no action is needed for its recovery. Two coheiresses to *A*'s estate in New Zealand were aged, illiterate, and humble. They did not know of their title to the property, and *D*, who did, induced them to sign an agreement whereby, in consideration of his acquainting them with this fact, they agreed to give him half the net property. At the same time, *D* verbally arranged to recover the property for them, and induced them to employ his solicitor in the matter. No litigation was contemplated, as the property was in the hands of the public trustee of New Zealand, and the title was clear.

---

[1] 40 Ch. Div. at pp. 485, 490. Cf. *Seear* v. *Lawson* (1880), 15 Ch. Div. 426.
[2] [1896] 2 Ch. 437; 65 L.J. Ch. 656. Applied in *Ford* v. *Radford* (1920), 64 S.J. 571.

ASSIGNMENT OF CHOSES IN ACTION 59

The property was recovered, the proceeds divided as agreed, and the executors of the coheiresses who had died sued *D* to have the documents set aside and cancelled. In this they succeeded, as it was held that the agreement was in the nature of champerty, and void. This decision was followed in *Wedgerfield* v. *De Bernardy*[1] and is consistent with several earlier cases. In *Stanley* v. *Jones* (1831)[2] the agreement was to exert influence to procure evidence upon condition of receiving a portion of the sum recovered and was held to be illegal. In *Sprye* v. *Porter* (1856)[3], the plaintiff agreed to give the defendant documents, which would prove his title to property, in return for one-fifth of the property recovered by such evidence; so far, the agreement was held to disclose neither champerty nor maintenance, because no suit was depending, and it did not stipulate for the commencement of any suit to recover the property, but merely for the communication of documents. But when it appeared that this agreement was merely colourable and had been preceded by a stipulation that the evidence should be supplied for the express purpose of using it to recover the property, and that the property should be recovered under the agreement it was held to be void for maintenance, for

the plaintiff purchases an interest in the property in dispute, bargains for litigation to recover it, and undertakes to maintain the defendant in a manner of all others the most likely to lead to perjury and to a perversion of justice[4].

It had been held earlier that if a person undertake to make out the title of another, and to prosecute suits to recover the claim, in return for part of the land, though the agreement be artfully drawn in order to keep it out of the statutes of champerty, he will not get specific performance in Chancery, but will be left to his remedy at law. The agreement was really an eight to one bet that the claimant was not entitled to the property[5].

In *Hutley* v. *Hutley* (1873)[6] the defendant promised that, in consideration of the plaintiff taking the necessary steps to contest

[1] (1908), 24 T.L.R. 497. 25 T.L.R. 21.   [2] 7 Bing. 369.
[3] 7 E. & B. 58, 80; 26 L.J.Q.B. 64.
[4] LORD CAMPBELL C.J. in 7 E. & B. at p. 81.
[5] *Powell* v. *Knowler* (1741), 2 Atk. 224.
[6] L.R. 8 Q.B. 112. Applied in *Ford* v. *Radford* (1920), 64 S.J. 571.

60 DEFENCES:

the will of J.H. and advancing money and obtaining evidence for such purpose and instructing an attorney, he would share with the plaintiff half the property which might result from such proceedings. The Court were unanimous that the agreement was champertous. Nor was it material that J.H. was the brother of the defendant and cousin of the plaintiff and that the defendant and plaintiff were consequently related, or that the plaintiff believed that the will which was to be contested revoked a former will by which J.H. had bequeathed property to the plaintiff. Neither of these was sufficient to give him a proper interest in proposed litigation. Kinship with the defendant was not enough *per se* to justify champerty[1] and even an honest belief on the part of the plaintiff that he would have benefited under the earlier will could not support an agreement that he should finance an action brought, not to recover his exact interest under that will but, to recover property in which he was to have half the proceeds[2].

If a bare agreement to share in the prospective proceeds of an action is unobjectionable, neither is it maintenance to purchase such proceeds outright[3]. But if the purchaser gives an indemnity against all costs that have been, or may be, incurred by the seller in the prosecution of the suit, this is maintenance[4]. The case deciding this is not well reported, and it has been criticized on that ground, and on the score of doubtful consistency with the previous law[5] and with general principle. Thus in *Hunter* v. *Daniel* (1845)[6], *A*, *B* and *C* who claimed as owners were litigating with *E*, *F* and *G*, who claimed as mortgagees of the lands in dispute. The plaintiff claimed to be a subsequent mortgagee. He contracted to purchase the interests of *E*, *F* and *G* in their principal moneys, arrears of interest,

[1] LUSH J. admitted that certain relationship would justify *maintenance.* Cf. *ante* p. 31, n. 3.

[2] Cf. the comment of CHITTY J. on this case in *Guy* v. *Churchill* (1888), 40 Ch. Div. at p. 490, and the Irish case of *Burke* v. *Green* (1814), 2 Ball & Beatty, 517.

[3] *Harrington* v. *Long* (1833), 2 Myl. & K. 590: *ante* 56.   [4] *Ibid.*

[5] WIGRAM V.-C. in *Hunter* v. *Daniel* (1845), 4 Hare, 420, and TURNER L.J. in *Knight* v. *Bowyer* (1858), 2 De G. & J., at p. 445, in referring to *Hartley* v. *Russell* (1825), 2 Sim. & Stu. 244. *Ante* 52. COZENS-HARDY L.J. in *Fitzroy* v. *Cave* [1905] 2 K.B. at p. 371.

[6] Last note.

ASSIGNMENT OF CHOSES IN ACTION 61

and securities, to pay the purchase money at certain times, and to pay and indemnify *E*, *F* and *G* against past and future costs of the proceedings. It was held that the plaintiff's interest as second mortgagee prevented the contract from being champertous. The Vice-Chancellor in referring to *Harrington* v. *Long* (*ante* p. 60), said: "If the purchaser might enforce his agreement, it is difficult to see why he might not indemnify the vendor"[1]. It might perhaps be suggested that a second mortgagee has a preceding interest in the property that he purchases which did not exist in the case of the purchaser of the debt in *Harrington* v. *Long*, but the latter case would still occasion difficulty on the point of indemnity, for it was admittedly not maintenance to purchase the subject of a suit, interest or no interest. *Knight* v. *Bowyer* (1858)[2] goes further than mere criticism of *Harrington* v. *Long*. *B* granted to six persons annuities out of his life interest in an estate. One of these annuities was purchased in *T*'s name, pending litigation as to its title. *T*, by the deed which transferred the share to him, covenanted to indemnify the vendors against past and future costs, and at the same time executed a declaration of trust shewing the purchase to be made on behalf of solicitors who acted in the suit (but not for the vendors). It was held that the purchase was not affected by the laws relating to champerty and maintenance, and even assuming it to be voidable as between the vendors and purchaser, objection could not be taken to it by third parties. TURNER L.J. admitted that *Harrington* v. *Long* as reported seemed to countenance the argument that this infringed the law of champerty and maintenance, but he said that the report did not shew what the contract was there, and he adopted the doubt of WIGRAM V.-C. in *Hunter* v. *Daniel*[3], whether the case were consistent with *Hartley* v. *Russell*[4]. He added, "I am not prepared to hold that, if the purchase would be valid without the covenant of indemnity, the covenant of indemnity could render it invalid"[5]. The conclusion seems to be that an agreement to

[1] 4 Hare, at p. 430.
[2] 2 De G. & J. 421.
[3] 4 Hare, at p. 430.   [4] *Ante* 52.
[5] 2 De G. & J. at p. 445. See also COZENS-HARDY L.J. in *Fitzroy* v. *Cave* [1905] 2 K.B. at p. 371.

62   DEFENCES:

indemnify against the costs of litigation where the prospective proceeds of such litigation have been sold by one person to another is perhaps maintenance, but that the transaction is not impeachable on that ground by persons other than the vendor or purchaser. Relief against such an agreement can probably be claimed by a party who is not *in pari delicto*. This is the deduction to be drawn from *Reynell* v. *Sprye* (1852)[1], where *S* knew that *R* was entitled to property and led *R* to believe that his title to it was precarious; nor did *S* remove this impression when he discovered that the title was not precarious. *R* sold one half of the property to *S*, *S* giving him an indemnity against all the costs of recovering the property. The case thus turned rather upon fraud and misrepresentation, but it was held that whether the agreement were champertous, or savoured of champerty, as the parties were not *in pari delicto*, *R*'s suit for relief against the agreement ought not to fail on the ground that he was a party to a contract against public policy, or illegal.

An undertaking to indemnify against the consequences of litigation apart from any lawful interest, or the transfer of any share in the suit, is certainly objectionable on the ground of maintenance. Thus an agreement to indemnify the defendant against costs in an action for libel, in consideration of previous publication by the defendant of such libel at the request of the promisor, and in consideration of the defendant agreeing to resist the action, is void. If the latter part of the consideration had stood by itself, the promise would still have been void as an act of maintenance[2]. Such indemnities are distinguishable from contracts of assurance against the illegal acts of others in that the former are given by one participator in the illegal act to another[3]. These cases may be compared with *Williamson* v. *Henley* (1829)[4] where the plaintiff, at the defendant's request and upon his undertaking to indemnify, defended an action for the recovery of £42 in which the defendant claimed an interest. The plaintiff himself had a very substantial interest,

---

[1] 21 L.J. Ch. 633; 1 De G. M. & G. 660.
[2] *Shackell* v. *Rosier* (1836), 2 Bing. N.C. 634; TINDAL C.J. at p. 645. See too COZENS-HARDY L.J. in *Fitzroy* v. *Cave* [1905] 2 K.B. at p. 371.
[3] *Smith (W. H.) & Son* v. *Clinton* (1908), 99 L.T. 840.
[4] 6 Bing. 299.

ASSIGNMENT OF CHOSES IN ACTION 63

not in the subject matter of the suit but, in the results of it; for one, Yeoman, had deposited £42 with him, and the plaintiff had at the defendant's request delivered this sum to the defendant. The report does not state whether the payment of the £42 by the plaintiff was based on some reasonable ground, but his parting with the money was not legal, for Yeoman recovered it from him. It was when Yeoman was threatening this litigation that the defendant gave the plaintiff the promise of indemnity; and it was held that this promise was not void for maintenance, and that the plaintiff could recover £42 under it. Questions as to the legality of promises to indemnify have been raised in several other cases in which solicitors were concerned. These can be better treated when we discuss the effect of maintenance and champerty on contract (*post* pp. 96–104).

Some rights are incapable of assignment at all without infringement of the law relating to champerty and maintenance. Thus the assignment to Navy agents of part of the subject of a pending prize suit amounts to champerty and is void. It was held that there was no completely vested interest in the prize before condemnation, and the judgment indicates that until then the captor had not even a contingent interest, for "the captured effects being condemned to the Crown, no right to any part of the produce can accrue to any one, except by the gift of the Crown"[1]. If that were so, what was assigned was not property but a mere right to litigate, and this is the key-note of a number of decisions which followed this case[2]. Consistently with it, the assignment of a bare right to get relief against fraud was held to be contrary to sound policy and void in *Prosser* v. *Edmonds* (1835)[3], and to savour of maintenance in *De Hoghton* v. *Money* (1866)[4]. In the first of these cases, it was pointed out that the assignee purchased nothing but a hostile right to bring the parties into a Court of Equity, and that where Equity

---

[1] *Stevens* v. *Bagwell* (1808). 15 Ves. Jr. 139, 152.

[2] Cf. *In re Paris Skating Rink Co.* (1877), 5 Ch. Div. 959, where the *ratio decidendi* is not champerty or maintenance.

[3] 1 Y. & C. 481, 496. Approved by STIRLING L.J. in *Dawson* v. *G.N. & City R. Co.* [1905] 1 K.B. at p. 271. This case was followed in *Ellis* v. *Torrington* [1920] 1 K.B. 399 and by FARWELL L.J. in *Defries* v. *Milne* [1913] 1 Ch. at pp. 109–110.

[4] L.R. 2 Ch. 164. Cf. *Twiss* v. *Noblett* (1869), Ir. Rep. 4 Eq. 64, 83.

64 DEFENCES:

recognizes the assignment of an equitable interest, it is such an interest as is recognized also by a third person and not merely by the party insisting on it[1]. In the second case, TURNER L.J. said that "the right to complain of a fraud is not a marketable commodity"[2]. On the other hand, it has been held that the purchase of shares in a company, for the purpose of instituting a suit to restrain the carrying out of an agreement alleged to be illegal, is not maintenance or anything savouring of it[3]. This case is clearly distinguishable from *De Hoghton* v. *Money*, for what it decided was that the purpose with which the shares were purchased did not in the circumstances make the purchase objectionable on the ground of maintenance. Whether the purchase would have given the buyer the right to effect his purpose, i.e. to sue for the prevention of carrying out an illegal agreement is quite another matter, and the report is silent upon it[4].

In re Cambrian Mining Co. (1882)[5], a company which was being wound up wished to sue *F*, in order to rescind a contract for the purchase of the Company's mine, and to recover the purchase price. As the company had no funds available for the litigation, a new company was formed, and an agreement under seal was made between it and the old company, whereby the mine and plant were assigned to the new company, which was to provide money not exceeding £30,000, partly for litigation against *F*, partly to prevent deterioration of the mine. *F* took out a summons for leave to sue to impeach the deed. It was held by KAY J. that the essence of the transaction was that it was a mode of converting the mines into money for the purposes mentioned; that, regarding it as a sale with a right of repurchase in a certain event, it was not the sale of a pretended right, but of the mines and plant; and that it was impossible to regard the purpose as one of promoting unnecessary litigation, as a large majority of the shareholders in the old company desired the action. It was therefore not maintenance. Nor was it champerty, for there was no agreement to divide the proceeds of the litigation.

---

[1] L.C.B., at p. 497.   [2] At p. 169.

[3] *Hare* v. *L. & N.W.R. Co.* (1860), Johns. 722.

[4] It was held that he could not sue for another reason—he was not, owing to a defect in the transfer, a shareholder.

[5] 48 L.T. 114.

ASSIGNMENT OF CHOSES IN ACTION 65

Dickinson v. *Burrell* (1866)[1] is a case not at all easy to reconcile with *Prosser* v. *Edmonds* (1835)[2]. The facts were that *A*, having executed a conveyance of real estate to *B*, which was liable to be set aside on equitable grounds, through improper conduct on the part of *A*'s solicitor in obtaining it, afterwards made a voluntary settlement of the same property in trust for himself for life, with remainders over to his children. It was held that a conveyance, whether voluntary or for valuable consideration, of property which the grantor has previously conveyed by a deed voidable in equity is not void on the ground of champerty; that the right of litigation so to avoid the deed passes to the grantee under the second conveyance; and that the infant children of *A* could maintain a bill, making *A* and the trustees of the settlement defendants, to set aside the conveyance to *B*. The facts in *Prosser* v. *Edmonds* were that *A*, who was entitled to property under his father's will, assigned the whole of it (except a reversionary interest) for valuable consideration to *B*, his father's executor; that *B* acted fraudulently in this assignment and that *A* subsequently assigned the whole of his interest under his father's will (including therefore the reversionary interest) to *C*. *C* now brought a bill to set aside the first assignment on the ground of fraud against *B*, and as *A* refused to join as plaintiff, *C* joined *A* as co-defendant. It was held that the bill was not maintainable, for an equitable interest not coupled with any partial interest in possession, and incapable of being reduced into possession without a suit, was not assignable in Equity.

Thus, in both *Prosser* v. *Edmonds* and *Dickinson* v. *Burrell*, *A* had made a transfer of property to *B*, voidable for fraud. In both cases, *A* had made a subsequent assignment of the property to *C*. In both cases, *C* sought to upset the original transfer and made *A* a co-defendant in the suit brought for this purpose. Yet the results were opposite in the two cases. LORD ROMILLY M.R. in *Dickinson* v. *Burrell* based his distinction of that case from *Prosser* v. *Edmonds* on the ground of a well-recognized difference between "the conveyance of the property itself and the conveyance of a mere right to sue"[3]. This is clear enough. What is by no means so clear is why the learned judge should have come

[1] L.R. 1 Eq. 337.   [2] 1 Y. & C. 481.   [3] L.R. 1 Eq. at p. 343.

W.L.P.   5

66   DEFENCES:

to the conclusion that the petitioner in *Dickinson* v. *Burrell* had acquired anything more than "a mere right to sue," when that was all that the petitioner got in *Prosser* v. *Edmonds*; and it is submitted, with respect, that the judgment does not really grapple with this problem at all[1].

A contract for the purchase of a litigated right is not the same thing as a contract for the purchase of a right which becomes disputable only subsequently to its creation; and this was the ground on which SHADWELL V.C. distinguished *Wilson* v. *Short*[2] from *Prosser* v. *Edmonds*. In the former case, *A* directed brokers to purchase iron on his account. They delivered to him bought notes purporting to be notes of the contract for the iron, not disclosing the seller's name. *A* paid the brokers their commission together with a deposit in part payment of the price of the iron, and he afterwards discovered that there was no principal seller of the iron other than one of the firm of brokers. *A* had obtained money on the security of the contracts from the plaintiffs, who filed a bill in Chancery against *A* and the brokers. The Court ordered the deposit to be repaid with interest, holding that there is no champerty where the right purchased was originally clear, but the litigation is the result of circumstances arising later or known later.

Here it may be remarked that a transfer which might otherwise be considered as an assignment of a mere right to litigate may be authorized by statute, e.g. by the Bankruptcy Acts. Thus, in *Seear* v. *Lawson* (1880)[3], the trustee in bankruptcy of a man who had conveyed away some real property absolutely, commenced an action against the grantee to have it declared that the conveyance was a mortgage, and that the deed ought to stand as security only for the money advanced.

---

[1] PARKER J. hinted at the difficulty in *Glegg* v. *Bromley* [1912] 3 K.B. at pp. 489–90. It was not taken into account in a reference to the two cases by STIRLING L.J. in *Dawson* v. *G.N. & City R. Co.* [1905] 1 K.B. at p. 271, nor by FARWELL L.J. in *Defries* v. *Milne* [1913] 1 Ch. at p. 106. *Prosser* v. *Edmonds* was followed in preference to *Dickinson* v. *Burrell* by the Irish Court of Chancery in *Keogh* v. *McGrath* (1879), 5 L.R. (Ir.), 478. SCRUTTON L.J. followed LORD ROMILLY'S principle in *Dickinson* v. *Burrell* in *Ellis* v. *Torrington* [1920] 1 K.B. at pp. 411–412. See his comment on *Prosser* v. *Edmonds* at p. 413.

[2] (1847), 6 Hare. 366.

[3] 15 Ch. Div. 426.

ASSIGNMENT OF CHOSES IN ACTION   67

The action had proceeded no further than the issue of the writ, when the trustee sold and assigned the subject-matter of the action to a purchaser for value. It was held by the Court of Appeal affirming the decision of BACON V.C. that the assignee from the trustee in bankruptcy was entitled to continue the action. The Court left open the question whether the bankrupt himself could have conveyed "this right or thing in action"[1]. But they did so, because it was unnecessary to their decision (which was unanimous) that the Bankruptcy Act, 1869, sect. 25, authorized the assignment by the trustee in bankruptcy[2].

How far, if at all, a right of action in tort is assignable is only a branch of the wider question which we have been discussing, and which has given us the clear rule that while property can be lawfully assigned, a bare right to litigate cannot. From the first case in which the relation of the law of maintenance to the assignment of choses in action was discussed[3] down to *Defries* v. *Milne*, a case decided quite recently[4], the general rule is that a right of action in tort is not assignable. At any rate this is the trend of judicial opinion, if not of judicial decision[5]. The reason suggested in Elizabethan times was that the damages in such an action are at the date of the purported assignment uncertain, "and perhaps the assignee may be a man of great power, who might procure a jury to give him greater damages"[6]. The first part of this reason is unconvincing and the latter obsolete. As the law now stands, the principle is that such an assignment is contrary to public policy[7] or savours of maintenance[8]. It is obvious that if the rule were otherwise, specula-

---

[1] JESSEL M.R. at p. 432. Cf. JAMES and BRETT L.JJ. at p. 434.
[2] See now the Bankruptcy Act, 1914, sects. 55, 56.
[3] Mich. 34 Hen. VI, f. 30. *Ante* 45–46.   [4] [1913] 1 Ch. 98.
[5] *Defries* v. *Milne* [1913] 1 Ch. 98 decides that what was there assigned was not a right of action in tort. It is true, therefore, that the emphatic remarks of FARWELL L.J. at p. 109, on the non-assignability of a right of action in tort were not necessary to the decision, but it is difficult to resist the conclusion drawn by the learned L.J. from *Prosser* v. *Edmonds* (1835), 1 Y. & C. 481 (*ante* 63, 65). Cf. Williams, *Pers. Prop.* ed. 17, pp. 168–171, and an article by the same author in *L.Q.R.* x at pp. 147–151.
[6] Argument in *Anon.* (39 & 40 Eliz.), Godbolt, 81.
[7] *Defries* v. *Milne* [1913] 1 Ch. 98.
[8] COZENS-HARDY L.J. in *Fitzroy* v. *Cave* [1905] 2 K.B. at p. 371.

5—2

68   DEFENCES:

tion in law suits of an undesirable kind would become common. There are, however, qualifications of the general rule. It is a familiar rule that if an undischarged bankrupt after his bankruptcy enter into transactions with any person dealing with him in good faith and for value, in respect of his after-acquired property, such transactions are, until the trustee intervenes, valid against the trustee[1]. In the case in which the rule was laid down, the bankrupt had assigned an action for conversion which he had already begun to one, Cohen. The action resulted in a verdict of £120 for the plaintiff, and this sum under the rule just stated was held to have become Cohen's as against the trustee in bankruptcy. No question was raised as to whether the bankrupt's assignment of the action were objectionable as being an assignment of a right of action in tort. But the report does not state the exact terms of the assignment, and it is not easy to understand how the case is consistent on this point with principle[2]. In any event, it is no authority for any general inference that rights of action in tort are assignable[3].

Another qualification of the general rule is the doctrine of subrogation as applied to contracts of insurance. A full statement of its principle will be found in the judgment of BRETT L.J. in *Castellain* v. *Preston* (1883)[4].

Whether there be any other qualification is doubtful. None has been traced so far as judicial decisions go, but the general rule is by no means so firmly settled that the matter is not still open to consideration, and we are not without hints that the Courts might take a distinction between assignment of an action for such a tort as slander[5], and assignment of an action for damages for (e.g.) running down a ship. The distinction was thought not unreasonable or inconsistent with law and morals

---

[1] *Cohen* v. *Mitchell* (1890), 25 Q.B.D. 262. The rule is now incorporated in the Bankruptcy Act, 1914.

[2] See the remarks of JESSEL M.R. and JAMES L.J. in *Seear* v. *Lawson* (1880), 15 Ch. Div. at pp. 432–434.

[3] See the careful statement of its effect in Williams' *Pers. Prop.* ed. 17 at p. 169 and in *L.Q.R.* x at pp. 149–150.

[4] 11 Q.B.D. at pp. 387 sqq. See also LORD BLACKBURN in *Burnand* v. *Rodocanachi* (1882), 7 A.C. at p. 339.

[5] As distinct from the fruits of such an action. *Glegg* v. *Bromley* [1912] 3 K.B. 474. *Ante* 56.

INTEREST OF OTHER KINDS 69

some eighty years ago[1]. It was presumably based on the idea that interference in litigation is more likely to be vindictive when it is concerned with a man's reputation than when it affects his property. But it must be added that this neglects the equally important idea in maintenance that the officious meddling comprised in it tends to harry a man with unnecessary legal expenses, quite apart from the fact that it may involve scandal to his reputation; and that consequence would follow just as much where a stranger maintains an action for negligence against him, as where he maintains an action for defamation.

Where judgment has been entered for damages in an action of tort, the damages become a judgment debt and are therefore assignable[2].

(9) INTEREST OF OTHER KINDS

As there is no broad principle underlying the exceptions to the law of maintenance and champerty, and as those which have acquired particular names are not exhaustive, the law recognizes a vague general exception under the heading of "interest." This is useful, as its very looseness makes it possible for the Courts to mould the older law of maintenance in such a way as to give expression to the needs of the modern community. But it also makes it difficult to say where interest ends and officiousness begins. The most that can be done is to examine the cases in which this defence has been pleaded, with a warning that they cannot be taken to tie the hands of the Courts in extending interest to include other cases.

BULLER J. more than a century ago thought that if a person had any interest in the thing in dispute, he might lawfully maintain an action[3], but this *dictum* must perhaps be confined by the context to cases where an interest has been acquired in property which is the subject of litigation, and, as we have seen in discussing the assignment of choses in action, it does not always follow that the acquisition of a title to such property

---

[1] PARK J. *obiter* in *Stanley* v. *Jones* (1831), 7 Bing. at p. 375.

[2] *Carrington* v. *Harway* (16 Car. II), 1 Keb. 803. *Goodman* v. *Robinson* (1886), 18 Q.B.D. 332. It is conceived that the Crown is at the present day in the same position with respect to an assignment of unliquidated damages as its subjects. Cf. *ante* 49.

[3] *Master* v. *Miller* (1791), 4 T.R. at p. 340.

70 DEFENCES:

gives an unlimited right to interfere in the litigation connected with it[1].

"Interest" was examined by LORD COLERIDGE C.J. in *Bradlaugh* v. *Newdegate* (1883)[2]. The plaintiff had sat and voted as a Member of Parliament without having taken the oath required by 29 & 30 Vict. c. 19. The defendant, also a Member of Parliament, procured *C* to sue the plaintiff for a penalty under that statute. *C* was too poor to pay the costs of the action if it were unsuccessful. After the action had commenced, the defendant gave *C* a bond of indemnity against all the costs and expenses which he might incur in consequence of the action. It was held that the action would not lie, and the plaintiff thereupon sued the defendant for maintenance, and in this he was successful, it being decided that the defendant and *C* had no common interest in the result of the action for the penalty[3]. LORD COLERIDGE, in quoting BULLER J.'s judgment in *Master* v. *Miller*[4], said that in all cases of common interest spoken of by him, the interest was an actual and valuable interest in the result of the suit itself, either present, or contingent, or future, or the interest which consanguinity or affinity to the suitor gives to the man who aids him, or the interest arising from the connection of the parties, or that which charity or compassion gives. He held that Newdegate had no common interest "except the interest which all the Queen's subjects have in seeing that the law of the land is respected, and the enactments of every Act of Parliament are obeyed."

Later general descriptions of "common interest" give us nothing more definite than this. "An interest in the subject-matter of the action at issue between the parties"[5]; "an interest recognized by law in the subject-matter of the action or some issue between the parties to the action"[6]; "such that the law

---

[1] See the preceding sub-sect. (8).   [2] 11 Q.B.D. 1, 11.

[3] It has been suggested that the ground of the objection to maintenance of a common informer's action for penalties is public policy. LORD PHILLIMORE in *Neville* v. *London Express Newspaper, Ld.* [1919] A.C. at p. 433.

[4] 4 T.R. at p. 340.

[5] LOPES L.J. in *Alabaster* v. *Harness* [1894] 1 Q.B. at p. 344. Quoted by SWINFEN EADY J. in *Oram* v. *Hutt* [1913] 1 Ch. at p. 267.

[6] LORD PARKER in *Oram* v. *Hutt* [1914] 1 Ch. at p. 104.

INTEREST OF OTHER KINDS 71

recognises it"[1]—these appear to be nebulous, but perhaps the law would gain little by attempts to make them less so, and the cases which raise the question of "common interest" lead to the same conclusion.

We have an early recognition of the rule that a mainpernor might legally maintain. In 14 Hen. VI, f. 6, the defendant to a writ of maintenance pleaded that G, his cousin, had been arrested by the plaintiff in an action of debt, and that the defendant had become his mainpernor. The Court held the plea good[2].

But any attempt to settle what degree of interference by the surety is justifiable is baffled by the elusiveness of the Year Book reports. In Hil. 32 Hen. VI, f. 24, John Doket sued a writ of maintenance against J. P. for maintaining A in a plaint brought by Doket against A in the Guildhall, City of London. J. P. alleged in defence a custom of the City of London under which he had become mainpernor for A in the action maintained, and stated that he had promised to reward A's attorney if he were diligent on his client's behalf. DANBY J. was of opinion that a mainpernor has a justification because he is liable if the person for whom he is mainpernor be attainted and be not found. PRISOT J. dissented, but whether from the general statement made by his brother judge or merely from some particular portion of it, does not appear,—probably the latter, for two years later he is reported as saying that one to whom another is bailed can come to the bar with him to see that he be recorded, otherwise not[3]; but that a mainpernor for another for surety of the peace cannot meddle though a *scire facias* against his principal be found for the King, for it was his own folly that he was a mainpernor. DANBY J. appears to have agreed to this[4].

There is a mere note in Mich. 18 Ed. IV, f. 12 that it was said by BRYAN C.J.C.P.[5] that it is a good plea in an action of

---

[1] VISCOUNT HALDANE in *Neville* v. *London Express Newspaper, Ld.* [1919] A.C. at p. 389.

[2] So too Br. *Abr. Maint.* 22. Fitz. *Abr. Maint.* 5 ("By the whole Court").

[3] Hil. 34 Hen. VI, f. 25. According to Br. *Abr. Maint.* 7, PRISOT J. said this of a mainpernor.

[4] The reporter states this as hearsay.

[5] And "Bridggs" (untraceable in Foss either as Bridges or Briggs).

72 DEFENCES:

maintenance to say that the maintainer was one who took the defendant in the first action in mainprise, provided that he meddled no further.

From this unsatisfying material we must try to deduce the existing law. Mainprise was appropriate to one who had been arrested on mesne process by *capias*, and arrest on mesne process has been largely abolished[1]. But procedure for the recovery of penalties under the Customs Acts may still involve the issue of a *capias* to the sheriff, who may have to make it effective by the issue of a special warrant for the arrest of the person named. This person must produce sureties for his appearance on a day fixed, and they are liable to forfeit the penalties due from their principal if he make default[2]. Further, it still remains to see whether the mediaeval cases give us any principle as to the cognate topic of bail.

Bail and mainprise were not identical even in early times[3]. By the 16th century, the distinction between them is that mainprise is delivery of one arrested by *capias* to certain persons who are amerced if they do not produce him by a certain day, while bail is the undertaking of sureties to produce a suspected felon for trial. The person mainprised is at large, the person bailed is not, being legally in the custody of his sureties[4]. But the point of similarity remains that both the mainpernor and the surety in bail have a strong pecuniary interest in the appearance of the person for whom they answer. Thus, the reason given by DANBY J. in Hil. 32 Hen. VI, f. 24 for the mainpernor's exemption from the law of maintenance can be applied equally to the surety in bail[5]; and it is submitted that no money or effort expended by the surety in inducing the accused to take his trial can possibly be an abuse of legal procedure[6]. True,

---

[1] Debtors' Act, 1869 (32 & 33 Vict. c. 62).
[2] 39 & 40 Vict. c. 36, sect. 247, 252.
[3] P. and M. II. 589–590. Holdsworth, H.E.L. I. 96, n. 2, and authorities there cited.
[4] *Termes de la Ley, sub nom.* "Mainprise" and "Bail." Hale, P.C. II. c. 15 adds another difference. *In re Nottingham Corporation* [1897] 2 Q.B. 502, 510.
[5] *Ante* p. 71.
[6] Cf. Petersdorff on Bail, p. 514, and NORTH J. in *Consolidated Exploration, etc. Co.* v. *Musgrave* [1900] 1 Ch. at p. 41.

INTEREST OF OTHER KINDS 73

the accused's defence may be entirely worthless, and the surety may know it to be worthless, but that is not the point to consider. What he is doing by his assistance is preventing the law from being mocked by the accused's escape. When the accused has surrendered to his bail and pleaded to the indictment, or has appeared in proceedings under the Customs Acts, then it may be relevant to inquire whether he should receive unlimited help from his former surety, in making a defence based possibly upon bribed or lying evidence; and it is submitted again that the maintainer, if he continue to aid the accused, must justify himself under some other exception from the law of maintenance than that of bail; nor is there anything inconsistent with this view in the Year Book cases which have been quoted.

So far as these conclusions relate to bail in criminal cases, they are subject to a modern decision that criminal proceedings are altogether outside the law of maintenance[1].

The next group of cases which requires analysis is that in which a body of persons, bound together by some common interest connected with land, have banded together in litigation; such are tithe-payers, commoners, parishioners or tenants.

In Pasch. 18 Ed. IV, f. 2, A sued a writ of trespass against B, whose defence was that the place of the alleged trespass was a properly consecrated churchyard, and that all he did was to erect a tomb and bury a fellow-parishioner there. C, another fellow-parishioner, maintained B in this defence, and A afterwards brought a writ of maintenance against C. It was held by all the Justices that all the inhabitants in the same vill could maintain an action of trespass brought against any one of them; but that the lord is not one of the inhabitants, though some say that he could maintain because he is lord of the town. The case was adjourned. There is an opinion of Coke's to the like effect in *Wanlace and Philipson's Case*[2].

There is a fair show of authority in favour of the legality of mutual maintenance by tithe-payers[3]. One decision to the

---

[1] *Grant* v. *Thompson* (1895), 72 L.T. 264. *Ante* pp. 5–6.
[2] 12 Jac. I (B.R.), 1 Roll. 57. Coke was then C.J.K.B.
[3] *Findon* v. *Parker* (1843), 11 M. and W. 675. *Dunch and Doyley's Case.* Hudson, 91 (presumably the same case as *Dunch* v. *Bannester* (14 Jac. I) mentioned in Vin. *Abr. Maint.* (O) 8). The law seems to have been doubtful before this. Hudson, *ibid. Stone* v. *Yea* (1822), Jac. 426.

74   DEFENCES:

contrary exists, and it is not of recent times[1]. But there is no reason for supposing that the mutual assistance may travel beyond the common purpose with impunity, as where a general agreement to oppose all demands of the tithe-owner is limited neither by time nor by residence in the parish[2].

The cases just discussed occurred before the Acts[3] commuting tithes, but as tithe rent charge is leviable parochially there is no need to reconsider the principle of the decisions.

To what, if any, extent a tenant may interfere to assist his lord in litigation is unknown. It is said that he may justify coming and standing with him at a trial[4], but this is too vague to be of practical application.

There is more authority on the question how far tenants may assert or protect a common interest against their lord. It is said to have been held in the Star Chamber that the tenants of a manor might all join together in a quiet and peaceable manner to defend the cause common to them all, in an action brought against them by the lord of the manor[5]; and there appears to have been a specific decision to that effect in a case where the tenants were interested in a particular custom[6]. In another Star Chamber case, tenants were fined for agreeing to contribute to expenses of suits commenced or to be commenced by the lord against any of them, and it was agreed that while such contribution is lawful for suit, custom, common or copyhold, it is not lawful where the claim is for several frank tenements or copyholds of inheritance in which the tenants have not an equal and joint interest[7]. Admitting that these cases are on criminal liability, there should be no doubt that the rules laid down in them are of general application[8].

[1] *Oliver* v. *Bakewell* (1792), 3 Gwillim's *Tithe Cases*, 1381.

[2] *Stone* v. *Yea* (1822), Jac. 426. *Lord Howard's Case*, Hudson, 91, which is possibly *Howard* v. *Bell* (14 Jac. I), a case referred by Roll. *Abr. Maint.* (O) 8 and Viner, *Abr. Maint.* (O) 8 to Hobart 91, 125, but which is not discoverable there.

[3] *Findon* v. *Parker* was decided in 1843, but the tithe litigation which preceded it began in 1832. The first Tithe Commutation Act (6 & 7 Will. IV. c. 71) passed in 1836.

[4] 1 Hawk. P.C. ch. 83, sect. 22.   [5] Vin. *Abr. Maint.* (O), 8.

[6] *Dunch* v. *Bannester* (14 Jac. I), Vin. *Abr. Maint.* (O) 8. No further reference is given. *Ante* 73, n. 3.

[7] *Amerideth's Case* (41 and 42 Eliz.), Moore, 562. Reported as *Meredith's Case*, Noy 99.

[8] See CHITTY J.'s opinion as to commoners in *Guy* v. *Churchill* (1888), 40 Ch. Div. at p. 489.

INTEREST OF OTHER KINDS 75

A hundred years ago, a Lord Chancellor said that if agreements relative to the expenses of suits were not permitted, in many cases the poor man would not get that to which he might be entitled[1]. Any one acquainted with the history of our law as to rights of common will appreciate this opinion, and will understand the injustice that would have been done to commoners who had the courage to resist inclosures if they had been held liable for maintenance[2].

The law in this paragraph has been summed up in the statement that, whenever persons claim a common interest in the same thing by the same title, they may maintain each other[3].

It is not clear whether a common religious belief is a good ground for maintaining a co-religionist in litigation connected with the belief[4].

The next heading may be roughly described as "common commercial interest."

Creditors may maintain the action or defence of a trustee or liquidator, who asserts or protects a claim for their common benefit[5].

Protection of commercial interest was examined in *British Cash & Parcel Conveyors, Ld.* v. *Lamson Store Service Co. Ld.*[6] The plaintiffs and defendants were rival manufacturers of apparatus for carrying cash from one part of business premises to another. The defendants obtained contracts for the hire of their apparatus from three persons already under a contract to use the plaintiffs' apparatus, and agreed to indemnify these customers against any claim by the plaintiffs for breach of contract. Two of these customers had formerly dealt with the defendants. The third had contracted with the plaintiffs believing that they were the defendants. The plaintiffs recovered damages

---

[1] *Wild* v. *Hobson* (1813), 2 Ves. & B. at pp. 112–113.
[2] Pollock, *Land Laws*, 182 sqq.
[3] 1 Hawk. P.C. ch. 83, sect. 18.
[4] FLETCHER MOULTON L.J. in *British Cash, etc. Ld.* v. *Lamson & Co. Ld.* [1908] 1 K.B. at p. 1014, thought that this had been accepted as an exception from the law of maintenance in *Holden* v. *Thompson* [1907] 2 K.B. 489; but the decision there was that charity is a good defence in spite of religious motives.
[5] *Guy* v. *Churchill* (1888), 40 Ch. Div. 481, 489, *ante* 57.
[6] [1908] 1 K.B. 1006. Distinguished by AVORY, J. in *Ford* v. *Radford* 1920), 64 S.J. 571.

76 DEFENCES:

for breach of contract against all three. The defendants paid these damages and costs under the indemnity. The plaintiffs claimed relief against the defendants on the ground of maintenance. RIDLEY J. held that the defendants had committed maintenance, directed the jury to find for the plaintiffs, ordered judgment to be entered for them for 40s., and granted an injunction restraining the defendants from unlawfully maintaining any legal proceedings between the plaintiffs and other persons. The Court of Appeal reversed this decision[1], holding that the defendants were acting in the legitimate defence of their commercial interests when they gave the contracts of indemnity. Similarly, where a society was formed to protect the copyright interests of its members, who assigned such interests to the society, it was held that this arrangement was made for legitimate business purposes and was not champertous, though it was a rule of the society that fees and damages recovered by the society were to be pooled and, after deduction of expenses, were to be divided among the members. This provision was only subsidiary to the real transaction[2].

The Courts were relieved of the necessity of trying actions in tort against trade unions by the Trade Disputes Act, 1906[3], which provides that an action against a trade union, whether of workmen or masters, or against any members or officials thereof on behalf of themselves and all other members of the trade union, in respect of any tortious act alleged to have been committed by or on behalf of the trade union, shall not be entertained by any court. This, of course, includes the tort of maintenance. It is needless to consider the extent to which the law previous to this Act sanctioned maintenance of their members by trade unions. At any rate, they stood in no privileged position then[4]; nor do they now with respect to the law of maintenance on its criminal and contractual side[5].

The relation between trustee and *cestui que trust* probably

---

[1] The form of the injunction was, in any event, objectionable. Report cited, at pp. 1011, 1017, 1018.
[2] *Performing Rights Society, Ld.* v. *Thompson* (1918), 34 T.L.R. 351.
[3] 6 Ed. VII. c. 47, sect. 4 (1).
[4] *Greig* v. *National Amalgamated Union, etc.* (1906), 22 T.L.R. 274.
[5] *Post* ch. II and III.

INTEREST OF OTHER KINDS 77

justifies either in supporting the other in civil proceedings connected with the subject of the trust. Blackstone states that unlawful maintenance was greatly encouraged by the first introduction of uses[1]. Be this as it may, their subsequent history shews that their benefit to the community discounts harm from their possible abuse. Several cases in the Year Books indicate this, though none of them actually decides the point[2].

Stepney v. *Wolfe*[3] is a Star Chamber case, but might reasonably be extended to the law of torts. Wolfe made a deed of gift of sheep to Dyo in consideration of Dyo being bound to Wolfe's creditors. One, Stepney, took the sheep. Dyo sued him, and Wolfe maintained Dyo, though Wolfe's debts were not yet due. POPHAM and ANDERSON C.JJ. and EGERTON C.S. held, on a bill of maintenance promoted by Stepney against Wolfe in the Star Chamber, that the maintenance was justifiable in respect of the reverting trust reposed in Dyo by Wolfe to have reassurance of the goods if he were not damnified for the debts[4].

It has been held that a mortgagee, though no party to a suit relating to the mortgaged premises, may expend money in supporting the title without committing maintenance, because of his interest therein[5].

The right of individual members of a corporation to help the corporation itself in litigation does not appear to have been seriously questioned. At any rate there is an old judicial opinion that a canon may justify maintenance of an action by the dean and chapter, because the dean and canons are one person in law[6].

Though there is no decided case on the point, it may be

---

[1] IV. 134.
[2] Hil. 15 Hen. VII, f. 2 (feoffor and feoffee in a trust each have a lawful interest to meddle). Mich. 34 Hen. VI, f. 30 (PRISOT C.J.C.P. *obiter* to same effect). Pasch. 2 Ed. IV, f. 2 (Lyttleton argued that maintenance by feoffee to uses is lawful; *quod fuit concessum*). In Hil. 9 Hen. VII, f. 18, one of the pleas to a writ of champerty was that one of the parties in the maintained action was seised to the use of the defendant. The Court is not reported as having dealt with this plea, though its opinion was otherwise in the defendant's favour.
[3] (43 Eliz.), Moore, 620. Noy 100. And see 1 Hawk. P.C. ch. 83, sect. 17.
[4] Cf. CHITTY J. as to *cestui que trust* of *chose in action* in *Guy* v. *Churchill* (1888), 40 Ch. Div. at p. 489.
[5] *Sharp* v. *Carter* (1735), 3 P.W. 375. Cf. *Hunter* v. *Daniel* (1845), 4 Hare, 420.
[6] *Per* JENNY J. in Pasch. 21 Ed. IV, f. 31.

78 DEFENCES:

inferred that persons who have no direct interest in a limited company have no legal right to prompt or to pay shareholders to take legal proceedings against the company[1].

A personal or sentimental interest in the result of an action is no excuse for maintenance of either party to it, though the maintainer may, on the same facts, have a good cause of action on his own account.

Alabaster v. *Harness*[2] is a leading case on this subject. The defendant was interested in the sale of electrical appliances for the treatment of disease. He employed T, an expert, to report thereon. T reported favourably. The plaintiffs, who were newspaper proprietors, published criticism adverse to T's report and to the appliances, and reflecting on T's expert qualifications, his conduct, and that of the defendant in connection with the report and the sale of the appliances. T sued the plaintiffs for libel, at the instigation of the defendant, who found the money for the action. T lost the action. The plaintiffs sued the defendant for maintenance. The Court of Appeal affirmed the decision of HAWKINS J.[3] and held that the action lay because the defendant had no common interest with T in the action for libel and was therefore not entitled to maintain him in bringing that action. It was true that the action for libel brought by T might have incidentally affected the defendant[4], but his character and conduct could be neither judicially condemned nor justified in that action[5]. His interest in it was sentimental, not legal[6].

Subsequent decisions follow this principle[7].

---

[1] The Courts will not allow themselves to be imposed upon by shareholders who are mere puppets in the hands of other persons for the purpose of instituting litigation; *Filder* v. *L.B. & S.C.R. Co.* (1863), 1 H. & M. 489; *Forrest* v. *M.S. & L.R. Co.* (1861), 7 Jur. N.S. 887; *Rogers* v. *Oxford, Worcester & Wolverhampton R. Co.* (1858), 2 De G. & J. 662. (Cf. *Bloxam* v. *Metropolitan Railway Co.* (1868), L.R. 3 Ch. 337); *Elliott* v. *Richardson* (1870), L.R. C.P. 744; *Hare* v. *L. & N.W.R. Co.* (1860), Johns. 722; and it is much more unlikely that they will countenance the machinations of the real litigants.

[2] [1895] 1 Q.B. 339. 64 L.J. Q.B. 76.   [3] [1894] 2 Q.B. 897.

[4] RIGBY L.J. [1895] 1 Q.B. at p. 345.

[5] HAWKINS J. [1894] 2 Q.B. at p. 904.

[6] LOPES L.J. [1895] 1 Q.B. at p. 344.

[7] *Greig* v. *National Amalgamated Union, etc.* (1906), 22 T.L.R. 274. *Scott* v. *N.S.P.C.C.* (1909), 25 T.L.R. 789. *Oram* v. *Hutt* [1913] 1 Ch. 259; [1914] 1 Ch. 98. Cf. *Breay* v. *Royal British Nurses Association* [1897]

INTEREST OF OTHER KINDS 79

It is not easy to say whether "common interest" as a defence to an action for maintenance includes assistance in litigation given from a sense of public duty. A generation ago, there were strong indications that it did not, for LORD COLERIDGE had expressed an opinion that "the interest which all the Queen's subjects have in seeing that the law of the land is respected, and the enactments of every Act of Parliament are obeyed" was not such a common interest[1]. But his decision related only to the support of a penal action brought by a common informer, and twelve years later it was held not to extend to the maintenance of a criminal prosecution on the ground that such a proceeding should not be hindered[2]. In *Neville* v. *London Express Newspaper, Ld.*[3], the defendant company had exposed in its newspaper the plaintiff's fraud, and had successfully maintained third parties in actions against the plaintiff for the recovery of the property of which they had been defrauded. When sued by the plaintiff for maintenance, the defendant company pleaded *inter alia* public duty, or alternatively *bonâ fide* belief in such duty. The Lord Chief Justice left to the jury the question whether there were such *bonâ fide* belief, and they negatived its existence. The learned judge held that, as a consequence of this verdict, the defendant company had no justification and entered judgment for the plaintiff. It will be noticed that he did so without considering the question whether the defendant company had acted from public duty, irrespective of its honest belief that it was so doing[4]. When the case came before the Court of Appeal[5], they unanimously ordered a new

2 Ch. 272, where, however, the question of maintenance was not raised; and *Hickman* v. *Kent Sheepbreeders Association* (1920), 36 T.L.R. 528, 37 T.L.R. 163. The question how far an approved society may assist a claimant under the National Insurance Act, 1911 (1 & 2 Geo. V. c. 55, sect. 11, sub-sect. 2) without committing maintenance was left open in *Skelton* v. *Baxter* [1916] 1 K.B. 321, 326, 328, 329–330.

[1] *Bradlaugh* v. *Newdegate* (1883), 11 Q.B.D. 1, 11.
[2] *Grant* v. *Thompson* (1895), 72 L.T. 264. *Ante* pp. 5–6.
[3] [1917] 1 K.B. 402.
[4] Need this question of belief have been put to the jury at all? If the plea of public interest were well-founded, belief in its goodness was irrelevant, the soundness of its foundation being a question of law; if it were ill-founded, previous decisions indicate that no amount of belief in its goodness would prevent the interference from being unlawful maintenance. *Ante* 14–15.
[5] [1917] 2 K.B. 564.

80 DEFENCES:

trial on the ground that the verdict of the jury was perverse, and once again there was no discussion as to whether the plea of public duty were a good defence. On further appeal to the House of Lords[1], a bare majority of the House ordered judgment to be entered for the defendant company for reasons unconnected with the plea of public duty, of which no account was taken, except by one of the dissentient law lords, VISCOUNT HALDANE, who thought that the conduct of the defendant company was a piece of journalistic enterprise not disclosing any interest recognized by the law and that it was therefore insufficient to support the plea[2].

On the surface, therefore, *Neville* v. *London Express Newspaper, Ld.* appears to leave the question of public interest where it was prior to that decision, but it must be remembered that the exceptions from liability to the law of maintenance are in a plastic condition, and that the modern tendency is to widen their scope.

We may conclude this section on "Defences" by stating that it has now been definitely settled by the highest judicial tribunal that the mere fact that the maintained action or defence was successful does not in itself constitute a defence to an action for damages for maintenance. Such was one of the decisions arrived at by the House of Lords in *Neville* v. *London Express Newspaper, Ld.*[3]

A brief sketch of the previous authorities is necessary in order to make the latest one intelligible, but it need be no more than brief, for the history of the matter was exhaustively treated in Neville's case. We need not pause long to investigate the ancient statutes or early reports and treatises, for the former upon close scrutiny give no solid reason for supposing that success in the maintained action or defence was essential to success in the action for maintenance, and the latter, though scanty and inconclusive, point in the same direction[4].

---

[1] [1919] A.C. 368.
[2] [1919] A.C. at p. 389.
[3] [1919] A.C. 368.
[4] Fitz. *Abr. Maint.* 26, citing Pasch. 33 Ed. III (unreported in Y.BB.): "a man shall have a writ of maintenance, although he be non-suited in the action in which the maintenance is supposed. Contrarium 7 Hen. IV coram Rege." It is pointed out by LORD PHILLIMORE in *Neville* v. *London Express Newspaper, Ld.* [1919] A.C. at p. 429 that Mich. 7 Hen. IV, f. 30 is not

INTEREST OF OTHER KINDS   81

The more modern cases begin with *Wallis* v. *Duke of Portland*[1], which at its lowest estimate strongly implies a similar view of the law. Wallis, an attorney, had maintained one, Tierney, in an election petition against the return of Jackson as Member of Parliament for a borough. Wallis alleged that he had been employed by the Duke of Portland for this purpose, and filed a bill of discovery against him in order to make good his demand for the payment of his bill of costs by the Duke. The Duke demurred to the bill on several grounds one of which was that such discovery should not be granted as it would disclose maintenance, and LORD LOUGHBOROUGH allowed the demurrer for this reason which, it would appear, was the chief ground on which the House of Lords upheld his decision. It will be noticed that no question was raised as to whether the result of the maintained proceedings were a material element in maintenance, but the inference is that neither LORD LOUGHBOROUGH nor the House of Lords thought that it was, for they regarded maintenance as having been committed, though Jackson, the person injured by it, had lost the election petition which had been the subject of Wallis's interference. This was one of the points which had to be considered by BRAY J. in *Scott* v. *N.S.P.C.C.*[2] at Birmingham Assizes, and he was of opinion that it was immaterial what the result of the maintained proceedings might be. This too was the opinion of LORD SUMNER when *Oram* v. *Hutt*[3] came before the Court of Appeal, though that case was one on contract, and not on maintenance as a tort.

Such was the law when *Neville* v. *London Express Newspaper, Ld.* first came before the Courts[4]. The facts which have already been stated in a highly condensed form in a previous section[5], must be given more fully here. Neville had instituted a competition which resulted in his receiving from each of some 2000

contrary to Pasch. 33 Ed. III. Finch (not mentioned in Foss as a judge) in Mich. 47 Ed. III, f. 9: "also a man shall have a writ of champerty... although the suit be still pending." Br. *Abr. Champ.* 2 attributes this to KIRKETON J. and Finch, and this is supported by another report of the case in 47 Lib. Ass. pl. 5.

[1] (1797), 3 Ves. 494. 8 Bro. P.C. 161. A case much debated by the H.L. in *Neville* v. *London Express Newspaper, Ld.* [1919] A.C. 368.

[2] (1909), 25 T.L.R. 789.   [3] [1914] 1 Ch. at pp. 107–108.
[4] [1917] 1 K.B. 402.   [5] *Ante* 79.

W.L.P.   6

82 DEFENCES:

subscribers three guineas in payment for the conveyance to each of a plot of land. The London "Express" Newspaper adversely criticized the competition, and the defendant company, which owned the paper, at its own expense maintained many of the competitors, irrespective of their pecuniary ability to sue on their own account, in actions in the Chancery Division against Neville for the recovery of the sums paid to him, on the ground of fraud. The actions succeeded, and Neville was ordered to refund the payments which he had received. He then sued the Newspaper Company in the King's Bench Division for damages for maintenance. VISCOUNT READING C.J. held that the failure of Neville's defence in the maintained action was immaterial, and gave judgment in his favour. The Court of Appeal[1] felt itself compelled by its previous decision in *Oram* v. *Hutt*[2] to follow the Lord Chief Justice's opinion on this point, but ordered a new trial on the ground of the perversity of the jury's verdict on the questions of fact in the court below. The plaintiff appealed to the House of Lords for restoration of the order of the King's Bench Division; the defendant company made a cross-appeal for entry of judgment in its favour[3]. The House delivered a considered judgment and by a majority of three to two[4] held that the maintainer's success in the maintained action or defence is not a bar to the right of action for maintenance. The previous authorities were carefully reviewed by most of the members of the Court, and the judgments of the majority were based mainly on the fact that the current of these authorities set in favour of the view that failure in the maintained litigation was immaterial, and that there was in effect a total absence of authority to the contrary in the statutes, reports, or text-books.

With all deference to the noble and learned lords who dissented, their adverse analysis of the authorities does not seem convincing. LORD SHAW OF DUNFERMLINE was emphatic on the point that all that the old statutes prohibited was *unlawful* maintenance, and that if the action maintained were successful the maintenance could not be unlawful. But, quite apart from

[1] [1917] 2 K.B. 564.   [2] [1914] 1 Ch. 98.   [3] [1919] A.C. 368.
[4] LORD FINLAY L.C., VISCOUNT HALDANE and LORD ATKINSON against the dissent of LORD SHAW OF DUNFERMLINE and LORD PHILLIMORE.

INTEREST OF OTHER KINDS 83

the fact that the preambles of mediaeval statutes often employed abusive terms of the wrong which they purported to remedy, it is very unlikely that it occurred to the framers of the statutes against maintenance that interference with legal proceedings, as they understood it, ever could be lawful[1]. Their object was to prevent the oppressive baron and the corrupt official from abusing legal procedure. These were not the men likely to assist litigants from motives of charity, or from a desire to benefit the public or anybody except themselves. If the legislators, when they spoke of maintenance as "unlawful," meant anything beyond abusive surplusage, they referred to it as "unlawful" because it did not enter their heads that it could be anything else. Such an epithet was a descriptive phrase, not a deliberate statement of a condition of liability, and the argument that the success of the maintained action made the maintenance a just and righteous act would have struck them as a complete inversion of ideas. It was precisely because maintenance was so successful in the Courts through their manipulation by great men that it was one of the crying scandals of mediaeval times.

But what held good of the mediaeval times does not necessarily apply to our own times. Maintenance may be, and frequently is, undertaken with a good motive, though very possibly not upon a ground recognized by the law as a sufficient defence. Allowing for change of circumstances, ought it to follow as of course that the success of the maintained action proves that the maintainer was justified? It is respectfully submitted that it ought not. To hold that maintenance ceases to be officious merely because the maintained person wins his action or makes good his defence seems to set up a possible confusion of justice according to law, with justice. A man may win his action in a law court through a perverse verdict, a judicial misdirection, failure of his opponent to produce vital evidence, incomplete legal argument, or decision in his favour of a highly technical point of law. This may be justice according to law, but it is

---

[1] A reservation like that in 28 Ed. I (Art. sup. Cart.). c. 11 of the right to have counsel of pleaders, or of learned men, or of relations or neighbours, is no real exception to this statement.

84 REMEDIES

not necessarily justice. That such cases are exceptional is beside the point. It is enough that they are possible.

It may be argued against this view that the law lags behind the needs of the community if the proprietors of a newspaper acting professedly in the public interest are to be held liable to an action for maintenance like that in *Neville's Case*. But this by no means follows. For, in the first place, it is not at all clear that "public interest" is no defence, and *Neville's Case* has been separately discussed with respect to this[1]; and, secondly, it may be suggested that, independently of the question whether public interest be in itself a defence or not, it can very well be served within the compass of the existing defences to maintenance without inviting all and sundry to apply for the maintainer's assistance. Reconstruct *Neville's* case on the supposition that the "Express" had offered help only to those who were too poor to sue Neville on their own account; then the newspaper proprietors would have been justified on the ground of charity. Was there any need for them to go beyond this?

REMEDIES

(a) *Action for damages*

§ 8. At the outset it is necessary to consider whether damage be of the gist of the action in maintenance. Early authorities are of no assistance after ruling out such as are certainly or possibly *dicta* or decisions on the criminal statutes concerning maintenance or champerty[2], and those in which the point at issue seems in truth to have been not so much whether there were *injuria sine damno* as whether there were any *injuria* at all[3]. In modern times, judges of the Court of Appeal twice

---

[1] *Ante* 79–80.

[2] Mich. 47 Ed. III, f. 9 (also in 47 Lib. Ass. pl. 5; Br. *Abr. Champ.* 2; Fitz. *Abr. Champ.* 4); this was a writ of champerty based on 28 Ed. I (Art. sup. Cart.). c. 11, and KIRKETON J. said that a man shall have champerty though he has lost nothing; so too 1 Hawk. P.C. ch. 84, sect. 8. Trin. 3 Hen. VI, f. 53 (Fitz. *Abr. Maint.* 2), where defendant in maintenance waived a plea that the plaintiff was not grieved because all the justices and serjeants were against him; the proceedings were under one of the statutes relating to maintenance, but whether they were civil or criminal does not appear.

[3] Trin. 3 Hen. VI, f. 53 (last note) is also a specimen of this. Another is Hil. 9 Hen. VII, f. 18, in which the opinion of the whole Court was that if a man shall say that he maintain, and then an action is brought and he does

REMEDIES 85

declined to commit themselves to an opinion one way or the other[1], and no case has been traced in which special damages were not claimed. Such was the authority, or the lack of it, when *Neville* v. *London Express Newspaper, Ld.* reached the House of Lords[2]. By a majority of three to two, that tribunal held that an action for damages for maintenance will not lie in the absence of proof of special damage[3]. Of the majority, the LORD CHANCELLOR'S reason[4] was that the action for maintenance at Common Law was not an action for the invasion of a right within LORD HOLT'S rule that "an injury imports a damage, when a man is thereby hindered of his right"[5]; LORD PHILLIMORE'S was that no private injury could ensue from support of a just action or a just defence owing to the absurdities which would result from the contrary view[6]; and LORD SHAW OF DUNFERMLINE concurred with the judgments of the LORD CHANCELLOR and LORD PHILLIMORE on this topic[7]. Of the dissentient lords, VISCOUNT HALDANE[8] held that, as the statutes relating to maintenance are silent as to the civil remedy, and as the right to protection from maintenance by the Courts is not confined to protection from maintenance of unjustifiable suits, the violation of the right imports an injury

not maintain, the action of maintenance is not applicable, because the person injured by the alleged maintenance is not damaged by this speaking, since the other party did nothing (the jumble of pronouns has been sorted). Cf. Keble *arguendo* Mich. 5 Hen. VII, f. 13. Another case of the same kind is Mich. 22 Hen. VI, f. 5 (continued from Mich. 21 Hen. VI, f. 15) where all the Court were of opinion that an abbot, who had given W. E. 40s. to labour a jury had committed maintenance, though W. E. had not approached the jury, nor had the plaintiff in maintenance suffered damage through the abbot (this is the case cited by counsel in Trin. 28 Hen. VI, f. 7. Cf. Fitz. *Abr. Maint.* 11, and Jenk. 101).

[1] COZENS-HARDY M.R. in *British Cash, etc. Ld* v. *Lamson & Co., Ld.* [1908] 1 K.B. at p. 1012. LORD SUMNER in *Oram* v. *Hutt* [1914] 1 Ch. at p. 107. See also Pollock, *Law of Torts* (ed. 1920), pp. 338–339.

[2] [1919] A.C. 368. The facts have been stated, *ante* pp. 81–82.

[3] LORD FINLAY L.C., LORD SHAW OF DUNFERMLINE, and LORD PHILLIMORE against the dissent of VISCOUNT HALDANE and LORD ATKINSON. This decision was applied in *Hickman* v. *Kent Sheepbreeders Association* (1920), 36 T.L.R. 528. 37 T.L.R. 163. [4] [1919] A.C. at pp. 379–380.

[5] *Ashby* v. *White* (1704), 1 Sm. L.C. (ed. 12), 266, 288; 2 Ld. Raym. 938, 955; 3 Ld. Raym. 320.

[6] [1919] A.C. at pp. 433–434. It will be remembered that Neville had lost the action maintained against him. *Ante* pp. 81–82.

[7] *Ibid.* at p. 421. [8] *Ibid.* at p. 392.

86　　　REMEDIES

independent of proof of legal damage, and thus falls within LORD HOLT's principle just quoted; LORD ATKINSON[1] based his judgment on the ground that the authorities shew that every subject has a legal right not to be harried in Courts of Justice by officious intermeddlers, and he cited the same principle to fuller effect. It must be confessed that the varying judgments of the House on the other question before it—whether failure in the maintained action be a bar to the action for maintenance[2] —were delivered in such terms that the dissentient judgments (whatever be the reasons of them) on the question of nominal damages being claimable appear to express the only logical view that could be taken.

This, it is submitted, is the real difficulty in *Neville's Case*, and it must now be discussed.

The House of Lords' decision which has just been examined shews that special damage must be proved. But upon what principle should its pecuniary equivalent be assessed? At one time the plaintiff seems to have been satisfied with the amount of his attorney's bill of costs in the action maintained[3], and still later to have claimed no more than party and party costs[4], but in *Bradlaugh* v. *Newdegate*[5] LORD COLERIDGE C.J. held that the plaintiff was entitled to the costs which he had incurred as between solicitor and client in the maintained action, and any legal expenses which he had had to bear, in addition, of course, to his own costs in the action for maintenance; in other words that he was entitled to an indemnity for everything which the maintenance had caused; and that if the parties could not agree as to the amount, the Official Referee must settle it. In following this decision in *Scott* v. *N.S.P.C.C.*[6] BRAY J. did not apparently frame the order quite so widely as LORD COLERIDGE seems to have done, as there is no reference to the recovery of legal expenses outside the costs as between solicitor and client which had been incurred in the maintained action (the costs of the action for maintenance of course would be the plaintiff's in any

---

[1] [1919] A.C. at pp. 405–406.　　　[2] *Ante* 82–84.
[3] *Pechell* v. *Watson* (1841), 8 M. & W. 691.
[4] This was BRAY J.'s interpretation of *Alabaster* v. *Harness* [1894] 2 Q.B. 897 in *Scott* v. *N.S.P.C.C.* (1909), 25 T.L.R. 789 (*nisi prius*).
[5] (1883), 11 Q.B.D. 1, 15.　　　[6] *Ubi sup.*

REMEDIES 87

event). However, VISCOUNT READING C.J. in *Neville* v. *London Express Newspaper, Ld.*[1] referred to *Scott* v. *N.S.P.C.C.* as well as *Bradlaugh* v. *Newdegate* as having decided that the plaintiff was entitled to recover an indemnity from the maintainer, and ordered the defendant company to pay by way of damages the costs which were ordered to be paid by Neville to the defendant company in the maintained action (which Neville had lost) and the costs as between solicitor and client incurred by Neville in defending that action. The Court of Appeal ordered a new trial on the ground of the perversity of the jury's verdict[2]; the House of Lords discharged this order and directed judgment to be entered for the defendant company[3], and their decision appears to lead to a very peculiar result on the question of damages. As has been pointed out already[4], the majority of the House held: (*a*) that an action for damages for maintenance will not lie in the absence of proof of special damage; (*b*) that the person injured by maintenance is not barred from suing the action for maintenance though he lost the maintained action. How, it may be asked, can he benefit by the concession in (*b*) in view of the restriction in (*a*)? *A* sues *B* for an alleged debt. *C* maintains *B* in defending the action. *A* loses the action, and proposes to sue *C* for damages for the maintenance. But what special damage can *A* prove? Not the debt claimed from *B*, for *ex vi termini* that was never legally due; nor the costs payable to *B*, for they followed the event in the action for debt; nor his own costs, for they were incurred in prosecuting a claim which had no legal existence. What other special damage can *A* prove that is not too remote? True, he can institute a criminal prosecution for maintenance against *C*, but while his civil remedy in theory exists, it appears to be of no practical use to him.

It might be thought that the mere fact of *C*'s intervention would very likely create two kinds of special damage. *A*'s costs might easily have been increased to a degree which they would not have reached if *C* had not interfered; e.g. *C*'s pecuniary help may have led *B* to brief King's Counsel and may thus have

[1] [1917] 1 K.B. 402. [2] [1917] 2 K.B. 564.
[3] [1919] A.C. 368. [4] *Ante* 82, 85.

88 REMEDIES

led *A* himself to seek more legal aid than he would have done otherwise. This would have put *A* to extra expense under two heads—the taxed costs which he must pay to *B*, and his own costs as between solicitor and client. Here then he would have material for proof of special damage, when he sues *C* for maintenance. But the LORD CHANCELLOR's judgment apparently excludes *A* from this course.

"It cannot," he said (at p. 380), "be regarded as damage sufficient to maintain an action that the plaintiff has had to discharge his legal obligations or that he has incurred expenses in endeavouring to evade them."

And, on this point, there was no difference of opinion between the noble and learned lords[1].

If this interpretation of *Neville's Case* be correct, the consequence of the decision in it appears to place any future plaintiff in an action for damages for maintenance in an embarrassing position, if he has been unsuccessful in the maintained proceedings. His dilemma will be that he cannot claim nominal damages because the law forbids it, and he will have considerable difficulty in proving special damages, though in theory he is entitled to do so.

Whether, and to what extent, his curious plight is modified, if the maintained action in which he was unsuccessful were one for the recovery of penalties under a statute, is not known. The question has never received a judicial answer and *obiter dicta* on it are conflicting. LORD COLERIDGE in *Bradlaugh* v. *Newdegate*[2], where the defendant had maintained an action for penalties against Bradlaugh, said that defendant's counsel had conceded that, if the House of Lords had not relieved Bradlaugh of the penalty, he would have been entitled to recover that as damages together with all the cost of defending himself; but as he had been relieved of the penalty the point did not arise. In *Neville* v. *London Express Newspaper, Ld.* the LORD CHANCELLOR thought that there was a difference in this respect between actions for penalties and actions for a debt due (which he considered

---

[1] VISCOUNT HALDANE at pp. 388, 393; LORD ATKINSON at p. 396; LORD SHAW OF DUNFERMLINE at p. 421; LORD PHILLIMORE at p. 434.

[2] (1883). 11 Q.B.D. 1, 15.

REMEDIES   89

irrecoverable by the plaintiff in maintenance), but he added that it was unnecessary to decide the point[1]. LORD ATKINSON, on the other hand, thought that counsel's admission in *Bradlaugh* v. *Newdegate* was a very rash one[2].

(b) *Other Remedies*

Penalties or forfeitures were fixed under several of the old statutes for the commission of maintenance, champerty, and kindred offences. Where these statutes remain in force, such penalties and forfeitures are in theory recoverable or enforceable, though the precise mode of procedure for exacting them is not always clear. Thus 3 Ed. I. c. 26 forbids any sheriff or other King's officer to take any reward for doing his office on pain of forfeiting twice the reward; and this is still unrepealed, though amended by the Sheriffs Act, 1887[3].

28 Ed. I (Art. sup. Cart.). c. 11 prohibits any one from taking upon him the business that is in suit, upon pain of forfeiture to the King of so much of his lands and goods as is equal in value to what he has purchased. It is easier to describe what the procedure was under this statute in Edward II's time than to state what it would be at the present day[4].

32 Hen. VIII. c. 9 explicitly gives two penal actions, one of which still survives[5]. Sect. 3 forbids any person unlawfully to maintain, or to cause or procure any unlawful maintenance in any

action, demand, suit or complaint, in any of the King's Courts of the Chancery, the Star Chamber, Whitehall, or elsewhere within any of the King's dominions of England or Wales, or the Marches of the same, where any person or persons have or hereafter shall have authority by virtue of the King's commission, patent, or writ, to hold plea of lands, or to examine, hear or determine any title of lands, or any matter or witnesses concerning the title, right or interest of any lands, tenements, or hereditaments.

---

[1] [1919] A.C. at p. 381.

[2] *Ibid.* p. 403. It is convenient to add here that a precedent for a statement of claim in an action for damages for maintenance will be found in Cunningham & Mattinson's *Precedents of Pleading* (ed. 1884), p. 387.

[3] *Ante* 42 n. *Post* 95.   [4] *Hist. of Abuse of Procedure*, ch. VI § 6.

[5] Sect. 2 which created the other was repealed by 60 & 61 Vict. c. 65, sect. 11.

90 THE BURDEN OF PROOF

A penalty of £10 for every offence is imposed, one moiety to be forfeited to the King, the other moiety "to him that will sue for the same by action of debt, bill, plaint or information in any of the King's Courts"[1].

A preventive writ based on 1 Rich. II. c. 4[2] exists in the printed *Registrum Brevium*[3], and Hawkins states that it is obtainable by one who fears that another will maintain his adversary[4]. There appears to be no modern instance of its application[5], and a preferable equivalent would be an action for an injunction, which, it is submitted, is procurable in a proper case[6].

According to Hawkins, a Court of record may commit anybody for an act of maintenance done in its face[7]. His authority for this is *Saulkell's Case*, where HUTTON C.J.C.P. committed to the Fleet one, Rudstone, for coming to the bar of the Court in an attaint in which his servant was concerned, and speaking in the matter as if he had been of counsel with his servant[8].

THE BURDEN OF PROOF

§ 9. Upon whom does the burden of proof lie in an action for maintenance or champerty? It is hardly worth while stating that it is for the plaintiff to prove that the defendant interfered, and interfered with some form of judicial proceeding falling within the limits already discussed[9]. But must he go further and prove that such interference was unlawful in the sense that it was unjustified by any of the defences which the law recognises, or is it for the defendant to shew that there was such a defence? It is submitted that the defendant must prove justification

---

[1] "Actions for penalties" for maintenance were mentioned by LORD FINLAY L.C. in *Neville* v. *London Express Newspaper, Ld.* [1919] A.C. at p. 380. Cf. LORD ATKINSON at p. 398.

[2] *Hist. of Abuse of Legal Procedure*, ch. VI § 6.

[3] f. 182 b; the last of the three writs on maintenance.

[4] 1 P.C. ch. 83, sect. 42.

[5] LORD FINLAY L.C. referred to it in *Neville* v. *London Express Newspaper, Ld.* [1919] A.C. at p. 383.

[6] The injunction to which the C.A. took exception in *British Cash, etc. Ld.* v. *Lamson & Co. Ld.* [1908] 1 K.B. 1006 was cast in an unacceptable form, even if there had been no other reason against its issue.

[7] 1 P.C. ch. 83, sect. 36.

[8] (3 Car. I, C.B.), Het. 78. A similar commitment occurred in *Anon* (3 Ed. VI), Moore 6.

[9] *Ante* pp. 4 et sqq.

THE BURDEN OF PROOF   91

of this kind, that the Year Books and later reports support this opinion[1], and that what has been said to the contrary is reducible either to a confusion of the law of maintenance with that of malicious prosecution, or to unhistorical inferences drawn from the use of the word "unlawful" as applied to maintenance in the ancient statutes and text-books.

It was held in *Pechell* v. *Watson*[2] that declaration in maintenance need not allege that the defendant was not interested in the action maintained, but that the defendant must plead that he was so interested. Two years later, this case was not followed on this point in *Flight* v. *Leman*[3], where there was a declaration in case that the defendant unlawfully and maliciously procured T to prosecute an action on the case against the plaintiff which resulted in the plaintiff's acquittal. Four judges unanimously held that no cause of action appeared because the declaration did not shew maintenance, since the action appeared not to have commenced when the defendant interfered[4], nor was want of reasonable and probable cause alleged; and two of the judges held that the action for maintenance was strictly analogous to that for malicious prosecution.

This analogy has been criticized in connection with another topic[5]. It is needless to repeat what has been said there, but it may be added that there is nothing in the history of the action upon the case in the nature of conspiracy which developed into the action for malicious prosecution to warrant the parallel, and that the weight of recent opinion in *Neville* v. *London Express Newspaper, Ld.* is against it[6]. Indeed, the decision of the majority of the House of Lords in this case conclusively disposes of any resemblance on one point. In the action for malicious prosecution, it must be proved that the proceedings complained of terminated in the plaintiff's favour, while it was definitely settled in *Neville's Case* that the result of the maintained proceedings is immaterial in the subsequent action for maintenance.

---

[1] So too Bullen & Leake (ed. 1915), 639.
[2] (1841), 8 M. & W. 691.   [3] (1843), 4 Q.B. 883.
[4] See the discussion on this part of the judgment, *ante* p. 11.
[5] *Ibid.*
[6] [1919] A.C. 368. LORD FINLAY L.C. at p. 385, and LORD ATKINSON at p. 404.

92 THE BURDEN OF PROOF

Some other modern cases have been reminiscent of the unfortunate comparison in *Flight* v. *Leman*[1], and its influence was traceable in *Neville* v. *London Express Newspaper, Ld.* when that case came before VISCOUNT READING C.J. in the King's Bench Division. He found himself unable to accept the argument that the defendants were not liable for maintenance unless they had no reasonable or probable cause for believing in the justice of the plaintiff's claim, and thought that it was correct to say that in *Flight* v. *Leman* the plaintiff failed because there was no allegation of want of reasonable and probable cause.

But the question turns on the meaning of the expression "reasonable and probable cause" in this connection. In my opinion it means nothing more than the absence of some lawful justification or excuse, and a plaintiff in order to succeed in an action of maintenance must prove not only that the defendant has assisted in the bringing of the suit but that he has done so without lawful justification or excuse[2].

The first part of the quotation puts a meaning on "reasonable and probable cause" which is intelligible and consistent with the previous law of maintenance, though the use of the phrase itself is regrettable and is merely a consequence of the unsound views put forth in *Flight* v. *Leman*[3]; but it is impossible to accept the rule laid down in the latter portion of the words cited. The Court of Appeal, in ordering a new trial, negatived any idea that the burden of proving the absence of lawful justification was on the plaintiff, for they said that an action for maintenance would lie unless the defendants could bring the case within the exceptions, thus casting the burden of proof on them[4]. The House of Lords ordered judgment to be entered for the defendants[5], but certainly not because the plaintiff had failed to prove lack of justification on the part of the defendants, and nothing occurs in the various judgments of the members of the Court to shew that they held any such view, except LORD SHAW OF DUNFERMLINE'S opinion that

---

[1] *Fischer* v. *Kamala Naicker* (1860), 8 Moo. Ind. App. 170; *Harris* v. *Brisco* (1886), 17 Q.B.D. 504; LORD SUMNER in *Oram* v. *Hutt* [1914] 1 Ch. at p. 108.
[2] [1917] 1 K.B. 402, at p. 406.   [3] (1843) 4 Q.B. 883.
[4] [1917] 2 K.B. 564.   [5] [1919] A.C. 368.

THE BURDEN OF PROOF 93

in any civil action in respect of maintenance it is necessary to establish.... that the maintenance was unlawful in the sense above described both in statutes and in text-books; that is to say, that it was to the hindrance or disturbance of common right, to the delay or distortion or withholding of justice[1].

If the noble and learned lord meant that the plaintiff must establish this, it is respectfully urged that this does not represent the law, and it has been submitted elsewhere that he attached a sense to "unlawful" which will not stand a historical examination of the statutes and text-books[2].

[1] *Ibid.* at p. 415. [2] *Ante* pp. 82–83

CHAPTER II

MAINTENANCE AND CHAMPERTY AS AFFECTING CONTRACTS

ARRANGEMENT OF CHAPTER

§ 1. In this chapter, the discussion will *mutatis mutandis* follow the lines adopted in Ch. 1, but a considerable amount of cross-reference will be needed, as many of the decisions on maintenance and champerty as torts are, in principle, of general application, and this is especially true of the defences which are pleadable. Moreover the sub-section on assignment of choses in action is necessarily implicated with contract. The matter may be divided as follows:

(1) *As to persons.*

(2) *As to place.*

(3) *As to the legal proceedings with which interference is possible.*

(4) *As to what constitutes such interference.*

(5) *As to the defences which can be pleaded.*

(6) *As to remedies.*

(7) *The burden of proof.*

AS TO PERSONS

§ 2. The law of maintenance and champerty as affecting contract is subject to the usual qualifications arising from the status of the parties which apply to any contract, and repetition of the text-books is not needed[1]. But a few peculiar modifications call for notice. Certain persons are under stricter liability than others owing to the greater opportunities of oppression or guile which they possess.

Royal and other officials. Statutes concerning royal and other officials, of which a historical account has been given elsewhere, are still in force[2]. Thus 3 Ed. I (St. West. I). c. 25 provides

---

[1] See the following books on the Law of Contract: Pollock (ed. 1911), ch. III; Leake (ed. 1911), Part II; Addison (ed. 1911), Bk. I, ch. VII.

[2] *Hist. of Abuse of Procedure,* 142 sqq.

AS TO PERSONS 95

that no officer of the King by himself or any other shall maintain pleas, suits or matters hanging in the King's Courts for lands, tenements, or other things, to have part or profit thereof by covenant made between them, and he that doth shall be punished at the King's pleasure; and c. 26 forbids any sheriff, or other King's officer to take any reward for doing his office on pain of forfeiting twice the reward, and being punished at the King's pleasure. As the Sheriffs Act, 1887, now allows sheriffs a percentage on sums collected by them under process of any court, that statute repeals 3 Ed. I. c. 26 in so far as it relates to a sheriff or sheriff's officer[1]. 3 Ed. I. c. 28 enacts that none of the King's clerks or justices shall receive without royal licence[2] the presentation of any church which is the subject of litigation in the King's Court, on pain of loss of the church and of the service; and that no clerk of any sheriff or justice shall maintain any suit depending in the King's Courts, subject to the same punishment or a more grievous one if necessary. The effect of 13 Ed. I. c. 49 is to forbid the Chancellor, Treasurer, Justices, Clerks of the Chancery, and members of the King's house from receiving any church, advowson, land or tenement in fee, by gift, purchase, champerty or otherwise, pending a plea. An act or bargain infringing the statute is punishable at the King's pleasure, whether the breach be committed by the seller or the purchaser[3].

Of these enactments, 3 Ed. I. c. 25 clearly prohibits champerty though not *eo nomine*, and parts of 3 Ed. I. c. 28 and 13 Ed. I. c. 49 forbid maintenance and champerty respectively. Agreements to commit crimes are illegal, not merely void, whether they be the offspring of the Common Law or statute[4]. Therefore agreements by the officials named in the statutes to commit the champerty or maintenance there described are illegal. They would also be illegal apart from the statutes, for the balance of historical analysis and the entire weight of modern opinion are

---

[1] 50 & 51 Vict. c. 55, sect. 20, 39.
[2] An exception omitted by the similar statute 13 Ed. I. c. 49.
[3] *Bona fides* is immaterial. 2 Inst. 484.
[4] Pollock, *Law of Contracts* (ed. 1911), pp. 290, 305, 307, 351. Leake, *Law of Contracts* (ed. 1911), pp. 516–517, 521, 524. Addison, *Law of Contracts* (ed. 1911), p. 75.

96 AS TO PERSONS

in favour of treating both maintenance and champerty as crimes at Common Law. The only difference that the statutes make, so far as the law of contract is concerned, is to add penalties to bargains which contravene them.

But what is to be said of 3 Ed. I. c. 26 (to the extent to which it is unrepealed) which forbids an offence akin to, but not exactly like, champerty, and 13 Ed. I. c. 49 which includes champerty in its purview, but is not limited to it? Are agreements to commit such offences illegal or merely void? The distinction is unimportant as between the immediate parties, but with respect to collateral transactions it may be vital. In both statutes the penalty would seem to recur on the making of every fresh agreement, and this, it is suggested, avoids the contract. Whether it be illegal so as to infect collateral transactions depends upon the construction of the statutes themselves[1]. Independently of these statutes, corrupt agreements by an under-sheriff[2] and a town clerk[3] have been held unlawful, but these cases involved no question of any accessory agreement, and throw no light upon it. Here, as elsewhere, the difficulty of distinguishing between "unlawful" (or "illegal") and "void" is increased by the tendency to use these terms interchangeably or as cumulative synonyms[4].

Solicitors. Solicitors occupy to some extent a peculiar position in the law of maintenance and champerty which vitiates certain transactions by them that would be unobjectionable in laymen. But, in addition to this, solicitors are subject to an independent rule that beneficial contracts obtained by them from their clients during their professional connection, and relating to the matter of the suit, are forbidden. Thus, in *Wood* v. *Downes*[5], such a beneficial contract was decreed by the Lord Chancellor to stand as security only for what was actually due, and purchases by the attorney were declared a trust. The decision also proceeded on the ground of champerty and maintenance. The principle

---

[1] Anson, *Law of Contract* (ed. 1920), pp. 229–230.
[2] *Morris* v. *Chapman* (23 Car. II), T. Jones, 24.
[3] *Hughes* v. *Statham* (1825), 4 B. & C. 187.
[4] Perhaps this applies to Shep. *Touch.* 370, where it is stated that an obligation to do an unlawful thing is void, and this is exemplified by an obligation to maintain a suit.
[5] (1811), 18 Ves. 120. The facts are inadequately stated.

AS TO PERSONS 97

underlying the rule has been variously stated as the policy of the law[1], or, more specifically, the opportunity which the attorney might have of imposing on his client from his superior knowledge of the value of the subject-matter of the suit[2]. More recently, it has been put on a higher ground than this. LORD ESHER M.R., while admitting that the fiduciary relation between solicitor and client was a reason for the rule, preferred to base it on the great responsibility of persons engaged in the profession of the law, and the necessity for regulating their conduct by the most precise rules of honour[3].

Such agreements are typified by a bargain indemnifying the client against costs in return for a share in, or a percentage on, the possible proceeds of the suit[4], but variations of this occur where there is not even a promise to indemnify[5]; or where the *res litigiosa* is purchased, not for the purpose of enabling the client to carry on the suit but, merely because he finds that the most convenient way of raising money[6]; or where the entire fruits of the action are assigned, in which case it is immaterial whether the actual assignment took place after judgment, if it were made in pursuance of an undertaking or agreement previously concluded; for the law will not allow itself to be stultified by the argument that, as such an agreement was void, the assignment cannot be referred to it[7].

In several of the cases cited, the ground of the decision was champerty or maintenance, and not the special rule which has been discussed[8]; in others, it was either the rule with main-

[1] *Strange* v. *Brennan* (1846), 15 Sim. 346. *Simpson* v. *Lamb* (1857), 7 E. & B. 84; LORD CAMPBELL C.J. at p. 93. *Anderson* v. *Radcliffe* (1858), E.B. & E. 806; WILLIAMS J. at p. 825. *Pince* v. *Beattie* (1862), 32 L.J. (N.S.), Ch. 734.
[2] LORD CAMPBELL C.J. in *Anderson* v. *Radcliffe* (1858), E.B. & E. at p. 817.
[3] *Pittman* v. *Prudential Deposit Bank, Ld.* (1896), 13 T.L.R. 110.
[4] *In re Masters* (1835), 1 H. & W. 348; 4 Dowl. P.C. 18. *Strange* v. *Brennan* (1846), 15 Sim. 346. *Thomas* v. *Lloyd* (1857), 3 Jur. N.S. 288. *Earle* v. *Hopwood* (1861), 30 L.J. (N.S.) C.P. 217; 9 C.B. N.S. 566. *Pince* v. *Beattie* (1862), 32 L.J. (N.S.), Ch. 734. *Hilton* v. *Woods* (1867), L.R. 4 Eq. 432. *Wild* v. *Simpson* (1919), *Times* newspaper, June 4.
[5] *In re Attorneys' and Solicitors' Act*, 1870 (1875), 1 Ch. Div. 573.
[6] *Simpson* v. *Lamb* (1857), 7 E. & B. 84.
[7] *Pittman* v. *Prudential Deposit Bank, Ld.* (1896), 13 T.L.R. 110.
[8] *In re Masters* (1835); agreement illegal for maintenance according to 1 H. & W. 348, for champerty according to 4 Dowl. P.C. 18. *Thomas* v.

W.L.P.   7

98   AS TO PERSONS

tenance and champerty as an alternative, or a mixture of the two[1]. Where it is champerty or maintenance, it is clear that the solicitor is in a worse position than a layman would be, for an absolute assignment *pendente lite* by the latter of the entire proceeds of litigation is valid[2], and if a client promise his solicitor a share in the profits of litigation, while the client is not disqualified from suing if his title be vested before the agreement, the solicitor presumably would be unable to sue in consequence of the maintenance which infects the agreement[3]. But whether his disability be due to the general law or to the special rule, it is reducible to his professional *status*, and this, on the other hand, gives him an advantage over the layman, for he cannot very well carry on business at all without an interference in litigation which has always been legally recognized[4].

Where his disability springs from his professional relation, independently of champerty or maintenance, the Court will consider whether the client had independent advice, and fully understood the purport of the agreement, irrespective of whether it were connected with what is really not a legal proceeding at all[5].

According to an Irish decision, a conveyance by a client to his solicitor, part of the consideration of which is a sum of money fixed upon as costs to be incurred in a contemplated suit, will not be allowed to stand any more than a contract to the like effect[6].

If the professional relation has not commenced at the date of the bargain, the rule has no application. Thus, a solicitor who takes an assignment of the subject-matter of the suit prior to his employment in that suit acquires a good title[7]. Much

Lloyd (1857), 3 Jur. N.S. 288. *Earle* v. *Hopwood* (1861), 31 L.J. (N.S.) C.P. 217; 9 C.B.N.S. 566 (void for maintenance). *In re Attorneys' and Solicitors' Act,* 1870 (1875), 1 Ch. Div. 573 (*semble,* agreement was champertous). *Wild* v. *Simpson* (1919), *Times* newspaper, June 4 (agreement unenforceable as being champertous).

[1] *Wood* v. *Downes* (1811), 18 Ves. 120. *Simpson* v. *Lamb* (1857), 7 E. & B. 84.
[2] E.g. *Tyson* v. *Jackson* (1861), 30 Beav. 384. *Ante* p. 52. See the principle stated p. 53.
[3] *Hilton* v. *Woods* (1867), L.R. 4 Eq. 432, 439.
[4] *Ante* pp. 22 et sqq.
[5] *Re Hoggart's Settlement* (1912), 56 Sol. J. 415 (a claim in connection with the North Sea outrage, 1904).
[6] *Uppington* v. *Bullen* (1842), 1 Con. & L. 291; 2 Dr. & War. 184. *Semble,* it is maintenance.
[7] *Davis* v. *Freethy* (1890), 24 Q.B.D. 519.

AS TO PERSONS 99

less should it apply where the relation has never existed at all, as where a share in the *res litigiosa* is assigned to one who covenants to indemnify the assignor against costs, and the assignee executes a declaration of trust as to his share shewing that the purchase is really on behalf of solicitors who acted in the suit, but not for the assignor. At any rate, even if such an assignment be voidable as between vendor and purchaser, it is not for third parties to claim that it is so. There is no rule of law "which prevents an attorney from purchasing what anybody else is at liberty to purchase, subject of course, if he purchases from a client, to the consequences of that relation"[1].

A client may lose his right to re-open a transaction by lapse of time. Where he voluntarily paid money to his attorney in pursuance of a champertous agreement, the Court would not compel the attorney to refund the sum after a period of 13 years; had the payment been made under pressure, the decision might have been otherwise[2]. It is useless to contend that an agreement by a solicitor savours of champerty when he has obtained a decree in a previous hostile suit on the foundation of that very agreement and the decree itself is not impeached[3].

An assignment to a solicitor by his client of the subject-matter of the suit by way of security for costs already due is legal at Common Law (of future costs something will be said almost immediately). This was the decision in *Anderson* v. *Radcliffe*[4]. *W* had recovered a verdict in an action of ejectment. Next day, *W* executed an indenture reciting that he was indebted in £100 (for money lent) to the attorney who had conducted the suit, and that he was unable to pay, and assigning the crop of potatoes on the land which had been in litigation as security for the £100. The Court unanimously held that the deed was unimpeachable. LORD CAMPBELL C.J.[5] distinguished the case of a sale outright on the ground that there the attorney's superior knowledge of the value of the subject might lead him to impose upon his client.

---

[1] *Knight* v. *Bowyer* (1858), 2 De G. & J. 421. *Per* TURNER L.J. at p. 444.
[2] *Ex parte Yeatman* (1835), 4 Dowl. P.C. 304, 310.
[3] *Bainbrigge* v. *Moss* (1856), 3 Jur. N.S. 58.
[4] (1858), E.B. & E. 806.   [5] At p. 816.

AS TO PERSONS

ERLE J.[1] thought that the law would be oppressive if the client might not raise money by charging his interest in that to which he claims to be entitled. The Court of Exchequer Chamber affirmed the decision of the Court below. WILLIAMS J.[2], in delivering a judgment in which his brethren concurred, said that neither public policy nor any of the statutes on champerty and maintenance or the text-book definitions applied to this case. He admitted that the Court should not rigidly confine itself to the definitions, if there had been an undertaking (before or after the actions were brought) that the attorney should have the estate or a share of it, in consideration of his future labours. But here the bargain was confined to payment of fees already due—"a most important consideration."

It is not clear whether a security for costs given to a solicitor by strangers to the suit is lawful. In *Pierson* v. *Hughes*[3], an obligation was given by three persons to an attorney, the condition being that if they did pay all monies that the attorney had expended in a suit between A and B, and all that he should expend in the prosecution of the said suit, then, etc. Judgment was given for the attorney in an action of debt upon this obligation, but it turned upon the procedural point that the defendant's demurrer did not shew whether the maintenance were lawful or unlawful, and it might be that the three persons were relations who might lawfully maintain. It is not a neat decision on the question whether, apart from any other legally recognized interest, they were justified in giving the security. According to another report of the case under a different name[4], ELLIS J. held that for fees past the attorney might lawfully take security of a stranger, and though security as to future fees were unlawful, yet it was good for those things which were lawful[5].

The Attorneys' and Solicitors' Act, 1870[6], sect. 4, enables an attorney or solicitor to make an agreement in writing with his

---

[1] E.B. & E. at p. 818.   [2] At p. 825.

[3] (24 Car. II), Freeman, 71, 81.

[4] *Pearson* v. *Humes* (23 Car. II), Carter, 227.

[5] A retainer of an attorney by a stranger on behalf of a party to an action is, according to an opinion in an Elizabethan case, maintenance. 1 Roll. *Abr.* 593 (Dett. 12) citing *Trussell* v. *Monslowe* (38 Eliz. B.R. No further reference given).

[6] 33 & 34 Vict. c. 28.

AS TO PERSONS

client as to the amount and manner of payment for the whole or any part of any past or future services, fees, charges, or disbursements in respect of business done or to be done by the attorney or solicitor, whether as attorney or solicitor or as advocate or conveyancer, either by a gross sum, or by a commission or percentage, or by salary or otherwise, and either at the same or at a greater or less rate as or than the rate at which he would otherwise be entitled to be remunerated. The Act, however, contains the following saving clause (sect. 11):

Nothing in this Act contained shall be considered to give validity to any purchase by an attorney or solicitor of the interest, or any part of the interest, of his client in any suit, action, or other contentious proceeding to be brought or maintained, or to give validity to any agreement by which an attorney or solicitor retained or employed to prosecute any suit or action, stipulates for payment only in the event of success in such suit action or proceeding.

Sect. 11 does not seem to have made any change in the previous law; at least, this is the inference from the cases which have arisen upon it, for where they exhibited objectionable agreements, there is nothing to shew that such agreements were not equally obnoxious to the law, apart from the Act[1]. The interpretation of other parts of the Act has caused a considerable amount of litigation which is only relevant here in so far as it touches abuse of legal procedure. One point of contact is the question as to the effect of an agreement by the solicitor to give his client a simple indemnity against costs, or to be satisfied with less than his usual remuneration, or none at all. A promise to carry on a suit at his own expense with a promise never to expect payment was formerly considered objectionable[2], and general principles appear to favour this view. The effect of such an agreement, it may be argued, will be either that the

---

[1] *Jennings* v. *Johnson* (1873), L.R. 8 C.P. 425. *In re Attorneys' and Solicitors' Act*, 1870 (1875), 1 Ch. Div. 573. *In re a Solicitor. Ex parte the Law Society* [1912] 1 K.B. 302. *Danzey* v. *Metropolitan Bank of England and Wales* (1912), 28 T.L.R. 327. Cf. *In re a Solicitor. Ex parte the Law Society* (1913), 29 T.L.R. 354.

[2] 1 Hawk. P.C. ch. 83, sect. 30. See HAWKINS J. in *Alabaster* v. *Harness* [1894] 2 Q.B. at p. 900. Freeman's editor, in a note to *Pierson* v. *Hughes* (23 Car. II), Freeman, 71, 81, refers to *Ashford* v. *Price* (1823), 3 Stark. 185 as authority for the statement that an attorney may conduct a course *gratis* from motives of charity. The report only shews that this was admitted in evidence.

102 AS TO PERSONS

solicitor, though he renounces his right to claim costs from his client, expects to get his taxed costs from the other party to the action, or that he does not wish to get his costs from anybody. On the first supposition, he is merely speculating in a suit discreditably to his profession and in defiance of one of the objects of the statutes against maintenance and champerty; on the second, assuming that he has no other defence, he is acting outside the scope of his calling altogether, and indulging in the very kind of interference which constitutes maintenance[1]. However, in *Jennings* v. *Johnson*[2], a case upon sect. 4 of the Attorneys' and Solicitors' Act, 1870, an opinion—not necessary to the decision—was expressed that an agreement by an attorney to charge his client nothing if he lost the action, and to take nothing for costs out of any money that might be awarded to him in such action, is not champerty. But this was an action by the client against the solicitor, not by the solicitor, and the practice of the Courts, even before the Act, when they inquired into agreements between solicitor and client, was to hold that such a promise was neither unfair nor unreasonable and to enforce it against the solicitor[3]. Later decisions on sect. 4 shew plainly that the Act has not altered the law here[4], and, as it has been held that the solicitor is precluded by such an agreement from recovering anything for costs either from the client[5] or from the opposite party[6], the possible mischief of maintenance is to that extent avoided.

Moreover, if the indemnity given to the client be a mask behind which the solicitor is in reality conducting the suit, using his client as a mere puppet, he will be held liable for all the expenses to which he has put the other parties by his conduct[7].

At one time it was doubtful whether a personal security for costs given by the client to the solicitor were permissible. In

---

[1] *Ante* pp. 26–27.   [2] (1873), L.R. 8 C.P. 425.

[3] *Per* LORD ALVERSTONE C.J. and BUCKLEY L.J. in *Clare* v. *Joseph* [1907] 2 K.B. at pp. 372, 378, and BUCKNILL J. in *Gundry* v. *Sainsbury* [1910] 1 K.B. at p. 104.

[4] See the cases last cited.

[5] Not even his out-of-pocket expenses unless there be a stipulation for them. *Turner* v. *Tennant* (1846), 10 Jur. 429 n. *Jones* v. *Reade* (1836), 5 Dowl. 216.

[6] *Gundry* v. *Sainsbury, supra.* Cf. *Adams* v. *London Improved Motor Coach Builders, Ld.* [1920] 3 K.B. 82.

[7] *Per* LORD HATHERLEY L.C. *In re Jones* (1870), L.R. 6 Ch. 497.

AS TO PERSONS 103

a case of Charles II's reign, it was agreed by all the judges that the client might give the attorney a bond for his fees, but this was an opinion expressed before the delivery of judgment on another point, and *curia advisare vult*[1]. But any hesitation which the Courts may have felt has long been resolved in favour of the rule that a solicitor may take security from his client for costs already due, whether in the form of a bond or a mortgage. It cannot be taken as covering more than the amount actually due[2]. Courts of Equity always recognized the possibility of undue influence by the attorney in procuring such an agreement, and, where that appeared, relieved the client from its consequences[3]; but though they viewed a security of this kind with jealousy, they would not restrain proceedings upon it at law merely because the client alleged it to be a nullity[4].

It was repeatedly held prior to the Attorneys' and Solicitors' Act, 1870, that a security given by the client for future costs was invalid[5]. But this is expressly allowed by the Act[6]. The Solicitors' Remuneration Act, 1881, enabled the solicitor to take from his client security for future costs in non-contentious business, and therefore restricted the application of the similar section in the earlier Act to contentious business[7].

If the agreement take the form of a mortgage, care should be taken that no unusual clauses are inserted unless their effect be fully explained to the client[8].

A mortgage which is security for something far beyond the mere costs of the action is tainted with champerty, and redemption will be decreed on payment only of the sums actually advanced; thus, a stipulation in the mortgage instrument that the solicitor shall be employed as such in the litigation is essentially an act of maintenance[9].

---

[1] *Pierson* v. *Hughes* (24 Car. II), Freeman, 71, 81.
[2] *Sanderson* v. *Glass* (1742), 2 Atk. 296. *Morgan* v. *Higgins* (1859), 1 Giff. 270.
[3] *Per* LORD HARDWICKE in *Walmesley* v. *Booth* (1741), 2 Atk. at pp. 29–30.
[4] *Jones* v. *Roberts* (1846), 9 Beav. 419.
[5] *Jones* v. *Tripp* (1821), Jac. 322. *Williams* v. *Piggott* (1822), Jac. 598. *Pitcher* v. *Rigby* (1821), 9 Price, 79.
[6] 33 & 34 Vict. c. 28, sect. 16.   [7] 44 & 45 Vict. c. 44, sects. 2, 9.
[8] *Cockburn* v. *Edwards* (1881), 18 Ch. Div. 449. *Jones* v. *Linton* (1881), 44 L.T. 601. See also the Mortgagees Legal Costs Act, 1895 (58 & 59 Vict. c. 25).   [9] *James* v. *Kerr* (1888), 40 Ch. Div. 449, 458.

104   AS TO PERSONS

As a solicitor is an officer of the Court, its control over him is not affected by the fact that he has made an agreement abroad which is to be carried out in this country and which would be void for champerty if made here[1].

Counsel. The barrister resembles the solicitor in that his profession is at once the justification for his interference in litigation, and the cause of his disability to make certain agreements.

He cannot recover his remuneration from his lay client by action, though it is of course recognized in taxation of costs. It has been stated that the reason for his incapacity is that his emoluments should not depend on the event of the cause, but ought to be the same whether that be successful or unsuccessful; hence the practice of payment of his fee on delivery of the brief[2]. But at the back of this is the professional theory that his employment is gratuitous, and this leads to the rule that no obligation inchoate or otherwise exists between him and his client. There is a careful modern analysis of this theory in *Kennedy* v. *Broun*[3]. ERLE C.J., in delivering the judgment of the Court, pointed out the wide powers which are conferred on advocates, and the need of a sustained sense of the corresponding duty which he owes to his client and the court, and said that if the law allowed the advocate to contract for hire, the performance of his duty might be guided by the words of his contract in preference to the principles of duty, that words sold and delivered for hire would fail to create sympathy and persuasion in proportion as they were suggestive of effrontery and selfishness, and that the standard of duty·throughout the whole class of advocates would be degraded. "It may also well be that, if contracts for hire could be made by advocates, an interest in litigation might be created contrary to the policy of the law against maintenance"[4]. Some of this reasoning is artificial, for a prosaic common juror is likely to think that forensic eloquence generally consists of "words sold and delivered for hire," but the main idea that the theory enhances the dignity of the profession is correct.

[1] *Grell* v. *Levy* (1864), 16 C.B.N.S. 73. *Post* 106–107 for facts of case.
[2] *Per* BAYLEY J. in *Morris* v. *Hunt* (1819), 1 Chitty at p. 551.
[3] (1863), 13 C.B.N.S. 677.
[4] *Ibid.* pp. 737, 738.

AS TO PERSONS 105

In the reports there is not much evidence of maintenance as a variant or additional element in the theory. It was held long ago that a bill in Chancery brought upon an agreement between a counsellor and his lay client for a fee of £200 was properly demurred to as unanswerable, because a reply to it would draw the defendant client under the penal law[1], and that a bond taken by a counsellor from his lay client to secure the conveyance to the counsellor of one-half of the estate, the recovery of which he undertook, must be set aside, except to secure what was actually laid out in recovering the estate[2]. In view of *Kennedy* v. *Broun* the bond would have been totally void at the present day[3]. But there is little need to pray in aid the law of maintenance and champerty, for in agreements like these, just as with those of solicitors, we have the independent rule that a professional legal adviser must not abuse his confidential position. If a barrister shortly after the suit in which his services were engaged is ended, gets a conveyance from his client of a large share of the property recovered, the conveyance must be set aside, for it must have been obtained either as a gift, and as such is improper because it follows so closely upon the period of professional relationship, or as the result of a contract which was objectionable unless the client had made it after getting advice elsewhere[4]. Had such separate advice been given, the decision might have been different. It is equally useless to attempt to hoodwink the court by an agreement which purports to be a mortgage, but which is really a "clandestine way of coming at fees"[5].

As to the recovery of fees by a barrister from the solicitor who briefed him, according to a case of Charles I's reign, a demurrer was successfully set up against a bill brought by a counsellor for his fees against a solicitor[6]. But the report is too brief to be of much value, and "solicitors" at that time very

---

[1] *Penrice* v. *Parker* (1673), Finch, 75. The head-note refers to the penal law as the statute of maintenance (which statute is unspecified). The report does not mention this.

[2] *Skapholme* v. *Hart* (1680), Finch, 477.

[3] (1863), 13 C.B.N.S. 677. Cf. Pollock, *Law of Contract* (ed. 1911), p. 712.

[4] *Broun* v. *Kennedy* (1864), 33 L.J. (N.S.), Ch. 342. Cf. *Penros Case, ante* p. 17.

[5] LORD HARDWICKE L.C. in *Thornhill* v. *Evans* (1742), 2 Atk. 330, 332.

[6] *Moor* v. *Row* (5 Car. I), 1 Rep. in Chancery, 21.

106 AS TO PLACE

likely included amateurs as well as those who made the law their sole business. More than 200 years later, KINDERSLEY V.C. dismissed a petition by a barrister for payment of fees by a solicitor, because no reported case could be produced in favour of the petition. The Vice-Chancellor expressed his unwillingness to derogate from the high position in which a barrister stands, which distinguishes him from an ordinary tradesman[1]. The weight of later judicial opinion is on the same side[2], and in *Wells* v. *Wells* the *ratio decidendi* was that fees owing to counsel are not "debts," it being held unanimously by the Court of Appeal that an action for such fees is no more applicable when the solicitor has received them from the lay client than when he has[3]. As far as principle is concerned, there is, of course, no risk of undue influence between the barrister and solicitor, as there is between lawyer and lay litigant, and it is difficult to see how the law of maintenance could be infringed if the barrister were allowed to sue. However, the suggested incapacity might be put on the ground that his duty is to see that the solicitor pays him on delivery of the brief, and that if he neglect this method of payment in advance, he has only himself to thank if he finds that he cannot recover his fees later[4].

Lastly, there is an indirect remedy in the possible disciplinary jurisdiction of the Court over solicitors who do not account to barristers for the fees which they have received[5].

AS TO PLACE

§ 3. It has been shewn elsewhere that the English laws of maintenance and champerty, are not of force as specific laws in India[6].

An agreement to be performed in this country which would

---

[1] *In re May* (1858), 4 Jur. N.S. 1169.

[2] All three L.JJ. *In re Le Brasseur and Oakley* [1896] 2 Ch. 487 (LINDLEY L.J. distinguished *In re Hall* (1856), 2 Jur. N.S. 1076, where counsel was admitted to prove for fees in the bankruptcy of solicitors). *Angell* v. *Oodeen* (1860), 29 L.J. (N.S.) C.P. 227.

[3] [1914] P. 157, 163. *In re Hall* (*ubi sup.*) and *Ex parte Colquhoun, In re Clift* (1890), 38 W.R. 688 were explained.

[4] It is foreign to the purpose of this work to consider the barrister's position with regard to fees for semi-professional and non-litigious work. See Pollock, *Law of Contract* (ed. 1911), pp. 713–714.

[5] *Re a Solicitor* (1894), 63 L.J.Q.B. 397. *Re a Solicitor* (1909), *Times* newspaper, 27th and 28th Jan. 1909. *Re a Solicitor* (1911), *ibid.* 5th Nov. 1911. [6] *Ante* p. 4.

PROCEEDINGS CAPABLE OF MAINTENANCE 107

be void for champerty if made here is not the less void because it was made in a foreign country, where such a contract would be legal. *Grell* v. *Levy*[1], the authority for this, related indeed to an agreement between solicitor and client, and the ground of it seems to be that its foreign origin could not affect the control of the Court over one of its officers, but the agreement would have been just as champertous here if one party to it had not been a solicitor. As champerty is forbidden by our law, the case really exemplifies either the principle of private international law that where a contract contemplated the violation of English law it cannot be enforced here, although it may have been valid by the law of the country where it was made, or (if we confine ourselves to the narrower procedural reason given by the Court) the twin principle that a contract in similar circumstances which conflicts with English ideas of essential public or moral interests is equally unenforceable here[2].

AS TO THE LEGAL PROCEEDINGS WITH WHICH INTERFERENCE IS POSSIBLE

§ 4. These have been dealt with in discussing maintenance and champerty as torts (*ante* ch. I, § 5).

AS TO WHAT CONSTITUTES INTERFERENCE

§ 5. Reference must be made on this topic to the corresponding matter, pp. 4–10, *ante*, and to the discussion of the assignment of choses in action as a defence to maintenance and champerty (*ibid.* pp. 44 sqq.). What is added here must be taken as supplementary to the matter there, and as peculiar to the law of contract.

To make an agreement champertous there need not be a collateral agreement to carry on the suit to its end. Any rule to the contrary would be futile, for the litigant might put all the money in his pocket and refuse to proceed on the ground that the agreement was champertous[3].

The Courts do not rigidly confine themselves to the definitions of maintenance and champerty in deciding whether an agree-

---

[1] (1864), 16 C.B.N.S. 73.

[2] Westlake, *Private International Law* (ed. 1905), §§ 214, 215. The learned author apparently takes the latter view.

[3] *Ball* v. *Warwick* (1881), 50 L.J. (N.S.) Q.B. 382.

108 AS TO WHAT CONSTITUTES INTERFERENCE

ment is to stand or not. If it be tainted with, or savour of, these offences, it will not be enforceable[1]. This pliancy of the law may occasionally make it a nice question whether a particular transaction falls on one side of the line or the other. A firm of brewers, one of whom was a magistrate, contracted with the tenant of a beerhouse that, in consideration of their paying all the costs of his application to the licensing magistrates for a license, he would tie the beer trade of the premises, when they were licensed, to the brewers and their successors for a specified term of years. It was necessary that this application should be backed by the name and business reputation of the brewers. ROMER J. upheld this contract in the absence of any proof that the consideration for it implied that the support of the tenant's application should take the shape of an attempt by the brewer magistrate to influence his brethren in granting the application. On appeal, it was argued that the agreement could not stand, because it was champerty or analogous to it—a point not taken in the Court below. The Court of Appeal affirmed the decision of ROMER J., all its members holding that there was no champerty, because an application for a license was not in any sense litigation, as magistrates' licensing sessions are merely statutory meetings of properly constituted persons, and not courts. On the further issue as to the analogy to champerty, LINDLEY M.R. took the view that there was no semblance of litigation. There was no fighting over the license, or division of it,

and to say that, because, without the license, you cannot carry on trade, and two persons are to share the profit of the beer which is to be sold in pursuance of the license, is stretching the doctrine of champerty to an absurdity[2].

CHITTY L.J. was of the same opinion, but COLLINS L.J. thought that the division of the profits to be made by the sale of the beer might bring it within the ambit of champerty, though it was unnecessary to decide this. With this may be compared *Rees* v. *De Bernardy*[3], where there was a contract to give information

[1] *De Hoghton* v. *Money* (1866), L.R. 2 Ch. 164. *Rees* v. *De Bernardy* [1896] 2 Ch. 437; 65 L.J. Ch. 656.
[2] *Savill Bros. Ld.* v. *Langman* (1898), 79 L.T. 44, 47.
[3] [1896] 2 Ch. 437. See also *Bainbrigge* v. *Moss* (1856), 3 Jur. N.S. 58.

DEFENCES WHICH CAN BE PLEADED 109

for the purpose of recovering property in return for a share in it, and to assist actively in its recovery. This was held to be in the nature of champerty and void as being contrary to the policy of the law, though no hostile proceedings were necessary to recover the property because it was in the hands of a public trustee. The distinction between this case and *Savill Bros. Ld.* v. *Langman* may perhaps be found in the fact that, though originally *ex parte* proceedings only would have been needed to realise the property in *Rees* v. *De Bernardy*, they might easily have developed into a contentious action[1]. But perhaps it would be wiser to take each of the cases of this kind as having been decided on its merits, than to snatch at artificial differences between them. It is a short step from the agreement which is champertous to the agreement which "savours of champerty," and a short step again to one which is "against the policy of the law," or "immoral." When that region is reached, contradictory decisions are likely to be plentiful[2].

THE DEFENCES WHICH CAN BE PLEADED

§ 6. In general, the exposition of this subject under maintenance and champerty as torts (*ante* pp. 21 sqq.) can be applied to contracts. But a few additional remarks on the section which dealt with "Interest of other kinds," are necessary, and these are directed to the legality of indemnities against litigation or its results, given by trade unions to their officials.

Comment has already been made on the immunity of trade unions from actions in tort. But within the domain of contract they are met by the doctrine of *ultra vires*, if they attempt to appropriate their funds for the purpose of unlawful maintenance. Unless, therefore, such appropriation can be reduced to some legally recognized justification for maintenance, it must be in breach of the rules which govern the union. This was the decision in *Oram* v. *Hutt*[3]. Johnson, the general secretary of a registered trade union had been slandered by a member of

---

[1] [1896] 2 Ch. at p. 449.
[2] Cf. *Jones* v. *Brinley* (1800), 1 East 1. The Court animadverted upon the immorality of an agreement to pay a percentage upon the day on which any money should be recovered by the defendant through the plaintiff's information.   [3] [1913] 1 Ch. 259. [1914] 1 Ch. 98.

110   DEFENCES WHICH CAN BE PLEADED

the union, who had made statements which defamed him not only personally but also in his official capacity. Johnson sued this member for slander, relying on a resolution of the trade union executive committee indemnifying him against the expenses of the action, and recovered £1000 damages and costs. The member could pay nothing. Oram, another member of the union, then contended that the promised indemnity was *ultra vires*, and sued Hutt and Johnson as representatives of the union claiming a declaration to this effect, and an order against Johnson for the repayment of money received by him as part of the indemnity. It was not contended for the defendants that the rules of the union authorized the resolution providing for the indemnity. SWINFEN EADY L.J. followed *Alabaster* v. *Harness*[1], and, in giving judgment for the plaintiff, held that the funds of the union had been applied in a way that conflicted with the law of maintenance, because the action for slander was for injury to the personal reputation of Johnson, who alone was entitled to whatever damages he had recovered, and the union had no legal (as distinct from sentimental) interest[2] in the action, and had therefore no common interest which justified its promotion of the action. The Court of Appeal, after consideration, unanimously affirmed this decision[3]. "A common interest," said LORD PARKER, "means an interest recognised by law in the subject-matter of the action or some issue between the parties in the action"[4], and he held that there was no such common interest here, though he recognized that it was vital for the union to controvert the allegations against Johnson from a business point of view. LORD SUMNER admitted that the union and Johnson had identical causes of action, but "a common cause is not a common interest"[5]. It may be questioned whether the Court of Appeal did not put a somewhat narrow construction upon the defence of common interest[6], but so long as we have no complete analysis of that term, so long will decisions on the border line occur.

---

[1] [1894] 2 Q.B. 897. *Ante* p. 78.
[2] Following LOPES L.J. in *Alabaster* v. *Harness* [1895] 1 Q.B. at p. 344.
[3] [1914] 1 Ch. 98.   [4] At p. 104.   [5] At p. 106.
[6] LORD PHILLIMORE in *Neville* v. *London Express Newspaper, Ld.* [1919] A.C. at pp. 425–426.

REMEDIES   111

It is quite possible that the rules of a trade union may be so framed as to make a resolution to indemnify in circumstances like those set out above *ultra vires* without having recourse to the law of maintenance[1].

REMEDIES

§ 7. Apart from the usual remedies which are available to one whose contract is affected with illegality, and which will be found in the standard works on the law of contract[2], a champertor or maintainer is penalized by some statutes which are still in force. By 28 Ed. I. (Art. sup. Cart.) c. 11, the taker of part of the thing in plea shall forfeit to the King so much of his lands and goods as amounts to the value of the part that he has purchased, but it has been hinted that the antiquarian mode of procedure for the enforcement of this part of the statute is difficult to adapt to modern conditions[3]. Reference has been made previously to the penal action which survives under 32 Hen. VIII. c. 9, sect. 3[4].

THE BURDEN OF PROOF

§ 8. See pp. 90–93 *ante*.

[1] *Alfin* v. *Hewlett* (1902), 18 T.L.R. 664.

[2] Pollock, *sub tit.* "Unlawful agreements" and "Equity." Leake, Part V, Addison, ch. VI.

[3] *Ante* p. 89.

[4] *Ibid*. It may be added here that a precedent of a plea of maintenance or champerty will be found in Bullen & Leake (ed. 1915), at p. 639.

CHAPTER III

MAINTENANCE AND CHAMPERTY AS CRIMES

The statute-book contains a number of unrepealed acts which make maintenance and champerty criminal or quasi-criminal offences. The youngest of these acts is over 350 years old, and there is an almost total lack of modern cases upon them. They passed in a state of society entirely unlike our own, and with the object of extirpating wrongs which nobody now is likely to commit. Their vitality depended on the existence of a feudal state of society dominated by powerful and lawless barons, under the nominal rule of a King,—often an incapable King—an ill-developed system of law administered by corrupt officials or abused by great men, and a legal profession infested by practitioners of indifferent repute. Maintenance at that time was "neither more nor less than chronic organised anarchy"[1]. With the advent of a strong central government, the ripening of the legal system, and the general improvement in official and professional morality, these statutes have become atrophied. Writing in 1883, Sir James Stephen said that no prosecution for maintenance had taken place within living memory, and that in modern times the crime had been swallowed up in conspiracies to defeat justice[2]. A historical account of the statutes has been given elsewhere[3], and it only remains to specify those which still survive. They are:

3 Ed. I. cc. 25, 26, 28.

13 Ed. I. (Stat. West. II) c. 49.

"Statutum de Conspiratoribus" of uncertain date.

28 Ed. I. (Art. sup. Cart.) c. 11.

1 Rich. II. c. 4.

32 Hen. VIII. c. 9, sect. 3.

---

[1] Stephen, *H.C.L.* III. 238. Stubbs, III. 532–540.

[2] In the 5th Report of the Criminal Code Commissioners, the abolition of maintenance and champerty as criminal offences is recommended. St. Dig. Cr. Law, Note III.

[3] *Hist. of Abuse of Procedure*, ch. VI § 6.

MAINTENANCE AND CHAMPERTY AS CRIMES 113

Authority has been shewn to exist for the view that maintenance and champerty are offences at Common Law independently of these statutes[1], and some of the highest judicial authorities expressed a very recent opinion that maintenance is still such a crime[2]. But when the modern text-books on criminal law are sifted, it is not easy to trace a single genuine criminal decision in them. Every modern, and nearly every ancient, authority cited illustrate maintenance and champerty either as torts or as affecting contracts. No doubt these decisions are valuable as analogies; for where they lay down that the circumstances constituted a good defence to an action in tort, or that they did not affect the validity of a contract, it may reasonably be inferred that they could not have been the subject of a prosecution[3]. But their value is negative. They indicate what is not criminal maintenance or champerty rather than what is. And where the decisions are the other way—where they settle that a given set of facts amounted to the tort of maintenance or of champerty, or made an agreement illegal on that account—they leave us in the dark as to whether this would have been criminal maintenance or champerty. It is impossible then to neglect the cases on the law of torts and of contract, and reference must be made to the exposition of it already given[4]. All that is left for discussion in this chapter is the small residue of cases which are genuinely criminal[5].

For the purpose of criminal law, maintenance has been defined as "the act of assisting the plaintiff in any legal proceeding in

---

[1] *Hist. of Abuse of Procedure*, ch. VI, § 6.

[2] *Neville* v. *London Express Newspaper, Ld.* [1919] A.C. 368. LORD FINLAY L.C. at p. 382. VISCOUNT HALDANE at p. 391. Cf. FLETCHER MOULTON L.J. in *British Cash, etc. Ld.* v. *Lamson & Co. Ld.* [1908] 1 K.B. at p. 1014.

[3] Cf. FLETCHER MOULTON L.J. cited in preceding note.

[4] *Ante* chs. I & II.

[5] It is believed that this fairly represents the case. See Russell, I. 587, Arch. 1146–1147 and in general modern books on criminal law. They found this part of their subject-matter on I Hawk. P.C. ch. 83, 84. Much of Hawkins' matter is traceable to civil cases, and even where the cases are on the criminal statutes, it must be recollected that our early criminal law and law of torts were not fenced off from each other. Thus 28 Ed. I. c. 11 would probably be described now as a criminal statute; yet Fitzherbert and Coke apparently make it the parent of the civil writ of champerty.

W. L. P.

114 MAINTENANCE AND CHAMPERTY

which the person giving the assistance has no valuable interest, or in which he acts from any improper motive"[1]. But even at the time at which this was written, it is doubtful whether it ever was law that maintenance could only be committed by assisting a plaintiff, and not a defendant; and it is almost certainly not law now[2]. Further, the phrase "valuable interest" is too narrow, and "improper motive" may easily be misconstrued[3]. Perhaps it is better to say that maintenance is interference in civil litigation not justifiable on the grounds recognized by law. This may err on the side of vagueness, but further precision is well nigh impossible. Champerty has been defined as "the unlawful maintenance of a suit in consideration of some bargain to have part of the thing in dispute, or some profit out of it"[4]. *Manutenentia ruralis* as well as *curialis* still exists but seems to be only a duplicate of common barratry[5].

There is some weight of opinion but no actual decision that a corporation cannot be indicted for maintenance[6].

It is said to have been held in the Court of Star Chamber that a mere agreement to maintain a suit and to divide the benefit of it is maintenance at Common Law, though no suit ensue. This was styled "the worst maintenance, because it giveth fuel to all suits"[7]. But against this emphatic resolution may be pitted an equally emphatic contrary opinion of the judges in Hil. 9 Hen. VII, f. 18 which is adopted by Hawkins[8];

---

[1] Stephen, *Dig. Cr. Law.* Art. 156.
[2] *Ante* pp. 17–18.   [3] *Ibid.* p. 13.
[4] 1 Hawk. P.C. ch. 84, sect. 5.
[5] *Hist. of Abuse of Procedure*, ch. VI § 2.
[6] LORD PARKER in *Oram* v. *Hutt* [1914] 1 Ch. at p. 103. VISCOUNT READING C. J. in *Neville* v. *London Express Newspaper, Ld.* [1917] 1 K.B. at p. 408. EARL OF SELBORNE L.C. in *Metropolitan Bank, Ld.* v. *Pooley* (1885), L.R. 10 A.C. at pp. 218–219 (but his opinion is possibly limited to the particular act of maintenance there alleged, and to a corporation in liquidation).
[7] Hudson, p. 91 cites the case of Egerton and Starky (14 Jac. I) without further reference. He also says that if a juror takes money to give a verdict, or a man undertakes to maintain, even if neither does anything further, both are punishable. He refers to Dyer 1 M. 5, and an unspecified case in 30 Lib. Ass. (probably pl. 15).
[8] With the qualification that the public manner in which the promise is made, or the power of the promisor, may make the promise maintenance. Probably his authorities are Mich. 22 Hen. VI, f. 5, Trin. 11 Hen. VI, f. 39, and Mich. 19 Ed. IV, f. 3. 1 Hawk. P.C. ch. 83, sect. 7. They do not help him much, and the examples given from which the qualification is deduced

AS CRIMES 115

and it is doubtful whether such an agreement is even tortious at the present day[1].

The extent to which motive is relevant in maintenance and champerty has been dealt with elsewhere. Whatever may have been the law upon this point in early times, it is submitted that the purchase of property in good faith pending an action for its recovery is not now criminal maintenance[2].

According to a judicial opinion, if a man request the sheriff to return a jury on his denomination, and the sheriff does so, it is misdemeanour on the part of the sheriff, and may be maintenance on the part of the instigator[3].

It has been seen that there is no very clear rule as to what a servant may do in maintaining his master's affairs without committing the tort of maintenance[4]. Here may be added *Lord Cromwell and Townsend's Case*[5], where a bill for maintenance against Townsend in the Star Chamber for procuring a partial jury to be returned was dismissed, on the ground that what he did was justifiable because he was the servant of the man whom he assisted. A suit had been brought relating to forfeiture of a copyhold, and the steward of the manor appeared likely to return a panel consisting only of the magnates of the country, who were themselves lords of manors, and therefore in favour of Lord Cromwell. Townsend procured the Earl of Arundel, who was lord of the manor, and Townsend's master to give him the book of the freeholders[6]. It was said that if Townsend had been a stranger and not a servant, it would have been maintenance in him, as it had lately been adjudged in the Star Chamber in *Gifford's Case*.

The Star Chamber also held that maintenance is justifiable in respect of an interest arising from a trust connected with the property which is the subject of the maintained litigation[7].

are rather in the nature of embracery or of contempt of court than maintenance.

[1] *Ante* ch. 1, § 6.
[2] *Ante* p. 14.
[3] *Per curiam* in *Turner* v. *Burnaby* (12 Will. III), 12 Mod. 564.
[4] *Ante* pp. 38–39.
[5] (28 Eliz.), 2 Leon. 133. The Chancellor was the only dissentient judge.
[6] To enable an indifferent selection of jurors to be made.
[7] *Stepney* v. *Wolfe* (43 Eliz.), Moore, 620. *Ante* p. 77.

8—2

116 MAINTENANCE AND CHAMPERTY AS CRIMES

Other Star Chamber cases illustrate the defence of common interest which tenants may have in defending an action[1].

The fact that the prosecutor lost the action which the defendant had maintained is, according to recent judicial opinion and analogy from civil cases, no defence to an indictment for maintenance[2].

According to an obscure case, if two be indicted for maintenance and one of them be acquitted, the conviction of his co-defendant is nevertheless good[3].

An unrepealed statute of Edward I relating to deceit or collusion practised by a Serjeant, pleader, or other in the King's Court may be noticed here. Whether his object be to beguile the Court or the party, he is punishable with imprisonment for a year and a day, and is disabled from pleading again in that Court. If he be no pleader, he is liable to the like term of imprisonment, or greater punishment at the King's pleasure[4].

We need not pursue the academic question as to what the exact punishment is for maintenance and champerty at Common Law. 1 Rich. II. c. 4, which is still in force, and forbids maintenance generally, fixes the punishment for those (other than Royal officials) at imprisonment and ransom. The Criminal Justice Administration Act, 1914, sect. 16, enables the court to add hard labour to the imprisonment[5].

---

[1] *Ante* p. 74. *Dunch* v. *Bannester* and *Amerideth's Case.*

[2] LORD SUMNER in *Oram* v. *Hutt* [1914] 1 Ch. at p. 107. *Neville* v. *London Express Newspaper, Ld.* [1919] A.C. 368.

[3] *R.* v. *Humphreys* (28 & 29 Car. II), 3 Keb. 739, 764. The collateral report, in 1 Vent. 302, is bad even as a specimen of that period. The indictment was on 32 Hen. VIII. c. 9.

[4] 3 Ed. I. c. 29.

[5] Cf. Arch. 1146–1147. The punishments peculiar to the special forms of maintenance and champerty in the old statutes are discussed in *Hist. of Abuse of Procedure*, ch. VI §§ 6 *et sqq.*

CHAPTER IV

AGREEMENTS AFFECTING LEGAL PROCEDURE OTHERWISE THAN BY WAY OF MAINTENANCE OR CHAMPERTY

ARRANGEMENT OF CHAPTER

§ 1. Certain agreements are objectionable because they stipulate for, or involve, an abuse of legal procedure, though they do not exhibit maintenance or champerty or any taint of either of these offences. They may be considered in the following order:

(1) *As affecting a contract otherwise unobjectionable.*
Here we have:
    (i) *Agreements in restraint of criminal procedure.*
    (ii) *Agreements in restraint of civil procedure.*
        (a) *Affecting bankruptcy jurisdiction.*
        (b) *Arbitrations.*
        (c) *Affecting other civil procedure.*
(2) *As grounding criminal liability.*

AGREEMENTS IN RESTRAINT OF CRIMINAL PROCEDURE

§ 2. The text to which agreements falling under § 1 (i) above are constantly referred is an *obiter dictum* of LORD LYNDHURST in *Egerton* v. *Brownlow* that "any contract or engagement having any tendency, however slight, to affect the administration of justice, is illegal and void"[1]. The special form of this rule with respect to criminal proceedings is that an agreement to stifle a prosecution is unlawful, and the earliest known variety of it goes back very far in the history of our law. Theft-bote, or the re-taking of one's chattels from a thief in order to favour and maintain him, was a heinous offence, and a judicial decision seems to have been needed to settle that the punishment for it was not capital[2]. As to the compromise of prosecutions for felony in general (those relating to less offences will be considered later), we find LYTTLETON J. in Hil. 18 Ed. IV, f. 28 putting

[1] (1853), 4 *H.L.C.* 1. 163.
[2] Fitz. *Abr. Corone*, 353 (3 Ed. III. It. North).

118   AGREEMENTS IN RESTRAINT OF

a hypothetical case in which he supposed himself bound by an obligation to hold *G* harmless in an appeal of robbery sued against him by a stranger. BRYAN C.J.C.P. demurred to this illustration on the ground that such a condition in a bond would be contrary to law, as it would imply meddling in a suit that would amount to maintenance. An appeal cannot be strictly described as a criminal proceeding, but *Jones' Case*[1] in Elizabethan times exemplifies the principle with respect to an indictment for felony. Jones had stolen the plate of Trinity College, Oxford. By the mediation of his friends, it was agreed that no evidence should be given against him, and that the College should be recompensed for the loss. Two of his friends bound themselves to the Rector of Lincoln College (but to the use of the Master and Scholars of Trinity College) that "if the said obligor paid £40 within six months after the said Henry Jones should be acquitted and released of the troubles wherein he now is, with the safety of his life, that then, &c." To an action of debt upon this obligation, the defendants pleaded that Jones was convicted, had his clergy, and was burned in the hand. WYNDHAM J. said that if the words had been to pay the money after Jones should be released and acquitted of the troubles in which he now is, without any more, the defendants would have been bound to pay the money. PERYAM J. was of the same opinion, but added that the words were: "with safety of his life," and he conceived that the intent of the obligation was that no evidence should be given, but as the defendants did not aver this, they could not take advantage of it. Judgment was given for the plaintiff. Here, there was no doubt about the purpose of the bond being unlawful, but a false move on the procedural chess-board disposed of the case, and the same thing occurred in *Brook* v. *King*[2], decided a year or so earlier, where the condition of the bond was to procure J. S. to recompense the plaintiff for certain beasts which J. S. was alleged to have stolen. As the condition merely stated that J. S. had unlawfully taken the beasts, the Court refused to imply that the condition was against the law, and even if it had expressly alleged that

[1] (31 Eliz.), 1 Leon. 203.
[2] (29 & 30 Eliz.), 1 Leon. 73.

CRIMINAL PROCEDURE   119

J. S. had stolen the beasts, the Court need not as a matter of course have held it to be unlawful in the absence of any promise not to prosecute, and a Court of our own times would not have done so[1]. In 1689, we get a neat decision that a condition in a bond "to shift off evidence of a felony" is against the law and avoids the bond[2].

The agreement, to be vicious, must bargain for the stifling of a prosecution. This may be considered, first, with respect to proof of the bargain, and secondly, as to what constitutes "stifling." As to the first point, it must distinctly appear that there was an agreement, express or implied, to abstain from prosecuting or from assisting the prosecution, where there is a legal duty to give such assistance. Such was the decision in *Wallace* v. *Hardacre*[3], and of four judges in *Ward* v. *Lloyd*[4] who refused to set aside a warrant of attorney given to secure a debt, on the ground that there was no agreement not to prosecute. The case is a strong one, for there had been a threat that unless the defendant went to the plaintiff's attornies and gave satisfactory security, the plaintiff would prosecute. It might be asked why a threat should not be objectionable when a mere agreement is? What difference is there between: "If you do not make good what you have stolen, I will prosecute you," and "If you make good what you have stolen, I will not prosecute you"? But this decision was followed in *Flower* v. *Sadler*[5], which may, however, be explained on the ground that such threats as were used were not an inducement for the giving of the bills of exchange, the real consideration of which was the transfer of a share in a patent[6]. Even if this case be taken as adopting *Ward* v. *Lloyd* in its entirety, neither of these cases nor *Jones* v. *Merionethshire etc. Society*[7], which will be con-

---

[1] *Ward* v. *Lloyd* (1843), 6 Man. & G. 785.
[2] *Mason* v. *Watkins*. 2 Ventris, 109.
[3] (1807), 1 Camp. 45.   [4] (1843), 6 Man. & G. 785.
[5] (1882), 9 Q.B.D. 81. Affirmed 10 Q.B.D. 572.
[6] BRETT L.J. was inclined to think, and COTTON L.J. was decidedly of opinion, that in an action by an indorsee of the bills against the acceptor for valuable consideration, it was no defence that the drawer indorsed the bills to the plaintiff in order to stifle a prosecution, but they refused to base their decisions on this ground.
[7] [1891] 2 Ch. 587. [1892] 1 Ch. 173.

120 AGREEMENTS IN RESTRAINT OF

sidered almost immediately, goes beyond the circumstances in which there was a genuine debt that the creditor was endeavouring to secure or recover. In *Flower* v. *Sadler*, COTTON L.J. said:

A threat to prosecute is not of itself illegal; and the doctrine contended for does not apply, where a just and *bond fide* debt actually exists, where there is a good consideration for giving a security, and where the transaction between the parties involves a civil liability as well as, possibly, a criminal act. In my opinion a threat to prosecute does not necessarily vitiate a subsequent agreement by the debtor to give security for a debt, which he justly owes to his creditor[1].

This is clear enough, and considering the expenses attendant upon a prosecution and the small likelihood in most cases of getting restitution except by such an agreement, no doubt moral justice was done.

It is impossible to ignore the question of reparation or to say that it should not be made[2], and it is a matter of common experience that a threat is occasionally the only mode of securing a reparation that would not otherwise be made. The difficulty is to imagine a case where an agreement "subsequent" to a threat is not also consequent upon it[3].

Whether there be any threat or not, a clear agreement to substitute payment of the debt for prosecution of the felony is unlawful[4].

In *Jones* v. *Merionethshire etc. Society*[5], *X*, the secretary of a building society, was threatened with a prosecution for embezzlement. *X* applied for help to his relatives, *Y* and *Z*, and they gave a written undertaking to make good the greater part of *X*'s defalcation, the expressed consideration being the forbearance of the society to sue *X* for that amount. *Y* and *Z*, in pursuance of this undertaking, gave two promissory notes and

---

[1] 10 Q.B.D. at p. 576. Cf. BRETT L.J. at p. 575.

[2] BOWEN L.J. in *Jones* v. *Merionethshire etc. Society* [1892] 1 Ch. at p. 185.

[3] Perhaps there is safety in the proffered compromise being put in such terms as "If you do not do such and such an act, I shall reserve all my legal rights against you." See LORD CRANWORTH L.C. in *Williams* v. *Bayley* (1866), L.R. 1 H.L. at p. 209.

[4] *Cannon* v. *Rands* (1870), 11 Cox C.C. 631. 23 L.T. 817. Two of the judges hesitated as to accepting this as the basis of their decision.

[5] [1891] 2 Ch. 587. [1892] 1 Ch. 173.

CRIMINAL PROCEDURE

some title deeds, as collateral security to the society. In doing this, their motive was to prevent X's prosecution, and the directors of the society knew this, but they made no promise that they would not prosecute. The Court of Appeal held (affirming the decision of VAUGHAN WILLIAMS J.) that it was an implied term in the agreement that there should be no prosecution, that the agreement was therefore founded on an illegal consideration and was void, and that the society could not recover on the promissory notes nor enforce the securities. *Ward* v. *Lloyd*[1] was distinguished on the ground that there was no agreement not to prosecute there.

When once an agreement not to prosecute has been proved, the mere fact that there is a genuine debt between the prosecutor and the accused, connected with the alleged felony, does not make the agreement any the less illegal. Thus, where a person indicted for embezzlement had been acquitted, counsel on each side compromised other indictments for embezzlement upon the accused's promise that he would bring no action for false imprisonment or malicious prosecution. LORD COLERIDGE C.J. expressed a strong dislike for agreements of this kind (which appear to have been common at that time at the Central Criminal Court) and thought that counsel for the prosecution could not escape this dilemma,—if the evidence did not warrant conviction, there was no consideration for the accused's promise not to bring an action, while if it did, counsel was foregoing a public duty for a private advantage[2].

What constitutes "stifling" a prosecution? We start with the principle that there is no legal duty on a person injured by the commission of a felony to institute a prosecution for it. The duty is a social one depending on the circumstances of each case, and so far the law does not interfere[3]. But it does interfere

---

[1] (1843), 6 Man. & G. 785.

[2] *Rawlings* v. *Coal Consumers' Association* (1874), 43 L.J. (N.S.) M.C. 111.

[3] This, it is suggested, is the correct inference from a number of conflicting *obiter dicta*. BOWEN L.J. in *Jones* v. *Merionethshire etc. Society* [1892] 1 Ch. at p. 183; and LUSH L.J. in *Whitmore* v. *Farley* (1881), 14 Cox C.C. at pp. 622–623 give weighty modern opinions in favour of it. The opinion of BACON (Ch. Judge in Bankruptcy) tends the other way *In re Mapleback. Ex parte Caldecott* (1876), 4 Ch. Div. at pp. 152–153. That of WILMOT L.C.J. in *Collins* v. *Blantern* (1767), 2 Wils. at p. 349 is decidedly

122   AGREEMENTS IN RESTRAINT OF

when the injured party attempts to make criminal proceedings the matter of a private bargain. Such a bargain may be in the shape of a forbearance to prosecute on condition of receipt of a particular sum of money or of a security, or in consideration of such money or security having been actually received. This is stifling a prosecution. So also is preventing a prosecution which has been instituted from running its ordinary course[1], and there is such prevention when a third person stipulates that his name shall be kept out of the proceedings. Thus, in *Lound* v. *Grimwade*[2], part of the consideration for a bond, which A gave to B, was an undertaking that criminal proceedings pending against X should be so conducted that either A's name should not be mentioned or that, if mentioned, A should be exonerated from all blame. It was held that this part of the consideration was illegal.

The particular stage which the prosecution has reached is immaterial, for even after sentence an agreement whereby money is deposited for payment to a person for his interest in soliciting a pardon is unlawful, and the money is irrecoverable[3]. On the other hand, there is nothing illegal in the prosecutor having the loss occasioned to him by the felony made good by the offender after he has been convicted[4]. And an agreement to postpone a prosecution is distinguishable from an agreement to put an end to it. At any rate it has been held that money paid in consideration of such postponement cannot be recovered from the prosecutor by the assignees of a bankrupt[5]. Discovery can be resisted on the ground that it would disclose composition of a felony[6].

so, but his view is more compatible with the sternness of the criminal law 150 years ago. It may be added here that the law as to misprision of a felony does not require more of a man, who knows that another has committed a felony, than that he shall give prompt information of what he knows to the King, or some servant of the King, like a judge or magistrate. Bract. III. f. 118 *b*. 3 Inst. 140. 1 Hale P.C. 374. 1 Hawk. P.C. ch. 59, sect. 2. Termes de la Ley *sub. tit.* "Misprision." 1 Chitty *Crim. Law*, 3-4. The law has been in a state of suspended animation since Bracton's time, and more than 50 years ago was said by LORD WESTBURY to have passed somewhat into desuetude (*Williams* v. *Bayley* (1866), L.R. 1 H.L. at p. 220).

  [1] *Per* COTTON and FRY L.JJ. in *Windhill Local Board* v. *Vint* (1890), 45 Ch. Div. at pp. 362, 364.   [2] (1888), 39 Ch. Div. 605.

  [3] *Norman* v. *Cole* (1800), 3 Esp. 252.

  [4] *Chowne* v. *Baylis* (1862), 31 Beav. 351.

  [5] *Harvey* v. *Morgan* (1816), 2 Stark. 17.

  [6] *Claridge* v. *Hoare* (1807), 14 Ves. 59.

CRIMINAL PROCEDURE 123

It seems that an agreement by a third person to make reparation for the loss occasioned by a felony, in consideration of the prosecutor's undertaking not to prosecute, is just as unlawful as a bargain to the like effect struck with the offender himself. A wife, in order to induce B to withdraw from the prosecution of her husband for larceny as a bailee, agreed to charge her separate estate, and title deeds of her property were accordingly deposited at a bank in the names of both parties. The magistrate was informed of this when A was brought before him on remand, and he allowed the prosecution to be withdrawn. The Court of Appeal decided that the agreement was unlawful and unenforceable and that the wife was entitled to a declaration for the delivery of the deeds. The consent of the presiding magistrate was beside the mark, for not even a judge of assize could sanction what was otherwise illegal,—in this case the compounding of a felony[1].

The curious case of *Fivaz* v. *Nicholls*[2] is another example. B had charged C with embezzlement, but agreed with A to abstain from further prosecution in consideration of C's drawing a bill of exchange on A and indorsing it to B. The bill was drawn accordingly, and A accepted it. B then indorsed the bill to D, a pauper, on the understanding that D should sue A upon it for B's sole benefit. D lost this action because the consideration for the acceptance was unlawful, but A, being unable to obtain his costs against D, sought to recoup himself against B. The Court unanimously held that the alleged injury arose out of an agreement to suppress the prosecution of a felony, and dismissed the action.

These cases fall short of deciding that a man can never assist a friend who is charged with a felony by recompensing the injured party. But it is one thing to be generous to the fallen, and quite another to procure condonation of a criminal offence. Exactly where the line is to be drawn between compassion and legal duty is not perfectly clear, but it is safe to say that when there is a distinct agreement that the prosecution shall not be begun or continued, this is a breach of the law. VAUGHAN

---

[1] *Whitmore* v. *Farley* (1881), 14 Cox C.C. 167, 45 L.T. 99.
[2] (1846), 2 C.B. 501.

124   AGREEMENTS IN RESTRAINT OF

WILLIAMS J. in *Jones* v. *Merionethshire etc. Society*[1] was at some pains to define what he regarded as an unlawful agreement by a third party. The substance of his conclusions may be thus stated: (*a*) The third party who gives the security to cover his friend's unlawful act must be cognizant of that act, and (*b*) his motive must have been to prevent a prosecution. (*c*) There must be on the side of the injured party an intention to prosecute, or a threat to do so. (*d*) The injured party must know that the promise or security is offered to him in consequence of the threat or probability of the prosecution. (*e*) There must be an undertaking by the injured party not to commence or not to continue the prosecution.

A variation of the promise to recompense by a third party, in order to stop a prosecution, is an agreement to adopt an instrument to which the third party's name has been forged. Several aspects of this have been examined in Courts both of law and of equity, and we may conveniently include among them cases in which there was no intervention of a third party. In *Brook* v. *Hook*[2], where an attempt had been made to ratify a signature forged to a promissory note, a majority of the Court of Exchequer made absolute a rule for a new trial, on the ground that there was evidence for the jury that there was no real ratification at all, but an agreement to submit to liability on the note, in consideration that the plaintiff would not prosecute the forger, in which case the agreement was against public policy and void as founded upon illegal consideration. But the Court were further of opinion that, as the forger's act was illegal and void, it was incapable of ratification, independently of any question as to whether the motive of the attempt to ratify were to save the forger from being prosecuted. It is quite possible that one whose name has been forged to a document may be estopped from setting up the forgery, if he has induced the holder to alter his position, but mere silence for a short period like a fortnight, during which the holder is in no way prejudiced, cannot be held to be an admission of liability or an estoppel[3]. Rescission

[1] [1891] 2 Ch. at pp. 596–597.   [2] (1871), L.R. 6 Ex. 89.
[3] *McKenzie* v. *British Linen Co.* (1881), 6 App. Cas. 82. LORD BLACK-BURN's *obiter dictum* at p. 99 cannot stand against *Brook* v. *Hook, ubi sup.* See also *Ogilvie* v. *West Australian etc. Corporation, Ld.* [1896] A.C. 257.

CRIMINAL PROCEDURE 125

of an accepted reparation for forgery may be refused by the Court on the maxim *in pari delicto, potior est conditio possidentis aut defendentis*. *A* confessed to *B* that he had forged *B*'s name to a bill of exchange, implored *B* to adopt the forgery, and promised to give him a bill of sale over his furniture, if he would do so. To this *B* assented. There was no evidence of any agreement not to prosecute *A*. In *A*'s bankruptcy, the Court of Appeal upheld this bill of sale by applying the above maxim. The bankrupt could not have recovered the proceeds of the bill of sale, and his trustee in bankruptcy stood in no better position than he did. The Court were of opinion that, had *B* been the plaintiff, he would have been in a very difficult position, for, though what he had done was neither compounding a felony, nor perhaps strictly misprision of a felony, yet it was a transaction intended to result, and actually resulting in, the prevention of a felony being discovered, and getting into the criminal's hands the most important piece of evidence[1]. When the consideration of an otherwise valid contract has been the deposit of some documents, which at a later date the depositary discovers to have been forged, a subsequent agreement not to prosecute for the forgery does not vitiate the original contract[2].

The oft-cited case of *Williams* v. *Bayley*[3] shews that there is a further principle in equity, which may make an agreement by a third party to compensate the person injured by the crime of another unenforceable. The very circumstances which led to his intervention may amount to the exercise of undue influence by the person to whom he is promising the compensation. A son had forged his father's name to promissory notes and carried them to a bank, of which he and his father were customers. The bankers, on discovering the forgery, insisted (but without directly threatening a prosecution) on a settlement to which the father should be a party. The father accordingly executed an agreement to make an equitable mortgage of his property, and

[1] *In re Mapleback. Ex parte Caldecott* (1876), 4 Ch. Div. 150. As there was no proof of an agreement not to prosecute, the case might have been placed on the same ground as *Flower* v. *Sadler* (1882), 10 Q.B.D. 572.

[2] *Ex parte Guerrier* (1882), 20 Ch. Div. 131. Cf. LORD WESTBURY in *Williams* v. *Bayley* (1866), L.R. 1 H.L. at pp. 219–220.

[3] (1866), L.R. 1 H.L. 200.

126 AGREEMENTS IN RESTRAINT OF

the notes were then delivered to him. The House of Lords decided that this agreement was invalid, for the father in such circumstances was not a free and voluntary agent, and they refused to enforce it. It is hard to disentangle the threads of argument interwoven in the judgments, but perhaps the following is a fair analysis of them. All the lords (LORD CRANWORTH L.C., LORD CHELMSFORD, and LORD WESTBURY) regarded the mere circumstances in which the father had been approached as raising a fiduciary relation between him and the bankers, and held that the agreement had been obtained by an abuse of that relation and undue influence on their part. The pressure in LORD CRANWORTH'S view was that the bankers in substance said to the father:

We have the means of prosecuting and so transporting your son. Do you choose to come to his help and take on yourself the amount of his debts—the amount of these forgeries? If you do we will not prosecute; if you do not, we will[1].

LORD WESTBURY also held that the agreement was making a trade of a felony, and seemed to infer, as LORD CRANWORTH did, that it prevented a prosecution. But if the noble and learned lords went as far as this, why, it may be asked, was it necessary to base their decision upon the ground of undue influence? It was not by any means the first case in which equity had dealt with such agreements, and in which equitable remedies had been applied to them for the neat reason that equity would no more countenance the stifling of a prosecution than the law would[2]. Another difficulty which, however, is only apparent, is the reconciliation of this case with *Ward* v. *Lloyd*[3], where it was held that a threat to prosecute for a felony, as distinct from an agreement not to prosecute for it, did not invalidate a warrant of attorney given to secure a debt. It was pointed out in a later case that in *Ward* v. *Lloyd* a debt really

---

[1] L.R. 1 H.L. at p. 212.

[2] LORD TALBOT L.C. in *Johnson* v. *Ogilby* (1734), 3 P. Wms. 277. *Claridge* v. *Hoare* (1807), 14 Ves. 59. *Dewar* v. *Elliott* (1824), 26 R.R. 214. 2 L.J. (O.S.) Ch. 178 (facts similar to those in *Williams* v. *Bayley*. The basis of a very briefly reported judgment was intimidation and duress of threats). *Osbaldiston* v. *Simpson* (1843), 13 Sim. 513.

[3] (1843), 6 Man. & G. 785.

CRIMINAL PROCEDURE 127

existed, and that the right to sue for it was upheld in spite of the threat of criminal proceedings, while in *Williams* v. *Bayley* the only consideration which the father received for making himself liable for his son's debt was the surrender to him of forged documents, in respect of which the son might have been prosecuted[1]. It may be added that LORDS CRANWORTH and WESTBURY in *Williams* v. *Bayley* certainly appeared to imply the agreement not to prosecute which did not exist in *Ward* v. *Lloyd*, and which, if it had existed there, would have made the agreement unlawful.

According to a later decision, the burden of proving pressure of the kind in *Williams* v. *Bayley* is on the plaintiff[2]. When such proof has been given, the Court will actively assist the oppressed party by directing money to be repaid, and will not stay its hand[3].

It was decided in *Wallace* v. *Hardacre* that, if the indorsee for value of a bill of exchange, to which the indorser had forged the acceptance of C, deliver the bill to the indorser on his solicitation, and receive in lieu thereof a bill accepted by D without consideration, the indorsee can sue D on this bill, unless there were an agreement between D and the indorsee to stifle a prosecution for forgery[4].

It will be seen when *Keir* v. *Leeman*[5] is discussed that a general rule was postulated there that, if an injured person has suffered actionable damages from a crime, he can compromise or settle his claim for damages in any way he may think fit. The breadth with which this is laid down would include the case in which the damages resulted not merely from a misdemeanour (as was the fact in *Keir* v. *Leeman*) but even from a felony. But the rule must be limited (and was intended by the Court to be limited) to agreements which do not stipulate for stifling the criminal remedy. If any use has been made of the rule in facts

---

[1] *Per* BRETT L.J. in *Flower* v. *Sadler* (1882), 10 Q.B.D. at p. 575. Cf. WILLIAMS J. in *Jones* v. *Merionethshire etc. Society* [1891] 2 Ch. at p. 594.

[2] *McClatchie* v. *Haslam* (1891), 17 Cox C.C. 402. W.N. 191.

[3] *Davies* v. *London etc. Insurance Co.* (1878), 8 Ch. Div. 469.

[4] (1807), 1 Camp. 45. LORD CRANWORTH L.C. in distinguishing this case in *Williams* v. *Bayley* (1866), L.R. 1 H.L. at p. 213, seemed to think that the decision was wrong, though its principle was right.

[5] (1844), 6 Q.B. 308. 9 Q.B. 371. *Post* 133.

128 AGREEMENTS IN RESTRAINT OF

which have constituted at one and the same time a felony and an actionable injury, it does not seem to have been the subject of reported litigation. Nor is there much likelihood that it will be, in view of the independent rule that it is not permissible to sue an action for damages where the same facts are a felony as well as a tort, unless it can be shewn that the defendant has been prosecuted, or that there is some reasonable excuse for his not having been prosecuted. This rule indeed is nothing but an application of the general principle that public policy requires offenders to be brought to justice, and therefore prohibits theft-bote or composition of felonies generally. At one time, the precise method by which this rule could be enforced was doubtful, but it is now settled that the proper course for the Court to adopt is to stay further proceedings in the action until the defendant has been prosecuted[1].

It may be noted here that it is an open question whether compounding a felony be an offence in Scots law[2].

The law relating to agreements to compromise prosecutions for misdemeanours or offences of less gravity has a history highly characteristic of much of the development of our Common Law. In 1734, Peere Williams was counsel in *Johnson* v. *Ogilby* which he incorporates in his reports[3]. X had begun a prosecution against a woman for a cheat and a fraud in levying a fine and suffering a common recovery as a *feme sole* when she was *covert*. Just before the trial, an agreement was made whereby X was to assign his right to the premises and to receive £580. The woman was acquitted for lack of prosecution. X sued upon the agreement. LORD TALBOT L.C., without assistance from the Bar, raised the point whether this were not an agreement to stifle a prosecution and therefore unenforceable. Peere Williams' reply was that this was true as to a prosecution for felony, but where the indictment was for a fraud and the party wronged agreed to be satisfied (as in conscience he ought to be) this was lawful, matters of fraud being cognizable and relievable as well in equity as at law; and no further insistence was made

[1] *Smith* v. *Selwyn* [1914] 3 K.B. 98, 105.
[2] *Lamson* v. *Paragon Supply Co. Ld.* (1914), S.C. 73, 78.
[3] 3 P. Wms. 277.

CRIMINAL PROCEDURE

on the objection. It was shortly afterwards held by LORD HARDWICKE in *Roy* v. *Duke of Beaufort*[1] that bonds given before magistrates by apprehended poachers which secured the injured land-owner against the commission of further trespass by the poachers "may be of great service in the preservation of the game, and an equal benefit to the obligors themselves, in taking them out of an idle course of life, which poaching naturally leads them into." But LORD HARDWICKE took it for granted that such agreements were made with the assent of the Court, and looked upon the bonds as "given by way of stated damages between the parties." *Johnson* v. *Ogilby* goes far beyond this, and it was inevitable that the principle upon which it purports to proceed should be reviewed later[2]. It is enough to say that if it had been adopted without qualification, one consequence of it would have been to make the stifling of a prosecution for an attempt to murder lawful on 23rd June, 1803 (when it was a misdemeanour), and unlawful on 24th June, 1803 (when it was made a felony). *Collins* v. *Blantern* (1767)[3] damaged its authority considerably, if it did not actually destroy it. This was an action for debt upon a bond for £700. Two of the obligors and three others had been indicted for perjury. Collins gave Rudge, the prosecutor, a promissory note for £350 in consideration of Rudge's not appearing to give evidence, and of Blantern and the two obligors indicted for perjury giving their bond (of even date with the promissory note) for £700 to Collins. When Collins gave Rudge the note for £350, the obligors (Blantern and the two others) executed the bond for £700 to Collins as an indemnity for the note. WILMOT L.C.J. would not tolerate the attempt to use the bond as a "cobweb varnish" for the note, but took the two instruments together as one entire agreement, and held that both were void. It was an agreement to stifle a prosecution for perjury and "the reason why the common law says such contracts are void, is for the public good"[4].

---

[1] (1741), 2 Atk. 190.

[2] The report is certainly below the standard of the majority of cases in Peere Williams; nor is it easy to believe that a judge of Lord Talbot's reputation should have approved such a specious argument in its entirety. His decision is reported, the reasons for it are not.

[3] 2 Wils. 347.   [4] *Ibid.* pp. 349–350

W. L. P

130 AGREEMENTS IN RESTRAINT OF

Johnson v. *Ogilby* cannot now be regarded as law unless it be taken either that the indictment for fraud was not really compromised, or that if there were a compromise it was of an indictment for a fraud which was not indictable at all[1]. If compromise be lawful then, it cannot since *Collins* v. *Blantern* be so merely because it is a compromise of a misdemeanour and not of a felony. In the period between this case and *Keir* v. *Leeman* (1844)[2], the Courts certainly conceded that some misdemeanours might be compromised, but they hesitated in fixing the boundaries within which this was allowable. Several cases tried by LORD KENYON display this oscillation. He had followed *Johnson* v. *Ogilby*[3] in 1794[4], and next year in *R.* v. *Lord Falkland*[5] acquiesced in the reference to arbitration of all matters in dispute between the prosecutor and the defendant arising out of indictments for conspiracy to cheat and for perjury. But this was inconsistent with what he did in *R.* v. *Rant* and *R.* v. *Coombs*[6] where cross bills of indictment for riot and assault had been preferred and submitted to arbitration. The Court expressed considerable surprise that a criminal prosecution should be so submitted, and distinguished cases where before verdict, or after verdict and before sentence, it was usual for the parties to talk together by recommendation of the Court, and, if they agreed, the Court imposed a nominal fine. But there the whole proceeding was under the inspection of the Court, and it was their sentence which was formally followed. In 1798, LORD KENYON held that a bond conditioned to be void if the obligor should remove certain public nuisances and not erect others, in return for which the obligee agreed not to prosecute the obligor, was good in law; but he added that if there were anything illegal in it the defendant should have pleaded it. LAWRENCE J. regarded the consideration as legal[7]. Even if it be presumed that the reason for the decision was that the compromise effected the main object of the prosecu-

---

[1] TINDAL C.J. in *Keir* v. *Leeman* (1846), 9 Q.B. at p. 393. LORD DENMAN C.J. *ibid.* (1844), 6 Q.B. at p. 317.
[2] (1844), 6 Q.B. 308. (1846), 9 Q.B. 371.
[3] *Ante* p. 128. [4] *Drage* v. *Ibberson.* 2 Esp. 643.
[5] Kyd, *Awards* (ed. 2), 66. [6] *Ibid.* 64.
[7] *Fallowes* v. *Taylor.* 7 T.R. 475.

CRIMINAL PROCEDURE 131

tion—the removal of the nuisance—this decision remains open to the criticism that a defendant who had infringed a public right was entirely freed from the punishment to which he was liable[1]; and it has been definitely held by the Court of Appeal that compromise of an indictment for obstructing a public road is unlawful[2].

With the beginning of the 19th century, the law takes a more decided turn in the direction of refusing to enforce agreements to compromise misdemeanours of a *public* nature. In *Edgcombe v. Rodd* (1804)[3], the plaintiff had been charged before the justices with the statutory misdemeanour of disturbing a dissenting congregation. As he could not find sureties, he was committed to prison under the statute till the next sessions. He subsequently sued the magistrates for false imprisonment. Their plea was that they had consented to an agreement between the prosecutor and the plaintiff whereby it was stipulated that the prosecution should be dropped; and that they had accordingly discharged the plaintiff in full satisfaction of the assault and imprisonment. The plea was held bad as disclosing an unlawful agreement. LORD ELLENBOROUGH C.J. said that it stopped the means of the Crown to recover the penalty of £20 if the plaintiff had been prosecuted and found guilty. GROSE J. pointed out that if the plaintiff were guilty, the agreement defeated public justice, and that if he were innocent, he was entitled as a matter of law to be discharged. LE BLANC J. placed his decision on the ground that this was a prosecution for a public misdemeanour, and not for any private injury to the prosecutor, and it was this passage in his judgment in particular that led to the approval of *Edgcombe v. Rodd* in later cases[4]. The inference from LORD ELLENBOROUGH'S judgment is that the case differed from those in which compromises sanctioned by the magistrates had been upheld, because here they were *functi officio* after committing the plaintiff to prison, and therefore incapable of judicially approving the subsequent agreement; but even if they had been acting judicially,

---

[1] TINDAL C.J. in *Keir v. Leeman* (1846), 9 Q.B. at pp. 393–394.
[2] *Windhill Local Board v. Vint* (1890), 45 Ch. Div. 351. See STIRLING J.'s criticism of *Fallowes v. Taylor* at p. 357.
[3] 5 East. 294.
[4] LORD DENMAN C.J. in *Keir v. Leeman* (1844), 6 Q.B. at p. 319.

9—2

132 AGREEMENTS IN RESTRAINT OF

the fact that the misdemeanour was of a public nature would perhaps have made their assent nugatory.

A few years afterwards, LORD ELLENBOROUGH again had occasion to consider the law in *Beeley* v *Wingfield*[1]. The result of this was to shew that there was nothing objectionable in a reduction of a sentence at Quarter Sessions for misdemeanour in ill-treating an apprentice, in return for a promissory note given by the misdemeanant to secure part payment of the costs of the prosecution. It was argued that this was a mere device to save the parish and country purses, and the agreement had certainly originated in a suggestion of the presiding magistrate. But the Chief Justice did not view it as stifling a prosecution or eluding the public interest. The sanction of the Court made it part of the punishment in addition to the imprisonment by which the defendant expiated his offence.

If we had seen any ground for suspecting that the authority of the Court had been used as an instrument of oppression or extortion, we should have watched the case jealously; but nothing of that sort appears[2].

Probably the Courts at the present day would take the same view of the facts. It is true that LORD DENMAN, over 40 years later, narrated in *Keir* v. *Leeman*[3] that he was present at these very Quarter Sessions, and always felt some doubt whether the proceeding sanctioned was quite correct, though he had no doubt that the principle on which the compromise of offences may be lawful was accurately stated[4]; the Court of Exchequer Chamber, however, endorsed LORD DENMAN's approval without sharing his doubts.

We may say then that it was recognized that misdemeanours not of a public kind might be compromised with the consent

---

[1] (1809), 11 East. 46.

[2] Another decision of LORD ELLENBOROUGH's was *Harding* v. *Cooper* (1816), 1 Stark. 467 (composition of civil rights, which did not include a stipulation to drop a prosecution, upheld).

[3] (1844), 6 Q.B. at p. 320.

[4] He mentioned without dissent *Kirk* v. *Strickwood* (1833), 4 B. & Ad. 421, a decision of four judges (including LORD DENMAN as C.J.). All held that the defendant should have urged his objection to the compromise when he was brought up for sentence, and not two years later. LORD DENMAN and TAUNTON J. considered that *Beeley* v. *Wingfield* applied.

CRIMINAL PROCEDURE 133

of the Court dealing with them, that it was also settled that assaults fell outside the category of public offences, and that such agreements respecting them were not only approved, but were frequently recommended by the Court. Thus, specific performance was decreed of a separation agreement between husband and wife, although it was made upon a compromise of indictments preferred by the wife against the husband and others for assaults upon her[1]; and a reference of assaults and the costs thereof to arbitration on the recommendation of the Court was held to be lawful[2].

Such then was the history of the law down to *Keir* v. *Leeman*[3] (1844–1846), which is the next landmark after *Collins* v. *Blantern*[4]. All the important previous cases were reviewed by LORD DENMAN C.J., and both his judgment and that of the Court of Exchequer Chamber affirming it were delivered after consideration. The plaintiff had indicted several for riot and an assault upon a constable in the execution of his duty, and for simple assaults. These offences were alleged to have been committed in impeding execution of a *fi. fa.* issued by the plaintiff against the goods of one of the persons indicted. The defendants, who were third parties, in consideration of the plaintiff refraining from further prosecution, promised to pay the balance remaining unsatisfied in the original action, and the costs of the prosecution. The plaintiff, in consideration of this, with the assent of the judge before whom the prosecution took place at the Assizes, forbore to prosecute further. LORD DENMAN C.J. held that the agreement was invalid as being grounded on an illegal consideration. It made no difference whether the party accused were innocent or guilty of the crime charged. If he were innocent, the law was abused for the purpose of extortion; if guilty, the law was eluded by a corrupt compromise, screening the criminal for a bribe. He considered most of the cases which have been detailed in the last section, and said that the result of them was that

---

[1] *Elworthy* v. *Bird* (1825), 2 Sim. & Stu. 272. Cf. *Garth* v. *Earnshaw* (1839), 3 Y. & C. 584, where the agreement was not for separation.
[2] *Baker* v. *Townsend* (1817), 7 Taunt. 422, following *Beeley* v. *Wingfield* (1809), 11 East. 46. Approved in *Keir* v. *Leeman* (1846), 9 Q.B. at p. 394.
[3] 6 Q.B. 308. 9 Q.B. 371.
[4] (1767), 2 Wils. 241. *Ante* p. 129.

134 AGREEMENTS IN RESTRAINT OF

some indictments for misdemeanour may be compromised, and that some may not. He considered that the line between them was correctly traced in the language of GIBBS C.J. in *Baker* v. *Townsend*[1]:

The parties have referred nothing but what they had a right to refer. They have referred the several assaults: these may be referred. They have referred the right of possession; that may be referred. The reference of all matters in dispute refers all other their civil rights, which may well be referred;

and in that of LE BLANC J. in *Edgcombe* v. *Rodd*[2]. He then laid down the rule that the law will permit a compromise of all offences, though made the subject of a criminal prosecution, for which offences the injured party might sue and recover damages in an action, this being often the only manner in which he can obtain redress. But if the offence be of a public nature, no agreement can be valid that is founded on the consideration of stifling a prosecution for it[3]. On the facts before him, there was not a mere personal injury, but riot and obstruction of a public officer in the execution of his duty. These were matters of public concern and therefore not legally the subject of a compromise. The approbation of the judge may properly be asked on all occasions where the indictment is compromised on trial, but it cannot make that legal which the law condemns.

The Court of Exchequer Chamber affirmed this decision on appeal, and its judgment was delivered by TINDAL C.J. He sifted out the unsatisfactory cases, and continued:

"But there is a class of cases, such as *Beeley* v. *Wingfield*[4] and *Baker* v. *Townsend*[5], which do not at all break in upon sound principles. These are cases where the private rights of the injured party are made the subject of agreement, and where, by the previous conviction of the defendant, the rights of the public are also preserved inviolate[6]." "We have no doubt," the judgment concludes, "that, in all offences which involve damages to an injured party for which he may maintain an action, it is competent for him, notwithstanding they are also of a public nature, to compromise or settle his private damage in any way he may think fit. It is said, indeed, that in the

[1] (1817), 7 Taunt. 422. *Ante* p. 133.
[2] (1804), 4 East. 294. *Ante* p. 131.
[3] 4 East at p. 321.
[4] (1809), 11 East. 46.
[5] (1817), 7 Taunt. 422.
[6] 9 Q.B. at p. 394.

CRIMINAL PROCEDURE 135

case of an assault he may also undertake not to prosecute on behalf of the public. It may be so: but we are not disposed to extend this any further."

The Court agreed entirely with what LORD DENMAN had said as to the immateriality of the judge's consent to the attempted compromise of what could not be legally compromised.

Upon the whole, there does not seem to be much difference between the language of LORD DENMAN C.J. and that of TINDAL C.J. According to the former, compromise of proceedings for any offence, whether of a public nature or not, is lawful provided that it does not take the form of stifling a prosecution, where the offence is of a public nature, the deduction being that even going so far as to stifle prosecution is not improper in the case of a "private" offence. TINDAL C.J. threw overboard the distinction between "public" and "private" offences, but apparently reached nearly the same practical result as LORD DENMAN by objecting to any agreement which would stifle a prosecution for any offence except perhaps assaults. Compromises within those limits he thought lawful if they were merely the means of securing settlement of a claim for damages resulting from the offence. The previous law had certainly not cramped prosecutors quite so much as this. Assaults were by no means the only kind of offence allowed to be compromised. Here, perhaps, the Court of Exchequer Chamber's opinion is more severe than that of LORD DENMAN.

Keir v. *Leeman* has been often followed, but curiously enough the later decisions tend to turn upon the question whether the offence which had been compromised were of a public nature,— a distinction which, as we have just seen, the Court of Exchequer Chamber abandoned. Thus, in *Clubb* v. *Hutson*[1] a promissory note had been given in consideration of the payee's forbearance to prosecute the maker for obtaining money by false pretences. ERLE C.J. held this to be illegal and unenforceable, because obtaining money by false pretences is not one of the misdemeanours in which the personal interest of the aggrieved party alone is concerned. In *Windhill Local Board* v. *Vint*[2], the plaintiffs had indicted the defendants for obstructing a

---

[1] (1865), 18 C.B. N.S. 414.   [2] (1890), 45 Ch. Div. 351.

136 AGREEMENTS IN RESTRAINT OF

public road. At the trial, a compromise was sanctioned by the judge and confirmed by a deed executed by the plaintiffs and defendants. The defendants covenanted to restore the road within seven years. The plaintiffs covenanted that, when this had been done, they would consent to a verdict of not guilty being entered on the indictment. STIRLING J. held that this agreement tended to affect the administration of public justice, and was illegal and void. This was affirmed by the Court of Appeal. COTTON L.J.[1] said that the Court would not allow any agreement which had the effect of withdrawing from the ordinary course of justice a prosecution when it was for an act which is an injury to the public. What was objectionable was that it took the administration of the law out of the hands of the judge and put it in the hands of a private individual. FRY L.J.[2] scouted the idea that the principle did not apply where the benefit secured by the agreement is to that of the public and not of some private individual. If this were so, a prosecution for manslaughter might be compromised by the payment of £1000 to the Chancellor of the Exchequer. This may be thought an extreme instance compared to the facts before the Court. The object of the compromise was the repair of the road, which was coincident with the object of the law. But the hardship of denying the lawfulness of such a compromise is only apparent, for other courses were open to the plaintiffs of attaining the same end[3]. An example of a lawful agreement is the acceptance of a letter of apology, with authority to make such use of it as may be deemed necessary, in lieu of prosecuting the apologist for infringement of a trademark. Civil and criminal remedies co-exist for this, and what the plaintiffs took by the compromise was much less than what was due to them[4] Keir v. Leeman[5] does not appear to have been cited before either the Vice-Chancellor or the Court of Appeal, and the extension of the doctrine of compromise to something which was not a mere

[1] 45 Ch. Div. at p. 362.   [2] At p. 364.
[3] See STIRLING J. at pp. 355–356.
[4] Fisher v. Apollinaris Co. (1875), L.R. 10 Ch. 297. JAMES L.J.'s comparison of the case with non-repair of a highway cannot stand. STIRLING J. in Windhill Local Board v. Vint (1890), 45 Ch. Div. at pp. 359–360.
[5] (1844), 6 Q.B. 308. 9 Q.B. 371.

CRIMINAL PROCEDURE 137

assault is perhaps more than the opinion of the Court of Exchequer Chamber in that case would have warranted. Be that as it may, the later case is not inconsistent with the *decision* in the earlier, and there is no reason to suppose that the Courts of to-day regard the list of offences, which may be compromised on the terms of not beginning or not continuing a prosecution, as incapable of expansion,—indeed they have not attempted to make such a list, and nothing but harm could have resulted if they had[1].

Even if the compromise of an offence like disobedience to a maintenance order be couched in such terms as to be unlawful, the plaintiff may be disabled from suing the parties, with whom he agreed, for the recovery of money paid in pursuance of the compromise, on the ground that he is *in pari delicto*[2]. But where this does not apply, it may be decreed that securities given by the plaintiff in order to prevent a prosecution shall be surrendered[3].

Some agreements, although they cannot be placed under the rubric of stifling prosecutions, are nevertheless unlawful because they adversely affect criminal procedure. A defendant who has been ordered to find bail for his good behaviour and who deposits the amount of the bail with his surety to protect the surety against the defendant's default cannot sue for its recovery[4]. It is beside the point that the defendant has committed no default. The mere deposit deprives the surety of any interest in taking care that the condition of the recognizance is performed[5]. Upon this principle, even if it be some person, other than the defendant, who has given the indemnity to the surety, the agreement is equally unlawful; for the surety has duties cast upon him, and corresponding powers conferred upon him, which are not transferable to another[6].

[1] Cf. Lush L.J. in *Whitmore* v. *Farley* (1881), 14 Cox C.C. at p. 623. Compromises for penalties under the excise laws *after* conviction have been upheld. *Sugars* v. *Brinkworth* (1814), 4 Camp. 46. *Pilkington* v. *Green* (1800), 2 B. & P. 151.

[2] *Goodall* v. *Lowndes* (1844), 6 Q.B. 464.

[3] *Osbaldiston* v. *Simpson* (1843), 13 Sim. 513 (the offence alleged was cheating at cards).

[4] *Hermann* v. *Jeuchner* (1885), 15 Q.B.D. 56. Such an agreement is a criminal conspiracy. *R.* v. *Porter* [1910] 1 K.B. 369.

[5] Cf. *Wilson* v. *Strugnell* (1881), 7 Q.B.D. 548.

[6] *Consolidated Exploration etc. Co.* v. *Musgrave* [1900] 1 Ch. 37.

138   AGREEMENTS IN RESTRAINT OF

Where there is an agreement to commit an abuse of legal procedure, which abuse is a substantive crime (*e.g.* champerty), through the agency of a third party, the agreement, it is submitted, is unlawful on the principle that *A* and *B* can no more lawfully bargain that *C* shall commit a crime than that either *A* or *B* himself shall commit one. The point was not entirely clear in mediaeval times, but it must surely be free from doubt at the present day[1].

Corrupt bargains with sheriffs or other officers of the law engaged the attention of the Courts at an early period. Mich. 2 Hen. IV, f. 9 reports a case in which a writ of debt for £40 was brought upon an obligation, the condition indorsed upon which was that, if the defendant kept the plaintiff without damage for four oxen taken in *withernam*, the obligation should be null. The plaintiff, who was bailiff of the sheriff, after taking the beasts in *withernam*, had delivered them to the defendant, and had taken the obligation from him to cover his own official liability. MARKHAM J. thought that the condition of the obligation was against the law of the land,

for I put it that if a writ be delivered to a sheriff against me, and I come to the said sheriff and oblige myself to him to keep him without damage in £20, if he wish to "embesiler" the writ[2], and he "embesile"

[1] In Hil. 42 Ed. III, f. 6, *M* brought a writ of debt against J. Penne for £40 on an obligation. They had covenanted that if *M* should at his own expense recover certain lands from *R*, by suing *R* in *C*'s name, then *C* should enfeoff *M* thereof; in default of *C* doing this, J. Penne was bound to *M* by the aforesaid obligation. This scheme was carried out up to the point of *C* being ready to enfeoff *M*, who then drew back "par doubt de Champartie," but ultimately hit upon the plan of getting *C* to enfeoff a stranger, who enfeoffed another. J. Penne contended that this satisfied the covenant. It was urged that the conditions of the bond were contrary to law, "et postea petens non prosequitur." But this is queried by the reporter who refers to Mich. 42 Ed. III, f. 24, where mere argument is reported which winds up, "et alii e contra."

[2] Make away with, or destroy, it. 5 Hen. IV. c. 14 affords contemporary evidence of the same meaning in making provision for the proof of feet of fines which have been "embeseilles." In *Rot Parl.* IV. 306 *a* (4 Hen. VI), a complaint is made of sheriffs for "embesillyng of Writtes." The word has an interesting history which cannot be detailed here, but it may be noted that the idea of "misappropriation" appears in *Rot. Parl.* IV. 155 *a* (11 Hen. VI); v. 509 *b* (4 Ed. IV) (embezzling of customs); II. 184 *a* (21 Ed. III, where it is contrasted with "destruction"); v. 236 *a* (31 Hen. VI, embezzlement by a tax collector): and that in the following passages it may be interpreted as "destruction" or "misappropiation":—*Rot. Parl.* II. 50 *b*, 75 *b*; III. 435 *b*, 439 *a*, 543 *b*; IV. 355 *a*; v. 34 *a*. Cf. Godefroy "Embeseiller" and Murray, *N.E.D.* "Embezzlement."

CRIMINAL PROCEDURE 139

this, whereby he is impleaded by bill in the Exchequer by him who bailed to him the writ, etc., and perhaps he lose damages to the said plaintiff, he shall never have an action against me upon such obligation of £20, because it was done upon a falsity &c. But the Court will well punish him who is plaintiff for his falsity.

RICKHILL J.:

There is no justice of discretion who wishes to hold that for such a falsity as delivering the beasts to the man from whom they were taken in *withernam*, he ought to recover his debt or damages for his own falsity, when he ought to have delivered to him who was plaintiff in the replevin.

THIRNING C.J., C.P. seemed to waver between holding the obligation void for illegality, and holding it valid for the defendant's folly in entering into it. The reporter states that he heard no more in that term except an emphatic repetition by MARKHAM J. of his former opinion.

A sheriff may appoint an under-sheriff, and may take from him an indemnity against escapes of prisoners. Far from prejudicing the object of the law, this really makes it more secure, for if the law permit the appointment of a deputy, it should equally approve safeguards for the execution of his duty. But if the sheriff agree with his deputy that the latter shall not levy any execution for more than £20 without first notifying the sheriff, this is void, for he cannot in delegating his powers abridge them, and it is against law and justice that the under-sheriff should be allowed to enter into a covenant which the sheriff himself certainly could not make[1].

The Statute 23 Hen. VI. c. 9 required sheriffs to release on bail all parties under arrest with certain exceptions[2]. This was repealed by the Sheriffs Act, 1887[3], sect. 14 (i) of which defines the sheriff's duties on the arrest of civil debtors. Sect. 29 (2) makes it a criminal offence for him to withhold a person bailable after he has offered sufficient security, and also to take any money other than the fees or sums allotted to him. The Levy

[1] *Norton* v. *Simmes* (12 Jac. I), Hob. 12; also reported as *Norton* v. *Syms* (11 Jac. I), Moore, 856. Cf. *Boucher* v. *Wiseman* (37 & 38 Eliz.), Cro. Eliz. 440.
[2] Cases upon its construction are *Dyve* v. *Manyngham* (4 Ed. VI), Plowden, 62. *Thrower* v. *Whetstone* (2 & 3 P. & M.), Dyer 118 *b*. Y.BB., 36 Hen. VI, f. 1, Pasch. 7 Ed. IV, f. 5.
[3] 50 & 51 Vict. c. 55, sect. 39.

140 AGREEMENTS IN RESTRAINT OF

of Fines Act, 1832, requires the sheriff to discharge any person arrested who gives security for his appearance at the following Quarter Sessions and for payment of the amount of the fine or forfeited recognizance[1]. Apart from his lawful dues, "the law knows of no promise to pay the sheriff for executing the King's writ,"[2] and an excess payment is recoverable from him[3].

AGREEMENTS IN RESTRAINT OF CIVIL PROCEDURE

§ 3. The first topic for discussion here is agreements affecting *bankruptcy proceedings*. It has long been held that agreements in fraud of the bankruptcy law are unlawful. Thus, in *Nerot* v. *Wallace*[4], the friend of a bankrupt who was on his last examination, promised that he would pay certain sums which the bankrupt was charged with having received and not accounted for, the consideration for this promise being that the assignees and commissioners would forbear to examine the bankrupt touching such sums. The Court unanimously held that this promise was void. The legislature had entrusted the examination of bankrupts to certain persons acting for the creditors' benefit, and its object would be defeated by such an agreement[5]. To say that the creditors were not prejudiced, because the agreement was to pay the whole debt, was to beg the question, for the examination might have disclosed something concealed, and what the assignees considered to be the whole debt might not in truth be so[6]. A century later, the Court of Appeal held an agreement to be unlawful by which the plaintiff, a friend of the bankrupt, promised to pay the solicitors of a petitioning creditor their costs, on their undertaking not to appear at the bankrupt's public examination, and not to oppose his discharge. The tendency of the bargain was obviously to pervert the course of justice, for "although the defendants were under no obligation to appear, they certainly were under an obligation not to

---

[1] 3 Geo. IV. c. 46, sect. 5.

[2] LORD ELLENBOROUGH in *Bilke* v. *Havelock* (1813), 3 Camp. 374.

[3] *Dew* v. *Parsons* (1819), 2 B. & Ald. 562. For illustrations of the various forms of extortion, see Chaster, *Powers of Executive Officers, sub tit.* "Extortion," pp. 181–188, and *Laws of England*, "Sheriffs," vol. xxv. § 1454.

[4] (1789), 3 T.R. 17.   [5] LORD KENYON C.J. at p. 23.

[6] ASHURST J. *ibid.*

CIVIL PROCEDURE

contract themselves out of the opportunity of appearing"[1]. There is also an offence against the bankruptcy laws where the object of a payment is to divert money from the general body of creditors in favour of particular creditors[2]. Suspicion of a fraudulent bargain to buy off opposition by creditors may justify the Court in ordering the application for the bankrupt's discharge to stand over for investigation[3].

The compulsory winding up of a company is on the same footing for this purpose as proceedings in bankruptcy against an individual. Therefore, an agreement by a shareholder that, in consideration of a pecuniary equivalent, he will endeavour to postpone the making of a call, or will support the claim of a creditor is illegal, as being contrary to the policy of the Winding-up Acts. The case, it was said, might fall within maintenance, but whether it did. or not, it interfered with the course of public justice. The policy of compulsory winding up by the Court is *inter alia* to get matters concluded within a reasonable time, and this agreement was contrary to it[4].

Arbitration. It has been repeatedly held that an agreement to refer all matters in dispute to arbitration is not sufficient to oust courts of law and equity of their jurisdiction[5]. If the law were otherwise, it would enable parties to exclude the ordinary tribunals in favour of a "domestic forum" of their own selection. Equity therefore refused specific performance of such an agreement[6]. At law, however, an action was held to lie for breach of it, though it could not bar proceedings in the courts[7].

On the other hand, an agreement in a lease to refer all

---

[1] *Kearley* v. *Thomson* (1890), 24 Q.B.D. 742, 745. *Hall* v. *Dyson* (1852), 17 Q.B.785. *Hills* v. *Mitson* (1853), 8 Ex.751. *Humphreys* v. *Welling* (1862), 1 H. & C. 7

[2] *Ex parte Wolverhampton & Staffs Banking Co.* (1884), 14 Q.B.D. distinguishing *In re Mapleback. Ex parte Caldecott* (1876), 4 Ch. Div. 150. Cf. *Davis* v. *Holding* (1836), 1 M. & W. 159.

[3] *In re Angerstein* (1863), 8 L.T. 223.

[4] *Elliott* v. *Richardson* (1870), L.R. 5 C.P. 744, 748–749; WILLES J. KEATING J. preferred not to base his judgment alternatively on maintenance, though he did not expressly differ from WILLES J. on this point.

[5] *Thompson* v. *Charnock* (1799), 8 T.R. 139.

[6] *Street* v. *Rigby* (1802), 6 Ves. 815. *Tattersall* v. *Groote* (1800), 2 B. & P. 131. *Cooke* v. *Cooke* (1867), L.R. 4 Eq. 77.

[7] *Livingston* v. *Ralli* (1855), 5 E. & B. 132.

142   AGREEMENTS IN RESTRAINT OF

differences to named arbitrators and to prosecute no suit, or to seek no remedy at law or in equity, without first submitting to arbitration, was held to be void[1]. Perhaps the distinction between these decisions is to be found in the more sweeping clause of the latter agreement. At any rate there is nothing improper in a covenant that no right of action shall accrue till a third person has decided on any difference that may arise between the parties to the covenant. This does no more than create a condition precedent to the bringing of an action, the fulfilment of which is necessary before recourse can be had to the legal remedy[2].

A clause in the articles of association of a limited company providing for forfeiture of the shares (on payment of their market value) of any shareholder, who commenced or threatened any legal proceedings against the company or its directors, was so obviously improper that the Court of Appeal refused to hear arguments the other way[3].

"Difference" in an agreement to refer to arbitration includes differences of law as well as of fact[4].

The Arbitration Act, 1889, consolidated the law on the subject. It deals with "submissions," which it defines as written agreements to submit present or future differences to arbitration, whether an arbitrator be named therein or not[5]. There is nothing in the Act to shew that agreements absolutely to exclude the jurisdiction of the courts are lawful.

An agreement between the parties to a building contract that valuations, certificates, orders and awards of the architect shall be final, and that no attempt shall be made to set them aside for any reason, or for any charge of fraud, is, in the absence of fraud on the part of either party in concluding the agreement, lawful, and not against public policy[6]. The decision seems

---

[1] *Horton* v. *Sayer* (1859), 4 H. & N. 643. Cf. Co. Litt. 53 *b*. *Lee* v. *Page* (1861), 30 L.J. (N.S.), Ch. 857.
[2] *Scott* v. *Avery* (1853), 8 Exch. 487, 497. 5 H.L.C. 811. POLLOCK C.B. in *Horton* v. *Sayer, ubi sup. Edwards* v. *Aberayron etc. Insurance Society* (1876), 1 Q.B.D. 563.
[3] *Hope* v. *International Financial Society* (1876), 4 Ch. Div. 327. JAMES L.J. at p. 334.
[4] *Randegger* v. *Holmes* (1866), L.R. 1 C.P. 679.
[5] 52 & 53 Vict. c. 49, sect. 37.   [6] *Tullis* v. *Jacson* [1892] 3 Ch. 441.

CIVIL PROCEDURE 143

inconsistent with the general principle. Had the agreement been that arbitration on such questions should exclude the jurisdiction of the courts it could not have been construed as valid. Yet such a stipulation for arbitration would have been less high-handed than the actual agreement which ruled out any settlement, lay or professional, of a dispute on the architect's certificates and other documents. But, if not strictly logical, the decision is a practical one, for opening an architect's certificate in a large work like a railway or large public building may result in enormous cost and litigation[1].

Agreements affecting other civil procedure. An agreement is corrupt and invalid whereby the payee of a bill of exchange promises to discharge the person liable upon it, in consideration that he will not move the Court against him, for an answer to the matters of an affidavit[2]. This may not be such a serious abuse of legal procedure as the stifling of a prosecution for perjury[3], but still it is an abuse, and the decision that it was so was followed in *Kirwan* v. *Goodman*[4], where a warrant of attorney given by an attorney to his client, with the object of inducing her not to institute proceedings for striking him off the roll, was ordered to be cancelled.

Again, an election petition against a member of Parliament is a proceeding instituted for the benefit of the public, and not of private individuals. Therefore an agreement by the petitioner to proceed no further with it, in consideration of a sum of money and of other terms, is unlawful. Such conduct is just as unlawful as taking a sum of money to stop a criminal prosecution. The petitioner, like the prosecutor, can drop the proceedings even after he has begun them, because he has not the money to continue them, but that is a very different thing from taking a bribe to abandon them[5].

---

[1] CHITTY J. *ibid.* p. 444. For the numerous cases on the details of the principles just considered, see Russell, *Arbitration and Award*.

[2] *Pool* v. *Bousfield* (1807), 1 Camp. 55.

[3] *Collins* v. *Blantern* (1767), 2 Wils. 241. *Ante* p. 129.

[4] (1841), 9 Dowl. P.C. 330.

[5] *Coppock* v. *Bower* (1838), 4 M. & W. 361, 366–367. The proceedings here were under the "Grenville" Act, 1770. The case is stronger still now that the trial of an election petition is strictly judicial under the Parliamentary Elections Act (31 & 32 Vict. c. 125).

144   AGREEMENTS IN RESTRAINT OF

An indemnity given to the printers and publishers of the indemnifier's newspaper against any claims that may be made against them in respect of any libel that may appear in the newspaper is unlawful. It differs from a contract of assurance against the unlawful acts of others in that it is an indemnity given by one participator in an unlawful act to another[1].

A person who conducts a legal aid society, and maintains proceedings in a claim for compensation which fails may be liable to the successful respondent for costs incurred in resisting the claim[2].

It is the policy of the Divorce Acts to prevent any one from recovering damages for a wife's adultery except under the control of the Court. Hence, an agreement by the petitioner, in a suit for dissolution of marriage, to withdraw from the suit in consideration of money paid and to be secured by the co-respondent is a fraud on the Divorce Act[3]. An agreement made abroad inconsistent with our law on this point will not be enforced here[4]. A promise to marry provided the promisee obtain a divorce is against public policy[5].

Where a warrant for commitment by the Lord Chancellor is really a civil execution, notes for the amount of the debt, in respect of which the commitment has been made, given in order to procure the discharge of the person committed, are based on a lawful consideration[6]. So, too, the release of goods taken under a *fi. fa.*, on the owner's promise to pay the debt, is a good consideration. The effect is the same as sale of the goods by the sheriff[7].

An agreement between the parties to a probate action that whichever of two wills in dispute be established, the costs of the proceedings shall be paid out of the estate is lawful. LAWRANCE J., who was pressed with LORD LYNDHURST's *dictum* in *Egerton* v.

---

[1] *Smith (W. H.) & Son* v. *Clinton* (1908), 99 L.T. 840.
[2] *Grassmoor Colliery Co.* v. *Workmen's Legal Friendly Society* (1912), 1 L.J. (C.C.), 92.
[3] *Gipps* v. *Hume* (1861), 2 J. & H. 517. Divorce Act (20 & 21 Vict. c. 85, sect. 33).
[4] *Hope* v. *Hope* (1857), D.M.G. 731.
[5] *Prevost* v. *Wood* (1906), 21 T.L.R. 684.
[6] *Brett* v. *Close* (1812), 6 East. 300.
Love's Case (5 Anne), 1 Salk. 28.

CIVIL PROCEDURE 145

Brownlow[1] and other authorities as to agreements affecting the administration of justice, said that none of them applied. "There is a broad distinction between an agreement which tends to divert the course of justice and prevent it reaching its proper goal, and an agreement which merely regulates the rights of the parties after the course of justice has reached its proper goal. It is clear that an agreement of the latter kind is not, merely as such, void; if it were, every judgment of a Court of justice would operate as a restraint on alienation of the property recovered"[2].

If a contract be made abroad, which is valid by the law of the country where it is made, but which conflicts with some essential principle of justice or morality prevalent here, the Court will not enforce it. A plaintiff, domiciled in France, sued in England on a contract made between himself and the defendant, a woman also domiciled in France, whom he had coerced into signing the contract by threats of a criminal prosecution against her husband for an offence which he had committed. The consideration for the contract was that the plaintiff would not prosecute the husband. There was evidence that the contract was not invalid according to French law. The Court of Appeal decided that, even if this were so, it would not enforce the contract. The decision is really one on undue influence, not abuse of legal procedure, for COLLINS M.R. refused to deal with the argument that the contract interfered with the course of justice, as he was not prepared to hold that, if valid according to French law, it might not be enforced here, though he expressed no final opinion on that question. He based his decision on the general principle that the Court will not enforce a contract obtained by means of such moral coercion as was used here; and the other Lords Justices seemed to be of the same opinion[3].

[1] (1853), 4 H.L.C. at p. 163. *Ante* p. 117.

[2] *Prince* v. *Haworth* [1905] 2 K.B. 768, 770. It was argued that Order LXV, r. 14 *a* ("The costs occasioned by any unsuccessful claim or unsuccessful resistance to a claim shall not be paid out of the estate unless the judge shall otherwise direct") made such an agreement invalid. But LAWRANCE J. regarded this as merely a rule of practice indicating what order should, in ordinary circumstances, be made by the Court, and not as affecting the conduct of the parties after the order had been made.

[3] *Kaufmann* v. *Gerson* [1904] 1 K.B. 591, 596, reversing decision of WRIGHT J. [1903] 2 K.B. 114. Cf. Westlake, *Private International Law*, § 215. *Hope* v. *Hope*, (1857) 8 D.M.G. 731. *Ante* p. 144.

W.L.P.

146 AGREEMENTS GROUNDING

AGREEMENTS GROUNDING CRIMINAL LIABILITY

§ 4. Under this heading, the first topic is that of *compounding offences*. Primary authority for the rules relating to it is surprisingly meagre. A great deal of what is to be found in the modern text-books on criminal law is drawn from the law of contract, the decisions cited being on the invalidity of agreements to stifle prosecutions, and not on any criminal liability resulting from them. What is left, after setting aside these and some *obiter dicta* which are of doubtful assistance even as analogies, is mainly conjecture.

The origin of the offence now known as compounding a felony is theft-bote to which a passing reference has already been made (*ante* p. 117). Its very name implies that it was familiar in the dawn of our law. Statutum Walliae (12 Ed. I. c. 4) describes it: "Hoc est de emenda furti capta sine consideratione regis"; and at that period both the justices in eyre, and the sheriffs in their towns, are directed to make inquiry of the offence[1]. In Edward III's reign, we get a judicial definition of it which, with trivial amendments, stands after the lapse of five and a half centuries. The justices said that theft-bote was properly where a man took his chattels from a thief to favour and maintain him, and they distinguished it from the case before them, where the accused had merely retaken his stolen horse from the thief[2]. The offence was regarded as so serious that the early law is said to have classified one who committed it as an accessory[3], and this is indirectly confirmed by the definition, which expresses the motive of the bargain made with the thief to be a desire to shelter him from the consequences of his act. This is exactly the idea involved in becoming accessory after the fact to a felony. The early lawyers took more account of this, than the other obvious motive of getting back one's property from the thief more quickly and cheaply than would be likely by process of law, or indeed of getting it back at all in times when conviction of felony is said to have entailed forfeiture even of the goods which the thief was convicted of stealing[4].

---

[1] Britton (ed. Nichols), Bk. I, c. XXI, sect. 11; c. XXX, sect. 3.
[2] 42 Lib. Ass. pl. 5.
[3] Bl. IV. 133. 1 Hawk. P.C. ch. 59, sect. 6.
[4] Br. *Abr.* Forfeiture de Terres 62, citing Pasch. 12 Ed. IV, f. 5.

CRIMINAL LIABILITY 147

Theft-bote seems to have been punishable capitally, until a judicial decision reduced the penalty to fine and imprisonment[1], and this holds good at the present day. There is not much to add for the purpose of stating the law as it now stands. There was at one time a tendency to make theft-bote a species of misprision of a felony[2], but the modern view is to regard the two offences as distinct[3], and there can be no doubt of the soundness of this. For, if the law of the 13th century put the offence on too high a level by making it as bad as theft itself, the law of the 18th century put it too low by making a corrupt bargain to recover the goods no worse than mere knowledge that a felony had been committed, without giving prompt information of it.

It has been held that if, after the alleged compounding of the theft, the compounder nevertheless prosecutes the thief to conviction, he should be acquitted[4]; but this can scarcely be regarded as law since the decision of the Court for Crown Cases Reserved in *R.* v. *Burgess*[5], where it was decided that it need not be alleged that the compounder desisted from prosecuting the felon, the offence being complete when the agreement not to prosecute is made. It was further held that it is possible for the crime to be committed by a person other than the owner of the stolen property, or a material witness to the prosecution. Coke and other authors had used expressions which might have raised the inference that it is only the owner who is capable of perpetrating theft-bote, but LORD COLERIDGE suggested that this may well have been because it never entered their heads that any one else would be likely to commit it. But it is not at all certain that Coke did not contemplate cases in which the compounder was not the owner. He speaks of "redoubbors," or "addoubeurs" who were "patchers, botchers, or menders of apparell, that take theft-bote of cloth (and change it into another fashion)" presumably for the purpose of making its identification by the owner difficult[6].

---

[1] Fitz. *Abr. Corone*, 353 (3 Ed. III. It. North.); Stanf. P.C. 40; 2 Hale P.C. 400; 1 Hawk. P.C. ch. 59, sect. 6. Imprisonment may be with hard labour (4 & 5 Geo. V. c. 58, sect. 16).   [2] 1 Hawk. P.C. ch. 59, sect 5.
[3] 1 Russ. 579. Arch. 1151.
[4] *R.* v. *Stone*, (1834), 4 C. & P. 379.
[5] (1885), 16 Q.B.D. 141.   [6] 3 Inst. 134.

10—2

148 AGREEMENTS GROUNDING

Closely allied to the offence of theft-bote is that of taking a reward for helping any person to stolen goods. So prevalent was this in the early days of George I's reign, that the notorious Jonathan Wild took the spoils of a gang of thieves who worked under him, and restored them at half price to the owners at a sort of public office. The impudence with which this was done led to the passing of 4 Geo. I. c. 11 which made the practice a felony punishable just as if the offender himself had stolen the goods, and, as Wild ignored this hint by the legislature, he was convicted and executed under the statute[1]. It did not immediately achieve its general object, for another statute, passed only two years later, recites the continuance of the crime, and offers a reward of £40 to any person who should discover, apprehend, and prosecute to conviction as a felon any such offender[2]. 4 Geo. I. c. 11 was repealed and replaced by 7 & 8 Geo. IV. c. 29, sect. 1, 58, which in turn was repealed by 24 & 25 Vict. c. 95 and replaced by the Larceny Act, 1861[3]. The present law is contained in the Larceny Act, 1916[4]:

> Every person who corruptly takes any money or reward, directly or indirectly, under pretence or upon account of helping any person to recover any property which has, under circumstances which amount to a felony or misdemeanour, been stolen or obtained in any way whatsoever, or received, shall (unless he has used all due diligence to cause the offender to be brought to trial for the same) be guilty of felony and on conviction thereof liable to penal servitude for any term not exceeding seven years, and, if a male under the age of sixteen years, to be once privately whipped in addition to any other punishment to which he may by law be liable.

This section differs from the corresponding section in the Larceny Act, 1861, in expressly mentioning the receipt of goods, and in reducing the age of eighteen in the earlier Act to sixteen.

The statutes of George I and George IV contained a saving clause in favour of those who had caused the apprehension and trial of the thief; but this was found to be unpractical, because it raised doubts as to whether the person who had received the

---

[1] Bl. IV. 132. Cf. Fielding's *Jonathan Wild*, Bk. IV, ch. 1 *sub fin.* and ch. 11.
[2] 6 Geo. I. c. 23, sect. 9.
[3] 24 & 25 Vict. c. 96, sect. 101.
[4] 6 & 7 Geo. V. c. 50, sect. 34.

CRIMINAL LIABILITY 149

reward for helping another to stolen goods could be convicted
where fulfilment of this saving clause was impossible owing to
the thief's death[1]. The later Acts of 1861 and 1916, by requiring
no more than "all due diligence" in causing the offender to
be brought to trial, removed this difficulty.

Several decisions under the older statutes are still instructive
on the similar provisions of the one now in force. Thus, a
prisoner was held to have been rightly convicted under 4 Geo. I.
c. 11, though he had no acquaintance with the original felon,
and though he never recovered, and had no power to recover,
the goods[2]. And in an Irish case upon the like statute applicable
to Ireland[3], a conviction was affirmed even though the person
with whom the agreement was made might not have committed
the larceny with which he was charged, and though the money
were not paid to the prisoner until after the property had been
returned. It was enough that he knew that he was to get the
money, and to return the property on that account, and that he
afterwards got the money[4]. A belief in one's capacity of discovering the thief (the money being consequently obtained for
that purpose) seems to be a good defence[5]; but any object of a
wicked nature at the time of taking the money suffices to constitute the offence, and such an object exists where there is no
intention to bring the thieves to justice. It is then immaterial
that there was no intention to screen them, or to share the money
with them, or to assist them in getting rid of the property by
procuring the owner to buy it[6].

[1] R. v. Drinkwater (1740), 1 Leach 15. The judges never publicly com-
municated their opinion on the point, and the prisoner was eventually discharged. Mere non-conviction (as distinct from impossibility of conviction)
of the thief would have been no defence, for in Jonathan Wild's case the
principal felon was not only not convicted, but appeared as a witness against
Wild. 2 East Pl. Cr. ch. xvi, sect. 155.
[2] R. v. Ledbitter (1825), 1 Mood. 76.
[3] 9 Geo. IV. c. 55, sect. 51. Repealed by 24 & 25 Vict. c. 95, sect. 1.
[4] R. v. O'Donnell (1857), 7 Cox, 337.
[5] R. v. King (1884), 1 Cox, 36. (7 & 8 Geo. IV. c. 29, sect. 58.)
[6] R. v. Pascoe (1849), 1 Den. 456. In R. v. Hicks (1845), 1 Cox, 145, it
was contended that an indictment was bad which charged the prisoner with
having received the money, not then having caused the offender to be apprehended, because this implied that a reasonable time had not been allowed
for such apprehension; but the argument was not accepted. The two cases
just cited were upon 7 & 8 Geo. IV. c. 29, sect. 58.

150 AGREEMENTS GROUNDING

One more topic related to theft-bote is the advertisement of rewards for the return of stolen property. LORD CHANCELLOR MACCLESFIELD declared such advertisements stating that "no questions will be asked" highly criminal "as being a sort of compounding a felony"[1]. The Larceny Act, 1861, enacts that,

Whosoever shall publicly advertise a reward for the return of any property whatsoever which shall have been stolen or lost, and shall in such advertisement use any words purporting that no questions will be asked, or shall make use of any words in any public advertisement purporting that a reward will be given or paid for property which shall have been stolen or lost, without seizing or making any inquiry after the person producing such property, or shall promise or offer in any such public advertisement to return to any pawnbroker or other person who may have bought or advanced money by way of loan upon any property stolen or lost the money so paid or advanced or any other sum of money or reward for the return of such property, or shall print or publish any such advertisement, shall forfeit the sum of fifty pounds for every such offence to any person who will sue for the same by action of debt, to be recovered, with full costs of suit[2].

This Act, in cutting down one form of abuse of legal procedure incidentally laid the seeds of another, for it brought upon the heads of printers and publishers a host of penal actions at the instance of common informers. This was reformed by the Larceny (Advertisements) Act, 1870, which required the assent of the Attorney-General or Solicitor-General as a preliminary to the bringing of such actions against printers or publishers and limited the time within which they could be brought to six months after the printer or publisher had incurred the forfeiture[3].

---

[1] 1 Hale P.C. 546 n.

[2] 24 & 25 Vict. c. 96, sect. 102 substantially re-enacting 25 Geo. II. c. 36, sect. 1 (repealed S.L.R. Act, 1867) which is also incorporated in 7 & 8 Geo. IV. c. 29 sect. 59 (repealed 24 & 25 Vict. c. 95). 8 & 9 Vict. c. 47, sect. 4 is similar with respect to advertisements of rewards for the return of stolen dogs (repealed 24 & 25 Vict. c. 95). In *Mirams* v. *"Our Dogs" Publishing Co.* [1901] 2 K.B. 564, it was held unanimously by the C.A. that a dog is included in "any property whatsoever" in the Larceny Act, 1861, sect. 102 *supra*.

[3] 33 & 34 Vict. c. 65, sect. 3. As to the meaning of "newspaper," see sect. 2 of this Act, sect. 2, 20–22 of 8 Ed. VII. c. 48, and *Wilkins* v. *Gill* (1903), 20 T.L.R. 3.

CRIMINAL LIABILITY 151

So far we have dealt with theft-bote only, which is usually reckoned as a species of the offence of compounding a felony. We have now to consider compounding a felony in general. This may appear to be an inversion of the correct order of discussion, but, as will be seen, there is some ground for questioning whether any other form of compounding a felony exists.

Our law started with no aversion from making composition for crimes,—even for a crime as grave as murder. Indeed, in Anglo-Saxon times, the idea was a welcome mitigation of the more barbarous outlawry and blood feud; for both these made the criminal's life and limb as insecure as those of a wild beast. If the offender would make *bót* to the injured party, and pay *wíte* to the King, he was at peace with both again. In the 12th century, *bót* and *wíte* had disappeared. They had become ruinously expensive, and were replaced, the one by discretionary money penalties, the other by damages assessed by the Court[1].

But there is a wide difference between these ancient compositions for crime approved by the state, and those which in later times are a mere matter of private arrangement; and so far as modern text-books go, we are repeatedly told that compounding a felony of any sort is an offence.

Every one commits a misdemeanour who, in respect of any valuable consideration, enters into an agreement not to prosecute any person for felony, or to show favour to any person in any such prosecution.

Such is the definition suggested by Sir James Stephen[2], but elsewhere he states that there is singularly little authority on the subject[3]. Moreover, the older text-books either speak of theft-bote as if that exhausted the topic, or, like Blackstone, regard "compounding a felony" as no more than an alternative description of theft-bote[4]. And when we turn to the reports, every case reported under the heading of "compounding a felony"

---

[1] P. & M. II. 449–462.

[2] Dig. Cr. Law, Art. 176. Cf. Russ. I. 579. Arch. 1151.

[3] H.C.L. I. 501–502.

[4] IV. 133. See also the citations, *ante* pp. 146-147, from Britton, Stanford, Hale, Hawkins. None of them speaks of "compounding a felony" nor does Foster nor *Termes de la Ley*. Blackstone is the first writer, so far as is known, who makes it equivalent to theft-bote.

152   AGREEMENTS GROUNDING

narrows down to compounding a larceny or, at most, some offence of dishonesty akin to it.

On the other hand, it cannot be denied that some of the 19th century judges were of opinion that the offence existed in its more general sense.

I apprehend the law to be this, and unquestionably it is a law dictated by the soundest considerations of policy and morality, that you shall not make a trade of a felony. If you are aware that a crime has been committed, you shall not convert that crime into a source of profit or benefit to yourself....If men were permitted to trade upon the knowledge of a crime, and to convert their privity to that crime into an occasion of advantage, no doubt a great legal and a great moral offence would be committed. And that is what, I apprehend, the old rule of law intended to convey when it embodied the principle under words which have now somewhat passed into desuetude, namely, "misprision of felony"[1].

Again, books of practice even before the 19th century include forms of indictment for procuring the compounding of offences other than larceny, e.g. rape[2]. Finally, it must be noted that theft-bote would, of necessity, be the commonest form which these corrupt agreements would take, and that in early times it is likely that no case is reported of compounding any other felony because of the comparative rarity of its commission. Larceny was almost the only known felony against property in which the opportunity of compounding would occur. There is nothing in the principles of our criminal law, either now or in the past, which would prevent it from including as an offence compounding any felony, whether a larceny or not. And it would be an absurdity if compounding a felony against the person, such as murder, were regarded as no offence, when compounding a felony against property, like larceny, is criminal[3].

[1] LORD WESTBURY in *Williams* v. *Bayley* (1866), L.R. 1 H.L. at p. 200. The last words of the quotation have been criticized as a confusion of misprision of felony with compounding a felony (Russ. 1. 579). But LORD WESTBURY was historically accurate, for in the 18th century theft-bote was regarded in some quarters as a species of misprision of a felony. *Ante* p. 147. And the LORD CHANCELLOR in this very case appeared to think that "compounding a felony" was an untechnical phrase, for he preferred LORD ELLENBOROUGH's expression, "stifling a prosecution" as more accurate (at p. 211).
[2] 4 Wentworth 327 (A.D. 1797). 2 Chitty, *Cr. Law*, 219.
[3] Cf. Draft Criminal Code (1878), Art. 127.

CRIMINAL LIABILITY   153

It will be noticed that the definition of compounding a felony given by Stephen (*ante* p. 151) makes valuable consideration an essential. It is conceived that a mere gratuitous agreement not to prosecute for a felony would be a conspiracy to defeat the ends of justice. Indeed, whatever be the doubts as to the existence of the offence of compounding a felony (apart from theft-bote), there seems to be little difficulty in regarding it as another and more reprehensible instance of this kind of conspiracy.

It is doubtful whether there be any offence known to the law as "compounding a misdemeanour"[1]. Early English law saw nothing objectionable in treating a misdemeanour as a private wrong for which a public penalty was also to be imposed. Thus a statute of Henry V gave the party injured by the making of false deeds a suit for damages, while it required the fabricator to make fine and ransom to the King[2], and it is but one example among many of the policy of mediaeval law with respect to misdemeanours[3]. This policy changed later, when the increased strength of the central government made it possible to do what was desirable,—to treat compensation of the party injured by crime as subordinate to punishment of the offender[4]. But what the law is now cannot be precisely stated. The question would be of greater practical importance if many of such agreements did not fall under criminal conspiracies to defeat the ends of justice. On considerations of pure principle, there seems to be little reason for distinguishing between the composition of felonies and the composition of misdemeanours. One flouts the law as much as the other does, though possibly in a less degree[5].

Actual and projected legislation of the last century points in

---

[1] Stephen (H.C.L. I. 502) thought not. Cf. Russ. I. 580. Arch. 1152–1154. Chitty's references (*Cr. Law*, II. 4) are to cases on contract, or on interference with witnesses.

[2] 1 Hen. V. c. 3.

[3] St. H.C.L. III. 180–181. Mich. 19 Hen. VI, f. 36 appears to have been a case on this statute. There was a reference to arbitration of a forgery of deeds, and no hint occurs that the mere reference was unlawful.

[4] West. Symb. Pt. II, f. 165 (A.D. 1647).

[5] Occasionally in a greater. "To stifle a prosecution for perjury seems to be a greater offence than compounding some felonies." *Per* WILMOT C.J. in *Collins* v. *Blantern* (1767), 2 Wils. at p. 373.

154 AGREEMENTS GROUNDING

the direction of putting them on the same footing. The Prosecution of Offenders Act, 1879, makes it the duty of every clerk to the justices, or to a police court, to transmit to the Director of Public Prosecutions a copy of the information and all depositions and other documents relating to any case in which the prosecution for an offence, instituted before such justice or court, is withdrawn, or is not proceeded with in a reasonable time[1]. The Draft Criminal Code, 1878, would have made every one guilty of an indictable offence who wilfully attempts in any way to obstruct, prevent, pervert, or defeat the course of justice, or the administration of law[2].

Two methods of ending a prosecution, neither of which is any real exception to the general principle that prosecutions should not be stifled, may be mentioned.

A prosecution may be terminated by a *nolle prosequi* being entered by leave of the Attorney-General or of the Court. The chief aim of this institution is to prevent abuse of legal procedure of the opposite kind, which takes the form of improper or vexatious attempts to oppress the defendant, as by repeatedly preferring defective indictments for the same alleged offence. It may also be granted where, in cases of misdemeanour, a civil action is depending for the same cause[3].

Distinct from a *nolle prosequi* is the practice by which the Court allows a defendant, after verdict has been returned, to "speak with" the prosecutor before any judgment is pronounced. If the prosecutor profess himself satisfied with this interview, a small punishment is inflicted, and the prosecution is thus in effect compromised. As the Court itself approves this, the practice is not inconsistent with the theory that prosecutions should not be stifled. Blackstone thought the practice a dangerous one unless confined to the prudence and discretion of the judges of the superior Courts. But he admits that the crimes so compromised are generally battery, imprisonment and the like (which are precisely the kind of crime tried by inferior courts), and that the policy of the law here is to reimburse the prosecutor for his expenses, and to make him some private amends without

[1] 42 & 43 Vict. c. 22, sect. 5. [2] Art. 127.
[3] 1 Chitty, *Cr. Law*, 478–479

CRIMINAL LIABILITY 155

the circuity of an action[1]. It cannot be said with certainty what crimes are within the boundary of this kind of compromise; much less can it be stated exactly whether attempted compromise of those which go beyond the boundary constitutes not merely an unlawful agreement, but also a criminal offence. In *R*. v. *Roxburgh*[2], COCKBURN C.J. approved such a composition in the case of a common assault. The accused had been indicted for a felonious assault, but, as the jury were unable to agree as to the felonious intent, they were discharged by arrangement, in order to allow the accused to plead guilty to common assault, to undergo a fine of 1*s*., and to pay £500 compensation to the prosecutor. Outside cases of assault, we are in the region of legal doubt. It is said that this permission to speak with the prosecutor applies to offences principally and more immediately affecting the individual[3]. It is at least clear that where compromise of an offence is not an unlawful agreement, it cannot be a criminal offence, and it is equally clear that where the Courts have upheld arbitration (or something in the nature of it) in criminal cases, an agreement to submit to such arbitration is no offence. But where such compromises and submissions have been regarded by the Courts as unlawful agreements, it by no means follows that they are criminal offences.

Some of the decisions on arbitration may now be considered. In *R*. v. *Hardey*[4], the Court were of opinion that it would have been unlawful to refer to arbitration an indictment for perjury and possibly one for conspiracy, even though the reference were embodied in a rule of Court; but they held that, in the circumstances, there had been no such reference.

"We think it quite clear," said PATTESON J. who delivered the judgment of the Court, "that the indictment for perjury could not legally be referred: and we do not mean to lay down as law that the indictment for conspiracy could, though such reference did take place in *R*. v. *Bardell*, in which case no objection was taken on that ground, and in which case the jury were discharged[5]. The rule is

[1] Comm. IV. 363–364. Russ. I. 580. St. I. H.C.L. 502.
[2] (1871), 12 Cox, 8.
[3] Russ. I. 580. Bl. IV. 363–364. St. I. H.C.L. 502.
[4] (1850), 14 Q.B. 529.
[5] (1836), 5 A. & E. 619. The decision was that 3 & 4 Will. IV. c. 42, sect. 39 (repealed by Arbitration Act, 1889) which took away the power of

156 AGREEMENTS GROUNDING

correctly stated by GIBBS C. J. in *Baker* v. *Townshend*[1]: 'Where a party injured has a remedy by action as well as by indictment, nothing can deter such party from referring the adjustment of the reparation which he is to receive to arbitration, although a criminal prosecution might have commenced.' It should also be added 'with leave of the Court.' When a verdict of guilty is taken, and the Court suspend judgment, and allow the questions between the parties to be referred, the matter is very different; for then it is only to enable the Court the better to see what sentence and judgment ought to be given[2]."

Reference of an indictment for nuisance, with the consent of the parties, and by order of the Court has passed unquestioned[3]. But where reference of an indictment for non-repair of a public highway was in effect a reference not only of the subject matter of the indictment but of the indictment itself, it was held that it could not be proceeded upon by action. The agreement was made before the jury were impanelled and without the consent of the Court (though later it was made a rule of Court); and the matter was one in which the injured party had no remedy by action in addition to that by indictment[4].

The Arbitration Act, 1889, excludes a "criminal proceeding by the Crown" from the powers of the Court to refer causes or matters for inquiry or report to any official or special referee[5].

The Criminal Appeal Act, 1907, authorizes the Court of Criminal Appeal to order reference of questions involving prolonged examination of documents or accounts or any scientific or local investigation to a commissioner for inquiry and report[6].

revoking submission to arbitration, does not extend to a reference agreed to on trial of an indictment; and that where such reference has been made at *nisi prius*, with a proviso for making the order a rule of Court, either party may, by himself or his attorney, still revoke the submission.

[1] (1817), 1 B. Moore, 120,124. Also *sub nom. Baker* v. *Townsend.* 7 Taunt. 422.   [2] 14 Q.B. pp. 541–542.

[3] *R.* v. *Moate* (1832), 3 B. & Ad. 237. This reference was ordered directly the case came on for trial. In *Dobson* v. *Groves, R.* v. *Dobson* (1844), 6 Q.B. 637 (also a case of nuisance) the reference was after a verdict of guilty, and the award was set aside for irregularity, but no objection was raised to the reference as such.

[4] *R.* v. *Blakemore* (1850), 14 Q.B. 544. In *Blanchard* v. *Lilly* (1808), 9 East 497, a reference of a prosecution for misdemeanour and all matters in difference between the parties was upheld. But the report is not a good one. See generally Russell, *Arbitration and Award* (ed. 1906), pp. 24–26.

[5] 52 & 53 Vict. c. 49, sect. 13 (1).   [6] 7 Ed. VII. c. 23, sect. 9.

CRIMINAL LIABILITY 157

A curious case of statutory composition occurs in the Larceny Act, 1861. The Act fixes the liability of the fraudulent trustee, but provides that nothing shall affect any agreement entered into or security given by him with the object of restoring or repaying the misappropriated trust property[1]. The statute 18 Eliz. c. 5, sect 3 prohibits any informer upon a penal statute from compounding or agreeing with any alleged offender against the penal statute until the information has been answered in Court, and then only with the consent of the Court. Sect. 4 punishes disobedience with the pillory (for which, in general, imprisonment[2] and fine at the discretion of the Court are now substituted by the Pillory Abolition Act, 1816), perpetual disablement from suing upon any popular or penal statute, and forfeiture of £10, half to the Crown and half to the party aggrieved. This forfeiture is recoverable by action of debt or information in any Court of Record. Sect. 5 provides that the statutory remedies against maintenance, champerty, buying of titles, or embracery shall not be affected[3]. A conviction under this statute was affirmed by all the judges, where the accused had taken the penalty from the person who had incurred it, but against whom there was no action or proceeding depending[4]. In a later case, it was held to be immaterial that no offence involving liability to a penalty had been committed by the person from whom the money was taken[5].

If the penalties be recoverable only on information before the justices, the statute has no application, for the legislature intended that so severe an enactment should be limited to compounding proceedings before the superior Courts[6].

---

[1] 24 & 25 Vict. c. 96, sect. 86. Lord Cairns was responsible for this section. Kenny, *Criminal Law* (ed. 1920), pp. 236–237.

[2] Which may be with hard labour (4 & 5 Geo. V. c. 58, sect. 16).

[3] The statute was made perpetual by 27 Eliz. c. 10 which was repealed by the S.L.R. Act, 1863. Portions of 18 Eliz. c. 5, not affecting the statement of the law above, have been repealed by 11 & 12 Vict. c. 43, sect. 36, the S.L.R. Act, 1863, and 42 & 43 Vict. c. 59.

[4] *R.* v. *Gotley* (1805), R. & R. 84.

[5] *R.* v. *Best* (1840), 2 Mood. 124.

[6] *R.* v. *Crisp* (1818), 1 B. & Ald. 282. BAYLEY, J. (at p. 287) thought that a case where the magistrate and the superior Courts had a concurrent jurisdiction would be within the Act. Cf. *R.* v. *Southerton* (1805), 6 East 126, some *obiter dicta* in which were discredited in *R.* v. *Crisp*.

CHAPTER V

CRIMINAL CONSPIRACY TO ABUSE PROCEDURE

PRELIMINARY

§ 1. The law of criminal conspiracy is likely to take the place of the obsolete law relating to maintenance and champerty as crimes, and in this chapter we have to consider its essentials where the object of the combination is to abuse legal procedure.

COMBINATION

§ 2. It was settled at an early date that one person alone could not be guilty of this offence. In 22 Lib. Ass. pl. 77, I. de W. and R. de B. were presented for false alliance and conspiracy in procuring the indictment of H. de C. of the death of one, Vesey. I. de W. appeared, R. de B. did not. I. de W.'s defences were that R. de B. was an indictor, and therefore by law could not conspire, and I. de W. could not conspire by himself; and secondly, that H. de C. admitted the death, but passed quit on the charge of it by justification, and that the defendant could not have known whether he were a felon or not. I. de W. was acquitted, but on which of these defences is not clear. More decisive is 28 Lib. Ass. pl. 12, where certain conspiracies and confederacies were presented against Adam M., and others. Adam did not appear. The others were acquitted. Adam came the next day, and demanded judgment on the ground that if the others had been acquitted, he could not be adjudged a conspirator or confederator; and he went quit[1]. But conviction of one conspirator was possible, where there was *ignoramus* as to another, but it had been found that the former *cum multis aliis* did conspire[2]; or where the only other conspirator

---

[1] So too Stanf. P.C. 173 E; 1 Hawk. P.C. ch. 72, sect. 8. *R.* v. *Salter* (1 Jac. II. B.R.), 2 Show. 456 is too compressed to be worth much. Defendant was indicted for conspiring to aggrieve one, Land, by pretending that Land had broken his (Salter's) arm, and exhibiting a complaint against him to the justices of the Peace. Indictment quashed because the matter was not indictable. Cf Wright, 39.

[2] *R.* v. *Herne* (7 Ann. B.R.); cited without further reference in *R.* v. *Kinnersley*, 1 Stra. 193.

COMBINATION

159

had died before the indictment was preferred[1]; for this involved no such contradiction as would arise where one was acquitted and the other convicted, and similarly judgment could be given against one of two conspirators if the other refused to come in. The Star Chamber, we are told, differed from the Common Law in punishing as conspiracy a false accusation by one person only, as in the case of Lee who practised to accuse reputable persons of the powder treason, and Pye who maliciously sought to indict Meyrick of felony[2].

It is said that no prosecution was maintainable against husband and wife only, because they are esteemed but one person in law, and are presumed to have but one will[3]. This rule rests upon an insufficient foundation which has been examined elsewhere[4], but it is repeated in contemporary books of practice as applying to the modern crime of conspiracy[5].

If combination were needed that was all that was needed. The definition of conspirators, 33 Ed. I, implies this in the first and commonest case to which it refers—combination falsely to indict, of falsely to move or maintain pleas[6]; and this is supported by 27 Lib. Ass. pl. 34, where certain people were arraigned of confederacy, because they were allied by the oath of each of them to maintain the others' quarrel, true or false, and though it was not supposed that anything had been put in execution, the parties were put to reply, because such a thing was forbidden in law[7]; and in Year Book 19 Rich. II there is an expression

[1] *R.* v. *Nichols* (1742), 13 East. 412 n.; *sub nom. R.* v. *Nicholls.* 2 Stra. 1227.
[2] Hudson 106; but he does not call their crimes conspiracies.
[3] Stanf. P.C. 174 A. 1 Hawk. P.C. ch. 72, sect. 8. Both cite Hil. 38 Ed. III, f. 3.
[4] *Hist. of Abuse of Procedure*, p. 64.
[5] Russell (ed. 7), 1. 146 n. Archbold (ed. 24), 1410–11.
[6] *Hist. of Abuse of Procedure*, p. 1.
[7] Repeated almost *verbatim* as a note in 27 Lib. Ass. pl. 44, between Articles 5 and 6 of a list of crimes to be inquired of by inquest of office in the King's Bench. Bryan, *Development of Eng. Law of Conspiracy*, 14–15, infers that bare combination was not punishable as late as 3 Hen. VII. c. 14. But he relies upon the recital of this statute, which merely states that conspiracies to destroy the King or his great officers have no remedy if actual deeds are not done, and appears to be reminiscent of the judicial construction put upon compassing treason under the Statute of Treason, 1351; and an argument of Kirton in Pasch. 42 Ed. III, f. 14 "assented to by the Court" that the King shall never have an indictment of conspiracy if a man speak of conspiring with others and nothing further be done; but the Court did

160 ACQUITTAL OF ACCUSED

of opinion to the same effect[1]. Coke in his report of *The Poulterers' Case*[2] notes that a false conspiracy shall be punished though nothing be put in execution, and that the usual commission of oyer and terminer gives power to the commissioners to inquire "de omnibus coadunationibus, confoederationibus, et falsis alligantiis"[3]. In *R.* v. *Spragg*, the Court, while it held that the conspiracy had been effected, said that if it had been unexecuted more weight might have been attached to the objections against the conviction, but gave no opinion on the degree of such weight[4].

All this still leaves open the question as to the precise point where agreement to do a thing passes into doing the thing, and this question, which is of more than theoretical importance, will now be discussed in connection with acquittal of the person falsely accused.

ACQUITTAL OF ACCUSED

§ 3. There is considerable difficulty in ascertaining whether prosecution of conspirators were possible if the person whom they accused were not acquitted. On a logical application of the rule that combination is the gist of conspiracy, it seems that the question answers itself. For if mere agreement to accuse falsely be a crime, there can surely be no necessity to require acquittal of the accused; for a great deal must have been done in pursuance of such agreement before any acquittal be possible. But this does not conclude the matter, and it will be seen that the development of the law in this connection was not only intelligible, but up to a certain point rational. In *Sydenham* v. *Keilaway*[5], a resolution of all the justices is reported that

not assent to this (in fact it is stated "non obstante le brē adjudge bon"), and even if it had done so, it would have emitted an *obiter dictum*, for the case was one on the writ of conspiracy. The more sweeping statement on p. 53, that the combination was not punishable apart from the act performed, cannot be accepted; it is submitted that Mr Bryan supports this view on authorities which lead to the opposite result (pp. 54–59).

[1] *Per* WADHAM J. (Bellewe).

[2] 9 Rep. 55 *b* (Mich. 8 Jac. I), Moore 813.

[3] So too in the next century, "*Et per* FORTESCUE J. falsis allegantiis is in the commission of oyer and terminer." *R.* v. *Kinnersley* (Trin. 5 Geo. I), 1 Stra. at p. 196. Cf. TWISDEN J. in *Timberley & Childe* (the title of the case is a blunder), (13 & 14 Car. II), 1 Sid. 68.

[4] (1760), 2 Burr. 993.   [5] (16 Eliz.), Cro. Jac. 7.

ACQUITTAL OF ACCUSED 161

conspiracy is indictable at Common Law, though the bill against the accused person were ignored, and thus there had been neither indictment nor acquittal. So far the Common Law Courts; and so far the Court of Star Chamber went with them[1]. Traces of its having acted upon this principle appear in Henry VIII's reign[2], and in the *Poulterers' Case*[3], of James I's reign, one, Stone, brought a bill in that Court against many of the Poulterers of London for a false and malicious confederacy and agreement to procure Stone's indictment of robbery, in consequence of which he was apprehended, but on proof of an *alibi* the grand jury ignored the bill. Counsel for the defendants contended that, admitting the combination to be false and malicious, no writ of conspiracy for the party grieved, or indictment or other suit for the King lay except where the accused had been *legitimo modo acquietatus*, and also pressed the Court with the possible risk of perversion of justice, by allegations on the part of notorious wrong-doers that there was a confederacy between those who would prosecute them. But upon good consideration it was resolved that the bill was maintainable, and it was agreed by COKE C.J.C.P., FLEMMING C.J., and EGERTON, the Chancellor, that by commission of the peace, and oyer and terminer, such confederacies are punishable by indictment at the suit of the King, though the party cannot have any action; and that they are also finable in the Star Chamber[4]. In *Sir Anthony Ashley's Case*[5] of the next year, it was resolved unanimously by all the Court of Star Chamber that a bill of Conspiracy was maintainable against those who had conspired to charge a man with murder, although he had not been acquitted[6]. The object of the "wicked and damnable con-

[1] Hudson (p. 105) says that no indictment for conspiracy will lie at Common Law unless the party [wrongfully accused by the conspirators] be indicted; but he cites no authority.

[2] Hudson, 106. Palin and Blackenball were sentenced for maliciously and without reasonable cause accusing Laughton for clipping money in 7 Hen. VIII. False accusation by Constance Young was questioned in 18 Hen. VIII. In neither case was there indictment or acquittal.

[3] (8 Jac. I), 9 Rep. 55 *b*. Moore, 813.   [4] Report in Moore at p. 814.

[5] (9 Jac. I), 12 Rep. 90. Moore, 816.

[6] The Lord Chancellor cited several precedents of censures in the Star Chamber for conspiracies and false accusations. They are summarized in Moore at p. 817.

W. L. P.   11

162   ACQUITTAL OF ACCUSED

spiracy" was to secure the forfeiture of Ashley's property, and its partition amongst his accusers. Once again, it was argued that, if the accusers were convicted of conspiracy, this would deter men from prosecuting great offenders, and that this was likely when the evidence for the prosecution might easily be rendered confused and contradictory by the severe separate examination of each witness which exhibition of a bill of conspiracy in the Star Chamber against the prosecutor might involve. The Court probably felt this difficulty, for while it denied the necessity for examining the crime falsely charged, yet it found evidence of the conspiracy in the fact that a witness had been bribed to accuse Ashley of Rice's murder 18 years after Rice's death, and in a written agreement for sharing the plunder. These facts might also be regarded as indirect proofs of Ashley's innocence, but the Court went further, and got direct proof of it from a great number of witnesses who said that Rice died, not by the alleged poisoning of Ashley but, by a disease due to his own dissolute life. Possibly the Star Chamber feared that if a Common Law Court tried Ashley first, it might through conspiracy or corruption have given a judgment against him, and that the Star Chamber would have felt bound by that judgment[1]. The knot was cut by taking the rare course of staying the proceedings at Common Law till the Star Chamber had heard the case.

In neither of the cases just discussed had the accused been indicted, for the bill of indictment was ignored in the *Poulterers' Case*, while in *Ashley's Case* none seems even to have been framed[2]. But how stood the law if an indictment were found? Had the accused to shew acquittal upon it in order to maintain a bill of conspiracy? There is a material difference between the two possible cases. If the accused has been indicted—if the grand jury have found a true bill—a body of persons independent of those who first brought the charge have said in effect, not that the accused is guilty but, that the charge needs further

---

[1] As much is hinted by Hudson, an experienced contemporary practitioner of the Court. (Star Chamber 17–18. *Collectanea juridica*, vol. II.) See also *Hurlestone* v. *Glaseour*. Goulds. 51.

[2] Mary Rice, the widow of Rice, accused Ashley in a petition to the king, who ultimately referred it to the Star Chamber. 12 Rep. at p. 91.

ACQUITTAL OF ACCUSED 163

investigation, that it has some basis which may be entirely lacking when they have ignored the bill of indictment. And we find, as we should expect to find, that the law took account of this difference, and that the Star Chamber required acquittal on the indictment before the accused could bring his counter-charge of conspiracy. Thus the rule that combination is the gist of conspiracy was subject to this qualification in the Star Chamber. In the later years of Elizabeth, it was laid down in that Court that a bill of conspiracy could not be had before the indictment had been traversed or otherwise avoided by error, because this would quash the trial at the Common Law and prevent it[1]; and Hudson states that when the party is indicted, and not *legitimo modo acquietatus*, no conspiracy can lie; as was adjudged in *Daniel Wright's Case*. He cites also *Baker* v. *Hall and Lumley* in which the defendants had prosecuted Baker for taking a woman against her will and marrying her; the indictment was avoided by error, and it was adjudged that Baker could not prosecute a conspiracy[2]. Hudson illustrates the rule by other cases from Henry VIII's reign[3].

There seems to be some doubt whether, on an indictment for conspiracy in a Common Law Court, as distinct from proceedings in the Star Chamber, the accused must prove that he had been acquitted. Coke states not only that he must[4], but that the acquittal must be by verdict which goes beyond the Star Chamber case, *Hurlestone* v. *Glaseour*; Hawkins questions the first part of this assertion, and implies that acquittal is not necessary[5]; Blackstone states that it is[6]. LORD HOLT said in *R.v.Best*,

it is a crime for several people to join and agree together to prosecute a man right or wrong. If in an indictment for such confederacy you proceed further, and shew a legal prosecution of the confederacy, there you must shew the event thereof, as *ignoramus* returned on the indictment, or an acquittal, or else the indictment fails; but where you rest upon *the confederacy*, it will be well without more[7].

In *R. v. Spragg*, the defendants were indicted for conspiracy

---

[1] *Hurlestone* v. *Glaseour*. Goulds. 51.
[2] Cf. *Hurlestone* v. *Glaseour, ubi sup.*
[3] 105–106. No further reference is given to the cases.
[4] 3 Inst. 143, 222. So too Hudson 105.   [5] 1 P.C. ch. 72 sect. 2.
[6] IV. 136.   [7] (3 Anne B.R.), 6 Mod. 185.

164 ACQUITTAL OF ACCUSED

to indict Gilmore of a capital offence, and the indictment alleged that they had actually indicted him. The report says nothing as to his acquittal, nor were the arguments directed to that point, but rather to the question whether the conspiracy had been executed, and it was on this ground that the conviction of the defendants was affirmed[1]. In *R.* v. *Jacobs*, the indictment alleged that *A* and *B* had falsely conspired to indict *C*, with intent to extort money, and that they had accordingly preferred the indictment. No proof of its falsity was given on the trial of *A* and *B*, but it was held that the truth or falsity of it was wholly immaterial except as showing the good or bad faith of the original prosecution. The point as to acquittal was thus raised by implication, and the inference seems to be that acquittal is unnecessary[2].

The result, if we take into account Star Chamber cases, seems to be that the balance of opinion and authority favours the view that at the present day acquittal of the accused is necessary where he has been indicted, and, according to Coke, that acquittal must be by verdict; but that if there has been no such indictment, no acquittal need be proved[3]. Of course, none need be proved where the conspiracy was to accuse publicly but not before a Court of Justice[4]. It may be argued on principle that no acquittal even on an indictment ought to be necessary, for otherwise we get the extraordinary consequence that if a man be falsely accused and convicted on indictment, his accusers cannot be prosecuted for conspiracy, though his conviction be due solely to the skill with which they manipulated the evidence and hoodwinked the Court. One of the resolutions in the ill-reported case, *Floyd* v. *Barker*[5], is that no witness nor any other person ought to be charged with conspiracy in the Star Chamber, or elsewhere, when the party indicted is convicted or attainted of murder or felony. In *R.* v. *McDaniel*[6], McDaniel and others procured

---

[1] (1760), 2 Burr. 993. [2] (1845), 1 Cox C.C. 173.

[3] Russell (ed. 7), 1. 162 cites 2 Hawk. P.C. ch. 72, sect. 3 for the statement that, "where the indictment has been preferred and tried it is not essential to prove acquittal." It is submitted, with deference, that this deduction is doubtful. We have been forced to state the conclusion in the text with more hesitation than Mr Bryan does (*Eng. Law of Conspiracy*, 53).

[4] *R.* v. *Kinnersley* (5 Geo. I), 1 Stra. 193.

[5] (5 Jac. I), 12 Rep. 53. [6] 19 St. Tr. 745.

FALSITY AND MALICE

Kelly and Ellis to be indicted and convicted of robbery in order to get a statutory reward for the apprehension of highwaymen. They were discharged on an indictment of them as accessories before the fact to this robbery; but were subsequently convicted of conspiracy on an indictment, which charged them with unlawfully and maliciously conspiring that one Blee should procure Kelly and Ellis to commit the robbery with intent that McDaniel and his fellow conspirators should cause Kelly and Ellis to be convicted of the robbery and so share the rewards mentioned[1]. It is remarkable that no reference to the indictment and conviction of Kelly and Ellis was made in the indictment, and the report is too condensed to shew whether any arguments or any *dicta* in the decision were directed to the absence of acquittal. This was in 1756, and in 1759 two of these same conspirators together with another person were indicted for conspiring to defeat public justice in causing one Kidden to be executed for a robbery of which they knew he was innocent, with intent to get a statutory reward. No evidence appeared and all were acquitted. This is practically the whole report[2]. It may be that the indictment in the first trial for conspiracy was deliberately drafted with a view to avoiding any difficulty as to acquittal of the accused person; it does not even allege, except as matter of intent, any accusation by the conspirators[3], and there is little doubt that at the present day under the broader definition of conspiracy persons who combine to procure a robbery, whatever be the ulterior motive, would be indictable for conspiracy. But the theoretical difficulty which was evaded or overcome in *R. v. McDaniel* remains unsolved, and might become one of practical importance[4].

FALSITY AND MALICE

§ 4. Stanford's statement that it ought to be charged in conspiracy that it is done falsely and maliciously without any good

---

[1] 19 St. Tr. at p. 808.

[2] 1 Leach 44 *sub nom. R. v. Macdaniel.* Foster, *Crown Cases*, 121, and 19 St. Tr. 745 do not report this.

[3] Cf. HOLT C.J.'s opinion, *ante* 163.

[4] The remarks of the C.C.C.R. in *R. v. Tibbits* [1902] 1 K.B. at p. 88 may be noted; but they relate to the very different case of conspiring to publish in a newspaper charges against persons who are on their trial for an offence to which these charges were irrelevant.

166 FALSITY AND MALICE

foundation may be taken to apply to both the writ and the indictment of conspiracy[1]. A case which shews the vacillation of the law between the principles of giving a man a free hand in litigation of his own, and forbidding malicious suits, occurs in Hil. 22 Ed. III. pl. 4. *A* was indicted for conspiring with others to implead *B* for the recovery of tenements in which *A* had already released all his right to *B*. It seemed to the Court that *A* could not be styled a conspirator, because it was his own plaint, but for the falsity and malice he made fine to the King. Stanford's rule is repeated by Hudson[2], by RICHARDSON J. in *Tailor and Towlin's Case*[3] and by Coke in his definition of the wrong, and also in his analysis of confederacy which "ought to be malicious, as for unjust revenge," and "ought to be false against an innocent"[4]. That innocence does not necessarily signify acquittal we have already seen[5]; and, on the other hand, even if there were an acquittal, it did not follow that the accusation was false. Thus in *Rochester* v. *Solm*, Rochester struck Solm's father on the head, and he died. Solm and his friends indicted Rochester for murder. He was acquitted, and preferred a bill of conspiracy in the Star Chamber, which refused to proceed, because the blow and the death which so soon followed it gave Solm just cause for the prosecution[6]. An indictment of rape was held to be both false and malicious where it was not brought for half a year after the alleged rape, and the accused was allowed to maintain a bill of conspiracy in the Star Chamber; HYDE C.J. said that upon probable proof a man might accuse another before any Justice of Peace, of an offence, and although the accusation were false, yet the accuser should not be punished, but he would be if the accusation were also malicious[7]. It was agreed by the Court, in *R.* v. *Best*, that several people may lawfully meet and consult to prosecute a guilty person, but not to charge one who is innocent, right or wrong, for that is

[1] P.C. 172 D, 173 C.
[2] 156; "for if it be maliciously, yet if it be true malice, it is a good informer, although a bad judge." Probably he means that if the motive be evil, the accusation may still not be false, as where there is sufficient evidence upon which it can be founded. [3] Godbolt (4 Car. I), 444.
[4] 3 Inst. 143. Note to *Poulterers' Case*, 9 Rep. at p. 57 *a*.
[5] *Ante* 160 sqq. [6] Hudson 105, 106.
[7] *Tailor & Towlin's Case* (4 Car. I), Godbolt, 444.

FALSITY AND MALICE 167

indictable[1]; and "associations to prosecute felons, and even to put the laws in force against political offenders are lawful"[2]. The indictment would, it seems, be sufficient if it allege that the defendants maliciously (without adding falsely) did conspire to indict, and falsely and maliciously did indict, because "falsely" appears in the latter part of the statement[3].

Hawkins gives the rule as to falsity and malice with the limitation of it to confederacy to maintain a suit, but from what follows this seems intended to include any accusation[4]. Though the practice is to charge offenders with having conspired "falsely," modern cases shew that this does not mean that the prosecution must prove that the charge was false in the sense that the crime charged was never committed, but that the conspirators had no belief in the charge. Where the jury found that A and B conspired to indict C with intent to extort money, but not falsely, the conviction was upheld, because it was immaterial whether the charge were false or not, except as shewing the good or bad faith of the original prosecution[5].

Under this heading we may include various defences, though there is rarely any express reference in the reports to lack of falsity and malice as the basis of such defences.

(1) *Indictors.* The oft-repeated rule that the writ of conspiracy does not lie against indictors (*i.e.* those who are now grand jurors) may be complemented with the rule that no criminal proceedings for conspiracy can be brought against them. This was soon settled in our law. Dozens might be amerced for false presentments, but conspiracy was inapplicable to them[6]. A case of Edward III's reign on the immunity of indictors has already been cited[7], and another, five years later, is more decisive. Several were presented for that by false alliance and conspiracy they had indicted J. de R. of the

---

[1] (3 Ann. B.R.), 1 Salk. 174.
[2] Russ. (ed. 7), 1. 162 citing *R.* v. *Murray* (1823), 1 Chit. Burn's Just. 817; Matt. Dig. 90.
[3] Hudson 105, 156. Cf. Indictments Act, 1915(5 & 6 Geo. V. c. 90), sect. 3(2), and App. to Rules, Form of Indictment, No. 13.   [4] 1 P.C. ch. 72 sect. 7.
[5] *R.* v. *Hollingberry* (1825), 4 B. & C. 329. *R.* v. *Jacobs* (1845), 1 Cox C.C. 173. Cf. *ante* p. 164.
[6] Eyre of Kent, 6 & 7 Ed. II, S. S. vol. XXIV, p. 153.
[7] 22 Lib. Ass. pl. 77; *ante* 158.

168 FALSITY AND MALICE

receipt of a felon. Four defendants pleaded that they were indictors, and they went quit upon production of the record[1]. Three years later still, two who were similarly indicted for causing others to be indicted of felonies and trespasses against the peace alleged that they were indictors, and so what they did was by their oath, and they too went quit when the record shewed this to be so[2]. In *Floyd* v. *Barker*, it seems that at first the grand jury who indicted William Price of murder were charged in the Star Chamber for conspiracy against him, and indicted and convicted, "which manner of complaint was never seen before." But the Court is reported to have resolved that no conspiracy lies for him, who is acquitted, against his indictors, *à multo fortiori* when he is lawfully convicted (as Price was)[3].

On the other hand, it was ruled that one who had procured a dozen to conceal offenders from the Eyre was indictable for conspiracy and trespass[4]; and procurement of oneself to be put upon the grand jury with intent to indict a neighbour maliciously was held to be in itself a statutory offence[5].

(2) *Jurors*. Of jurors as distinct from indictors the early law says little. In 27 Lib. Ass. pl. 73, the presentment was that Adam M. sued an *elegit* on a judgment against J. C., and that certain persons conspired to make the extendors put in their extent that J. C. had other lands in another county when he had not, so that the whole of his lands were taken in execution under guise of their not exceeding one half. The defence set up was that the proceedings by extent were by the oath of twelve, and had not since been reversed; and the defendants passed quit on this point. This throws no light on the liability of the jurors themselves.

In *Floyd* v. *Barker*[6], the petty jury who, on a plea of not guilty, convicted Price were charged in the Star Chamber for con-

---

[1] 27 Lib. Ass. pl. 12. Cf. pl. 13.
[2] 30 Lib. Ass. pl. 21; so too 1 Hawk. P.C. ch. 72, sect. 5. For a harsher view at an earlier date see *Abb. Plac.* 322.
[3] 12 Rep. 23; this seems to be the joint effect of resolutions (1) and (2).
[4] Eyre of Kent 6 & 7 Ed. II (vol. 11.), S. S. vol. xxiv. p. 145.
[5] Under 11 Hen. IV. c. 9. *Scarlet's Case* (10 Jac. I), 12 Rep. 98. Scarlet had conspired with the clerk who read the panel to get himself inserted in it.
[6] 12 Rep. 23.

FALSITY AND MALICE 169

spiracy against him, and indicted and convicted. But the Court is said to have resolved that a person convicted shall not charge the jury who found him guilty, and, again, that no person ought to be charged with any conspiracy in the Star Chamber or elsewhere, when the party indicted is convicted or attainted of murder or felony. The rule is stated for certain by Hawkins[1] that no one is liable to any prosecution whatsoever in respect of any verdict given by him in a criminal matter, either upon a grand or a petty jury, for they could not well perform their duties with a prosecution hanging over them.

(3) *Witnesses.* One who was sworn to inform the jurors pleaded this unsuccessfully, in 27 Lib. Ass. pl. 12, to a presentment for conspiracy. According to *Floyd* v. *Barker*, witnesses on a trial for murder, where there is a conviction, are not to be drawn in question in the Star Chamber for any conspiracy, nor ought they to be charged with conspiracy there or elsewhere when the party indicted is convicted of murder or felony; but if a witness conspire out of Court, and afterwards swear in it, his oath shall not excuse him. He differs from the juror in being produced by the party, not by the Sheriff, and the jurors are sworn as indifferent persons[2]. Hawkins puts the rule in a harsher form, by laying it down that it is no defence to plead that the defendant intended merely to give testimony in the course of justice, against the other party. But the weak side of this (the possibility of prejudging the good faith of a man's evidence before he had given it) could be avoided in practice by an application to the Court to stay the trial of the confederacy till determination of the cause in which the evidence was to be given[3]. The command of a Justice of the Peace to a complainant to prefer a bill of indictment at the next Sessions, and to give evidence, appears to have been a good defence to both the Justice and the prosecutor[4], and even without such compulsion the latter, if he had probable cause, was according to a judicial opinion excusable[5].

---

[1] 1 P.C. ch. 72, sect. 5. For the present law as to misconduct of jurors, see *Hist. of Abuse of Legal Procedure*, ch. VII.

[2] 12 Rep. 23. [3] 1 P.C. ch. 72, sect. 4.

[4] *Per* MOUNTAGUE C.J. in *Anonymous* (3 Ed. VI), Moore 6.

[5] *Per* HOLT C.J. in *Tailor & Towlin's Case* (4 Car. I), Godbolt 444.

170   THE PURPOSE OF THE COMBINATION

(4) *Judges*. Judicial acts were not indictable as conspiracies. One of the defendants in 27 Lib. Ass. pl. 12 said that he was a justice by commission in the Sessions at which the aggrieved party had been indicted, so that he was bound by his office to inform for the King to the best of his ability, and as to the time preceding the execution of his duty he pleaded not guilty[1]. And afterwards he put himself in the mercy of the King. The reporter notes that he was not excused for the whole time, as an indictor was. Stanford says that a Justice of the Peace shall not be punished as a conspirator for a thing done in open Sessions as Justice, since his oath compels him to execute his office duly[2]. *Floyd* v. *Barker* states the same law with more emphasis to judges generally,—"and the law will not admit any proof against this vehement and violent presumption of law." But this would not protect a Justice for a previous conspiracy out of Court[3].

THE PURPOSE OF THE COMBINATION

§ 5. We are told that in the Star Chamber conspiracy to indict for trespass was punishable, as well as conspiracy to prosecute for treason or felony; and malicious indictment for barratry was a common variety of it, because it tended to the ruin of a man's reputation; another example was false presentation in the leet for suffering a felon to escape[4].

Moreover, there is reason to think that at an early date conspiracy to sue a false civil action was indictable[5]. And, in our own times, a combination to sue for a debt known not to be due has been held to be a criminal conspiracy[6].

Early in the 18th century, it was settled that a combination to accuse of some offence is indictable, though the accusation

---

[1] "& quant a nul temps devant, de rien culp̄. Et puis il se mist en la grace du Roy."

[2] P.C. 173 B, C.

[3] 12 Rep. at p. 24. So too *Anonymous* (3 Ed. VI), Moore 6, *ante* 169. 1 Hawk. P.C. ch. 72, Sect. 6, where the reasons for the immunity are stated. *R.* v. *Mawbey* (1796), 6 T.R. 619. For other offences of judges, see ch. VII. *post*, and Russ. (ed. 7), 1. 601–3, 614, 627.

[4] Hudson 107. Writ No. 4 in Reg. Brev. f. 134 is the civil remedy for the last-mentioned wrong.

[5] Y.B. Hil. 22 Ed. III, pl. 4 (*ante* p. 166).

[6] *R.* v. *Taylor* (1883), 15 Cox C.C. 265.

THE PURPOSE OF THE COMBINATION 171

was made merely to neighbours as distinct from a Law Court. In *R.* v. *Tymberley*[1], there was a motion to quash an indictment for conspiracy to charge the prosecutor with being the father of a bastard child. The indictment was held good, for though fornication be a spiritual offence, yet the Court considered that it had cognizance of every illegal thing whereby damages might come to the party, and here, if the charge were true, he would be liable for the maintenance of the child. TWISDEN J. said that the matter was inquirable by the Court, otherwise the words in their commission, "de omnibus coagulationibus" would be void and idle. It is clear from the facts and the indictment that the conspiracy here was to accuse, but not to accuse before any Court, and WYNDHAM J. said that the conspiracy would be punishable by the Common Law, although no prosecution were had thereon[2]. In *R.* v. *Armstrong*[3], where an accusation of immorality, with a view to extort money, was made only to the prosecutor himself, a motion in arrest of judgment was unsuccessful[4].

If then the combination need not be to accuse before a Court of any sort or of any crime, much less would the nature of the crime charged (where one was charged) before a Court of justice be material to the issue[5]. Combinations to prevent or to obstruct the course of justice are criminal conspiracies, and are exemplified in an agreement to fabricate evidence by the production of a false certificate as to the repair of a road[6], whether the evidence be actually used or not[7]. So too, a combination to interrupt the proceedings of a Court, and to suppress the truth by keeping back a necessary witness, is criminal[8]. So is an agreement with

---

[1] 1 Keble 254 (13 & 14 Car. II. B.R.), 1 Lev. 62. 1 Sid. 68 (as *Timberley and Childe*, the bastard child apparently having crept into the name of the case).

[2] So too *R.* v. *Best* (3 Anne), 6 Mod. 185.

[3] (28 & 29 Car. II. B.R.), 1 Vent. 304.

[4] Cf. *R.* v. *Grimes* (4 Jac. II), 3 Mod. 221, where the conspiracy was to extort money by wrongfully withholding goods.

[5] Cf. 1 Hawk. P.C. ch. 72, sect. 3. But the authorities cited in ed. 1777 are either altogether irrelevant, or refer to action on the case in the nature of conspiracy.　　　　　　　　　　　[6] *R.* v. *Mawbey* (1796), 6 T.R. 619.

[7] *R.* v. *Vreones* [1891] 1 Q.B. 360.

[8] *R.* v. *Steventon* (1802), 2 East 362. *R.* v. *Roderick* (1906), Glamorgan Assizes. 1 Russ. 164 *n.*

172   THE PURPOSE OF THE COMBINATION

other persons by a witness, who has been bound over to prosecute and to give evidence, not to appear at the trial; and it is immaterial that the immediate object of the conspirators is not the perversion of the course of justice[1].

The principle underlying the law as to bail for an accused person, is to make the person who gives bail responsible for the appearance of the accused at his trial. If, therefore, the bail gets an indemnity against his liability, he loses all interest in the discharge of this responsibility, and it is obvious that criminals, especially if wealthy, would often abscond from justice. Hence, an agreement by an accused person to indemnify his bail is illegal, in that it tends to produce a public mischief, and the parties to the agreement are guilty of conspiracy, although they may have had no direct intent to pervert or to obstruct the course of justice[2].

Many of the acts which fall under this head are contempts of Court. Such certainly is adverse comment in a newspaper on the conduct of a person who is being tried criminally. And if this be the result of a combination, it is also a criminal conspiracy. During the course of the trial of two persons for felony, a newspaper reporter sent to the editor articles affecting the conduct and character of the accused, which would have been inadmissible in evidence against them. The editor published the articles, and after conviction and sentence of the accused, he and the reporter were convicted on an indictment charging them with unlawfully attempting to pervert the course of justice, and with conspiring to do so. The Court for Crown Cases Reserved affirmed the conviction. They attached no weight to the fact that the persons who had been the subject of the newspaper comment were convicted of the felony laid to their charge.

To give effect to such a consideration would involve the consequence that the fact of a conviction, though resulting, either wholly or in part, from the influence upon the minds of the jurors at the trial of such articles as these, justifies their publication. This is an

[1] *R. v. Hamp* (1852), 6 Cox C.C. 167.
[2] *R. v. Porter* [1910] 1 K.B. 369, 373.   Cf. LORD LYNDHURST C.B. in *Bloomfield* v. *Blake* (1833), 6 C. & P. 75.

THE PURPOSE OF THE COMBINATION 173

argument which we need scarcely say reduces the position almost to an absurdity, and indeed, its chief foundation would appear to be a confusion between the course of justice and the result arrived at[1].

It has been seen that if the necessary consequence of the act agreed upon is to pervert the course of justice, the absence of any desire to commit such perversion is immaterial. On the other hand, evil motive may turn a presumptively innocent act into a perversion of justice. Thus, it would seem that the conveyance of an estate from one brother to another, in order to give the latter a colourable title to kill game, and therefore to get rid of an information pending against him, is an indictable conspiracy[2].

Associations to prosecute felons and even to put the law in force against political offenders appear to be lawful[3].

Conspiracy of the kind treated in this chapter is a misdemeanour now punishable by fine, imprisonment (which may be with hard labour[4]), and sureties for good behaviour[5].

---

[1] *R. v. Tibbits* [1902] 1 K.B. 77, 88.
[2] *Doe d. Roberts* v. *Roberts* (1819), 2 B. & Ald. 367. BEST J. *obiter* at p. 370.
[3] ABBOTT C.J. in *R. v. Murray*, 1 Chit. Burn's Just. 817. Matth. Dig. 90. Cited in 1 Russ. 162 *n*.
[4] 4 & 5 Geo. V. c. 58, sect. 16.
[5] Leach's note to 1 Hawk. P. C. (ed. 1787), ch. 72, sect. 9. Bl. IV. 136–137. *R.* v. *Best* (3 Ann. B. R.), 6 Mod. 186. 1 Russ. 202. Cf. *Hist. of Abuse of Legal Procedure*, pp. 99–102.

CHAPTER VI

MALICIOUS PROSECUTION[1]

§ 1. The roots of the action for malicious prosecution are in the action upon the case in the nature of conspiracy[2], and some special reference to their growth is implied in an attempt to depict the present elements of the remedy. The essentials to success in it are:

(1) There must have been a prosecution by the defendant of the plaintiff.

(2) The prosecution must have ended in the plaintiff's favour.

(3) It must have been instituted without reasonable or probable cause.

(4) It must have been malicious.

These must be successively discussed.

WHAT CONSTITUTES A PROSECUTION

§ 2. The tentative definition of a prosecutor by LOPES J. in *Danby* v. *Beardsley*[3] as "a man actively instrumental in putting the law in force" needs restriction in one direction and expansion in another. It is too wide in that it might include a man whose acts result in the false imprisonment of another,—a tort which needs sharp distinction from malicious prosecution; and it leaves open the question of what is active instrumentality.

An oft-cited example of the difference between acts which may make one liable for false imprisonment, and those which may form one of the elements in malicious prosecution, is that of two parties being before the magistrate, and one of them making against the other a charge upon which the magistrate orders that other to be taken into custody and detained till the matter can be investigated. Here the party making the charge

[1] See H. Stephen, *Malicious Prosecution* (1888).
[2] For its history, see *Hist. of Abuse of Legal Procedure*, ch. II.
[3] (1881), 43 L.T. 603.

WHAT CONSTITUTES A PROSECUTION 175

is not liable to an action for false imprisonment, because he does not set in motion a ministerial officer, but a judicial one[1]. The great Common Law judge who gave this illustration was dealing with a case in which the defendant, after his wife had given the plaintiff into custody on an unfounded charge, signed the charge-sheet on an inspector's refusal to incur the responsibility of detaining the plaintiff, unless the defendant did so. On the next day the magistrates discharged the plaintiff, who sued the defendant in the County Court for false imprisonment, ex-pressly disclaiming any cause of action for malicious prosecution. The County Court judge treated the signing of the charge-sheet as the commencement of a malicious prosecution, and ruled that all the proceedings were one continuous transaction, that the false imprisonment could not be separated from the rest, and that he had consequently no jurisdiction. On appeal, the Court directed a new trial. WILLES J. held that the false imprisonment lasted so long as the plaintiff remained in the custody of a ministerial officer of the law, whose duty it was to detain him until he could be brought before a judicial officer, and that until he was so brought, there was no malicious prosecution. But it does not follow that mere signature of the charge-sheet will make the signer responsible for an arrest already made by some one else. He has possibly gone one step towards making himself liable for malicious prosecution, but he has not committed the tort of false imprisonment[2].

When can a man be said to have been "actively instrumental" in putting the law in force so as to have satisfied this head of liability in malicious prosecution? Mere narration of the facts of a wrong which the defendant has sustained to a ministerial officer, like a policeman, who, without further instruction, arrests the plaintiff, is not sufficient, even though one of the facts narrated implicates the plaintiff, e.g. a statement that the stolen property was last seen in the plaintiff's possession. "The stone set rolling was a stone of suspicion only"[3].

Similarly, if a man does no more than tell the story of his

---

[1] WILLES J. in *Austin* v. *Dowling* (1870), L.R. 5 C.P. 534, at p. 540.
[2] *Sewell* v. *N.T.C. Ld.* [1907] 1 K.B. 557, 560.
[3] *Danby* v. *Beardsley* (1881), 43 L.T. 603. *Per* LINDLEY J.

176 WHAT CONSTITUTES A PROSECUTION

loss to a judicial officer, such as a magistrate, leaving him to determine whether the facts amount to a felony, he does not maliciously procure the magistrate to issue his warrant. Much less can the perversion of such a story by the clerk who frames the warrant into a charge of felony be imputed to the complainant[1]. But where the story told is known by the teller to be false, the Judicial Committee have held in an Indian appeal that the teller is liable. The peculiar frequency of such lying charges in India was a special justification of this decision, but its general reasonableness adds to its persuasive authority here[2].

Whatever be the activity of the defendant in making a charge, he cannot be liable if no arrest of the plaintiff be made. Where the defendant wrote to a chief constable charging the plaintiff with murder and requiring his arrest, and also sent a similar charge and request to the superintendent of police, who tried unsuccessfully several times to arrest the plaintiff, it was held that no prosecution had been instituted before a judicial officer[3].

When a judicial, as distinct from a ministerial, officer is set in motion, that may be malicious prosecution on the part of the mover; and as a magistrate is justified in issuing a warrant on suspicion of a felony, a statement to him by the defendant that he suspects the plaintiff, upon which the magistrate issues the warrant, is the commencement of a prosecution[4]. Nor need the charge have been taken down in writing; it may be oral[5].

Being bound over merely to give evidence does not make the person so bound over liable for malicious prosecution[6]; but it is otherwise if he give evidence in support of a charge and represent himself as preferring it, though it be preferred at another's expense[7]. There is, however, a material difference

---

[1] *Cohen* v. *Morgan* (1825), 6 D. & R. 8 (ABBOTT C.J. strongly deprecated such official editing). *Leigh* v. *Webb* (1800), 3 Esp. 164.

Pandit Gaya Parshad Tewari v. *Sardar Bhagat Singh* (1908), 24 T.L.R. 884.

[3] *Harris* v. *Warre* (1874), 4 C.P.D. 125. *Gregory* v. *Derby* (1839), 8 C. & P. 749.

[4] *Elsee* v. *Smith* (1822), 1 D. & R. 97. *Davis* v. *Noak* (1816), 1 Stark. 377.

[5] *Per* BOSANQUET J. in *Clarke* v. *Postan* (1834), 6 C. & P. 423. *Dawson* v. *Vasandeau* (1863), 11 W.R. 516.

[6] *Eager* v. *Dyott* (1831), 5 C. & P. 4. Cf. *Browne* v. *Stradling* (1836), 5 L.J. (C.P.) 295.

[7] *Clements* v. *Ohrly* (1848), 2 C. & K. 686.

WHAT CONSTITUTES A PROSECUTION 177

between instituting a prosecution and merely attending the hearing upon a proceeding already commenced by another; the continuation by the defendant of such a proceeding does not make the lack of reasonable and probable cause, which might be evidence against that other, evidence against him[1].

Binding over a person to prosecute is, on the face of it, an act which connects him more nearly with the prosecution than simply binding him over to give evidence. Yet this does not necessarily make him a mover of the prosecution, for he may have been bound over against his will. Hence, 'a man who had been robbed whilst drunk and who was compelled the next day to go before a magistrate, by whom he was bound over to prosecute the plaintiff, was held not to have put the law in motion. He gave no evidence against the plaintiff, and made no charge against him. All that he did was to state that he had lost his watch, and he would gladly have avoided a share in proceedings which must have revealed his discreditable condition when he was robbed[2].

But where the first step in the accusation is that of the defendant, who must have seen the probability of further steps being taken, he cannot shelter himself behind an order of the Court that he shall prosecute. A trustee in bankruptcy is an officer of the Court, but not in the sense that he can fasten upon it the responsibility of his own individual acts. If he reports to the Court that, in his opinion, the bankrupt has been guilty of any offence under sect. 16 of the Debtors Act, 1869[3], and the Court thereupon orders him to prosecute, an action for malicious prosecution against him by the bankrupt ought not to be stayed as frivolous and vexatious[4]. Still stronger is the case against one who has maliciously procured himself to be bound over to prosecute. It does not lie in his mouth to argue that he has acted under compulsion[5].

[1] *Weston* v. *Beeman* (1857), 27 L.J. Exch. 57.
[2] *Browne* v. *Stradling* (1836), 5 L.J. (C.P.) 295. *Dubois* v. *Keats* (1840), 11 Ad. & E. at p. 332.
[3] Repealed and re-enacted by the Bankruptcy Act, 1914 (4 & 5 Geo. V. c. 59), sect. 161, 168.
[4] *Mittens* v. *Foreman* (1888), 58 L.J. (Q.B.) 40.
[5] *Dubois* v. *Keats* (1840), 11 Ad. & E. 329.

W. L. P.

178 WHAT CONSTITUTES A PROSECUTION

What is to be said of one who, in the course of a civil action and with the sole object of winning his case, tells a lie which leads the Court entirely against his wish to bind him over to prosecute the other party? This was the problem for the Court of Exchequer Chamber in *Fitzjohn* v. *Mackinder*[1]. *M* sued *F* in the County Court for debt. *F* claimed a set-off, in answer to which *M* produced his ledger containing an acknowledgment signed (as he falsely swore) by *F*. *F* denied the signature, and alleged it to be a forgery. The County Court judge, induced partly by *M*'s perjured statement, partly by *F*'s conduct in Court, committed *F* for trial for perjury, and bound over *M* to prosecute. *F* was acquitted, and sued *M* for malicious prosecution. COCKBURN C.J. and BRAMWELL and CHANNELL B.B. held that the action was maintainable. The Chief Justice regarded the prosecution as commencing with the preferment of the indictment, and the defendant as having set the law in motion because the act of the County Court judge was a natural consequence of *M*'s perjury, though his motive in committing it was not that of getting the plaintiff prosecuted.

A prosecution, though in the outset not malicious, as having been undertaken at the direction of the judge or magistrate, or, if spontaneously undertaken, from having been commenced under a bonâ fide belief in the guilt of the accused, may nevertheless become malicious in any of the stages through which it has to pass, if the prosecutor, having acquired positive knowledge of the innocence of the accused, perseveres malo animo in the prosecution, with the intention of procuring per nefas a conviction of the accused[2].

This language was wider than was needed to support the decision, but it is submitted that it is sounder in principle than the views of the two dissentient judges. Of these, BLACKBURN J. held that the defendant had not procured himself to be bound over to prosecute,—in fact it was probably the last thing he desired; and WIGHTMAN J. thought that the defendant's perjury in the County Court was too remote a cause of the prosecution to make the defendant liable. BLACKBURN J.'s opinion really comes round to this. But surely a reasonable man would foresee that a lie told by a party in a Law Court, which implies that

---

[1] (1861), 9 C.B. N.S. 505.   [2] At p. 531.

WHAT CONSTITUTES A PROSECUTION 179

his opponent has committed perjury, is likely to lead to the prosecution of the opponent for perjury. That the false swearer did not desire such a prosecution is not to the point. The question is whether a reasonable man would have foreseen its likelihood. It is a trite saying that a man is often liable in the law of torts for consequences which he did not desire.

At an early date the action was held to lie against one who exhibited a bill of indictment against another[1]. LORD HOLT described the three kinds of damage any one of which might ground the action upon the case, which is the parent of the action for malicious prosecution. Briefly, they are damage to a man's fame, person, or property. The Court of Appeal has recently applied this test to a class of proceedings greatly multiplied by modern statutes,—summary proceedings before magistrates to secure the performance of some public duty. If these be promoted maliciously and without probable cause, can they be regarded as "prosecutions" for the purpose of malicious prosecution? They create but a remote possibility of interference with the accused's personal freedom; they do not cause damage to his property beyond the loss of his costs as between solicitor and client (a head of damage not recognized by law); and therefore they satisfy Lord Holt's analysis only if they involve scandal to the reputation. A vast number of them do not do this, and we must now take it as law that, unless they do, their improper institution cannot be regarded as a malicious prosecution. A century ago it was held that an indictment for a violent assault implied no such scandal as would ground the action for malicious prosecution[2]; and this case was noticed by the Court of Appeal, in 1914, in *Wiffen v. Bailey and Romford Urban Council*[3]. The defendant had made a complaint under sect. 95 of the Public Health Act, 1875, against the plaintiff, who was the occupier of a house, for non-compliance with a notice stating that a nuisance existed at the house arising from the want of cleansing of certain rooms, and requiring him to

[1] *Payn v. Porter* (16 Jac. I), Cro. Jac. 490.
[2] *Byne v. Moore* (1813), 5 Taunt. 187. Cf. *Freeman v. Arkell* (1823), 3 D. & R. 669.
[3] [1915] 1 K.B. 600.

180 WHAT CONSTITUTES A PROSECUTION

abate the same. The justices dismissed the complaint, and awarded the plaintiff £5. 5s. which represented his costs as between party and party. He sued the defendant for malicious prosecution, and recovered £250 damages. Against judgment for that amount the defendant successfully appealed. BUCKLEY L.J. held that the proceedings did not naturally and necessarily convey an imputation affecting the plaintiff's fair fame. True, they were in a sense criminal, for they might have resulted in the imposition of a fine for failure to comply with a statutory obligation. But that did not conclude the question. They no more injured the plaintiff's reputation than similar proceedings for keeping pigs in an improper place, or for letting dogs wander about unmuzzled, would have done[1]. And the learned Lord Justice distinguished *Rayson* v. *South London Tramways Co.*[2], an earlier decision of the Court of Appeal. A close (and perhaps inevitable) adherence to this decision had led to the mistaken judgment by the Court of first instance in *Wiffen's Case*[3]. In *Rayson's Case*, it had been held that proceedings under sect. 51 of the Tramways Act, 1870, against any traveller who attempts to avoid payment of a tramway fare, or who wilfully travels beyond the distance covered by his fare, without making an additional payment, are criminal proceedings, and may ground an action for malicious prosecution. Here, as the Court of Appeal pointed out in *Wiffen's Case*, the charge imputed that the plaintiff was attempting to cheat the defendants[4], and thus cast a slur on his reputation, which the charge against Wiffen did not. The notice to repair might have been served upon him as a mere occupier, who had gone in the day before, who was in no way responsible for the lack of repair, and whose fair fame was therefore unaffected. Unfortunately the Court in *Rayson's Case* had uttered *dicta* which were insufficiently guarded and tied to some extent the hands of a puisne judge in a later case. BUCKLEY L.J. had no difficulty in disposing of the other two possible grounds for Wiffen's claim. To the argument that his liberty of person had been endangered, he replied that

---

[1] At pp. 608–609.　　　　　　　　　　　　[2] [1893] 2 Q.B. 304.
[3] [1914] 2 K.B. 5.
[4] [1915] 1 K.B. at pp. 608, 612, 614.

FAVOURABLE ENDING OF PROSECUTION 181

though, if the summons had succeeded, a fine might have been imposed, and on non-payment of it a warrant of distress might have been issued, and in default of goods to satisfy the distress, imprisonment might have followed, yet the imprisonment would not have been by virtue of the proceedings[1]. Nor had the plaintiff suffered any pecuniary damage, for the excess of his costs as between solicitor and client over those as between party and party was not damage in the eye of the law[2].

WHAT IS A FAVOURABLE ENDING OF THE PROSECUTION

§ 3. The Courts in moulding the action upon the case, which was not tied down to any precise form, could ignore some troublesome limitations that attached to the formed writ of conspiracy. Thus, an early and persistent distinction taken was that case would lie against one only, whereas conspiracy must be brought against two at least. CLENCH J. in *Shotbolt's Case* thought that this was the sole difference[3], and that acquittal of the plaintiff on the original accusation was necessary; and an averment to that effect was required according to *Nyn* v. *Taylor*[4]. It was, however, very soon held that there was sufficient acquittal if the bill of indictment had been ignored. YELVERTON J. in *Barnes* v. *Constantine* (2 Jac. I. B.R.) speaks of

---

[1] I.e. the imprisonment was too remote a consequence. Cf. PHILLIMORE L.J. at p. 610.

[2] It may be added that the Court of Appeal thought that the finding of the jury as to malice was against the weight of evidence, and that the damages were excessive, but they found it unnecessary to deal with these points specifically.

[3] Other cases shewing that the action would lie against one only are *Marsh* v. *Vauhan* (41 & 42 Eliz. B.R.), Cro. Eliz. 701 (*obiter dictum*), *Lovet* v. *Fawkner* (11 Jac. I. B.R.), 2 Bulst. 270, where COKE C.J. said that this was ruled in *Jerom* v. *Knight* (1 Leon. 105, Cro. Eliz. 70, 134), and DODDERIDGE J. took the distinction as "a sure rule." *Smith* v. *Cranshaw* (1 Car. I. B.R.), W. Jones 93 (second resolution of the Court). *Mills* v. *Mills* (7 Car. I. B.R.), Cro. Car. 239. *Palke* v. *Dunnyng* (9 Car. I. B.R.), Rolle, *Abr.* 111. *Damont, Ruddock and Sherman's Case* (16 Car. I. B.R.), Rolle, *Abr.* 112. *Price* v. *Crofts* (1657), T. Raym. 183. *Skinner* v. *Gunton* (or *Gunter*) (21 Car. II. B.R.), 2 Keb. 473. Raym. 176. 1 Ventr. 12, 18. *Pollard* v. *Evans* (31 Car. II. B.R.), 2 Shower 50. *Savile* v. *Roberts* (10 Will. III. B.R.), 1 Lord Raym. 374. Note by HOLT C.J. to *Muriell* v. *Tracy* (3 Ann. B.R.), 6 Mod. 170. *Subley* v. *Mott* (21 Geo. II), 1 Wils. 210.

[4] Roll. *Abr.* 114 (5 Jac. I. B.R.).

182 FAVOURABLE ENDING OF PROSECUTION

this as having been already adjudged[1], and there was little difficulty in adhering to this rule when scandal to the reputation came to be one of the main props of the action[2]. In *Marham* v. *Pescod*[3], one of the early cases in the history of this remedy, all the Court agreed that there was no need to state of what felony in particular the plaintiff had been acquitted[4], though proof of some act evidencing the charge was necessary[5]. One report of the case indicates that no acquittal of any sort was required[6], and in *Wine* v. *Ware* the verdict of the jury for the plaintiff in the action, which found the indictment to be false and malicious, was held to dispense with any allegation of acquittal or *ignoramus*[7]. *Skinner* v. *Gunton* (or *Gunter*) is to the same effect[8]. There it was moved in arrest of judgment that the declaration was insufficient, because it was not shewn that the first proceedings were determined; but all the Court were of opinion for the plaintiff. But this doctrine cannot now be regarded as law. At first sight it did not inflict upon the defendant any conspicuous injustice, for if the jury found that he had acted falsely and maliciously, one piece of evidence upon which their finding was based was presumably the failure of the criminal proceedings against the plaintiff; or, if he had been convicted thereon, that might have been due to especial subtlety on the part of the defendant. But awkward consequences might ensue if the plaintiff were allowed to have the action on the case without any proof of what had happened in the criminal prosecution

---

[1] Yelv. 46. So too *Hord* v. *Cordery* [or *Whorewood* v. *Corderoy*] (10 Jac. I), Hutton 49. *Deney* v. *Ridgy* (19 Jac. I. B.R.) cited in *Wright* v. *Black* (20 Jac. I. C.P.), Winch 54. *Smith* v. *Cranshaw* (1 Car. I), W. Jones 93. *Pollard* v. *Evans* (31 Car. II), 2 Shower 50. BULLER J. in *Morgan* v. *Hughes* (1788), 2 T.R. 225.

[2] *Payn* v. *Porter* (16 Jac. I. B.R.), Cro. Jac. 490. See too the first resolution of the Court in *Smith* v. *Cranshaw* (1 Car. I), W. Jones 93.

[3] (4 Jac. I. B.R.), Cro. Jac. 130.

[4] TANFIELD J. said he well knew this difference between case and conspiracy to be agreed in *Knight* v. *Jermin* [*Jerom* v. *Knight, ante* 181] after long debate and advisement. This does not appear in the report. Later cases on the same point are *Bell* v. *Fox* (7 Jac. I, B.R.), Cro. Jac. 230, Yelv. 161 (but this may have been conspiracy, not case). *Best* v. *Aier* (11 Jac. I. B.R.), Roll. *Abr.* 113–114. *Taylor's Case* (17 Jac. I. B.R. *Vin. Abr.* Act. Case. Consp. p. 33. Reference to Palmer, 44, is untraceable). *Anon* (26 Car. II. B.R.), 1 Vent. 264. *Haynes* v. *Rogers* (3 W. & M.), Shower 282.

[5] Last case in note 3, p. 181, and *Saunders* v. *Edwards*, 1 Sid. 95.

[6] Noy 116.   [7] (12 Car. II), 1 Siderf. 15.

[8] (21 Car. II. B.R.), 2 Keb. 473. Raym. 176. 1 Vent. 12, 18.

FAVOURABLE ENDING OF PROSECUTION 183

against him. If he had been convicted there, and then won his action on the case, it proved the futility of trial by jury. And if the defendant were to demur that the plaintiff had not shewn what had become of the prosecution, it would have been impossible to argue that this was solved by the jury finding falsity and malice, for *ex hypothesi* they had so far found nothing at all. The defendant did so demur in *Parker* v. *Langley*[1], and judgment was given for him. PARKER C.J. in delivering the resolution of the Court, said that the declaration should have shewn that the former action was false and hopeless, for, as it stood, *non constat* whether the first suit were determined, deserted, or going on. If it were determined, *non constat* whether for or against the plaintiff; if deserted, that would have shewn the proceeding to be false and hopeless; if going on, then the action upon the case was brought too soon[2]. No man could say of an action still depending that it was false and malicious. The plaintiff must shew in his declaration what became of the indictment. The judgment adds that a verdict or plea in bar admitting the first action to be false and hopeless might cure the defect in the declaration, but that if it were to be held good in spite of the omission, this would introduce the absurdity of inconsistent and incongruous verdicts in different actions; and that though there might be this danger if the defendant were nonsuited in the first action, yet the possibility of such a verdict should not prevent the plaintiff suing case[3]. This last sentence raises the inference that nonsuit of the defendant was a sufficient termination of the proceedings in the plaintiff's favour, and LORD HOLT C.J. had already hinted as much in an earlier case, where the question was whether a *nolle prosequi* maintained the plaintiff's allegation of exoneration from the charge. LORD HOLT doubted whether it did, for a *nolle prosequi* only put the accused *sine die*, and differed from a nonsuit in that the indictment still stood[4]. As to acquittal on a defective indictment, it

---

[1] (12 Ann. B.R.), 10 Mod. 145, 209.   [2] He cited 2 Rich. III, f. 9.

[3] The principle in this case was regarded as settled law in *Fisher* v. *Bristow* (1779), 1 Dougl. 215, and the case itself was followed in *Morgan* v. *Hughes* (1788), 2 T.R. 225, where the mere allegation of discharge from imprisonment was held insufficient.

[4] *Goddard* v. *Smith* (3 Anne B.R.), 1 Salk. 21. 3 Salk. 245. 6 Mod. 261. 11 Mod. 56. Some learned authors consider that this case is inconsistent

184 FAVOURABLE ENDING OF PROSECUTION

was at first held that this prevented the plaintiff from suing[1], but this rested on too close an adherence to the "legitimo modo acquietatus" borrowed from the old writ of conspiracy, and in *Smithson* v. *Symson* the Court took the contrary view[2] which was settled to be the law in *Jones* v. *Gwynn*[3]. The fact that the malicious proceedings were *coram non judice* is no defence, for the vexation of the plaintiff is the same[4].

It seems that if the plaintiff be indicted for and convicted of an offence similar to, but graver than, that with which the defendant charged him, the defendant is still liable in an action for malicious prosecution of the graver offence. At least this is the inference from *Boaler* v. *Holder*[5] where the defendant at first charged the plaintiff with knowingly publishing a libel, and then withdrew the charge, the plaintiff being committed for trial for the less serious offence of merely publishing a libel. He was however indicted for the more serious offence, but was convicted of publishing only; and this conviction was held to be no bar to an action for malicious prosecution for knowingly publishing the libel.

On the other hand, if the accused were convicted on the prosecution, he cannot bring the action. This was held unanimously in *Willins* v. *Fletcher*[6], and was possibly the reason for a similar decision in *Vanderbergh* v. *Blake*[7]. The rule is open to the criticism that if the conviction be solely due to the ingenuity of the malicious prosecutor in influencing the tribunal, it is grossly unjust to the accused, and especially so where he cannot appeal against the conviction. This was actually the case in *Basébé* v. *Matthews* (1867)[8], but the Court unanimously held that the accused could not sue; if the rule were otherwise, BYLES J. thought that every case would have to be retried on its

with later authorities. *Enc. Laws of Eng.* VIII. 515. *Laws of Eng.* vol. XIX. § 1445. But these authorities are colonial or American.

[1] *Hunt* v. *Lines* (8 Car. I. B.R.), Roll. *Abr.* f. 110.

[2] 3 Keble 141 (25 Car. II. B.R.). Cf. *Gardner* v. *Jollye* (1649. *Vin. Abr.* Act. Case. Consp. Qc. sect. 8) and editor's note to *Pedro* v. *Barrett* (8 Will. III), 1 Lord Raym. 81.

[3] 1 Salk. 15. 12 Mod. 148, 214 (12 Anne B.R.). Followed in *Chambers* v. *Robinson* (12 Geo. I), 1 Stra. 691, and *Wicks* v. *Fentham* (1791), 4 T.R. 247.

[4] *Atwood* v. *Monger* (1653), Style 378.   [5] (1887), 3 T.LR. 546.

[6] (10 Jac. I. B.R.), 1 Bulst. 185.

[7] (13 Car. II. Exch.), Hardres 194.   [8] L.R. 2 C.P. 684.

FAVOURABLE ENDING OF PROSECUTION 185

merits, and MONTAGUE SMITH J. feared that they would be constituting themselves a court of appeal in a case where the legislature allowed none. With deference, it may be suggested that neither of these reasons is convincing, for the burden of proof in malicious prosecution is quite heavy enough to hinder profuse employment of it by convicted persons as an indirect method of appeal, and though *Basébé* v. *Matthews* now represents the law there are *dicta* of at least two masters of the Common Law which lend some support to this criticism[1]. A reversal of the accused's conviction by a higher tribunal was held in *Reynolds* v. *Kennedy*[2] to make the action inapplicable. The Court seems to have held that the original condemnation shewed that there was probable cause for the prosecution, and that its reversal did not entitle them to infer malice. Whether the Courts at the present day would go the length of this is not clear. In a recent case where the conviction had not been reversed, COLLINS M.R. referred to the principle that "as long as a conviction stands, 'no one against whom it is producible shall be permitted to aver against it'"[3]. It must be noted that there is no need to shew that the malicious proceedings terminated in the plaintiff's favour where they were incontrovertible[4].

Evidence of acquittal is obviously sufficient if it consist in the production of the original record by the official who has it in custody[5]. At any rate this is so in the case of misdemeanours. Where the original accusation was of a felony, the authorities

---

[1] LORD CAMPBELL C.J. in *Churchill* v. *Siggers* (1854), 3 E. & B. at p. 937. WILLES J. in *Fitzjohn* v. *Mackinder* (1860), 8 C.B. N.S. at p. 92. The reasoning in *Basébé* v. *Matthews* seems however to have commended itself to the C.A. in *Bynoe* v. *Bank of England* [1902] 1 K.B. 467.

[2] (1748), 1 Wils. 232 (commented on in *Sutton* v. *Johnstone* (1786), 1 T.R. at p. 505). The opposite view might be inferred from *Mellor* v. *Baddeley* (1834), 2 Cr & M. 675, but the point was not discussed.

[3] *Bynoe's Case (supra)*. Cf. Smith, L.C. (ed. 11), I. 270, II. 478. *Smith* v. *Sydney*, L.R. 5 Q.B. 203 (there cited) was an action for assault and false imprisonment.

[4] *Steward* v. *Gromett* (1859), 7 C.B. N.S. 191. *Gilding* v. *Eyre* (1861), 10 C.B. N.S. 592 proceeds rather upon the assumption that there were no judicial proceedings which the plaintiff could have disputed (malicious suit of *ca. sa.* upon a judgment). For some of the American authorities see *Laws of England*, vol. XIX. § 1445, note (*d*).

[5] *Morrison* v. *Kelly* (2 Geo. III), 1 W. Bl. 384.

186 FAVOURABLE ENDING OF PROSECUTION

are confused as to whether the leave of the Court which tried the case is necessary in order to obtain a copy of the acquittal. As the result of a historical accident, there was, until 1916, a rule that, if the person acquitted of felony desired a copy of the *indictment* he must get a special order of the judge. This rule originated in a temporary increase in the number of actions against prosecutors during Charles II's reign. The judges thought that this hindered just prosecutions, and as a copy of the indictment was then needed by the plaintiff in such an action, they made an order at the Old Bailey in 16 Car. II that no copies of any indictment for felony should be granted without a special order[1].

The rule had no application to misdemeanours[2], nor to high treason or misprision of it[3]; and if a true copy of the indictment were surreptitiously obtained, it could not be refused as evidence, though the officer responsible for its issue committed a contempt of Court[4]. The Indictments Act, 1915, has reduced this to antiquarian matter by providing that it shall be the duty of the clerk of assize or the clerk of the peace at Quarter Sessions, after a true bill has been found on any indictment, to supply to the accused person a copy of the indictment free of charge[5]. But the historical outline was necessary, as it throws some light on the method of proving an acquittal as distinct from an indictment As to this, HOLT C.J. in *Groenvelt* v. *Burwell*[6], said *obiter* that if *A* be indicted of felony and acquitted, and be

[1] Kelyng 3. *Morrison* v. *Kelly*, 1 W. Bl. 384, note (*d*). *R.* v. *Brangan* (1742), 1 Leach C.C. 27 is more guarded. All that it decided was that a copy of the indictment could not be obtained from the trial judge, because it was not necessary that *he* should grant it. See 2 Russ. 2146 *n.* for doubt and criticism of the rule even before the Indictments Act, 1915, abolished it.

[2] *Jordan* v. *Lewis* (13 Geo. II), 2 Stra. 1122. As to prosecutions for misdemeanour by the Attorney-General or Solicitor-General, 60 Geo. III & 1 Geo. IV. c. 4, sect. 8 makes a copy of the indictment or information obtainable by the accused free of charge.

[3] 7 & 8 Will. III. c. 3, sect. 1. (The proviso that the accused must pay for the copy is impliedly repealed by rule 13 (1) in Sched. 1 of the Indictments Act, 1915.)

[4] *Legatt* v. *Tollervey* (1811), 14 East 302. The plaintiff who procured it apparently did not. *Ibid.* 305 *n.*

[5] 5 & 6 Geo. V. c. 90, Sched. 1, rule 13. If the bill of indictment be ignored, the plaintiff would presumably prove this in the same way as any other judicial document.

[6] (9 Will. III), 1 Ld Raym. 252.

LACK OF REASONABLE CAUSE 187

minded to bring an action, the judge will not permit him to have a copy of the record, if there were probable cause of the indictment, and he cannot have a copy without leave. Possibly HOLT C.J. had in mind the order of the judges at the Old Bailey in 16 Car. II referred to above, which makes the assent of the judge necessary to procuring a copy of an indictment for felony. And perhaps the same applies to an *obiter dictum* of LORD MANSFIELD's about 70 years later that leave of the Court which acquitted the accused is necessary to get a copy of the record in order to ground an action for malicious prosecution of a felony[1]. If these opinions were merely loose expressions of the order of 16 Car. II, they occasion no difficulty. But if they are taken literally, they go far beyond that, and make the consent of the acquitting Court necessary to obtaining a copy of the acquittal of a felony. They are then in conflict with an opinion of WILLES L.C.J. that every prisoner, upon his acquittal, has an undoubted right to a copy of the record of such acquittal for any use he may think fit to make of it, and that a refusal by the proper officer to make it out after demand is punishable[2]. It is submitted that this opinion is now more likely to be the one adopted by the Courts. The opposite view is destitute of any reason, and is a mere technicality inconsistent with the spirit of modern criminal procedure.

Whatever be the rule on this point, it has long been unnecessary to produce in any proceedings even a copy of the record of an acquittal of any indictable offence. A certificate by the clerk of the Court where the acquittal has taken place that the paper produced is a copy of the record of the acquittal, omitting the formal parts thereof, is sufficient[3].

LACK OF REASONABLE AND PROBABLE CAUSE

§ 4. It is not long after the action had been established that we get a neat decision making lack of probable cause an essential to success in it; and this is implied from the historical outset of the action, which we have placed in Elizabethan times. Thus in *Fuller* v. *Cook*[4], the plaintiff declared that the defendant had

---

[1] *Morrison* v. *Kelly* (2 Geo. III), 1 W. Bl. 384.
[2] *R.* v. *Brangan* (1742), 1 Leach C.C. 27.   Cf. Roscoe, *Crim. Ev.* (ed. 1921) 244.
[3] 14 & 15 Vict. c. 99, sect. 13.   [4] (26 Eliz. K.B.), 3 Leon. 100.

188 LACK OF REASONABLE

informed a Justice of the Peace that the plaintiff had stolen the defendant's hogs, and the Justice thereupon issued a warrant for the plaintiff's apprehension. On arrest and examination he was bound over, and none appearing against him at the next Sessions he was discharged. All this was found by special verdict, and thereupon judgment was given for the plaintiff. The Court took the distinction that praying a Justice to examine into the stealing, on which examination then takes place, would not ground the action, but alleging to a Justice that one has stolen your goods and procuring a warrant thereon will ground the action. Here, it will be noticed, the facts were found by the jury, while the Court pronounced what their effect was. In *Knight* v. *Jermin*[1], GAWDY J. was of opinion that if the defendant had acted upon "good presumptions" he ought to plead them, and with this WRAY C.J. agreed. This is what the defendant did in *Varrel* v. *Wilson*[2] a few years later. The plaintiff demurred to the defence, and here the Court considered the plea of reasonableness, without aid from the jury. In *Pain* v. *Rochester*[3], *Chambers* v. *Taylor*[4] and *Wale* v. *Hill*[5] the procedure was the same. In *Marham* v. *Pescod*[6], where the plea also set out the special matter shewing cause of suspicion, it was found for the plaintiff, for whom judgment was then given. It was moved in error on behalf of the defendant that the plea was ill, *sed non allocatur* because, had the plea been true, it would have justified what the defendant had done. The result of these cases seems to be that early in James I's reign, the Court decided the question of probable cause upon facts found by the jury or admitted by the plaintiff, and this is the law as it stands at the present day[7]. *Dogatte* v. *Lawry*[8] is not inconsistent with this

---

[1] (31 Eliz. B.R.), Cro. Eliz. 134.   [2] (36 Eliz.), Moore 600, pl. 828.
[3] (41 Eliz.), Cro. Eliz. 871.   [4] (44 & 45 Eliz.), Cro. Eliz. 900.
[5] (8 Jac. I. B.R.), 1 Bulst. 149.   [6] (4 Jac. I. B.R.), Cro. Jac. 130.
[7] *Lister* v. *Perryman* (1870), L.R. 4 H.L. 521. *Abrath* v. *N.E.R. Co.* (1886), 11 A. C. 247. (See the direction of the judge to the jury which was held by the House of Lords to be correct.) *Cox* v. *English etc. Bank, Ld.* [1905] A.C. 168. *Panton* v. *Williams* (1841), 2 Q.B. 169. Cf. H. Stephen, *Mal. Pros.* 41, 57. The learned author's statement there is a little liable to misapprehension, as it might imply that the question of probable cause was in the earliest history of the action one for the judge solely. It is submitted that the authorities support the view above stated.
[8] (5 Jac. I. B.R.), Cro. Jac. 190.

AND PROBABLE CAUSE 189

view. The circumstances of suspicion were specially pleaded by the defendant there, to which the plaintiff replied "de son tort demesne sans tiel cause," and the jury found for the plaintiff. The Court refused to arrest judgment, "for the plaintiff having laid it to be falsely and maliciously, and the jury having found it to be *sans tiel cause*, it all appears to be without any ground." Here the finding "sans tiel cause" may be taken to signify that the jury negatived the facts alleged by the defendant, and not that the jury settled the question of probable cause to the exclusion of the judge[1]. Later cases clearly recognize the defence of probable cause[2], and in *Anon.* (2 Anne B.R.)[3] there is a strong direct statement of the rule. "If the person be ever so innocent, yet if there were *a probable cause* of prosecution, an action for malicious prosecution will not lie"[4].

Malice was not always kept distinct from lack of probable cause. It is not clear whether the "falso et malitiose," imported from the writ of conspiracy proper, implied respectively lack of probable cause and malice[5]. But be this as it may, it was held in *Manning* v. *Fitzherbert*[6] that *ex malitia* implied *falso*, in an allegation by the plaintiff that the defendant had *ex malitia* charged the plaintiff's wife with stealing a hog. But the plaintiff had further alleged that the defendant had falsely and maliciously testified to the charge, and perhaps this influenced the Court's decision, and Rolle C.J. in delivering a similar opinion in 1653, said that repetition of *falso* throughout the record was unnecessary[7]. Hale C.B. in *Vanderbergh* v. *Blake*[8] separated malice from absence of just cause, in the strongest terms. In *Jones* v. *Gwynn*[9], the first and most material objection to the

---

[1] *Golding* v. *Crowle* (1751), Sayer 1, indicates the provinces of judge and jury.
[2] *Anon.* (10 Jac. I. B.R.), Roll. *Abr.* f. 112. *Payn* v. *Porter* (16 Jac. I. B.R.), Cro. Jac. 490. *Atwood* v. *Monger* (1653), Style 378 (*per* Rolle C.J.).
[3] 6 Mod. 25, 73; at p. 25.
[4] So too Holt C.J. in *Muriell* v. *Tracy* (3 Ann. B.R.), 6 Mod. 170.
[5] Hale C.B in *Vanderbergh* v. *Blake*, Hardres at p. 196 implies that they did.
[6] (8 Car. I), Cro. Car. 271. Cf. *Moore* v. *Rock* (14 Car. I. B.R.), Roll. *Abr.* f. 115.
[7] *Kitchinman's Case.* Style 374.
[8] (13 Car. II, Exch.), Hardres at p. 196.
[9] (12 Ann. B.R.), 10 Mod. 148, 214.

190 LACK OF REASONABLE

action was that the indictment of the plaintiff was declared to be brought *falso et malitiose*, without adding *absque rationabili et probabili causâ*.

"This action," said PARKER C.J., in delivering the resolution of the Court, "cannot, indeed, be supported, unless the indictment was groundless, and without a probable cause; but no one authority was cited to prove that these very words are necessary to be used. ... But the true answer to this objection is, that the word '*malitiose*' implies it to be *absque rationabili et probabili causâ*, and a great deal more"[1].

This statement does not go beyond a concession to pleaders that probable cause need not be expressly alleged. But since *Farmer* v. *Darling*[2] and *Sutton* v. *Johnstone*[3] it must be, and there is a cogent reason for the entire separation of malice from lack of probable cause, since a man may with a malicious motive prosecute real guilt, and is not liable in that case to the action[4]. There is not, on principle, any reason for arguing from acquittal of the accused to lack of probable cause for the accusation. In the ordinary course of things, the prosecution would run the gauntlet of an inquiry by the magistrate, another by the grand jury, and finally one by the petty jury. If it break down at the second or third of these stages, the plaintiff certainly is "acquitted" for the purposes of suing an action of malicious prosecution, but his committal by the magistrate shews that there was some reason for suspecting him. Nor does it follow that,

---

[1] Books of Entries shew that the practice prior to this decision though not settled tended to make the allegation of lack of reasonable or probable cause advisable. Aston (1661) 40. Browne (1671) 38. Brownlow (1693) 50, 61. Clift (1703) 24, 25, 27, 28, 29, 32, 35 (No. 12). Vidian (1684) 36. Winch (1680) 74. On the other hand there is no such allegation in Browne 19, 37, 82; Brownlow 65; Clift 31, 33, 34 (No. 9); Winch 95. In *Box* v. *Taylor* (32 & 33 Car. II. B.R.), 2 Show. 154, "absque justa causa" was held insufficient, because that did not exclude probable cause, and then it could not be malicious. But "absque aliqua causa," or "sine causa justa vel probabili" would have been good. The statement in Bryan, *Eng. Law of Conspiracy*, 43, as to the recognition that "the absence of probable cause is nothing but a more or less accurate test or measure of malice," probably is based on *Jones* v. *Gwynn* (12 Anne), 10 Mod. 148, 214. If so, a reference to that case is needed to make the statement historically more intelligible.

[2] (7 Geo. III. B.R.), 4 Burr. 1971. "Malice (either express or implied) and the want of probable cause must both concur" (*per* three judges at p. 1974).

[3] (27 Geo. III), 1 T.R. 493.

[4] LORDS MANSFIELD and LOUGHBOROUGH, 1 T.R. at p. 545.

AND PROBABLE CAUSE 191

even if the magistrate dismissed the charge on the preliminary examination, there was no probable cause. For a mistake might be made as to the identity of the accused which that examination alone could clear[1]. That there was no necessary connection between acquittal and lack of probable cause in the early history of the action appears from the authorities. In *Knight* v. *Jermin*, the plaintiff had been acquitted, but two of the judges implied that if the defendant had acted upon good cause and pleaded it, his defence would have been sound[2]. In *Varrel* v. *Wilson*, in spite of the plaintiff's acquittal, the defendant's suspicion on finding stolen goods in his possession was held to be reasonable, and to make the action inapplicable[3]. Succeeding cases are to the same effect[4], with one or two exceptions which cannot be regarded as seriously affecting the general rule[5]. Indeed, when there was some doubt as to whether acquittal of any sort were necessary, it could scarcely have been otherwise. LORD HOLT C.J. in *Savile* v. *Roberts* said that if the indictment had been found against the plaintiff, the defendant would not be bound to shew probable cause, but that the plaintiff would have to shew express malice and iniquity in the prosecution; but that if the bill of indictment had been ignored, and it contained neither matter of scandal nor cause of imprisonment or loss of life or limb, no action would lie[6]. If the first of these propositions were meant to imply that the finding of a true bill made proof of probable cause by the defendant (or lack of it by the plaintiff) unnecessary, it does not now represent the law, which is that

---

[1] Cf. *Musgrove* v. *Newell* (1836), 1 M. & W. 582. The opinion of FLEMING C.J. in *Wale* v. *Hill* (8 Jac. I. B.R.), 1 Bulst. 149, that, if the plaintiff be acquitted on a prosecution in which defendant persists after the magistrate refuses to commit, the defendant is liable, was not necessary to the decision.
[2] (31 Eliz. B.R.), Cro. Eliz. 134.   [3] (36 Eliz.), Moore 600, pl. 828.
[4] *Pain* v. *Rochester* (41 Eliz.), Cro. Eliz. 871 (Plaintiff wilfully absented himself, and was ultimately acquitted. Resolved sufficient cause for defendant's suspicion). *Chambers* v. *Taylor* (44 & 45 Eliz.), Cro. Eliz. 900 (Plaintiff's answers before magistrate various and uncertain). *Webb* v. *Welles* (14 Jac. I), 1 Rolle 438 (*sub nom. Weal* v. *Wells*, Bridg. 60). *Palke* v. *Dunnyng* (11 Car. I. B.R.), Roll. *Abr.* f. 111.
[5] CROKE J. in *Hercot* v. *Underhill.*(12 Jac. I), 2 Bulst. 331. But the opinion barely implies that acquittal suffices. C.J. in *Anonymous* (30 Car. II. C.B.). 2 Mod. 306 (Acquittal proves the prosecution to be false. Perhaps this was intended to apply only to malicious prosecution for a trespass).
[6] (10 Will. III. B.R.), 1 Lord Raym. 374.

192   LACK OF REASONABLE

the burden of proving lack of probable cause is on the plaintiff, and he does not remove that burden by mere proof of his innocence, which does not involve other circumstances so as to shew this lack of probable cause[1]. Nor is it now true that if the grand jury throw out a bill of indictment, the accused person cannot successfully sue malicious prosecution, unless the accusation imperils his reputation or personal security.

It has been said that reasonable cause is such as would operate on the mind of a discreet man, probable cause such as would operate on the mind of a reasonable man[2]. But this was really a belated attempt to distinguish two adjectives inherited from the pleader's *absque rationabili et probabili causa* of the old writ upon the case. He inserted variant terms like this on the drag-net principle, and with little regard to their scientific meaning[3]. The attempt has not been of much assistance to judges, though it has been repeated in some decisions and text-books. The difficulty is to picture a reasonable man who is not discreet.

One peculiarity of this essential of liability is that the plaintiff is compelled to prove a negative. It is not for the defendant to shew that he had reasonable and probable cause, but for the plaintiff to shew that he had none. Another anomaly has been pointed out as having been established early in James I's reign, —that while the facts are found by the jury, it is the judge who must decide whether they shew lack of reasonable and probable cause[4]. This splitting of a function usually assigned to the jury is firmly fixed in our law, and if constant repetition

---

[1] *Abrath* v. *N.E.R. Co.* (1883), 11 Q.B.D. 440 (affirmed 11 A.C. 247). *Per* BOWEN L.J. at p. 462. See also H. Stephen, *Mal. Pros.* ch. XI.

[2] *Per* TINDAL C.J. in *Broad* v. *Ham* (1839), 5 Bing. N.C. at p. 725.

[3] "Without reasonable and probable cause" is not a common phrase in the early forms of pleading. Books of Entries indicate various forerunners of it, such as "sine aliqua causa" (Aston, 40, A.D. 1661), "injuste" (Winch, 96, A.D. 1678), "absque ulla legitima vel vera causa" (Brownlow, 21, A.D. 1693). In Clift (A.D. 1703), which is wealthy in pleadings of this action, "absque alia rationabili vel probabili causa" occurs in several of the precedents (e.g. pp. 29, 32); but variations are also given such as "sine causa rationabili," "absque aliqua vera seu probabili causa" (*ibid.* 24, 25, 27). But as late as 1791, "without any just or probable cause" seems to have been satisfactory (Lilly, 1. 63); and in 1671 there is at least one precedent which relied upon the "falso et malitiose" of the old writ of conspiracy without any reference to lack of reasonable and probable cause (Browne, 19).

[4] *Ante* pp. 187 et sqq.

AND PROBABLE CAUSE 193

of the rule in the reports be a test of its soundness it certainly has that. Fifty years ago some members of the House of Lords expressed a preference for letting the jury answer the entire question, but went no further than this[1]. One consequence of the rule is that if there be undisputed evidence which, in the opinion of the judge shews lack of reasonable and probable cause, this part of the case will not go to the jury at all[2]. On the other hand, where the probable cause consists partly of matter of fact, partly of matter of law, the judge is warranted in leaving the question to the jury[3].

There is no formula which expresses what is reasonable and probable cause[4], and the House of Lords has stated that no definite rule can be laid down here for the exercise of judicial discretion[5]. All that can be usefully done is to select examples on each side of the line from the numerous cases in which the question has been raised. Thus, withdrawing from the prosecution is not in itself conclusive proof of lack of reasonable and probable cause, but it is certainly an element which ought to be taken into account[6]. Disbelief of the defendant in the charge seems at one time to have been some evidence of want of probable cause[7], but later decisions go further than this, and such disbelief has been held to entitle the judge to rule that there was no such cause[8]. If, however, there be an honest belief that the plaintiff committed the offence, it is still reasonable and probable, even though it be mistaken[9]. And unless there be some evidence of the absence of such belief, the case ought not to be left to the jury[10]. It is not essential that facts should

---

[1] *Lister* v. *Perryman* (1870), L.R. 4 H.L. 521.
[2] *Blachford* v. *Dod* (1831), 2 B. & Ad. 179. *Davis* v. *Hardy* (1827), 6 B. & C. 225.   [3] *M'Donald* v. *Rooke* (1835), 2 Bing. N.C. 217.
[4] Cf. POLLOCK C.B. in *Busst* v. *Gibbons* (1861), 30 L.J. Exch. at p. 76.
[5] *Lister* v. *Perryman* (1870), 4 H.L. 521.
[6] *Hilliar* v. *Dade* (1898), 14 T.L.R. 534.
[7] *Broad* v. *Ham* (1839), 5 Bing. N.C. 722. LORD DENMAN C.J. in *Turner* v. *Ambler* (1847), 10 Q.B. 252, said that this must be qualified by the necessity of *proof* of the absence of belief, when reasonable and probable cause appears.
[8] *Haddrick* v. *Heslop* (1848), 12 Q.B. 267. *Williams* v. *Banks* (1859), 1 F. & F. 557. *Shrosbery* v. *Osmaston* (1877), 37 L.T. 792.
[9] *Hicks* v. *Faulkner* (1878), 8 Q.B.D. 167.
[10] *Bradshaw* v. *Waterlow & Sons, Ld.* [1915] 3 K.B. 527. Cf. *Abrath.* v. *N.E.R. Co.* (1886), 11 A.C. at pp. 250, 254, 255.

W.L.P.   13

194   LACK OF REASONABLE

be established which would be admissible as evidence to the
jury upon an issue as to the actual guilt of the accused. "The
distinction between facts to establish actual guilt and those
required to establish a *bonâ fide* belief in guilt should never
be lost sight of in considering such cases"[1]. But this does not
entitle a man, in making an accusation, to shut his eyes to the
existence of facts which would lead any reasonable person to
infer that the other party's conduct was not criminal. Where
there is evidence of a reasonable claim of right, like a lien on
the defendant's goods openly asserted by the plaintiff before
he took them, but the defendant commences the prosecution in
spite of this, he acts without reasonable and probable cause.
"An assertion of right is not a felony"[2]. Nor can he give
evidence of the plaintiff's character being generally suspicious in
order to prove reasonable and probable cause[3]. The question
whether the defendant took reasonable care to inform himself
of the facts before he instituted the prosecution should not be
left to the jury unless there be some evidence of absence of
his honest belief in the charge[4].

    There may be facts sufficient to make the defendant or any
reasonable person believe the truth of the charge which he
made, but if those facts came to his knowledge only after he
had made the charge, he cannot use them as evidence of reasonable and probable cause[5]; but the burden of proving that such
facts were unknown to the defendant is on the plaintiff[6]. The
converse of this occurs when the defendant, after he has charged
the plaintiff, comes to know of a fact which shews that the
plaintiff did not commit the offence. If the defendant then
persists in the prosecution, he cannot contend that the probable
cause with which he commenced the charge continued throughout the proceedings. But if the new fact were a mere representa-
tion as to the character of the plaintiff, the defendant does not

---

    [1] *Hicks* v. *Faulkner*, (1878), 8 Q.B.D. at p. 173.
    [2] WATSON B. in *Huntley* v. *Simson* (1857), 2 H. & N. 600, at p. 604.
James v. *Phelps* (1840), 11 A. & E. 483.
    [3] *Newsam* v. *Carr* (1817), 2 Stark. 69.
    [4] *Bradshaw* v. *Waterlow & Sons, Ld.* [1915] 3 K.B. 527.
    [5] *Delagal* v. *Highley* (1837), 3 Bing. N.C. 950, 959–960.
    [6] *Brooks* v. *Blain* (1869), 39 L.J. (C.P.) 1. *Per* BYLES and BRETT JJ.

AND PROBABLE CAUSE 195

cease to have reasonable and probable cause because he goes on with the proceedings. In *Musgrove* v. *Newell*[1] the defendant had reasonable and probable cause for supposing that the plaintiff had assaulted him with attempt to rob him. He fetched a constable who recognized the plaintiff, and assured the defendant that he was a respectable man, and that he (the constable) would be answerable for the plaintiff appearing to meet the charge. In spite of this, the defendant gave the plaintiff into custody, and on the next day preferred the same charge against him before a justice who dismissed it. In an action for malicious prosecution, the judge directed the jury that in his opinion reasonable and probable cause ceased on the constable's explanation. This direction was held to be wrong. LORD ABINGER C.B. said that the constable's evidence as to the plaintiff's character could not remove the probable cause afforded by the original facts, however much it might weaken the inference to be drawn from them[2]. Just as little does a new fact affect the reasonable and probable cause of a prosecution, if it merely shews that the defendant has mistaken the identity of the plaintiff, but still leaves it open whether the plaintiff committed the offence or not[3].

There is an opinion that if the defendant be mistaken merely in a point of law, that is not enough to negative reasonable and probable cause[4]. But perhaps this cannot be pressed beyond a submission that the defendant is not blameable because he did not form a clear opinion upon a matter which an astute lawyer took considerable time to enforce upon the Court[5]. Nor is it by any means clear that, even if he acted in good faith upon counsel's opinion (however erroneous that opinion may be), this will be reasonable and probable cause[6]. Certainly an opinion given by counsel on an incorrect statement of facts will not

---

[1] (1836), 1 M. & W. 582. [2] *Ibid.* 588–589.
[3] *Harrison* v. *National Provincial Bank of England* (1885), 2 T.L.R. 70, affirming decision in 1 T.L.R. 355.
[4] *Per* BRAMWELL B. in *Johnson* v. *Emerson* (1871), L.R. 6 Exch. at p. 365.
[5] *Phillips* v. *Naylor* (1859), 4 H. & N. at p. 568.
[6] In *Ravenga* v. *Macintosh* (1824), 2 B. & C. 693, BAYLEY J. thought that it would be, but HOLROYD J. declined to commit himself. LITTLEDALE J. is reported as concurring (apparently with HOLROYD J.). Cf. *Abrath* v. *N.E.R. Co.* (1883), 11 Q.B.D. 440, 445. 11 A.C. 247, 249.

13—2

196　　　　　　　　　　MALICE

shelter the defendant[1], nor perhaps will an opinion given by a weak and ignorant man[2].

If there be several charges in an indictment, some of which were made maliciously and without probable cause, the defendant is liable in an action for malicious prosecution, even though there be good ground for the rest of the charges[3].

MALICE

§ 5. It was only natural that the phrase "falso et malitiose" inherited from the writ of conspiracy should affect the action upon the case. It was apparently held in *Nyn* v. *Taylor*[4] that the plaintiff in that action must aver malice, and in *Wale* v. *Hill*[5] it was distinguished from lack of probable cause[6]. PARKER C.J. analysed the word in *Jones* v. *Gwynn*[7], and said: "Among the Romans it [*malitia*] signified a mixture of hatred and fraud, and what was utterly repugnant to simplicity and honesty..... Thus it is used in the civil law, and thus in ours." Other judicial attempts to define malice have not carried it much further in clearness[8]. "Some other motive than a desire to

---

[1] *Hewlett* v. *Cruchley* (1813), 5 Taunt. 277.

[2] *Ibid.* HEATH J. at p. 283. Where the Attorney-General has granted his fiat for a prosecution on facts not shewn to have been put unfairly before him, the Court of Appeal has indicated that there cannot be absence of reasonable and probable cause. *Bradshaw* v. *Waterlow & Sons, Ld.* [1915] 3 K.B. 527.

[3] *Reed* v. *Taylor* (1812), 4 Taunt. 616. In *Delisser* v. *Towne* (1841), 1 Q.B. 333, 339 *n.*, LORD DENMAN C.J. thought that *Johnstone* v. *Sutton* (1786), 1 T.R. 493, conflicted with *Reed* v. *Taylor*, but declined giving any opinion as to the doctrine of each. The decision in *Delisser* v. *Towne* was that a plaintiff who has got a verdict and damages in malicious prosecution is not entitled to the costs of witnesses, who were not called at the trial, but who were brought to answer a case which it was supposed that the defendant would attempt to make as to nine out of ten assignments for perjury contained in the malicious indictment.

[4] (5 Jac. I. B.R.), Roll. *Abr.* 114.

[5] *Per* FLEMING C.J. 1 Bulst. 149 (8 Jac. I. B.R.).

[6] Not always. See HUTTON's opinion in *Mankleton* v. *Allen* (22 Jac. I. C.P.). Winch 73. *Anonymous* (30 Car. II. C.B.), 2 Mod. 306 makes the C.J. say in one sentence that indicting the plaintiff proved the malice, and in the next that after acquittal the prosecution should be accounted malicious.

[7] (12 Anne. B.R.), 10 Mod. 214, 148. The report in Gilbert 185 is rambling; that in 1 Salk. 15 is a mere note.

[8] Cf. ALDERSON B. in *Stevens* v. *Midland Counties R. Co.* (1854), 10 Exch. at p. 356 ("Any motive other than that of simply instituting a prosecution for the purpose of bringing a person to justice, is a malicious motive"); BOWEN L.J. in *Abrath* v. *N.E.R. Co.* (1883), 11 Q.B.D. at p. 455 (Proceedings initiated from "an indirect and improper motive, and not in

SCOPE OF ACTION AS TO PERSONS   197

bring to justice a person whom he [the accuser] honestly believes to be guilty" seems to ignore the frequency with which motives are mixed[1]. A learned author suggests "a wish to injure the party rather than to vindicate the law," and this would form a good basis for directing a jury[2].

It was said in *Johnstone* v. *Sutton* that malice may be, and most commonly is, inferred from want of probable cause[3]; but we cannot now interpret this to mean that it can be inferred from that alone[4]. In any event, the question of malice is one for the jury[5], and the burden of proving it is on the plaintiff[6].

SCOPE OF THE ACTION AS TO PERSONS

§ 6. A reiterated rule was that the old writ of conspiracy did not lay against indictors, and that they were equally immune against the action upon the case appears from a resolution in *Stowball* v. *Ansell* that case would not lie against a juror for indicting the plaintiff of barratry, even though he acted maliciously[7]. Here "indictors" must be taken to mean grand jurors. But if we use it in its loose modern sense of "prosecutors," we find that the Courts held indecisive views at first as to whether they were suable. This, of course, is merely stating in another form that it was doubtful at first whether the action upon the case would lie against anybody at all. An indictment, it was pointed out, was an ordinary proceeding of the law, and one who promoted it should not be liable for doing his duty as

furtherance of justice"). PARKE J. in *Mitchell* v. *Jenkins* (1883), 5 B. & A. 588. LORD DAVEY in *Allen* v. *Flood* [1898] A.C. at pp. 172–173. LORD BRAMPTON in *Quinn* v. *Leathem* [1901] A.C. at pp. 524–525.

[1] CAVE J. in *Brown* v. *Hawkes* [1891] 2 Q.B. at p. 723. CAVE J. himself recognized anger as a proper motive. *Ibid.* p. 722.

[2] H. Stephen, *Mal. Pros.* at p. 37. Cf. Pollock, *Torts* (ed. 1920), 321. Addison, *Torts* (ed. 1906), 254. Examples of malice are endeavouring to concoct a case against another person (*Heath* v. *Heape* (1856), 1 H. & N. 478); or prosecuting him for the purpose of frightening others and thereby deterring them from committing depredations on the prosecutor's property (*Stevens* v. *Midland Counties R. Co.* (1854), 10 Exch. 352, 356).

[3] (1786), 1 T.R. at p. 545.

[4] *Brown* v. *Hawkes, ubi sup.* LORD ESHER M.R. at p. 726. BOWEN L.J. at pp. 727–728. *Mitchell* v. *Jenkins* (1833), 5 B. & Ad. 588. *Hicks* v. *Faulkner* (1878), 8 Q.B.D. at p. 175.

[5] See last two cases cited in note 4.

[6] *Abrath* v. *N.E.R. Co.* (1883), 11 Q.B.D. 440, 455, 11 A.C. 247.

[7] (1 W. & M. B.R.), Comb. 116.

198   SCOPE OF ACTION AS TO PERSONS

a citizen. But this was never urged to the extent of protecting him where he had acted maliciously, and after some hesitation the liability of the prosecutor was established and with it the action for malicious prosecution itself[1].

A justice of the peace who issued a warrant for the arrest of a person upon another's accusation, and so caused that person's arrest was thought in Elizabeth's reign to be excusable, but not if he caused of his own malice a person to be arrested whom nobody else had accused[2]. Two centuries later the Court held that the appropriate action was not case but trespass, though it did not dissent from the substantial part of the earlier opinion[3]. But the judges did not relish such actions, for KELYNG C.J., in dismissing another similar action against a justice who had procured witnesses to appear against the plaintiff and had got his own name indorsed on the indictment, censured the plaintiff for suing at all, and said that strict proof of malice in the case of a justice was necessary. Justices, he pointed out, ought to cause any person who can give evidence against one, who is indicted, to do so[4].

Officers in the naval or military service of the Crown have perhaps a qualified exception from liability. In the famous case of *Sutton* v. *Johnstone* the Court was of opinion that even if proceedings in a court-martial have been instituted without probable cause, courts of law will not interfere with the discretion of an officer acting in a matter of discipline[5]. This opinion was necessary neither to this decision nor to those in *Dawkins* v. *Rokeby*[6] and other later cases in which it has been followed, but the weight of it cannot be ignored. Quite recently, however, the principle that matters of military discipline and

[1] See *Knight* v. *Jermin* (29 Eliz.), Cro. Eliz. 70, 134. *Throgmorton's Case* (39 Eliz.), Cro. Eliz. 563. *Sherington* v. *Ward* (41 Eliz. B.R.), Cro. Eliz. 724. *Arundell* v. *Tregono* (5 Jac. I), Yelv. 116. *Nyn* v. *Taylor* (5 Jac. I), Roll. *Abr.* 114. *Blackman* v. *Trunkett* (9 Car. I), 1 Roll. *Abr.* 114. *Shapcott* v. *Rowe* (10 Car. I), *Ibid. Mankleton* v. *Allen* (22 Jac. I), Winch 73.

[2] *Windham* v. *Clere* (31 Eliz. B.R.), Cro. Eliz. 130.

[3] *Morgan* v. *Hughes* (1788), 2 T.R. 225.

[4] *Girlington* v. *Pitfield* (21 Car. II. B.R.), Vent. 47. 2 Keb. 572. The liability of a magistrate for an improper *conviction* rests upon a different basis, and is dealt with *post* ch. VII.

[5] (1786), 1 T.R. 493, 510, 784.

[6] (1866), 4 F. & F. 806, 832, 833.

SCOPE OF ACTION AS TO MATTER 199

duty are cognizable only by a military tribunal, and not by a court of law, has been declared to be still open to discussion, at any rate in the House of Lords. And that court gave the plaintiff an opportunity of testing the question[1]. Considering its constitutional gravity, it is all the more regrettable from the lawyer's point of view that the opportunity was not taken[2]. Corporations are now amenable to the action, though the law has shewn some hesitation in reaching this conclusion[3].

SCOPE OF THE ACTION AS TO MATTER

§ 7. The action upon the case was not confined to malicious indictments. One of the first examples of its application was where the defendant had procured the outlawry of the plaintiff by maliciously suing out *ca. sa.* against him[4]. It was held to cover the procurement of excommunication in an ecclesiastical court, though no worse result in the shape of imprisonment or damages ensued; but it did not extend to actions between party and party (as distinct from citations *ex officio*) in such a court, for there the successful defendant is regarded as adequately compensated by getting his costs[5]. In *Vanderbergh* v. *Blake*, a false and malicious information was alleged to have been laid in the Exchequer against the plaintiff, and though the defendant had judgment given in his favour, it was upon the score either of the plaintiff's conviction in the Exchequer proceedings or of defects in his pleading. No intrinsic objection was taken to the action itself[6], which in modern times has been extended to maliciously procuring the arrest of a ship[7]. In *Vanderbergh* v. *Blake*, HALE C.B., in giving examples of litigation where no acquittal was possible, said that the action would lie for causeless making of a man bankrupt, or if process of a court were unduly

---

[1] *Fraser* v. *Balfour* (1918), 87 L.J.K.B. 1116.

[2] The composition of the army during the recent war and general democratic tendencies set against the principle.

[3] *Cornford* v. *Carlton Bk.* [1899] 1 Q.B. 392 [1900] 1 Q.B. 22. For earlier cases see Stephen, *Mal. Pros.* 86–97.

[4] *Bulwer* v. *Smith* (26 Eliz. K.B.), 4 Leon. 52.

[5] *Hocking* v. *Matthews* (22 Car. II. B.R.), 1 Vent. 86. *Gray* v. *Dight* (29 Car. II. B.R.), 2 Show. 144 Cf *Fisher* v. *Bristow* (1779), 1 Doug. 215.

[6] (13 Car. II), Hardres 194.

[7] *Redway* v. *McAndrew* (1873), L.R. 9 Q.B. 74. *The Collingrove* (1885), 10 P.D. 158. *The Walter D. Wallet* [1893] P. 202.

200   SCOPE OF ACTION AS TO MATTER

served. About 100 years afterwards, LORD MANSFIELD held that the feasibility of the action in the first of these illustrations was too clear for argument[1], and though MARTIN B. in *Johnson* v. *Emerson* (1871) expressed doubt upon this point[2], he was adequately answered by the Lords Justices in *Quartz Hill Gold Mining Co.* v. *Eyre* (1883), who adopted the view that the action is in these circumstances based upon the scandal which arises from an attack upon a man's credit[3]. The forms which this abuse of procedure may take are numerous. An example is that of taking bankruptcy proceedings as part of a fraudulent scheme to prevent the plaintiff from getting his just due[4]. And whether such abuse be sufficient to ground the action or not, it is well to remember that there is "no reason why the process in bankruptcy should not be affected by the same species of fraud, which would affect and set aside any other process in any other Court," and that the Court will stop proceedings accordingly[5]. It would do so if the real object of their institution were to put an end to a valuable lease[6], to stay proceedings against a third person[7], to dissolve a partnership[8], to defeat an action[9], or to extort money from a debtor[10]. As in the action for malicious prosecution, the plaintiff must prove lack of reasonable and probable cause, but the proof appears to be lighter than in the former. For in general very slight evidence in proving a negative is sufficient to force the other party to prove the affirmative, especially where the nature of the affirmation is such as to admit of proof by witnesses, and cannot depend upon matters lying

---

[1] *Brown* v. *Chapman* (3 Geo. III), 1 W. Bl. 427.

[2] L.R. 6 Exch. at p. 377.

[3] 11 Q.B.D. 674. See pp. 683, 689. As in the action for malicious prosecution, the proceedings must have terminated in the plaintiff's favour. *Whitworth* v. *Hall* (1831), 2 B. & Ad. 695. Approved by H.L. in *Metropolitan Bank* v. *Pooley* (1885), 10 A.C. 210.

[4] *Owen* v. *Lavery* (1900), 16 T.L.R. 375.

[5] *Per* LORD ELDON L.C. *Ex parte Gallimore* (1816), 2 Rose 424 at pp. 431–432.

[6] *Ibid.*

[7] *Ex parte Kemp* (1841), 1 Mont. D. & De G. 657.

[8] *Ex parte Browne* (1810), 1 Rose 151. *In re Christie* (1833), Mont. & B. at p. 351. *Ex parte Johnson* (1842), 2 Mont. D. & De G. 678. *Ex parte Phipps* (1844), 3 Mont. D. & De G. 505.

[9] *Ex parte Bourne* (1826), 2 Gl. & J. 137.

[10] *Re Davies* (1876), 3 Ch. Div. 461.

SCOPE OF ACTION AS TO MATTER

exclusively within the party's own knowledge, as in some cases of criminal prosecution it may do[1].

It is no defence to shew that the adjudication of bankruptcy could not have been legally made even if the facts falsely alleged by the petitioner had been true[2].

It is doubtful whether it is necessary to prove pecuniary damage. According to one opinion it is not, for bankruptcy proceedings attack a man's fair fame[3], and if this be conceded, it should be immaterial whether they are taken against a trader or any one else, for they cast a slur on reputation in either case, though the material damages are likely to be more marked in one than in the other[4]. But a later opinion leaves the question open, with a slight inclination in favour of regarding proof of special damage as unnecessary. All that the decision amounted to was that the Court would not stop an action for malicious proceedings in bankruptcy as frivolous merely because there was no allegation of such damage in the statement of claim[5].

Under statutes now extinct, there was a special remedy for maliciously or fraudulently taking bankruptcy proceedings; but these in no wise derogated from the Common Law remedy[6]. At the present day, the Bankruptcy Act, 1914, apparently gives no special remedy.

False and malicious presentation of a winding-up petition against a company also grounds an action, on the same principles as are applicable to the action for malicious proceedings in bankruptcy[7].

HALE C.B., when he referred in *Vanderbergh* v. *Blake*[8] to undue service of the process of the Court, may have had in mind

---

[1] *Per* LORD TENTERDEN C.J. in *Cotton* v. *James* (1830), 1 B. & Ad. at p. 133.

[2] *Farley* v. *Danks* (1855), 4 E. & B. 493.

[3] BRETT M.R. in *Quartz Hill Gold Mining Co.* v. *Eyre* (1883), 11 Q.B.D. at p. 684.

[4] See however 11 Q.B.D. at pp. 691–692, where BOWEN L.J. does not go beyond applying the principle to proceedings against a trader. Cf. LINDLEY M.R. in *Wyatt* v. *Palmer* [1899] 2 Q.B. 106.

[5] *Wyatt* v. *Palmer* [1899] 2 Q.B. 106.

[6] *Chapman* v. *Pickersgill* (1762), 2 Wils. 145. *Brown* v. *Chapman* (1763), 3 Burr. 1418. 1 W. Bl. 427.

[7] *Quartz Hill Gold Mining Co.* v. *Eyre* (1883), 11 Q.B.D. 674.

[8] (13 Car. II), Hardres 194.

202   SCOPE OF ACTION AS TO MATTER

Waterer v. *Freeman*[1]. There the plaintiff sued the defendant for bringing a second writ of *fi. fa.* against him when he had already got one. The Court held the plaintiff was entitled to judgment, since he had been twice vexed and grieved wilfully. This leads to a much wider question. Will the action lie for any malicious civil proceeding? As a matter of history there is no reason why it should not. In tracing the progress of the writ of conspiracy it has been shewn that it lay for improper civil actions, and that there the writ was properly one of trespass or deceit[2]. It is precisely the organic growth of these three actions together that made it possible for the Courts to extend the law without perceptible effort, and at the same time made it difficult for them to prevent the elasticity of the actions from doing harm. Thus HOBART C.J. in the case last cited denied that the mere bringing of an action upon a false surmise could be regarded as a reason for a counter-action by the defendant, for "executio juris non habet injuriam." But he added that if a suit were utterly without ground of truth, and that to the knowledge of the plaintiff, the action upon the case would lie for the undue vexation and damage caused; and he mentioned several earlier cases, two of which were on the writ of deceit[3]. But whatever may have been the tendency in the past, the law now probably is that no action will lie for malicious suit of a civil cause though it be without probable grounds[4] (apart from the exceptions under discussion). The costs which the Court allows to a successful defendant will, it is said, sufficiently compensate him.

An action upon the case closely analogous to that in the nature of conspiracy was the action for maliciously causing arrest. It is traceable in the reports from the latter half of the 17th century[5], and was held to lie on the same conditions as the

---

[1] Hob. 205, 266 (15 Jac. I). It was cited to him. Cf. *Clissold* v. *Cratchley* [1910] 2 K.B. 244.

[2] *Hist. of Abuse of Procedure*, Index "Deceit."   [3] Hob. at pp. 266–267.

[4] *Per* BOWEN L.J. in *Quartz Hill Gold Mining Co.* v. *Eyre* (1883), 11 Q.B.D. at pp. 688–691. *Wiffen* v. *Bailey Council* [1915] 1 K.B. at pp. 606, 612. Cf. *Castrique* v. *Behrens* (1861), 3 E. & E. 720 and *Redway* v. *McAndrew* (1873), L.R. 9 Q.B. 74, and note thereon in H. Stephen, *Mal. Pros.* 20.

[5] E.g. *Daw* v. *Swaine* (21 Car. II. B.R.), 1 Siderf. 424. The cases down to 1829 are collected in Petersdorff *Abr. sub. tit.* "Malicious Arrest." See too H. Stephen, *Mal. Pros.* 19. *Laws of England*, vol. XIX. §§ 1476–1481.

SCOPE OF ACTION AS TO MATTER   203

action for malicious prosecution[1]. Abolition of arrest on mesne process has cut the ground from under it, but it is still conceivable in a case where, under the Debtors Act, 1869, the imprisonment of a debtor has been maliciously procured by his creditor on a false allegation that he is about to abscond[2]; and in procedure for the recovery of penalties under the Customs Acts[3]. No action lies against a sheriff or his officer for arresting a person attending as a witness under an order of Court, though it be alleged that the person was privileged and that the sheriff or his officer knew of this, and made the arrest maliciously. For the privilege is not that of the witness, but of the Court which he attends. Such Court can order the release of the witness, and also punish the sheriff (if he has acted maliciously) for contempt[4].

Maliciously procuring the issue of a search warrant for goods is also actionable, and there seems to be no need to discuss it as a particular case, unless it were arguable that the issue of the warrant is a ministerial and not a judicial act, and that the applicant for the warrant cannot be styled a "prosecutor." If that were so, the action would resemble one for false imprisonment rather than one for malicious prosecution. But the facts that the action is upon the case, that the points which the plaintiff must prove are identical with those in malicious prosecution, and that the magistrate in issuing the warrant acts judicially and not merely ministerially[5] unquestionably shew that the analogy is to malicious prosecution and not to false imprisonment. Whether further it is malicious prosecution pure and simple or only analogous to it, is a question of correct terminology which depends upon whether the applicant for the warrant can be described as a prosecutor[6].

---

[1] *Churchill* v. *Siggers* (1854), 3 E. & B. 929.
[2] 32 & 33 Vict. c. 62. Addison, *Torts* (ed. 1906), 182.
[3] 39 & 40 Vict. c. 36, sect. 247, 252.
[4] *Magnay* v. *Burt* (1843), 5 Q.B. 381.
[5] *Elsee* v. *Smith* (1822), 1 D. & R. 28. Cf. *Jones* v. *German* [1896] 2 Q.B. 418. [1897] 1 Q.B. 378.
[6] *Hope* v. *Evered* (1886), 17 Q.B.D. 338, and *Lea* v. *Charrington* (1889), 23 Q.B.D. 45, 272, shew that the similar action for malicious procurement of a search warrant under 48 & 49 Vict. c. 69, sect. 10 is related to the action for malicious prosecution.

204 SCOPE OF ACTION AS TO MATTER

It seems that wrongful registration of an order under the Judgments Act, 1838[1], if made maliciously and without reasonable and probable cause, is actionable[2].

A special action on the case was held to lie where A and B maliciously conspired to defeat C of execution for a judgment for £100 against A, by procuring A to confess a judgment for £160 in favour of D to whom A really owed nothing[3]. We are not told why the old writ of conspiracy was not selected by the plaintiff. Apparently it would have sufficed, but he seems to have preferred an action on the case, and the experiment was justified, for the defendants got nothing on a writ of error in Parliament.

[1] 1 & 2 Vict. c. 110, sect. 19.
[2] *Gibbs* v. *Pike* (1842), 9 M. & W. 351, 362.
[3] *Smith* v. *Tonstall* (2 & 3 Jac. II), Carthew 3.

CHAPTER VII

ABUSE OF PROCEDURE BY JUDICIAL OFFICERS

ARRANGEMENT OF CHAPTER

§ 1. This topic will be handled in the following way:

(1) *Abuse by judicial officers in general:*

(i) Civil remedies	(a) Acts within jurisdiction.
(ii) Criminal remedies	
(iii) Other remedies	(b) Acts beyond jurisdiction.

(2) *Abuse by Justices of the Peace:*

(i) Civil remedies	(a) Acts within jurisdiction.
(ii) Criminal remedies	
(iii) Other remedies	(b) Acts beyond jurisdiction.

The separation of Justices of the Peace from other judicial officers is justified, not on the ground of any marked difference in the principles of liability, or of exemption from it, but because questions with respect to their position are of much more frequent occurrence and the principles depend to some extent on statutory provisions peculiar to this kind of judicial officer.

ABUSE BY JUDICIAL OFFICERS IN GENERAL

Civil remedies. Acts within jurisdiction

§ 2. If he act within his jurisdiction, "no action lies for acts done or words spoken by a judge in the exercise of his judicial office, although his motive is malicious and the acts or words are not done or spoken in the honest exercise of his office"[1]. These words were possibly wider than were needed to decide the case before the Court of Appeal, which was an action against the judges of the Supreme Court of Trinidad and Tobago, but they express a principle which has been repeatedly approved and acted upon throughout our legal history. If it were otherwise, the administration of justice would lack one of its essentials,— the independence of the judges. It is better to take the chance

[1] *Anderson* v. *Gorrie* [1895] 1 Q.B. 668. LORD ESHER M.R. at p. 671.

206 ABUSE BY JUDICIAL OFFICERS IN GENERAL

—happily a rare one now—of judicial incompetence, irritability, or irrelevance, than to run the risk of getting a Bench warped by apprehension of the consequences of judgments which should be given without fear or favour. Moreover, to say that there is no civil remedy for judicial misconduct is far from admitting that there is no remedy whatever. But of this more will be said later.

This exemption from liability to civil proceedings has been rather unfortunately styled a "privilege." But that might imply that the judge, witness, or advocate, has a private right to be malicious, whereas its real meaning is that in the public interest it is not desirable to inquire whether acts of this kind are malicious or not. It is rather a right of the public to have the independence of the judges preserved than a privilege of the judges themselves[1].

§ 3. There are traces of recognition of this exemption early in the reports. In Henry VI's reign, BABINGTON C.J.C.P. was of opinion that one shall never have an action against a justice of record[2], and it has been shewn that judges and those sharing in the administration of the law could plead the exercise of their functions against various remedies for abuse of legal procedure[3]. According to Coke's Reports, "the law will not admit any proof against this vehement and violent presumption of law, that a justice sworn to do justice will do injustice; but if he hath conspired before out of Court, this is extra-judicial"[4]. BABINGTON'S opinion hints a distinction between a justice of record and other justices[5], but nothing turns upon that in modern times, for even inferior judges and those not of record cannot be called in question for an error of judgment, so long as they act within their jurisdiction[6]. A court-martial is not a court of record[7], yet a witness before a mere military Court of

---

[1] CHANNELL J. in *Bottomley* v. *Brougham* [1908] 1 K.B. at pp. 586–587.
[2] Hil. 9 Hen. VI, f. 60. [3] *Hist. of Abuse of Legal Procedure*, p. 78.
[4] *Floyd* v. *Barker* (5 Jac. I), 12 Rep. 23.
[5] HOLT C.J. in *Groenvelt* v. *Burwell* (11 Will. III), 1 Ld Raym. 454, at p. 467, describes a justice of record as one who has power to fine and imprison, a judge as one who has power to punish an offence by imprisonment.
[6] LORD TENTERDEN C.J. *obiter* in *Garnett* v. *Ferrand* (1827), 6 B. & C. at p. 626.
[7] KELLY C.B. in *Scott* v. *Stansfield* (1868), L.R. 3 Exch. at p. 223.

ABUSE BY JUDICIAL OFFICERS IN GENERAL 207

Inquiry has been protected[1]. And as to a court-martial itself, if the act be done within the limits of its jurisdiction, probably no action lies against its members, even though they acted maliciously and without reasonable or probable cause[2].

At one time some of the judges seem to have had doubts whether judicial exemption holds where the act has fallen within jurisdiction, but has been done maliciously or without reasonable or probable cause. But the *dicta* which express these doubts must be taken to refer to criminal liability[3], or to Justices of the Peace (whose liability is to some extent still doubtful and is discussed later)[4], or, if they go beyond this, they cannot now be accepted. Thus it might be inferred from *Ackerley* v. *Parkinson* that if an ecclesiastical judge act with malice, but within his jurisdiction, he is liable[5], and LORD WYNFORD, in a Scots law appeal to the House of Lords, thought that subordinate judges at any rate were liable if malice were clearly proved[6]. Again, COCKBURN C.J. in *Thomas* v. *Churton*[7] left open the question of the liability of a judge who abuses his office by using slanderous words maliciously and without reasonable and probable cause.

On the other hand, it has been held that no action will lie against a judge of a superior Court for a judicial act, although it were alleged to have been done maliciously and corruptly[8], and LORD COLERIDGE C.J. in a later case, while stating that his personal opinion tallied with that of COCKBURN C.J. in *Thomas* v. *Churton*, admitted that the authorities were too strong against it[9]. LORD ESHER M.R. in *Anderson* v. *Gorrie* said that if the question had come before COCKBURN C.J. he must and would, after considering the previous authorities, have decided that the

---

[1] *Dawkins* v. *Rokeby* (1875), L.R. 7 H.L. 744.

[2] *Jekyll* v. *Moore* (1806), 6 Esp. 63. *Dawkins* v. *Rokeby* (1873), L.R. 8 Q.B. 255; (1875) L.R. 7 H.L. 744. *Sutton* v. *Johnstone* (1785), 1 T.R. 493.

[3] E.g. LORD TENTERDEN C.J. in *Garnett* v. *Ferrand* (1827), 6 B. & C. at p. 626.

[4] LORD DENMAN C.J. in *Kendillon* v. *Maltby* (1842), Car. & M. at p. 409. *Post* § 12.

[5] (1815), 3 M. & S. 411.

[6] *Allardice* v. *Boswell* (1830), 1 Dow. & Cl. at p. 515. See too LORD CHELMSFORD L.C. in *Hamilton* v. *Anderson* (1858), 3 Macq. at pp. 374–375.

[7] (1862), 2 B. & S. at p. 479.

[8] *Fray* v. *Blackburn* (1863), 3 B. & S. 576.

[9] *Seaman* v. *Netherclift* (1876), 1 C.P.D. at p. 544.

208 ABUSE BY JUDICIAL OFFICERS IN GENERAL

action would not lie[1]; and LORD CRANWORTH in *Hamilton* v. *Anderson* was of opinion that adding that the act was done maliciously amounted to nothing at all[2]. Other modern cases are still more emphatic. In *Scott* v. *Stansfield*, it was held that words alleged to have been spoken by a County Court judge, in his capacity as such, falsely, maliciously, and without any reasonable, probable, or justifiable cause, and not *bonâ fide* but wholly irrelevant to the matter before him, were not actionable[3], and a similar allegation was held to be equally useless in an action against a Justice of the Peace, in *Law* v. *Llewellyn*[4].

§ 4. *Persons exercising judicial functions.* Judges of the superior Courts are protected[5]; so are those in Ireland; thus, a warrant by the Irish C.J.K.B. in Chambers to arrest a party for a breach of the peace has been decided to be such a judicial act as will protect him against an action for false imprisonment[6].

Judges at Quarter Sessions are also exempted from civil liability. It has been held that no action will lie against the Recorder of London and other judges for a wrongful commitment to prison at Sessions any more than for an erroneous judgment[7].

The sheriff was a constituent part of the old County Court, and issued his warrants in a judicial capacity. Hence trespass would not lie against him for the act of his bailiff in mistakenly taking the goods of the wrong person under a warrant issued by the sheriff, in execution of a judgment of the County Court[8]. Though he acted under the direction of the suitors of the Court, it was he who ordered the bailiff to execute a writ, and he therefore stood in a situation quite different from that in which he executes the process of the superior Courts. There he is the party primarily ordered to execute the process[9]. So too, where sheriffs have a customary Court of record, there is no remedy against them by action on the case if, without fraud or corruption[10], they take insufficient bail. The case is just the same as if

[1] [1895] 1 Q.B. at p. 671.
[2] (1858), 3 Macq. at p. 378.
[3] (1868), L.R. 3 Exch. 220. [4] [1906] 1 K.B. 487.
[5] *Fray* v. *Blackburn* (1863), 3 B. & S. 576.
[6] *Taaffe* v. *Downes* (1813), 3 Moore P.C.C. 36.
[7] *Hamond* v. *Howell* (26 Car. II), 1 Mod. 184.
[8] *Tinsley* v. *Nassau* (1827), Mood. & M. 52.
[9] *Tunno* v. *Morris* (1835), 2 Cr. M. & R. 298. [10] But see § 3 *ante.*

ABUSE BY JUDICIAL OFFICERS IN GENERAL 209

insufficient bail were taken by any of the superior courts, where two authorities are united in one person, and it shall be taken to be done by that authority by which they have power to bail, and that is as judges of the Court, and not as gaolers[1]. The stewards of Courts baron and hundred Courts are similarly protected as judicial officers in the exercise of their authority, e.g. where the bailiff of the Court by error takes the goods of the wrong person in execution[2].

County Court judges are also exempted[3]. So is a Coroner. He is a judge of a Court of record, and no action will lie against him for an act done in his judicial capacity, such as turning a person out of a room where he is about to make his inquisition[4], or speaking falsely and maliciously in his address to the jury[5].

A Vice-Chancellor exercising judicial authority under the charter of a University is immune against the consequences of an erroneous judgment[6]. Other tribunals reckoned as judicial are the Court of the County Palatine of Durham[7], the Censors of the Royal College of Physicians[8], Commissioners of Appeal as to judgments in certain cases declared by statute to be final[9], ecclesiastical Courts[10], and the Official Receiver, for he is under a statutory authority to make a judicial inquiry[11].

The immunity also applies wherever there is an authorized inquiry which, though not before a Court of justice, is before a tribunal which has similar attributes[12]. On this principle an ecclesiastical commission appointed by a bishop under statutory authority is a judicial tribunal[13]. So is a military Court of

---

[1] *Metcalfe* v. *Hodgson* (8 Car. I), Hut. 120.
[2] *Holroyd* v. *Breare* (1819), 2 B. & Ald. 473. *Bradley* v. *Carr* (1841), 3 Man. & G. 221.
[3] *Scott* v. *Stansfield* (1868), L.R. 3 Exch. 220.
[4] *Garnett* v. *Ferrand* (1827), 6 B. & C. 611.
[5] *Thomas* v. *Churton* (1862), 2 B. & S. 475.
[6] *Kemp* v. *Neville* (1861), 10 C.B. N.S. 523.
[7] *Peacock* v. *Bell* (1667), 1 Saund. 74 (a superior Court).
[8] *Groenvelt* v. *Burwell* (11 Will. III), 1 Ld. Raym. 454, 467 (they are justices of record).
[9] *Radnor* v. *Reeve* (1801), 2 Bos. & P. 391.
[10] *Ackerley* v. *Parkinson* (1815), 3 M. & S. 411. Cf. *ante* p. 207.
[11] *Bottomley* v. *Brougham* [1908] 1 K.B. 584.
[12] LORD ESHER M.R. in *Royal Aquarium Society Ld.* v. *Parkinson* [1892] 1 Q.B. at p. 442. Cited by COLLINS M.R. in *Barratt* v. *Kearns* [1905] 1 K.B. 504, at p. 510.   [13] *Barratt* v. *Kearns* (*ubi sup.*).

W.L.P.   14

210 ABUSE BY JUDICIAL OFFICERS IN GENERAL

Inquiry, though it cannot administer an oath[1]. Much more then is a Court Martial[2], or a select Committee of Inquiry of the House of Commons, which can administer such an oath[3]. Again, the judge of a Consular Court has the same exemption as a judge of a Court of record here, though his Court may not have been created a Court of record in the sense of English law[4]. Provincial magistrates in India are on the same footing as those of English Courts of similar jurisdiction[5].

The duties of a returning officer at a Parliamentary election are neither entirely ministerial nor wholly judicial, but a mixture of the two. He must exercise a certain amount of discretion in accepting or rejecting a vote. If he is merely mistaken in the exercise of it, he is not liable; if he acted maliciously he is[6].

It should be added that the exemption extends also to witnesses in a Court. They incur no liability for what they say if it has reference to the inquiry on which they are testifying[7]. And the protection accorded to counsel is at least as large, and is referable to the same principle, as that of a judge or a witness[8]. Jurors are also free from liability[9].

But a meeting of the London County Council for the purpose of granting music and dancing licences is not a Court for this purpose. "Judicial" has two meanings in this connection. It may refer to the discharge of duties exercisable by a judge (whether in a law Court or in a private room) or to administrative duties which need not be performed in Court, but in respect of which it is necessary to use a judicial mind,—a mind to determine what is fair and just as to the matters under consideration. Licensing meetings of a County Council fall under this

---

[1] *Dawkins* v. *Rokeby* (1875), L.R. 7 H.L. 744.
[2] *Ante* pp. 206–207.
[3] *Goffin* v. *Donnelly* (1881), 6 Q.B.D. 307.
[4] *Haggard* v. *Pélicier Frères* [1892] A.C. 61 (J.C.).
[5] *Calder* v. *Halkett* (1839), 3 Moore P.C.C. 28. *Post* §§ 12 sqq.
[6] *Cullen* v. *Morris* (1819), 2 Stark. 577, 587. Qu. as to malice making any difference? *Ante* § 3.
[7] *Seaman* v. *Netherclift* (1876), 2 C.P.D. 53. See PIGOT C.B.'s elaborate review of the English authorities in *Kennedy* v. *Hilliard* (1859), 10 Irish C.L.R. 195. This review commended itself to LORD COLERIDGE C.J. in *Seaman* v. *Netherclift* (1876), 1 C.P.D. at p. 546.
[8] *Munster* v. *Lamb* (1883), 11 Q.B.D. 588.
[9] *Bushell's Case* (1670), 6 St. Tr. 999.

ABUSE BY JUDICIAL OFFICERS IN GENERAL 211

second head[1]. Bodies like this, such as the Inns of Court and the General Medical Council do well enough with such protection as quasi-judicial functions imply[2].

§ 5. There is an important distinction between superior and inferior Courts as to proof of jurisdiction, when the exemption is claimed. Nothing shall be intended to be out of the jurisdiction of a superior Court but that which specially appears to be so, and nothing shall be intended to be within the jurisdiction of an inferior Court but that which is expressly so alleged[3]. But though it must be proved in defence of an act presumptively wrongful, done under process of an inferior Court, that the Court had jurisdiction, this does not apply to officers of the Court, for they are punishable as ministers of the Court for disobedience if they do not carry out its commands[4].

Civil remedies. Excess of jurisdiction

§ 6. It must be observed at the outset that the protection accorded to judicial acts cannot be extended to ministerial acts. It has been said that where there is a ministerial act to be done by persons, who on other occasions act judicially, the refusal to do the ministerial act is just as actionable as if no judicial functions were on any occasion entrusted to them, or as if they had acted beyond their jurisdiction. This appears to represent the law, though the actual decision of the House of Lords in which the opinion was given related to a refusal by a Presbytery to take on his trials a presentee to a church in Scotland[5]. Where the act is not merely ministerial, but it appears that there has been absence or excess of jurisdiction, the judge is also liable[6]. Such is the case where a revising barrister turns a man out of his Court on the ground that he has misconducted himself not

---

[1] *Royal Aquarium Society, Ld.* v. *Parkinson* [1892] 1 Q.B. 431. LOPES L.J. at p. 452.

[2] FRY L.J. *Ibid.* at p. 447.

[3] *Peacock* v. *Bell* (1667), 1 Saund. 73. *Carratt* v. *Morley* (1841), 1 Q.B. 18. *Trevor* v. *Wall* (1786), 1 T.R. 151.

[4] *Moravia* v. *Sloper* (1737), Willes 30. *Mayor of London* v. *Cox* (1867), L.R. 2 H.L. 239.

[5] LORD CAMPBELL in *Ferguson* v. *Earl of Kinnoull* (1842), 9 Cl. & Fin. 251, at pp. 312–313. Cf. *Green* v. *Hundred of Buccle-churches* (31 Eliz.), 1 Leon. 323.

[6] *Case of the Marshalsea* (10 Jac. I), 10 Rep. 68 *b*, 76 *a*.

14—2

212 ABUSE BY JUDICIAL OFFICERS IN GENERAL

then but at a previous sitting of the Court[1]. So too, if the steward of a hundred Court, instead of taking the regular course of directing process to the bailiff of the Court, issues the writ to special bailiffs nominated by the attorney of one of the parties, taking an indemnity to protect himself from the consequences of their misconduct, he so far mixes himself up personally with the party as to sanction what these special bailiffs do in executing the process[2]. Again, officers of a Court-Martial are liable for the trial of a person not subject to their jurisdiction[3].

These are simple illustrations, but difficulties must necessarily arise in deciding at what point a judge goes beyond his proper province. Where the question is one of words spoken by him, it has been held in Scots law that the only sound rule is to grant the protection unless it can be shewn so clearly that no man of ordinary intelligence and judgment could honestly dispute it that the words used had no connection with the case in hand[4].

Criminal remedies. Acts within jurisdiction

§ 7. There is not much authority on this. Such as it is, it appears to be in favour of criminal liability in some form or other. A case of Edward III's reign is inconclusive. A justice assigned to hear and determine felonies and trespasses was arraigned for having entered on his record that certain persons who had been indicted of trespass were indicted of felony, and judgment was demanded on his behalf, because he could not as a matter of law contradict his own record. And it was advised by the justices that the presentation was null, and thereon it was adjourned[5]. According to Coke, however, it is a criminal conspiracy if a judge suborn witnesses, or engage in false and malicious prosecutions out of Court[6], and there is other evidence

---

[1] *Willis* v. *Maclachlan* (1876), 1 Exch. Div. 376.
[2] *Bradley* v. *Carr* (1841), 3 Man. & G. 221.
[3] *Comyn* v. *Sabine* (11 Geo. II): unreported, but cited in 1 Sm. L.C. 671 (ed. 12).
[4] *Per* LORD MONCREIFF in *Primrose* v. *Waterston* (1902), 4 F. (Court of Session) at p. 793.
[5] 27 Lib. Ass. pl. 18.
[6] *Floyd* v. *Barker* (5 Jac. I), 12 Rep. 24.

ABUSE BY JUDICIAL OFFICERS IN GENERAL 213

that corruption, neglect of duty, and misconduct in it, are and always will be punishable by public prosecution[1]. No modern instance can be given of criminal proceedings against judges of the Supreme Court for misconduct in office. County Court judges are criminally liable for such misconduct, but if the party injured has already memorialized the Lord Chancellor, who has declined to interfere, he cannot institute a criminal information against the judge. The object of each proceeding is punishment, and if the complainant has elected to pursue the one, he cannot have the other[2].

Misconduct of Coroners has been dealt with by the Coroners Act, 1887[3]. If the Coroner be guilty of extortion, corruption, wilful neglect, or misbehaviour in discharge of his duty, he commits a misdemeanour, and in addition to any other punishment may, unless his office of Coroner is annexed to any other office, be removed from it by the Court which convicts him[4]. He also commits a misdemeanour if he acts as solicitor to prosecute or defend a person for any offence of which he is charged on an inquisition taken before the Coroner[5], or if he refuses on the written request of a majority of the jury to summon as a witness a legally qualified medical practitioner named by them, or to direct a *post mortem* examination by such practitioner[6]; and if he does not, in cases of murder and manslaughter, comply with the provisions of the Act as to the delivery of the inquisition or the taking and delivery of depositions and recognizances, he may be fined summarily[7]. The Common Law illustrates what is misconduct on the part of the Coroner. It may take the form of excluding some of the jurors who have been sworn[8], or inserting the names of persons in the finding of the jury[9], or refusing to receive the evidence of the person implicated[10]. And it is clear from these cases that

---

[1] LORD TENTERDEN C.J. in *Garnett* v. *Ferrand* (1827), 6 B. & C. at p. 626.
[2] *R.* v. *Marshall* (1855), 4 E. & B. 475.
[3] 50 & 51 Vict. c. 71. Extended to deputy coroners by 55 & 56 Vict. c. 56, sect. 1 (5).
[4] 50 & 51 Vict. c. 71, sect. 8 (2).   [5] Sect. 10.
[6] Sect. 21 (3).   [7] Sect. 9.
[8] *R.* v. *Stukely* (13 Will. III), 12 Mod. 493.
[9] *R.* v. *Marsh* (undated), 3 Salk. 172. The Coroner was convicted of forgery.
[10] *R.* v. *Scorey* (22 Geo. II), 1 Leach 43. Held to be a misdemeanour.

214 ABUSE BY JUDICIAL OFFICERS IN GENERAL

the Coroner is amenable to the ordinary criminal law independently of his statutory liability.

Criminal remedies. Excess of jurisdiction

§ 8. The Bench in early times certainly did not lack men with an itching palm, and several instances occur of the punishment of judges for bribery and corruption. THOMAS DE WEYLAND C.J.C.P. was charged with these offences in 1280, and so were the rest of the judges. All except two were convicted and heavily fined. He was also attainted of the graver offences (apparently extra-judicial) of instigating his servants to commit murder and screening them from punishment. For this he was ultimately compelled to abjure the realm. Again, in 1289, Adam de Stratton, a chamberlain of the Exchequer, was charged with corruption and felony. He was dismissed from his office and suffered imprisonment, forfeiture of his property, and a fine. The procedure against WILLIAM DE THORPE C.J.K.B. who confessed in 1350 to having received bribes from various persons, who had been indicted before him, was before five specially appointed royal commissioners, who were given authority to inquire into and punish his offences. He was committed to the Tower and all his lands and goods were seized by the King till the royal pleasure should be made known. The King ordered a further judgment that he be degraded and hanged, but this was commuted to imprisonment. Parliament confirmed the judgment, but in the next year he was pardoned[1]. The more familiar cases of Francis Bacon in 1621, and the Earl of Macclesfield in 1725[2], were tried on impeachment. Both were charged with corruption, Bacon for taking bribes of suitors, the Earl for selling offices contrary to law and taking extortionate payments for them. Both were convicted and punished, and both were to some extent victims of a vicious system that connived at bribery of the sort which they committed if it did not always condone it. The system has disappeared and the judicial atmosphere of modern times is such as to make a repetition of these offences or anything like them highly improbable. Altogether

[1] Foss, *Lives of the Judges*. Coke, 3 Inst. 145 sqq.
[2] 16 St. Tr. 767.

ABUSE BY JUDICIAL OFFICERS IN GENERAL 215

different was the later case of JOHNSON J. of the Irish Bench, who in 1805 was indicted for, and convicted of, publishing a libel extra-judicially[1].

Other remedies

§ 9. Quite apart from ordinary civil or criminal proceedings, there are other means of dealing with judicial incompetence or dishonesty. By 38 & 39 Vict. c. 77, sect. 5, judges of the High Court and of the Court of Appeal, with the exception of the Lord Chancellor, hold office during good behaviour, subject to a power of removal by the Crown on address by both Houses of Parliament. The view generally taken of this in text-books is that such judges are removable only on address by both Houses of Parliament. A more likely interpretation of it seems to be that they hold office as regards the Crown during good behaviour, as regards Parliament also during good behaviour, though the two Houses may extend the term so as to cover any form of misconduct which would destroy public confidence in the judge[2].

Judges of other kinds are removable in various ways. Thus the County Courts Act, 1888[3], provides for the removal of judges of the County Court, and fines, remedies, and penalties against officers of the County Court for misconduct[4]. Again, a Coroner may be removed by the Lord Chancellor for such misconduct as inexcusable delays in holding inquests or intoxication whilst executing his office[5], and these are no more than examples.

Habeas corpus. Inapplicability of judicial exemption

§ 10. 16 Car. I. c. 10, which abolished the jurisdiction of the Star Chamber and of the Court of the President and Council in Wales and elsewhere, fixed heavy penalties on judges offending against it, besides awarding treble damages to the party injured[6]. It also gives the like amount to any one who has applied to a

---

[1] 29 St. Tr. 81–502. The speech of Mr Burrowes in the Irish Court of Exchequer is a good specimen of a style of forensic rhetoric now extinct. It moved LORD AVONMORE to tears in Court and to embraces out of it. Col. 244.

[2] Anson, *Law of the Constitution*, vol. II. Pt. I, ch. III, sect. viii, § 2.

[3] 51 & 52 Vict. c. 43, sect. 15, 50, 51.

[4] See also *Ex parte Ramshay* (1852), 18 Q.B. 173.

[5] *In re Hull* (1882), 9 Q.B.D. 689. *In re Ward* (1861), 30 L.J. Ch. 775.

[6] Sect. 6, 7.

216   ABUSE BY JUSTICES OF THE PEACE

judge for a writ of *habeas corpus* to free him from imprisonment by the Courts abolished, and who has been refused a grant of the writ[1].

The Habeas Corpus Act, 1679, imposes a £500 penalty on any judge who, in Vacation time, denies the writ of *habeas corpus*[2]. There are further penalties for sending a person to gaol abroad,—treble costs and damages which are not to be less than £500 in any event. The offence is also punishable as an offence under the Statute of Praemunire[3].

Time limitation for proceedings

§ 11. The Public Authorities Protection Act, 1893, requires any action, prosecution, or proceeding against any person for any act done in pursuance, or execution, or intended execution of any Act of Parliament, or of any public duty or authority, or in respect of any neglect or default in the execution of any such Act, duty, or authority, to be commenced within six months next after the act, neglect, or default complained of, or, if it be a continuing injury or damage, within six months next after the ceasing thereof[4].

ABUSE BY JUSTICES OF THE PEACE
Civil remedies. Acts within jurisdiction

§ 12. Whether an action against a Justice of the Peace for an act done by him in the execution of his duty will lie in any circumstances is doubtful. Sect. 1 of the Act for the Protection of Justices of the Peace, 1848[5], provides that every action hereafter to be brought against any Justice of the Peace for any act done by him in the execution of his duty as such Justice, with respect to any matter within his jurisdiction[6] as such Justice, shall be an action on the case as for a tort; and that in the declaration it shall be expressly alleged that such act was done maliciously and without reasonable and probable cause, and if at the trial of any such action, upon the general issue

---

[1] Sect. 8.   [2] 31 Car. II. c. 2, sect. 10.   [3] Sect. 12.

[4] 56 & 57 Vict. c. 61, sect. 1. The section also deals with costs and tender of amends.

[5] 11 & 12 Vict. c. 44.

[6] See *Kendall* v. *Wilkinson* (1855), 4 E. & B. 680.

ABUSE BY JUSTICES OF THE PEACE 217

being pleaded, the plaintiff shall fail to prove such allegation, he shall be nonsuit, or a verdict shall be given for the defendant.

It will be observed that the section nowhere creates any remedy, but merely assumes the existence of one. If, therefore, it can be proved that there is no such remedy at Common Law, Justices of the Peace are not liable. Moreover, the Common Law is organic and is constantly developing and changing. Therefore, it does not follow that because there may have been a civil remedy at Common Law in 1848 (the date of the passing of the Act) against Justices of the Peace for acts done in the execution of their duty, there is any such remedy at the present day. For the Common Law may have changed on this point, and may have reached the conclusion that there is no such remedy. If that be so, the Act of 1848 merely regulates what does not exist. True, it assumes that there is such an action, and labels it an action on the case. But if the assumption be unfounded, sect. 1 only baptizes something that never existed or has since died. We have now to examine this assumption, and it may be said at once that, while there is no decision that such an action will not lie, it is at least open to the Courts even now to give such a decision without being hampered by the Act of 1848.

Before that Act, there are certainly traces that an action did exist. Against this view there is the opinion of LYTTELTON J. in Edward IV's reign that a Justice of the Peace is a judge of record, and that the party ought not to punish him[1], and WYNDHAM J. in Elizabeth's reign doubted whether an action on the case would lie against a Justice of the Peace for refusing to take the oath of the party robbed, because a Justice of the Peace is a judge of record[2]. Again, Lambard, though he speaks of criminal remedies against Justices of the Peace, says nothing of any civil remedy[3]. But shortly before Lambard's book was published, the statute 7 Jac. I. c. 5 not only assumes that action upon the case, trespass, battery, or false imprisonment

---

[1] Pasch. 9 Ed. IV, f. 3. Cf. BABINGTON C.J.C.P. in Hil. 9 Hen. VI, f. 60, that one shall never have an action against a justice of record.

[2] *Green* v. *Hundred of Buccle-churches* (31 Eliz.), 1 Leon. 323. See too TWISDEN J. in *Anon.* (16 Car. II), Siderf. 209.

[3] *Eirenarcha* (1614), 370, 630, 631.

218 ABUSE BY JUSTICES OF THE PEACE

could be brought against a Justice of the Peace for a wrong done in virtue of his office, but shews in its preamble that the very reason why the Act passed was because Justices of the Peace had been troubled by frequent and vexatious actions against them for acts done in the due execution of their duty[1]. And in *Lane* v. *Santeloe*, at *nisi prius*[2], an action for malicious prosecution was successfully brought against a Justice who had committed the plaintiff, and the existence of civil liability is recognized expressly or impliedly in many other cases[3]. Nor are examples of its recognition lacking after the Act of 1848 came into operation[4]. *Gelen* v. *Hall* (1857)[5] is entirely inconclusive, but the very fact of its inconclusiveness after considerable forensic argument perhaps marks the turn of the tide in the direction of holding that Justices of the Peace are not liable for acts done in the execution of their office. In that case, one of the counts in a declaration alleged that the defendant, a Justice of the Peace, maliciously and without reasonable or probable cause, took an information against the plaintiff and convicted him, and that the conviction was quashed. For this the plaintiff recovered heavy damages. It was moved in arrest of judgment that the verdict was against evidence, and that the count disclosed no cause of action. The Court said that after much consideration they were not then prepared to hold the count bad, but they ordered a new trial apparently on the ground that the verdict was against evidence. One of the arguments of counsel was that the Act of 1848 was a restraining

---

[1] Repealed 56 & 57 Vict. c. 61, sect. 2.

[2] (4 Geo. I), 1 Stra. 79.

[3] By LORD MANSFIELD, with some hesitation, in *R.* v. *Young* (1758), 1 Burr. at p. 562; and more unreservedly in the following cases: *R.* v. *Palmer* (1761), 2 Burr. 1162; *R.* v. *Fielding* (1759), 2 Burr. 719 (where such an action had been actually commenced against a Justice of the Peace, for the prosecutor was put to his election between that and the prosecution); *Weston* v. *Fournier* (1811), 14 East 491; *Burley* v. *Bethune* (1814), 1 Marsh. 220 (a decision on 43 Geo. III. c. 141 repealed by the Act of 1848). See too LORD ABINGER C.B. in *West* v. *Smallwood* (1838), 3 M. & W. at pp. 420–421; and TINDAL C.J. in *Cave* v. *Mountain* (1840), 1 Man. & G. at p. 263.

[4] *Linford* v. *Fitzroy* (1849), 13 Q.B. 240, 247. *Kirby* v. *Simpson* (1854), 10 Exch. 358. LORD CAMPBELL C.J. in *Kendall* v. *Wilkinson* (1855), 4 E. & B. 680 at p. 689 (the decision was that an action would not lie, because no malice was alleged, as required by sect. 1 of the Act of 1848).

[5] 2 H. & N. 379.

ABUSE BY JUSTICES OF THE PEACE 219

Act in favour of Justices of the Peace, and that it did not give a new remedy where there was none before. As has been pointed out, this did not prove that there was no remedy before the Act; in fact, the evidence is the other way. But from this point onwards, it is impossible to resist the conviction that the trend of opinion is against the liability of Justices of the Peace to an action for having done something within the scope of their jurisdiction. This is to be inferred from the strong opinions which have been expressed in favour of judicial immunity generally in such cases as *Anderson* v. *Gorrie*[1], and from the decision of the Court of Appeal in *Law* v. *Llewellyn*[2] that no action of slander will lie against a Justice of the Peace for words spoken in the discharge of his office. There is nothing in the judgment of the Court adverse to the conclusion that, if an action of slander will not lie, there is no reason why any other action should lie.

In any event, if there be such a remedy, the plaintiff must allege and prove that the act was done maliciously and without reasonable and probable cause[3]; and there would be a wide distinction between an action against a prosecutor for malicious prosecution, and one against a magistrate for malicious conviction. The question in the latter would be whether *upon the hearing* there appeared to be no actual ground for imputing the crime to the plaintiff[4].

§ 13. *Law* v. *Llewellyn*[5] cited at the end of the preceding section well illustrates an act done within jurisdiction. The magistrate in allowing the prosecutor to withdraw a charge commented severely on his conduct in having made it at all. Now a criminal charge cannot be withdrawn as a matter of course, and what less can a magistrate do in fairness to the accused person than state the reason why he allows it to be withdrawn at all?[6]

But when a question as to excess of jurisdiction arises, can

---

[1] [1895] 1 Q.B. 668. See other cases cited in §§ 3 et sqq. *ante*.
[2] [1906] 1 K.B. 487.
[3] 11 & 12 Vict. c. 44, sect. 1. *Ante* p. 216.
[4] *Burley* v. *Bethune* (1814), 5 Taunt. 580, 583–584.
[5] [1906] 1 K.B. 487.
[6] For remarks made extra-judicially v. *post* § 16. *Paris* v. *Levy* (1860), 9 C.B.N.S. 342.

220 ABUSE BY JUSTICES OF THE PEACE

the Justice of the Peace give himself jurisdiction by assuming in his favour the existence of a fact upon which his jurisdiction depends? The rule is that if, supposing the alleged facts to be true, the magistrate would have had jurisdiction, his exemption from liability is not affected by the truth or falsehood of those facts, nor by the sufficiency or insufficiency of the evidence adduced to establish them[1]. Thus a Justice of the Peace may have given himself jurisdiction only by calling a 74-gun ship a boat, but it is a fallacy to assume that the fact which he has to decide is that which gives him jurisdiction[2]. Supposing that he may convict if the bird be a partridge, but not if it be a thrush, it is for him to decide whether it be a partridge or not[3]. On the other hand, no Court of limited jurisdiction can give itself jurisdiction by a wrong decision on a point collateral to the merits of the case upon which the limit to its jurisdiction depends[4]. This still leaves open for decision on each particular occasion the question whether a point is collateral or not. At any rate, it is collateral when the judge unreasonably decides that an objection is not *bonâ fide* and thus assumes to himself jurisdiction which that very objection would exclude[5].

§ 14. Where any poor rate has been made, allowed, or published, no action shall be brought against a Justice of the Peace who has issued a distress warrant against a person named and rated therein by reason of any irregularity or defect in the rate, or by reason of such person not being liable to be rated therein[6]. But the Justice must have acted within his jurisdiction to entitle him to this exemption[7]. No action can be brought against a Justice of the Peace for the exercise of a discretion

---

[1] *Cave* v. *Mountain* (1840), 1 Man. & G. 257. *Secus* if he had acted from any malicious or improper motive. TINDAL C.J. at p. 263.

[2] *Brittain* v. *Kinnaird* (1819), 1 Brod. & B. 432, 442. Approved in *R.* v. *Bolton* (1841), 1 Q.B. 66, 74.

[3] *Per* BUCKLEY L.J. in *Livingstone* v. *Westminster Corporation* [1904] 2 K.B. at pp. 118–119.

[4] COLERIDGE J. in *Bunbury* v. *Fuller* (1853), 9 Exch. at p. 140. Cited by ERLE J. in *R.* v. *Nunneley* (1858), E.B. & E. at p. 861.

[5] See *R.* v. *Bloomsbury Income Tax Commissioners* [1915] 3 K.B. 768 LORD READING C.J. at pp. 782–783.

[6] 11 & 12 Vict. c. 44, sect. 4.

[7] *R.* v. *Justices of Great Yarmouth* (1850), 4 New Sess. Cases 313.

ABUSE BY JUSTICES OF THE PEACE 221

conferred upon him by any Act of Parliament[1]. And he cannot be sued in the County Court for any act done in the execution of his office if he object[2]. If he refuse to act when he should do so, he may be compelled by a rule of the King's Bench Division made absolute, and then no action can be brought against him for having obeyed such rule[3].

If the act complained of were done by the Justice in the execution of his office, the plaintiff cannot recover more than twopence nor any costs[4] if it be proved that he was actually guilty of the offence of which he was convicted, or that he was liable by law to pay the sum he was ordered to pay, and that he suffered no greater punishment than that assigned by the law[5].

Civil remedies. Acts in excess of jurisdiction

§ 15. We may begin here, as in the corresponding section dealing with judges generally, by pointing out that a Justice of the Peace appears to be liable for a ministerial, as distinct from a judicial, act[6]. In *Green* v. *Hundred of Buccle-churches*[7], all three judges agreed *obiter* that a Justice who refused to act in his ministerial, as opposed to his judicial, capacity, could be sued; and two of them thought that a refusal to examine a complainant was a refusal to perform a ministerial act, but the other judge held that such examination was a judicial act[8]. It has been held that the duty of a magistrate with respect to admitting to bail cannot be split into functions partly judicial, partly ministerial, but that it is a judicial duty, and that mistaken or omitted execution of it is not actionable unless the magistrate act with malice[9].

---

[1] 11 & 12 Vict. c. 44, sect. 4.

[2] *Ibid.* sect. 10 as amended by the Public Authorities Protection Act, 1893 (56 & 57 Vict. c. 61) and the Statute Law Revision Act, 1894 (57 & 58 Vict. c. 56). See *Weston* v. *Sneyd* (1857), 1 H. & N. 703.

[3] 11 & 12 Vict. c. 44, sect. 5.

[4] But as to costs, see the Public Authorities Protection Act, 1893 (56 & 57 Vict. c. 61), sect. 2 (*d*).

[5] 11 & 12 Vict. c. 44, sect. 13. "Such action" must be construed by reference to "action" in sect. 8.

[6] *Ante* § 6.   [7] (31 Eliz.), 1 Leon. 323.

[8] In *Anon.* (21 Car. II), 1 Vent. 41, the Court directed a party to bring an action of debt for a statutory forfeiture against a Justice of the Peace who had refused to come and view a force.

[9] *Linford* v. *Fitzroy* (1849), 13 Q.B. 240, 247. Qu. whether it is now actionable in any circumstances? *Ante* § 12.

222 ABUSE BY JUSTICES OF THE PEACE

§ 16. Where there has been absence or excess of jurisdiction, an action will lie. The reports afford numerous illustrations of this. If there were an attempt to exercise jurisdiction when the proper number of justices was not present, or costs were inflicted where there was no power to inflict them[1]; if no reference were made in the warrant of arrest to the sworn information, or if the deposition on oath were taken by the Justices' clerk, the Justice neither being present then, nor at any time seeing, examining, or hearing the deponent[2]; if the proceeding were for an offence under a statute then repealed[3]; if the defendant were convicted twice for the same offence[4]; if a person suspected of felony were detained for examination beyond the proper time[5], or had his examination improperly postponed by a committal to prison in the first instance[6]; if a warrant for commitment be issued in circumstances which make it inapplicable[7],—in all these cases, the Justice would have no defence to the action. And it would appear that there is no exemption for remarks made extra-judicially, such as adverse comments on a trade circular made to a newspaper reporter after the close of public business at the Court[8].

Where the acts are those of a Justice of the Peace not duly qualified (e.g. because he has not taken the oath at the general sessions), they are not absolutely void. He indeed may be liable, but a person seizing goods under a distress warrant signed by such a Justice is not a trespasser[9].

If a person has paid money under protest to escape imprisonment under a warrant which magistrates had no jurisdiction to issue, he can recover the whole amount from them[10].

§ 17. The Act for the Protection of Justices of the Peace,

---

[1] *George* v. *Chambers* (1843), 11 M. & W. 149.

[2] *Caudle* v. *Seymour* (1841), 1 Q.B. 889.

[3] *Ward* v. *Stevenson* (1844), 1 New Sess. Cases 162.

[4] *Crepps* v. *Durden* (1777), 2 Cowp. 640.

[5] *Scavage* v. *Tateham* (43 Eliz.), Cro. Eliz. 829. *Davis* v. *Capper* (1829), 10 B. & C. 28.

[6] *Edwards* v. *Ferris* (1836), 7 C. & P. 542.

[7] *Robson* v. *Spearman* (1820), 3 B. & Ald. 493. *Prickett* v. *Greatrex* (1846), 8 Q.B. 1020.

[8] *Paris* v. *Levy* (1860), 9 C.B.N.S. 342, 363. Cf. *Law* v. *Llewellyn* [1906] 1 K.B. 487. *Ante* § 13.

[9] *Margate Pier Co.* v. *Hannam* (1819), 3 B. & Ald. 266, 271.

[10] *Clark* v. *Woods* (1848), 2 Exch. 395.

ABUSE BY JUSTICES OF THE PEACE 223

1848, sect. 2[1], provides that for an act done by a Justice of the Peace without jurisdiction or in excess of it, an action may be maintained against him as might have been done before the Act, without any allegation of malice or of lack of reasonable and probable cause, provided the conviction or order shall have been quashed. It also exempts him from any such action for an act done under a warrant to compel appearance, if a summons were previously served and not obeyed[2].

Sect. 1 has already been stated and discussed[3]. What the relation of that is to sect. 2 is a riddle that has not been answered. The Act is ill-drawn, and the solution of the problem was attempted by the Queen's Bench with little success in *Barton* v. *Bricknell*[4], where the Court seems to have reached the conclusion that to order an illegal punishment is an act done within jurisdiction, and therefore within sect. 1, but that to carry out such an order is in excess of jurisdiction, and therefore within sect. 2[5].

§ 18. Other provisions of the same Act afford exemption in certain circumstances. If one Justice of the Peace make a conviction or order, and another Justice *bonâ fide* and without collusion grant a warrant of distress or of commitment thereon, no action shall be brought against the latter because of any defect in such conviction or order, or for want of jurisdiction in the Justice who made the same, and who alone is liable to the action, if any[6].

If a warrant shall have been issued on a defective conviction or order, no action shall be brought against the Justice who issued the warrant if the conviction or order shall have been affirmed on appeal[7]. And affirmation by Quarter Sessions is enough, though the conviction be ultimately quashed on *certiorari*[8].

---

[1] 11 & 12 Vict. c. 44.

[2] But this does not apply to a summons and warrant issued *after* the conviction with a view to the levying of penalties. *Bessell* v. *Wilson* (1853), 1 E. & B. 489.   [3] *Ante* § 12.   [4] (1850), 13 Q.B. 393.

[5] Cf. JERVIS J. in *Ratt* v. *Parkinson* (1851), 20 L.J. (M.C.) at p. 212. For an example of excess of jurisdiction under sect. 2, see *Leary* v. *Patrick* (1850), 15 Q.B. 266. Cf. *Pease* v. *Chaytor* (1861), 1 B. & S. 658.

[6] 11 & 12 Vict. c. 44, sect. 3.   [7] Sect. 6.

[8] *McVittie* v. *Marsden* [1917] 2 K.B. 878.

224 ABUSE BY JUSTICES OF THE PEACE

The following provision of the Act seems to apply whether the Act be done within jurisdiction, or in excess of it. If any action be brought against a Justice of the Peace, where the Act makes such action inapplicable, a judge of the Court where the action is brought may, on the defendant's application and affidavit of the facts, set aside the proceedings[1].

Criminal remedies. Acts within jurisdiction

§ 19. "The Statutes," says Lambard, "do now and then correct the dulnesse of these Justices, with some strokes of the rodde, or spur. And therefore generally, if a Justice of peace will not give remedy to a party grieved in any thing that he may hear, determin, or execute: then upon complaint to the Justices of assize, or to the Lord Chancellor, he shall not only be put out of the commission by the Lord Chancellor, but shal also be punished according to his demerites"[2].

He states elsewhere that by the opinion of some Justices, if a Justice of the Peace do anything of record ignorantly that he shall not be punished, but that if he craftily "embesill"[3] an indictment which was never found by the jury, then his misdemeanour may be inquired of by commission (due to a resolution of all the Justices assembled before the King in the Star Chamber, 2 Rich. III) by the oaths of twelve men, and he may be fined[4]. This Lambard calls the punishment at Common Law. At the present day the criminal remedies are information or indictment, and these may be separately treated.

§ 20. *Information.* In 1758, all the judges agreed in *R.* v. *Young*[5] that an information would lie against Justices for partiality, malice, or corruption in the exercise of their jurisdiction (though none of these appeared in the case before them), and three years later it was held that punishment by information was an extraordinary course, and inapplicable if the Justice acted honestly without oppression, malice, revenge or any ill intention; and that, unless this were proved, the party would

---

[1] 11 & 12 Vict. c. 44, sect. 7.
[2] *Eirenarcha* (1614), p. 370. He cites 4 Hen. VII, c. 12 (repealed S.L.R. Act, 1863). As to removal now, v. *post* § 23.
[3] For the meaning of this v. *ante* p. 138, *n.* 2.
[4] *Eirenarcha*, 630, 631.   [5] 1 Burr. 556.

ABUSE BY JUSTICES OF THE PEACE 225

be left to his ordinary legal remedy by indictment[1]. This then is the test. It will not help the applicant to show that the act was not strictly right[2], and that apparently is the rule whether the Justice's conduct be challenged by information or by indictment[3].

§ 21. *Indictment.* There is little to add to what has been said on this in the preceding section, which shows that an indictment is less hampered in the evidence required to support it than an application for an information is. But examples of conviction on such an indictment are not easy to find[4], and *R. v. Skinner* throws doubt on the very existence of the remedy. There, a motion to quash an indictment against a Justice of the Peace for scandalous words spoken by him to a grand jury at general sessions was successful. He called them seditious, scandalous, corrupt, and perjured. LORD MANSFIELD thought the words extremely improper and that if the party were a borough Justice this might have been a ground for applying to the Lord Chancellor to get him removed; but that to go on an indictment would be subversive of all ideas of a constitution[5]. The distinction may, however, be taken that the Justice was here acting at general, not Petty, Sessions[6].

Criminal remedies. Excess of jurisdiction

§ 22. Here again the proceedings may be by information or indictment, and if the former be selected, it must be clearly shewn that the Justice of the Peace acted illegally, oppressively, or corruptly, and not from mere mistake, or error of judgment[7].

It has been said that fraud or misconduct of Justices at Quarter Sessions may ground a criminal proceeding against them, and that there have been instances in which a criminal

---

[1] *R. v. Palmer* (1761), 2 Burr. 1162. So too *R. v. Jackson* (1787), 1 T.R. 653.

[2] *Per* PATTESON J. in *Ex parte Fentiman* (1834), 2 A. & E. at p. 129.

[3] ABBOTT C.J. in *R. v. Borron* (1820), 3 B. & Ald. 430, at p. 434.

[4] In *R. v. Constable* (note to *Caudle* v. *Seymour* (1841), 1 Q.B. at p. 894), a Justice was fined £100 for illegally sentencing a party when neither he nor his witnesses were before the Justice. But it does not appear whether the proceedings were by information or indictment. And could such an act be regarded as within his jurisdiction at all?

[5] (12 Geo. III), Lofft 55.   [6] See § 22 *post.*

[7] Short & Mellor, *Crown Office Practice* (ed. 1908), p. 158, and cases there cited.

W.L.P.

226 ABUSE BY JUSTICES OF THE PEACE

information has been granted against them in such circumstances[1]. The reports exemplify applications for such an information[2], and in one case at least the applicant was successful[3]. But its grant has been much commoner against magistrates for acts done in Petty Sessions[4], such as illegal and corrupt discharge of a person committed as a vagrant[5], or rejection of bail (otherwise sufficient) on the ground of the character or opinions of the bail[6]. But the party complaining cannot get an information against a Justice of the Peace for improperly convicting him, unless he make an exculpatory affidavit that he is innocent[7].

An information will be granted against Justices of the Peace, not for mere refusal to grant a licence but, for a corrupt motive in such refusal, e.g. because the applicants would not exercise their Parliamentary vote in the way in which the Justices desired[8]. So too where an improper grant of the licence has been made, for the mischief is infinitely greater here in that it may injure the whole community, whereas an improper refusal only affects the applicant[9].

Justices of the Peace have been convicted on indictment for illegal acts, and here it has been held that absence of corruption is no defence, though it may be to an application for an extraordinary remedy like an information[10].

Other remedies

§ 23. A Justice of the Peace may be removed from office by a writ of discharge under the great seal, or by a writ of *supersedeas* similarly authenticated. The latter suspends the power of all the Justices concerned, but does not totally destroy it[11].

---

[1] LORD KENYON C.J. in *R. v. Seton* (1797), 7 T.R. 373.
[2] *R. v. Shrewsbury Justices* (1733), 2 Barnard 272. *R. v. Eyres* (1733). *Ibid.* 250. *R. v. Seaford Justices* (3 Geo. III), 1 W. Bl. 432. *R. v. Davie* (1781), 2 Dougl. 588.
[3] *R. v. Phelps* (1757), 2 Ld Kenyon 570.
[4] *R. v. Mather* (1733), 2 Barnard. 250.
[5] *R. v. Brooke* (1788), 2 T.R. 190.
[6] *R. v. Badger* (1843), 4 Q.B. 468.
[7] *R. v. Webster* (1789), 3 T.R. 388. See Crown Office Rules (1906), r. 37, and r. 36. Short & Mellor, *Crown Office Practice* (ed. 1908), pp. 161–162.
[8] *R. v. Williams* (1762), 3 Burr. 1317. *R. v. Hann* (1765), *ibid.* 1716, 1786.
[9] *R. v. Holland* (1787), 1 T.R. 692.
[10] *R. v. Sainsbury* (1791), 4 T.R. 451. ASHURST J. at p. 457.
[11] Bl. *Comm.* 1. 353.

BRIBERY

Time limitation for proceedings

§ 24. It must be added that the time limitation of six months under the Public Authorities Protection Act, 1893, applies to proceedings against Justices of the Peace[1].

BRIBERY

§ 25. This is the offence committed by a judge or other person concerned in the administration of justice, who takes any undue reward to influence his behaviour in his office[2]. It appears at one time to have been confined to those "in a judicial place"[3]. Some examples of it have been given in a previous section[4]. It was an offence at Common Law. Thus, in *R.* v. *Steward*[5], *A* paid £5 to *B* to vote for Steward's election as an alderman, and an information was granted against all three, for the offence was against public policy and concerned an office which, in addition to its other duties, involved those of a Justice of the Peace. The punishment is forfeiture of the offender's office, fine, and imprisonment[6], and those who offer a bribe, though it be refused, are just as amenable to these penalties as those who accept it[7].

A statute (repealed in modern times for no apparent reason) required certain judicial officers to be sworn not to appoint any Justice of the Peace, sheriff, or other royal officer for any gift, brocage, favour, or affection[8]. But another ancient statute, still in force on this point, inflicts on any one who sells, takes or promises a reward for, any office concerning the administration or execution of justice, forfeiture of the office or of the nomination thereto, and disables the giver of the reward or promise from enjoying such office[9]. And this disablement has been held to be permanent[10]. The statute has been construed to apply to the chancellor, register, and commissary in ecclesi-

---

[1] *Ante* § 11.

[2] Bl. IV. 139. This has been adopted as a definition in preference to the clumsier ones given by Coke (3 Inst. 145) and Hawkins (1 P.C. ch. 67, sect. 1, 2). For the history, see St. H.C.L. III. 250–255.

[3] Coke and Hawkins, *ubi sup.*   [4] *Ante* § 8.   [5] (1831), 2 B. & Ad. 12.

[6] Which may be with hard labour. 4 & 5 Geo. V. c. 58, sect. 16 (1).

[7] 1 Hawk. P.C. ch. 67, sect. 6. Bl. IV. 139.

[8] 12 Rich. II. c. 2. Repealed 34 & 35 Vict. c. 48.

[9] 5 & 6 Ed. VI. c. 16, sect. 2.

[10] *R.* v. *Bishop of Norwich* (undated), Hobart 75.

228 EXTORTION

astical Courts, on the ground that the jurisdiction of such Courts is not merely *pro salute animarum*, but extends to legitimation, matrimony, and legacies, and that they are therefore Courts of Justice[1]. Much of this ground has been cut away owing to the transfer of most of these matters to other jurisdictions, but the general tendency of modern criminal law against bribery of any sort may well be invoked to supply a fresh *ratio decidendi*.

Offices in fee are outside the statute.

EXTORTION

§ 26. This is distinguished by Coke from Bribery in that it extends also to ministerial officers, and is not confined to judicial officers[2]. Broadly, it signifies any oppression under colour of right. More strictly, it means the taking of money by any officer, by colour of his office, where what is demanded is not due at all, or is not yet due, or is more than is due. It is punishable at Common Law by fine and imprisonment[3], and by removal from the office in the execution of which it is committed[4].

---

[1] *Trevor's Case* (8 Jac. I), Cro. Jac. 269.
[2] 3 Inst. 147.
[3] Which may be with hard labour. 4 & 5 Geo. V. c. 58, sect. 16 (1).
[4] 1 Hawk. P.C. ch. 68, sect. 1, 5.

CHAPTER VIII

PREVENTIVE PROCEEDINGS

ARRANGEMENT OF CHAPTER

§ 1. There are certain means by which abuse of legal procedure can be prevented altogether or at least stopped very soon after it has begun. These are extremely useful where civil procedure is concerned, mainly of course in the interest of the persons attacked, but also in a secondary degree in the interest of monomaniacs who would otherwise fritter away their money in foolish litigation. The subject may be handled in the following way:

(i) Criminal procedure.

(ii) Civil procedure:

    (a) The Vexatious Actions Act, 1896.

    (b) Summary interference of the Court:

        (1) In virtue of its inherent jurisdiction.

        (2) Under the Rules of the Supreme Court.

(iii) The writ of prohibition.

CRIMINAL PROCEDURE

§ 2. The two chief modes of accusation of a crime (other than one punishable on summary conviction) are information and indictment. There is little likelihood of any abuse of the former which is under the control of Crown officials. But indictments can be initiated by private persons, and such restrictions as exist on their freedom to make this kind of accusation are unsatisfactory, not in their essence but, in their limited scope.

The Vexatious Indictments Act, 1859[1], sect. 1 enacts that no bill of indictment for any of the offences mentioned below shall be presented to, or found by, any grand jury[2], unless: (1) the prosecutor or other person presenting the indictment has been bound over to prosecute or to give evidence against the accused; or (2) the accused has been committed to, or detained in, custody, or has been bound over to appear to answer such

---

[1] 22 & 23 Vict. c. 17.   [2] V. *post* p. 235.

230 CRIMINAL PROCEDURE

indictment; or (3) such indictment for such offence, if charged to have been committed in England, be preferred by the direction or with the consent in writing of a judge of the High Court, or of the Attorney-General or Solicitor-General, or, if charged to have been committed in Ireland, by the like direction or consent of a judge of the Supreme Court in Ireland or of the Attorney-General or Solicitor-General in Ireland, or in the case of an indictment for perjury by the direction of any Court, Judge, or public functionary, authorized by the Criminal Procedure Act, 1851[1], to direct a prosecution for perjury.

The offences within the scope of this Act, unhappily illustrate the application of a wholesome principle in a hesitating and niggardly fashion. There is no reason why it should not have included all indictable offences. In fact, it was limited to: (1) Perjury and subornation of perjury[2]. (2) Conspiracy. (3) Obtaining money or other property by false pretences. (4) Keeping a gambling or a disorderly house. (5) Any indecent assault.

If, as appears to have been the fact, the framers of the Act wished to restrain the promotion of indictments for particularly scandalous offences, there were plenty such (e.g. forgery) omitted from the Act. And the absurdity of such omissions was shewn by a judicial decision that an attempt to obtain money by false pretences did not fall within the Act, though the actual obtaining of course does[3]. But the point need not be laboured. The mistake was to make any attempt to earmark one offence more than another as "scandalous." The true principle ought to have been to wipe out the anomaly that "in this country any one and every one may accuse any one else, behind his back and without giving him notice of his intention to do so, of almost any crime whatever"[4].

The later history of the Act is exactly what one might have expected it to be, for it resembles statutory amendment of the law in many another direction,—a series of half-hearted and sporadic extensions of a principle maimed at its birth by an unsound limitation and even then not consistently applied. In

---

[1] 14 & 15 Vict. c. 100. Repealed and re-enacted on this point by the Perjury Act, 1911 (1 & 2 Geo. V. c. 6).

[2] Repealed and re-enacted by the Perjury Act, 1911, *supra*.

[3] *R. v. Burton* (1875), 13 Cox 71. [4] St. H.C.L. I. 293.

CRIMINAL PROCEDURE   231

the course of some sixty years, eight small groups of offences—
apparently (but by no means certainly) those regarded as especially scandalous—have been added to the Act. These are: (1) All
misdemeanours under Part II of the Debtors Act, 1869 (32 & 33
Vict. c. 62, sect. 18) and the Bankruptcy Act, 1914 (4 & 5
Geo. V, c. 59, sect. 164). (2) All libels or alleged libels (44 & 45
Vict. c. 60, sect. 6). (3) All misdemeanours under the Criminal
Law Amendment Act, 1885 (48 & 49 Vict. c. 69, sect. 17).
(4) All indictable offences under the Merchandise Marks Act,
1887 (50 & 51 Vict. c. 28, sect. 13). (5) Offences under the
Prevention of Corruption Act, 1906 (6 Ed. VII. c. 34, sect. 2 (2)).
(6) Offences under the Punishment of Incest Act, 1908 (8 Ed.
VII. c. 45, sect. 4 (1)). (7) Misdemeanours under Part II of
the Children Act, 1908 (8 Ed. VII. c. 67, sect. 35). (8) Any
felony under the Defence of the Realm (Amendment) Act, 1915
(5 Geo. V. c. 34, sect. 1 (4)). In Offences under (5) and (6),
the sanction of the Attorney-General is also required, unless
in cases under (6) the prosecution is commenced by the Director
of Public Prosecutions[1].

As will be seen shortly, grand juries were suspended during
the war[2], so that for the time being a private person cannot
abuse an indictment through their agency. If the suspension
becomes permanent, an abuse will be wiped out by destruction
of the thing abused, and we shall owe to the accident of a war
a change in the law which itself produces an accidental reform.

Justices of the Peace sitting in, and acting for, one petty
sessional division of a county make a sufficient committal for
the purposes of this Act if they commit for trial on a charge
in another petty sessional division of the same county, for
county Justices have jurisdiction throughout the county[3].

If the mode adopted of complying with sect. 1 of the Act
be the obtaining of a Judge's written consent to the prosecution,
the section is satisfied if there be no previous summons or notice
to the party accused, or even if there be no affidavit of the facts[4].

In considering the sufficiency of a recognizance to prosecute

[1] 6 Ed. VII. c. 34, sect. 2 (1). 8 Ed. VII. c. 45, sect. 6.
[2] *Post* p. 235.
[3] *R. v. Beckley* (1887), 20 Q.B.D. 187, 190.
[4] *R. v. Bray* (1862), 3 B. & S. 255.

232   CRIMINAL PROCEDURE

under sect. 1, reference may be made to the accompanying depositions to ascertain particulars of the offence to be charged[1].

The *fiat* of the Attorney-General may be issued even where magistrates have already refused to commit for trial[2], and, in any event, it is unnecessary to produce and prove the *fiat* for presentment of an indictment under sect. 1. It is enough that it has been deposited with the Clerk of the Court of trial[3]. Nor need the performance of any of the conditions in the Act appear upon the record or be proved before the petty jury. Indeed it would be very inconvenient if the rule were otherwise, for the performance of such conditions might then be put in issue, and it would be necessary in every case within the Act for the petty jury to decide whether the accused had been committed or bound over to answer the indictment[4].

Where a prisoner was committed upon one charge only of false pretences, but an indictment was preferred containing a second charge for which no leave as required by sect. 1 had been obtained, and was found by the grand jury, it was held that the part of the indictment which related to the second charge should have been quashed[5].

On a charge of conspiracy against three persons, the prosecutors were bound over to prosecute and the accused to appear at the next session, and an indictment was there found, and the defendant surrendered, but trial was postponed and the recognizances respited till the next sessions because a material witness was absent. Before the next sessions, the Solicitor-General directed an indictment for conspiracy against the three defendants and a fourth person, which indictment was found against all four. It was held that the indictment had been preferred with the proper authority and that the recognizances had been duly entered into, as the charge on which the defendants were tried was the same as that to which their recognizances related[6].

---

[1] *R.* v. *Bell* (1871), 12 Cox 37.   [2] *R.* v. *Rogers* (1902), 66 J.P. 825.
[3] *R.* v. *Dexter* (1899), 19 Cox 360. Cf. *R.* v. *Metz* (1915), 84 L.J. (K.B.) at p. 1464.
[4] *Knowlden* v. *R.* (1864), 9 Cox 483. COCKBURN C.J. at p. 488.
[5] *R.* v. *Fuidge* (1864), 9 Cox 430. See however the Criminal Law Amendment Act, 1867, sect. 1, *post* p. 235.
[6] *Knowlden* v. *R.* (1864), 5 B. & S. 532. As to exercise of the magistrate's discretion, see *R.* v. *Bennett* (1908), 72 J.P. 362.

CRIMINAL PROCEDURE

Sect. 2 of the Vexatious Indictments Act, 1859, provides that, where any charge or complaint shall be made before a Justice of the Peace that any person has committed an offence to which the Act applies within the jurisdiction of the Justice, who refuses to commit or to bail the person accused for trial, then if the prosecutor desire to prefer an indictment for the offence, the Justice must take the recognizance of such prosecutor to prosecute, and transmit it and the information and depositions, if any, to the Court in which such indictments ought to be preferred in the same manner as the Justice would have done if he had committed the accused for trial.

There has been some litigation as to what is a refusal to commit within this section. It has been held that dismissal of a *bonâ fide* charge of a substantial character on the ground that there is lack of evidence to support it is a refusal to commit within this section, and that the prosecutor may require the Justice of the Peace to take his recognizance to prosecute in such circumstances[1].

Where the magistrate committed the accused for trial for certain offences and no further evidence was called in respect of other charges, the magistrate neither being asked to commit, nor expressing any opinion on them, but counts were subsequently added to the indictment in respect of such other charges, it was held that these facts amounted to a refusal to commit, and the counts thus added were quashed. Sect. 1 of the Act had not been satisfied; nor had there been any binding over to prosecute as required by sect. 2, apparently because the prosecutor had expressed no desire to prefer an indictment[2].

The magistrate cannot be compelled under sect. 2 to take the recognizance of the prosecutor where what is charged is obviously not an indictable offence of any sort, e.g. a charge of conspiracy against members of either House of Parliament for making false statements in the House[3].

If a prosecutor is bound over under sect. 2, but fails to send up a bill to the grand jury, at the sessions for which he is bound

---

[1] *R.* v. *Lord Mayor of London. Ex parte Gostling* (1886), 16 Cox 77.
[2] *R.* v. *Coyne* (1905), 69 J.P. 151. The case might have been more clearly reported.   [3] *Ex parte Wason* (1869), L.R. 4 Q.B. 573.

234 CRIMINAL PROCEDURE

over, before that body is discharged, the Court cannot enlarge his recognizances till the next sessions[1].

The section does not apply until after a summons or warrant has been granted[2].

As has repeatedly happened in the history of abuse of legal procedure, the remedy devised by the Act of 1859 was itself twisted into an abuse. Delay and inconvenience in the working of the criminal law often occurred, because it was objected at the trial of a prisoner that he had either not been charged with, or had not been committed for, the precise offence stated in the indictment, although the depositions clearly shewed that the charge made in the indictment was materially the same as that which had been investigated by the magistrates. This was remedied by the Criminal Law Amendment Act, 1867[3], sect. 1 of which provides that sect. 1 of the Vexatious Indictments Act, 1859, shall not prevent the presentment to, or finding by, a grand jury[4] of any bill of indictment containing a count or counts for any of the offences in the said Act if such counts may[5] be lawfully joined with the rest of such bill, and if the count or counts be founded (in the opinion of the Court before which the bill be preferred) upon the facts disclosed in any examinations or depositions taken before a Justice of the Peace in the presence of the accused, and transmitted to such Court. Nor shall the Act of 1859 prevent the presentment or finding of any bill of indictment if such bill be presented with the consent of the Court in which it may have been preferred[6].

Getting the consent of the Court under the latter part of this section is not a mere formality and counts must be quashed if it has been obtained on material insufficient for the exercise of the Court's discretion[7]. Consent is not needed for the addition of counts for offences within the Vexatious Indictments Act before the bill is presented to the grand jury, if the facts on

---

[1] *R. v. Eayres* (1900), 64 J.P. 217.

[2] *R. v. Bather* (1880), 42 L.T. 532.

[3] 30 & 31 Vict. c. 35.   [4] V. *post* p. 235.

[5] The word "now" which follows has been expunged by 5 & 6 Geo. V. c. 90, sect. 9.

[6] Cf. *R. v. Brown* [1895] 1 Q.B. 119. *R. v. Kopelewitch* (1905), 69 J.P. 216.

[7] *R. v. Bradlaugh* (1882), 15 Cox 156.

CRIMINAL PROCEDURE 235

which the counts are based appear upon the depositions[1]. But if the added counts be embarrassing, the Court can apparently refuse to allow evidence to be given in support of them[2].

The Indictments Act, 1915[3], provides that nothing in the Act shall prevent an indictment being open to objection if it contravenes or fails to comply with the Vexatious Indictments Act, 1859, as amended by the Criminal Law Amendment Act, 1867, or any other enactment; but that it shall not be open to objection under these Acts on the ground that a count is joined with the rest of the indictment which could not at the time of the passing of the Criminal Law Amendment Act be lawfully joined, if that count can be lawfully joined under the law for the time being in force.

Where a person is acquitted of an offence included in the Act of 1859 for which he has been indicted without having been committed to, or detained in, custody, or bound by recognizance to answer the indictment, the Court before which he is acquitted may order the prosecutor to pay the whole or any part of the costs of defence (including any proceedings before the examining Justices) as taxed by the proper officers of the Court[4]. Grand juries were suspended by the Grand Juries (Suspension) Act, 1917, until six months after the termination of the war[5]. But the Act safeguards an accused person against vexatious indictments by providing that where he has been committed for trial, or where the written consent or direction of a judge of the High Court, or of the Attorney-General or Solicitor-General for the presentment of an indictment has been given, but in no other case, an indictment may be presented without having been found by a grand jury, and that in such case the Court may authorize the addition of other counts to the indictment, or the presentment of any further indictment against the accused, if such counts or indictment are founded

[1] R. v. Clarke (1895), 59 J.P. 248.
[2] R. v. Harris (1900), 64 J.P. 360. It is apparently necessary to get consent where it is desired to prefer a fresh bill of indictment, whether it charge offences disclosed on the depositions or not, as is the practice of the Central Criminal Court. R. v. Crabbe (1895), 59 J.P. 247.
[3] 5 & 6 Geo. V. c. 90, sect. 7.
[4] Costs in Criminal Cases Act, 1908 (8 Ed. VII. c. 15), sect. 6 (2).
[5] 7 Geo. V. c. 4.

236 CIVIL PROCEDURE

on facts disclosed in any examination or deposition taken before a Justice of the Peace in the presence of the accused. And where a person is bound by recognizance to prosecute the accused who is not committed for trial, the recognizance must require him to get the consent of the High Court or of the Attorney-General or Solicitor-General to present an indictment. If such consent be refused, the recognizance shall be void[1].

CIVIL PROCEDURE
The Vexatious Actions Act, 1896

§ 3. By this Act, if the Attorney-General satisfies the High Court that any person has habitually and persistently instituted vexatious legal proceedings without any reasonable cause, whether in the High Court or in an inferior Court, and whether against the same person or different persons, the Court may, after hearing such person or giving him an opportunity of being heard, order that he shall institute no legal proceedings in any Court, without the leave of the High Court or some judge thereof obtained after satisfying the High Court or such judge that such legal proceeding is not an abuse of the process of the Court, or that there is *primâ facie* ground for such proceeding[2].

It appears from a case decided shortly after the Act passed, that some such safeguard against foolish litigation was urgently needed. Within the five years preceding the Act, a person had brought 48 civil actions against the Speaker of the House of Commons, the Archbishop of Canterbury, the Lord Chancellor and others. With a single exception, not one of these actions had been successful. Some of them had been dismissed, some stayed as vexatious, some were still pending. The Court made the order required, laying down the rule that the number, general character, and result, of the actions brought must be taken into account[3]. It need scarcely be added that the number need not reach anything like the figure in this case in order to justify the Court's interference. In another decision, only five actions had been brought, but every one of them had been stayed and one of

---

[1] 7 Geo. V. c. 4, sects. 1 (2) and 1 (3).
[2] 59 & 60 Vict. c. 51, sect. 1.
[3] *Re Chaffers* (1897), 45 W.R. 365. 76 L.T. 351.

CIVIL PROCEDURE 237

them had been dismissed as frivolous and vexatious, and there was evidence that the plaintiff had no money, and merely desired to force the defendants to spend their own[1]. The power under the Act is wider than that inherent in the jurisdiction of the Court so far as actions are concerned, but narrower with regard to persons. Apart from the Act, the Court can stay one particular action only, or all applications of any sort in such action. Under the Act a stop can be put upon litigation generally, but it is only on the application of the Attorney-General that this is possible, whereas any litigant can ask the Court to exercise its summary powers of dealing with vexatious litigation.

"Legal proceedings" in the Act have been construed not to include criminal proceedings. Therefore an order under the Act will bar neither an application to a magistrate for a summons upon a sworn information, nor the presentment of an indictment[2]. This conclusion was reached only after a division of opinion in the Court below, and its affirmation in the Court of Appeal was also weakened by a dissenting judgment. There was some examination of the policy of extending the Act to criminal proceedings, but it is of little moment whether it ought to have been so extended or not. If it had been, it would not have achieved the object so imperfectly conceived by the legislature in the Vexatious Indictments Act, 1859[3]. What ought to be made impossible is the entire freedom (apart from that Act) of any person to accuse another before a grand jury. That would not have been effected by making the Vexatious Actions Act applicable to criminal proceedings, for it would not have struck at the root of the abuse. It would only mean that, after a man had already made a number of groundless accusations, he could be stopped from making any more. What would be the use of gagging him when he would have already done incalculable mischief by indulging in lying accusations of innocent persons? The evil is not merely that the victims of a Titus Oates may be gone beyond recall, but that irreparable

[1] *In re the Vexatious Actions Act (In re Jones)* (1902), 18 T.L.R. 476.
[2] *In re Boaler* [1914] 1 K.B. 122. [1915] 1 K.B. 21.
[3] *Ante* § 2.

238 SUMMARY INTERFERENCE OF THE COURT:

damage may have been done to a man's reputation merely by an accusation, though that accusation is at once rejected by a grand jury. What is really needed is to prevent the institution of the first prosecution, and that could be done much better by extending the Vexatious Indictments Act to all indictable offences than by applying the Vexatious Actions Act to all proceedings. A dozen vexatious actions against a man will not do him one tithe the harm that one vexatious prosecution may do.

SUMMARY INTERFERENCE OF THE COURT
(1) INHERENT JURISDICTION

§ 4. There is a power inherent in the jurisdiction of every Court of justice to protect itself from abuse of its own procedure[1]. In the High Court this certainly exists independently of Rules of the Supreme Court, and apparently other Courts possess it apart from anything of the sort which may have been conferred upon them by enactment. Hence, the High Court may strike out frivolous and vexatious matter in a pleading[2]. And its inherent jurisdiction to dismiss an action is expressly reserved to it by the Judicature Act, 1873[3]. But it should be very sparingly exercised and only in very exceptional cases. It should not, for example, be applied merely because the story told in the pleadings is highly improbable[4]. It has been exercised where allowing an action to proceed would be merely vexatious and a waste of time and money, such as an action for libel against a state official in a matter wherein he obviously has absolute privilege[5]. An action by the father of an infant, ostensibly as his next friend but really brought for the sole object of extorting money, has been dismissed[6]; so too an action in which groundless allegations of fraud were made[7], and one which was sued to try a hypothetical case[8].

---

[1] EARL OF SELBORNE L.C. in *Metropolitan Bank Ld.* v. *Pooley* (1885), 10 App. Cas. at p. 214. *Norman* v. *Matthews* (1916), 85 L.J. (K.B.) 857, 859, 861.
[2] *Reichel* v. *Magrath* (1889), 14 App. Cas. 665.   [3] Sect. 24 (5).
[4] LORD HERSCHELL in *Lawrence* v. *Norreys* (1890), 15 App. Cas. at p. 219.
[5] *Chatterton* v. *Secretary of State for India* [1895] 2 Q.B. 189, 191. Cf. *Salaman* v. *Secretary of State for India* [1906] 1 K.B. 613.
[6] *Huxley* v. *Wootton* (1912), 29 T.L.R. 132.
[7] *Lawrence* v. *Norreys* (1888), 39 Ch. Div. 213. Affirmed 15 App. Cas. 210.
[8] *Glasgow Navigation Co.* v. *Iron Ore Co.* [1910] A.C. 293.

INHERENT JURISDICTION 239

This Common Law power is a useful adjunct to the statutory power, for it has the advantage that in its exercise all the facts can be examined and evidence can be laid before the Court on affidavit[1] or otherwise[2].

If repeated frivolous applications have been made to the Court by the same parties, they may be ordered to make no further application without its leave[3].

Again, the Court has inherent jurisdiction to prevent any proceeding before it from being made the vehicle for scandal or impertinence by ordering it to be amended or struck out[4]; and it seems to be immaterial whether the attention of the Court be drawn to the scandalous matter by a motion of the Court, by a party to the action who is not injured, or even by a mere stranger[5]. But charges of the most offensive kind may be inserted in pleadings if they are relevant to the issue. If they are irrelevant, they become scandalous[6].

Courts other than the High Court seem to have a similar inherent jurisdiction. At any rate it has been decided that a County Court judge to whom an action has been transferred under 30 & 31 Vict. c. 142, sect. 10 (now replaced by 51 & 52 Vict. c. 43, sect. 66) has power to stay proceedings until the plaintiff has paid the costs of a previous action brought by him in the High Court against the same defendant[7]; and the later decision that he is able, quite apart from his statutory power under the County Courts Act, 1888, sect. 164, to stay or to dismiss an action which is frivolous and vexatious was put on a ground broad enough to be of general application[8].

---

[1] *Willis* v. *Howe* [1893] 2 Ch. 545, 551, 554.

[2] *Critchell* v. *L. & S.W.R. Co.* [1907] 1 K.B. 860.

[3] *Grepe* v. *Loam* (1887), 37 Ch. Div. 168. *Kinnaird* v. *Field* [1905] 2 Ch. 306.

[4] *Re Miller* (1884), 54 L.J. Ch. 205.

[5] *Cracknall* v. *Janson* (1879), 11 Ch. Div. 1, 13.

[6] MALINS V.-C. in *Rubery* v. *Grant* (1872), L.R. 13 Eq. at p. 447. *Millington* v. *Loring* (1880), 6 Q.B.D. at p. 196. *Blake* v. *Albion Life Assurance Society* (1876), 45 L.J. (C.P.), 663.

[7] *R.* v. *Bayley* (1882), 8 Q.B.D. 411.

[8] *Norman* v. *Matthews* (1916), 85 L.J. (K.B.) 857. By Ord. VIII, r. 2 of C.C. Rules, he can stay proceedings where several actions are brought by different plaintiffs in respect of the same cause of action.

240 SUMMARY INTERFERENCE OF THE COURT:

SUMMARY INTERFERENCE OF THE COURT
(2) RULES OF THE SUPREME COURT

§ 5. By Order XXV, r. 4, the Court may order any pleading to be struck out on the ground that it discloses no reasonable cause of action or answer, and in any such case, or in case of the action or defence being shown by the pleadings to be frivolous or vexatious, the Court may order the action to be stayed or dismissed or judgment to be entered accordingly, as may be just.

Independently of this, the Court can rely on its inherent jurisdiction to prevent abuse of its own procedure (*ante* § 4). But this rule considerably extends its powers by enabling it to stay an action on wider grounds than exist at Common Law. Thus, at Common Law, the Court informs itself by affidavits on an application of this kind[1], but in procedure under r. 4 affidavits are from the very terms of the rule inadmissible[2]. If the pleading is not bad on the face of it, but extrinsic evidence is needed to prove that it is, r. 4 does not apply[3].

There is nothing to prevent the same application being made under both the inherent jurisdiction and r. 4[4]. R. 4 is to be acted on only in plain and obvious cases, and the powers under it should be exercised with extreme caution[5]. Except in frivolous cases it was not intended that it should be a mere substitute for demurrers (which Ord. XXV, r. 1, abolished), and the Court will not entertain an application under it if the pleading raises an important question of law[6]. If a defendant wish to raise the question whether, assuming a statement of claim to be proved, it entitles the plaintiff to relief, and the case requires argument and careful consideration, he should proceed not under r. 4, but under Ord. XXV, r. 2, which entitles a party

---

[1] *Metropolitan Bank Ld.* v. *Pooley* (1885), 10 App. Cas. 210. LORD BLACKBURN at pp. 220–221.

[2] *Republic of Peru* v. *Peruvian Guano Co.* (1887), 36 Ch. Div. 489. CHITTY J. at p. 498.

[3] A. L. SMITH L.J. in *A.-G. of Duchy of Lancaster* v. *L. & N.W.R. Co.* [1892] 3 Ch. at p. 278.

[4] *Coxon* v. *Gorst* [1891] 2 Ch. at p. 71.

[5] SWINFEN EADY L.J. in *Moore* v. *Lawson* (1915), 31 T.L.R. at p. 419.

[6] *A.-G. of Duchy of Lancaster* v. *L. & N.W.R. Co.* [1892] 3 Ch. 274. COZENS-HARDY M.R. in *Dyson* v. *A.-G.* [1911] 1 K.B. at p. 414.

RULES OF THE SUPREME COURT   241

to raise by his pleading any point of law[1]. R. 4 is appropriate to cases in which any master or judge can say at once that the statement of claim as it stands is insufficient, even if proved, to entitle the plaintiff to what he asks[2]. Thus an action which involves a serious investigation of ancient law and questions of general importance is not within r. 4[3]. "The pleading will not be struck out unless it is demurrable and something worse than demurrable"[4]. And it cannot be said that there is "no reasonable cause of action," unless the Court is clear that the pleadings, either as they stand or with reasonable amendment, disclose no cause of action[5].

Examples of the application of r. 4 occur where an action in tort is brought against a trade union contrary to the Trade Disputes Act, 1906[6], or where the action is on a contract which either does not exist[7], or is legally unenforceable[8], or where the claim is barred by lapse of time[9], or is against the late directors and official liquidator of a company which has been wound up[10].

Again, an action is frivolous or vexatious which makes solicitors or other persons parties to it without seeking relief against them[11], or which attempts to make the trustee in bankruptcy of a lunatic a defendant because he declines to prosecute a right of action vested in him[12].

[1] By r. 3, if the decision of that point substantially disposes of the whole action, the Court may dismiss the action.

[2] *Hubbuck* v. *Wilkinson* [1899] 1 Q.B. at p. 91.

[3] *Dyson* v. *A.-G.* [1911] 1 K.B. 410. Cf. *Wyatt* v. *Palmer* [1899] 2 Q.B. 106.

[4] CHITTY J. in *Republic of Peru* v. *Peruvian Guano Co.* (1887), 36 Ch. Div. at p. 496.

[5] *Woods* v. *Lyttleton* (1909), 25 T.L.R. 665. VAUGHAN WILLIAMS L.J. at p. 670. For staying an action with leave to amend, see *Smith* v. *Selwyn* [1914] 3 K.B. 98. Cf. *Richmond* v. *Branson* [1914] 1 Ch. 968.

[6] *Vacher & Sons Ld.* v. *London Society of Compositors* [1913] A.C. 107. The name of the trade union was struck out of the writ and subsequent proceedings on the ground that no reasonable cause of action was disclosed.

[7] *South Hetton Coal Co.* v. *Haswell Coal Co.* [1898] 1 Ch. 564.

[8] *Humphreys* v. *Polak* [1901] 2 K.B. 385.

[9] *Price* v. *Phillips* (1894), 11 T.L.R. 86.

[10] *Coxon* v. *Gorst* [1891] 2 Ch. 73. For a motion to stay an action which was held to be premature, see *Wright* v. *Prescot Urban Council* (1916), 30 T.L.R. 82.

[11] *Burstall* v. *Beyfus* (1884), 26 Ch. Div. 35.

[12] *Farnham* v. *Milward & Co.* [1895] 2 Ch. 730. For the form and mode of application under r. 4, see *Annual Practice*, 417.

W.L.P.   16

242   RULES OF THE SUPREME COURT

Order XIX, r. 27, establishes another mode of summary inter-ference by the Court, which may at any stage of the proceedings order to be struck out or amended any matter in any indorse-ment or pleading which may be unnecessary or scandalous, or which may tend to prejudice, embarrass, or delay the fair trial of the action, and may in such case, if it think fit, order the costs of the application to be paid as between solicitor and client.

An application under this rule may be combined with one under Ord. XXV, r. 4[1]. It should be made at Chambers by a summons for directions under Ord. XXX or by notice under r. 5 of that Order[2].

An example of scandalous matter occurs where a plaintiff alleges fraud, but in his reply states that he does not intend to ask for any relief on that ground[3].

As to matter that is embarrassing, the Courts seem to be disposed to interpret liberally the words, "fair trial of the action," and to hold that a pleading which tends to prejudice, embarrass, or delay the plaintiff at any stage of the proceedings in the action, not merely so as to prevent him from fairly trying at the actual trial but, so as to prevent him from ever trying on fair terms the real issue, would affect the fair trial of the action[4].

While mere prolixity in pleading is not embarrassment[5], setting out at great length immaterial documents is[6]. So is a defence to an action for defamation which alleges at length the defendant's own version of what he said, which differs materially from the words set out in the statement of claim[7]; so are allegations in a statement of claim repeated from a former statement of claim with a view to relitigating the question raised in it[8].

[1] *Mutrie* v. *Binney* (1887), 37 Ch. Div. at p. 617. *Republic of Peru* v. *Peruvian Guano Co.* (1887), 36 Ch. Div. 489 (where the application was framed alternatively).   [2] *Annual Practice*, 358–359.
[3] *Brooking* v. *Maudslay* 55 L.T. 343. Cf. *Smith* v. *British Insurance Co.* (1883), W.N. 232. *Lumb* v. *Beaumont* (1884), 49 L.T. 772.
[4] THESIGER L.J. in *Berdan* v. *Greenwood* (1878), 3 Exch. Div. at p. 256.
[5] *Heap* v. *Marris* (1877), 2 Q.B.D. 630, 633.
[6] *Davy* v. *Garrett* (1877), 7 Ch. Div. 473.
[7] *Rassam* v. *Budge* [1893] 1 Q.B. 571.
[8] *Knowles* v. *Roberts* (1888), 38 Ch. Div. 263. See too *Mudge* v. *Penge Urban Council* (1916), 85 L.J. Ch. 814.

WRIT OF PROHIBITION 243

A defence must be amended as embarrassing if it does not shew what it is that is admitted[1]. But pleadings are not necessarily embarrassing because they are inconsistent[2].

In a libel action, if there be payment into Court by the defendant with a denial of liability, there must be a specific statement as to that part of the cause of action in respect of which the payment is made; otherwise this may embarrass the plaintiff in ascertaining what he has to meet[3].

As a general rule, no appeal will be allowed from an order striking out a pleading as embarrassing[4], unless the judge below has acted on a wrong principle[5].

Security for costs of an appeal. Ord. LVIII, r. 15, enables the Court to direct the giving of this in special circumstances, e.g. where the contemplated appeal is presumptively an abuse or threatened abuse of procedure owing to the appellant's claim being substantially the same as that in a former action against the same defendants which was dismissed as frivolous[6].

WRIT OF PROHIBITION

§ 6. This writ, which is of very ancient origin, is designed to prevent inferior Courts from exceeding their jurisdiction. It issues from a Court of superior jurisdiction and is directed to the inferior Court to prevent it from usurping a jurisdiction which it does not possess[7].

---

[1] *British etc. Association Ld.* v. *Foster* (1888), 4 T.L.R. 574. *Stokes* v. *Grant* (1878), 4 C.P.D. 25.

[2] *Re Morgan* (1887), 35 Ch. Div. 492.

[3] *Fleming* v. *Dollar* (1889), 23 Q.B.D. 388. Cf. *Davis* v. *Billing* (1891), 8 T.L.R. 58. *Whitworth* v. *Darbishire*, 41 W.R. 317. 68 L.T. 216.

[4] *Golding* v. *Wharton Saltworks Co.* (1876), 1 Q.B.D. 374.

[5] *Watson* v. *Rodwell* (1876), 3 Ch. Div. 380.

[6] *Weldon* v. *Maples, Teesdale & Co.* (1887), 20 Q.B.D. 331.

[7] See Shortt, *Informations, Mandamus and Prohibition* (1887), Pt. IV. Shortt and Mellor, *Crown Off. Pract.* (1908), 252–269.

16—2

INDEX

Abuse of procedure. *See* Table of
  Contents
Accessory, 146
Addoubeurs, 147
Advertisement for stolen goods, 150
Affidavit, 143, 240
Agreements
  civil procedure, affecting, 140–145.
    See Civil Procedure, Main-
    tenance
  criminal, 146–157. *See* Com-
    pounding Offences, Main-
    tenance (criminal), Stifling
    Prosecution
  illegal, 95
  unlawful, 95
  void, 95
  See also Contracts, Stifling Prose-
    cution
Appeal
  accusation by, 118
  Commissioners of, 209
  criminal, 156
  security for costs of, 243
Arbitration, 141–143
  criminal cases, in, 155–156
Architect, 142
Army officers, 198, 206, 209–210,
  212
Arrest
  malicious, 202
  witness, of, 203
Assault, indecent, 230
Assignment of choses in action, 44–
  69. *See* Choses in Action
Association to prosecute felons, 173
Assurance, 144
Attorney. *See* Solicitor
Attorney-General, 230, 232, 235, 236

Bacon, Francis, 214
Bail
  indemnity for, 137, 172
  insufficient, 208–209
  judicial function, 221
  mainprise distinguished, 72
  refusal of, 226, 233
  sheriff, 139
Bailiff, 208, 209, 212
Bankrupt
  cannot sue maintenance, 3*n.*
Bankruptcy procedure
  contracts affecting, 140–141. *See*
    also Maintenance

Bankruptcy procedure (*contd.*)
  malicious, 199–201
  offences in, 231
  trustee in, 241
Baron, court, 209
Barratry, 114, 170
Barrister
  champerty, 27–28
  collusion, 116
  contempt, 28
  contracts, 104–106
  conveyance, 105
  deceit, 116
  exemption, 210
  fees, 104–106
  maintenance, 27–28, 43
Blood feud, 151
Bót, 151
Bribery, 214
Brocage, 227
Building contract, arbitration, 142

Campi partitio, 6
Ca. sa., maliciously suing, 199
Case, action upon, 41, 202, 203, 217
Censors of Royal College of Physicians, 209
Cestui que trust, 76
Champerty, 1–116
  agreement for, 12–15, 138. *See*
    Maintenance (contract)
  bonâ fides, 14. *See* Maintenance
    (motive)
  burden of proof, 90–93
  church, 95
  collateral agreement, 107
  conspiracy, 158
  contract, affecting, 94–111. *See*
    Maintenance (contract)
  criminal, 112–116
    abolition recommended, 112
    definition, 114. *See* Mainten-
      ance (criminal)
  defences to, 21–84. *See* Mainten-
    ance (defences)
  definition, 2, 114
  derivation, 6
  feoffment for, 15–17
  interference, what is. *See* Main-
    tenance (interference)
  mediaeval, 112
  motive, 14–15, 52–54
  plea, precedent of, 111*n.*
  precedent of plea, 111*n.*

INDEX

245

Champerty (*contd.*)
  proof, 90–93, 111
  purchase in good faith, 14
  remedies, 84–90, 111. *See* Maintenance (remedies)
  species of maintenance, 1
  tort, as a, 1 sqq.
    action, what is, 4–10
    corporation, 3–4
    India, 4
    interference, what is, 10–21
    locality, 4
    personal disabilities, 3–4
    proceedings capable of, 4–10
    status, 3–4
    suit, what is a, 4–10
    unaffected by 18 Eliz. c. 5, 157
    writ of, 1, 113n.
  See also Maintenance.
Chancellor
  ecclesiastical court, of, 227
  Lord, 215, 224, 225
  See also Officials
Chancery, maintenance of suit in, 6–7
Chapter, 77
Charity, defence to maintenance, 40–41
Children, 231
Choses in action, 44–69
  apprentice, assignment of, 51
  assignable
    by statute, 66
    not at first, 44
  assignment of, 44–69
    absolute, 54
  attorney, 52, 56–57
    letter of, 50
  bankrupt, 66–67, 68
  bankruptcy, trustee in, 57
  bill of exchange, 50
  champerty, 44–69
  consideration, 50
  covenant, 51, 55
  damages, unliquidated, 49, 69n.
  debt, 46, 48, 49
    judgment, 69
    uncertain, 51. *See also* 49, 67, 69n.
  dilapidations, 57
  entry, 46
  Equity, 49
  evidence, procuring, 59
  exchange, bill of, 50
  indemnity, 61–63
  information, 58
  insurance, 68
    marine, 54
  judgment debt, 69

Choses in action (*contd.*)
  King, 46–49, 69n.
  kinship, 60
  Lands Clauses Act, 55
  lease, 51, 55
  legacy, 55
  lien, 52
  litigation
    proceeds of, 56, 60
    right of, 55, 63
  maintenance, 44–69
  mixed, 47
  mortgage, 60–61
    of suit, 56, 57
  motive, 52
  obligation, 49–50
  personal, 47
  prize suit, 63
  property, 55
  real, 47
  recognizance, 48
  rent, 47
  security, 56
  shares, 64
  solicitor, 52, 56–57
  statute, assignable by, 66
  stranger
    gift to, 50
    sale to, 50
  subrogation, 68
  surety, 50
  title, making out, 59
  tort, action in, 67. *See also* 49, 69n.
  wardship, 47
Church. *See* Ecclesiastical
Civil procedure, contracts affecting, 140–145
  abroad, contract, 144, 145
  affidavit, answer to, 143
  arbitration, 141–143
  architect, 142
  assurance, 144
  attorney, 143
  bankruptcy, 140–141
  building contract, 142
  commitment, 144
  company
    shares, 142
    winding-up, 141
  conflict of laws, 145
  divorce, 144
  election petition, 143
  Equity, 141
  execution, 144
  foreign contract, 144, 145
  French law, 145
  indemnity, 144
  legal aid society, 144
  libel, 144

246 INDEX

Civil procedure, contracts affecting (*contd.*)
  petition, election, 143
  private international law, 145
  probate action, 144
  release of goods, 144
  shareholder, 141
  shares, 142
  solicitor, 143
  undue influence, 145
  winding-up of company, 141
  See also Champerty, Maintenance (contract)
Civil proceeding, malicious, 202
Clerks. *See* Officials
College of Physicians, 209
Collusion, 116
Combination. *See* Conspiracy
Commissary, ecclesiastical, 227
Commission, ecclesiastical, 209
Commissioners of Appeal, 209
Commitment, 144. *See* Contempt
Common barratry. *See* Barratry
Commoners, 73
Commons, House of, 210
Company
  forfeiture of shares, 142
  maintenance by, 3–4
  winding-up
    abuse of, 141
    petition, 201
  See also Corporation
Compounding offences, 146–157
  accessory, 146
  adoubbeurs, 147
  advertisement for goods, 150
  agreement unfulfilled, 147
  appeal, criminal, 156
  arbitration, 155–156
  conspiracy, 153
  court, assent of, 155–157
  definition, 151
  discontinuing prosecution, 154
  dogs, advertising for, 150
  felony, 146–153
  informer, 157
  judge, assent of, 155–157
  misdemeanour, 153–154
  misprision, 121–122, 147, 152
  "no questions asked," 150
  nolle prosequi, 154
  printer of advertisement, 150
  publisher of advertisement, 150
  redoubbors, 147
  "speaking with" prosecutor, 154–155
  stolen goods, reward for, 148–149
  stranger, 147
  theft-bote, 146–148, 151, 152

Compounding offences (*contd.*)
  third person, 147
  trustee, 157
  usual, once, 151, 153
  verdict, after, 156
  withdrawing prosecution, 154
  witness, 147
Composition. *See* Civil Procedure, Compounding Offences, Stifling Prosecution
Confederacy, 158, 160, 161, 163, 166, 167, 169
Conflict of laws, 145
Conspiracy
  criminal, 137*n.*, 212
  to abuse procedure, 158–173
    acquittal
      of accused, 160–165
      of one, 158
    agreement, mere, 159
    association to prosecute felons, 173
    bail, indemnity to, 172
    barratry, 170
    combination, 158–160
    confederacy, 158, 160, 161, 163, 166, 167, 169
    contempt, 172
    conviction of one, 157
    defences, 167–170
    falsity, 165–170
    ignoramus of indictment, 160–165
    indictment for, 167
    indictors, 167–168
    judge, 169
    jurors, 168–169
    Justice of Peace, 169, 170
    malice, 165–170
    motive, 173
    punishment, 173
    purpose, 170–173
    wife, 159
    witnesses, 169
  defeat justice, to, 153
  indictment for, 230, 232
  judgment, to defeat, 204
  maintenance, and, 20
  writ of, 202, 204
Consular court, 210
Contempt, 28, 115*n.*, 144, 172, 203
Contracts
  abroad, 145
  abusing legal procedure, 117–157. *See* Champerty, Choses in Action, Civil Procedure, Compounding Offences, Conspiracy, Maintenance, Stifling Prosecution

INDEX

247

Contracts (*contd.*)
affecting legal procedure otherwise than by champerty or maintenance, 117–157
champerty, affecting,12–15,94–111
civil procedure, affecting, 140–145. *See* Civil Procedure, Champerty, Conspiracy, Maintenance
collateral transactions, 96
criminal, 146–157. *See* Champerty, Compounding Offences, Conspiracy,Maintenance, Stifling Prosecutions
criminal procedure, affecting, 117–140
foreign, 106–107, 144, 145
illegal and void, 95
maintenance affecting, 10–12, 94–111, 114
penalized, 95–96
prosecutions, stifling, 117–140. *See* Stifling Prosecutions
restraining criminal procedure, 117–140
solicitors. *See* Solicitors
stifling prosecutions, 117–140. *See* Stifling Prosecutions
theft-bote, 117
undue influence. *See* Undue Influence
unlawful and void, 95
void and unlawful, 95
See also Champerty, Choses in Action, Civil Procedure, Compounding Offences, Conspiracy, Maintenance, Stifling Prosecutions
Coroner, 209, 213, 215
Corporation
maintenance, 3–4, 77
malicious prosecution, 199
Corruption
judicial, 214
offences, 231
Costs
prosecutor, payment by, 235
security for, 243
Counsel. *See* Barristers
County Council, London, 210
County Court
modern, 209, 213, 215, 221, 239
old, 208
Court
assent to compromise. *See* Compounding Offences, Stifling Prosecutions
baron, 209
collusion in, 116

Court (*contd.*)
Criminal Appeal, of, 156
ecclesiastical, 7, 199, 207, 209
hundred, 209, 212
inferior, 243
Inquiry, of, 206–207, 209–210
Martial, 198, 206, 210, 212
payment into, 243
power to prevent abuse of procedure, 238–243
prevention of abuse, inherent power of, 237, 238, 240
protection of. *See* Judicial Officers, Maintenance (defences), Malicious Prosecution
Rules of Supreme, 240–243
summary interference of, 238–243
Courtesy, defence to maintenance, 42–44
Creditors, 75
Crime
compounding. *See* Compounding Offences
duty to prosecute. *See* Stifling Prosecutions
Criminal Appeal, Court of, 156
Criminal conspiracy to abuse procedure. *See* Conspiracy (criminal)
Criminal procedure, contracts affecting, 117–140. *See also* Maintenance
Crown
choses in action of, 46–49, 69n.
judges removable by, 215
Customary court, 208

Dean, 77
Debtors' offences, 231
Deceit, 116, 202
Defence of Realm, 231
Demurrer, 240
Discharge, writ of, 226
Dismissing action, 240
Disorderly house, 230
Divorce
contract affecting, 144
maintenance, 10
Dozens, 167, 168
Durham, 209

Ecclesiastical commission, 209
Ecclesiastical court, 7, 199, 207, 209
Editor, contempt by, 172
Election petition, 7–8, 143
Embarrassing pleading, 242
Embesiler, 138
Embesill, 224
Embezzlement, derivation, 138n.
Embracery, 115n., 157

248 INDEX

Equity, arbitration, 141
Exchequer, malicious information, 199
Excommunication, malicious, 199
Execution
  contract affecting, 144
  wrongful, 209

False imprisonment, 174
False pretences, 230
Felons, prosecution of, 173. *See also* Compounding Offences, Misprision, Stifling Prosecutions
Felony
  compounding, 146–153
  misprision, 121–122, 152
  stifling. *See* Stifling Prosecutions
Feme covert. *See* Wife
Feoffment, champertous, 15–17
Fiat of Attorney-General, 232
Fi. fa., abuse of, 202
Friendship, defence to maintenance, 42–44
Frivolous pleading, 238–243

Gambling house, 230
General Medical Council, 211
Grand juries, 235

Habeas corpus, 215
House of Commons Committee, 210
Houses of Parliament, address by, 215
Hundred court, 209, 212
Husband and wife, conspiracy by, 159

Impeachment, 214
Imprisonment, false, 174
Incest, 231
Indecent assault, 230
Indemnity
  bail, for, 137, 172
  libel, 144
  sheriff, 139
  steward of court, 212
India, 4, 106, 176, 210
Indictment, vexatious, 229
Indictor
  conspiracy, 167–168
  malicious prosecution, 197
Inferior courts, 211, 243
Information, vexatious, 229
Informer, 157
Inherent power of court, 237, 238, 240
Inns of Court, 211
Inquiry, Court of, 209–210
Insurance, 54, 68, 144
International law, private, 145
Irish judges, 208

Johnson, Mr Justice, 215
Judges
  abuse of procedure by, 205, 228. *See also* Judicial Officers, Justices of Peace
  champerty, 95
  consent to prosecution, 230 sqq.
  consent to withdrawing prosecution, 155–157
  criminal conspiracy, 169
  maintenance, 95
Judgment, conspiracy to defeat, 204
Judicial officers
  abuse of procedure by, 205–228
  acts beyond jurisdiction, 211–212, 214–215, 225–226
  acts within jurisdiction, 205–215, 216–221, 224–225
  address by Parliament, 215
  Bacon, Francis, 214
  bail, 208–209
  bailiff, 208, 209, 212
  baron, court, 209
  behaviour, good, 215
  bishop, 209
  bribery, 214, 227, 228
  capacities, two, 208–209
  Censors of Royal College of Physicians, 209
  Chancellor
    ecclesiastical court, 227
    Lord, 215
  civil remedies, 205–214, 216–225
  College of Physicians, 209
  Commission, ecclesiastical, 209
  Commissioners of Appeal, 209
  Commons, Committee of House of, 210
  conspiracy, criminal, 212
  consular court, 210
  coroner, 209, 213, 215
  corruption, 207, 208, 214
  counsel, 210
  County Council, London, 210
  County Court, 208, 209, 213, 215
  County Palatine, 209
  court
    baron, 209
    hundred, 209, 212
    Inquiry, of, 206–207, 209–210
    Martial, 206, 210, 212
  criminal remedies, 214, 225–228
  Crown, removal by, 215
  customary court, 208
  delay, 215
  drunkenness, 215
  Durham, 209
  ecclesiastical
    commission, 209

INDEX

249

Judicial officers (*contd.*)
  ecclesiastical (*contd.*)
    court, 207, 209, 227–228
    excess of jurisdiction, 211, 214
    execution, taking, 209
    General Medical Council, 211
    good behaviour, 215
    habeas corpus, 215
    history of exemption, 206–208
    House of Commons Committee, 210
    hundred court, 209, 212
    impeachment, 214
    incompetence, 215
    indemnity, 212
    independence of, 205
    India, 210
    inferior, 206, 211, 216–227
    Inns of Court, 211
    Inquiry, Court of, 209–210
    intoxication, 215
    Irish, 208
    Johnson, Mr Justice, 215
    "judicial," meaning of, 210
    jurisdiction
      acts beyond, 211–212, 214–215, 225–226
      acts within, 205–215, 216–221, 224–225
      excess of, 211, 214
      proof of, 211
    jurors, 210
    Justice of Peace. *See* Justices of Peace
    London County Council, 210
    licensing meeting, 210
    Macclesfield, Earl of, 214
    magistrates
      Indian, 210
      Quarter Sessions, 208. *See* Justices of Peace
    malice, 205, 207, 210
    malicious prosecution, 198, 212
    Medical Council, General, 211
    military court, 206–207, 209–210, 212
    ministerial act, 211, 221
    misconduct, 213, 214, 215
    mistake, 210
    motive, 205, 207
    neglect, 213
    officers of court, 211
    Official Receiver, 209
    oppression, 228
    Palatine, County, 209
    Parliament, address by, 215
    Physicians, Royal College of, 209
    praemunire, 216
    presumption of jurisdiction, 211

Judicial officers (*contd.*)
  "privilege," 206
  probable cause, no, 207
  Quarter Sessions, 208
  quasi-judicial exemption, 211
  reason for exemption, 205–206
  reasonable cause, no, 207
  record, court of, 209, 210
  record, judges of, 206
  Recorder, 208
  Register in ecclesiastical court, 227
  remedies
    civil, 205–214, 216–225
    criminal, 214, 225–228
    other, 215, 226
  removal, 215, 228
  Returning Officer, 210
  Revising Barrister, 211
  Royal College of Physicians, 209
  Scots Law, 212
  selling office, 227
  sheriff, 208
  slander by, 207
  steward, 209, 212
  Stratton, Adam de, 214
  superior courts, 208, 211
  Supreme Court, 213
  Thorpe, William de, 214
  time limit for remedies, 216
  Vice-Chancellor, 209
  Weyland, Thomas de, 214
  who are, 208–211
  witnesses, 206–207, 210
  See also Judges, Justices of Peace
Jurors
  criminal conspiracy, 168
  exemption, 210
  grand, 235
  maintenance, 19, 20, 41–42, 115
  malicious prosecution, 197
Justices of Peace
  abuse of procedure by, 216–228
  action against, setting aside, 224
  Assize, Justice of, complaint to, 224
  bail, 221, 226
  battery, action of against, 217
  bribery, 227
  brocage, 227
  case, action upon, against, 217
  champerty, 108
  Chancellor, Lord, 224, 225
  civil liability, 216–224
  commission, putting out of, 224
  conviction by brother J.P., liability for, 223
    defective, 223
    malicious, 219
  costs, 221
  County Court, liability in, 221

250 INDEX

Justices of Peace, (*contd.*)
  criminal conspiracy, 169, 170
  criminal liability, 224–226
  discharge, writ of, 226
  discretion, 220–221
  "embesilling" indictment, 224
  execution of duty, 216
  extortion, 228
  extra-judicial remarks, 222
  false imprisonment, liability for, 217
  fraud, 225
  Indian, 210
  indictment against, 225, 226
  information against, 224–226
  judicial act, 221
  jurisdiction
    absence of, 222, 225
    acts within, 216–221
    excess of, 221–224, 225–226
    explained, 219
  King's Bench Division, rule of, 221
  license, 226
  malice, 216, 219, 221, 223
  malicious
    conviction, 219
    prosecution, 198, 218, 219
  ministerial act, 221
  misconduct, 225
  oppression, 228
  poor rate, 220
  probable cause, 216, 219, 223
  proceedings against, setting aside, 224
  punishment, illegal, 223
  rate, poor, 220
  reasonable cause, 216, 219, 223
  record, judge of, 217
  remarks, extra-judicial, 222
  remedies against,
    civil, 216–224
    criminal, 224–226
    other, 226
  removal, 224, 225, 228
  rule of King's Bench Division, 221
  scandalous words, 225
  sentence, illegal, 223
  slander, action of, against, 219, 225
  supersedeas, 226
  suspension, 226
  time limit for remedies, 227
  tort, action in, against, 216
  trespass, action of, against, 198, 217
  unqualified, 222
  vexatious indictments, 230, 231, 232, 234
  warrant, 222, 223
  See also Judges, Judicial Officers

King, assignment of choses in action, 46–49, 69n.
Kinship
  champerty, 28–31
  maintenance, 28–31

Legal aid society, 144
Libels, 231
License, 226
Licensing meeting, 210
Litigation, vexatious, 229–243. *See also* Preventive Proceedings
Livery, 34, 35, 38, 39
London County Council, 210
Lunacy proceedings, maintenance of, 8–10

Macclesfield, Earl of, 214
Magistrate. *See* Justices of Peace, Judicial Officers
Mainpernor, 71
Mainprise, 72
Maintenance, 1–116
  action, of unsuccessful, 80, 87, 116
  barristers, 27–28, 104–106
  bona fides. See Motive, *infra*
  bribery of jurors, 36, 38
  burden of proof, 90–93
  champerty, a species of, 1
  Chancellor, 95
  clerks, 95
  conspiracy, 20, 158
  contracts, affecting, 94–111
    abroad, 106–107
    barristers, 104–106
    Chancellor, 95
    choses in action. *See* Choses in Action
    clerks, 95
    defences, 109–111. *See* Defences, *infra*
    foreign, 106–107
    India, 106
    information, 108–109
    interference in legal proceedings, 107–109
    judges, 95
    persons, 94–106
    place, 106–107
    proof, 111
    remedies, 111
    sheriff, 95
    solicitor, 96–104
    status, 94–106
    Treasurer, 95
    See also Choses in Action, Champerty
  corporation, 3, 114
  counsel, 27–28, 104–106

INDEX

251

Maintenance (*contd.*)
  criminal, 112–116
    abolition recommended, 112*n.*
    acquittal of co-defendant, 116
    co-defendants, 116
    Common Law offence, 113
    contract, 114
    corporation, 114
    defences, 115–116. *See also* 21–
      84, 109–111, and Defences,
      infra
    definition, 113
    interest, 116
    motive, 114, 115
    plaintiff unsuccessful, 116
    servant, 115
    sheriff, 115
    statutes, 112
    trust, 115
  criminal proceedings, of, 79
  damage, special, 85
  defences, 21–84, 109–111, 115–116
    advice, 42–44
    assignment of choses in action.
      See Choses in Action
    attornies, 23–27, 96–104
    bail, 72
    barristers, 27–28, 35–36, 104–106
    brother, 29, 30, 31*n.*
    brother-in-law, 31*n.*
    burden of proof, 90–93
    cestui que trust, 76
    chapter, 77
    charity, 31*n.*, 40–41, 52, 84
    child, 28, 30
    choses in action. *See* Choses in
      Action
    commercial interest, 75
    common interest, 69–84, 109–
      111
    commoners, 31*n.*, 73
    compulsion by law, 41–42
    corporation, 77
    counsel, 27–28, 35–36, 104–106
    courtesy, 42–44
    cousin, 29*n.*, 30
    creditors, 75
    dean, 77
    duty, public, 79
    father, 28, 30
    friendship, 42–44
    godfather, 31*n.*
    guardian, 30*n.*
    heir, 31
    interest, 69–84, 109–111, 114, 116
      definition, 70–71
      public, 84
    jurors, 41–42
    kinship, 28–31, 60

Maintenance (*contd.*)
  defences (*contd.*)
    landlord, 31*n.*, 32
    legal help, 22–28, 35–36, 96–106
    lessor, 31*n.*, 32
    mainpernor, 71
    mainprise, 70
    master and servant, 31*n.*, 34–39,
      115
    mortgage, 77
    nephew, 31*n.*
    officials, 42
    parents, 28
    parishioners, 73
    poor, 40–41, 52
    poverty, 40–41, 52
    proof, 90–93
    public duty, 79
    public interest, 84
    religion, 75
    remainderman, 32
    reversioner, 31
    sentiment, 78
    servant and master, 31*n.*, 34–
      39, 115
    solicitors, 23–27, 52, 96–104
    son, 28, 30
    son-in-law, 29, 31*n.*
    surety, 71
    tenant, 32, 73
    tithe-payers, 73
    trade-union, 76, 109
    trustee, 76
    warranty, 33
    witness, 41
  defendant, assisting, 114
  definition, 1–2, 113
  election petition, 81
  failure of maintained action, 80
  interference in action, what is, 10–
    21, 107–109, 114–116
    advice, 20
    agreement, 10–12, 20
    assignment of debt, 20. *See also*
      Choses in Action
    defendant, assisting, 17–18
    evidence, 20
    feoffment, 15–17
    gift, 19
    innocent purchase, 13–17
    jurors, 19, 20
    loan, 19
    plaintiff, assisting, 17–18
    service, 19
  judges, 95
  jurors
    bribing of, 36, 38
    return of, 115
  loss of maintained action, 80

INDEX

252

Maintenance (*contd.*)
malicious prosecution, 11, 91
mediaeval, 83, 112
motive, 13–15, 52–54, 79, 114, 115
officials, 94
plaintiff, assisting, 114
plaintiff, unsuccessful, 116
plea, precedent of, 111*n.*
precedent of plea, 111*n.*
probable cause, 91–92
proof, 90–93, 111
prosecution, of, 79
purchase in good faith, 14
rarity in modern times, 2*n.*
reasonable cause, 91–92
remedies, 84–90, 111, 116
commitment, 90
contract, in, 111
criminal, 116
damages, 84–89
forfeiture, 89–90
injunction, 90
penalties, 89–90
writ, 90
servant and master, 34–39
sheriff, 95
solicitors, 22–27, 96–104
special damage, 85
statement of claim, 89*n.*
status, 3–4, 94–106, 114, 116
stifling prosecution, 118
success of maintained action, 80, 116
tort, as a, 1–93
action, what is, 4–10
bankrupt, 3*n.*
burden of proof, 90–93
Chancery, of suit in, 6–7
child, action for custody of, 8*n.*
company, 3–4
corporation, 3–4
defences. *See* Defences, *supra*
divorce, 10
ecclesiastical court, in, 7
election petition, 7–8
India, 4
information, 5
interference, what is, 10–21
locality, 4
lunacy proceedings, 8–10
malicious prosecution, and, 5–6, 11
penal action, 5
personal disabilities, 3–4
Prize Court, 8
proceeding, pending, 17
proceedings capable of interference, 4–10
proof, 90–93

Maintenance (*contd.*)
tort (*contd.*)
prosecution, maintenance of, 4–6
remedies, 84–90
status, 3–4
suit, what is, 4–10
unaffected by 18 Eliz. c. 5, 157
"unlawful," 82
writ of, 1
See also Champerty
Malice. *See* Judicial Officers, Maintenance, Malicious Prosecution, Motive
Malicious
action, 202
bankruptcy proceedings, 199–201
ca. sa., 199
causing arrest, 202
civil proceedings, 202
excommunication, 199
fi. fa., 202
information, 199
prosecution. *See* Malicious Prosecution
registration of order, 204
search warrant, 203
ship, arrest of, 199
winding-up petition, 201
Malicious prosecution, 174–204
acquittal, 181–187, 190, 191
certificate of, 187
copy of, 186
impossible, where, 199
probable cause, and, 190, 191
proof of, 185
army officers, 198
arrest
causing, 202
essential, 176
attending hearing, 177
bankruptcy
proceedings, 199–201
trustee, in, 177
belief in charge, 193
binding over, 176, 177
bonâ fide, where originally, 178
ca. sa., 199
cause, reasonable and probable, 187–196
certificate of acquittal, 187
character, suspicious, 194
charge sheet, signing, 175
charges, partly malicious, 196
civil proceedings, malicious, 202
committal by magistrate, 190
company, 201
conspiracy
judgment, to defeat, 204
writ of, 202, 204

INDEX

253

Malicious prosecution (*contd.*)
  contempt, 203
  conviction
    of graver offence, 184
    reversal of, 185
  coram non judice, 184
  corporations, 199
  counsel's opinion, 195
  court, functions of, 188, 192
  Court Martial, 198
  deceit, writ of, 202
  disbelief in charge, 193
  ecclesiastical court, 199
  essentials of, 174
  evidence
    acquittal, of, 185
    giving, 176
  Exchequer, 199
  excommunication, 199
  facts
    later, 194
    new, 194
  false imprisonment, 174
  false statement, 178
  falsity, 189
  favourable ending of prosecution,
    181–187
  fi. fa., abuse of, 202
  ignoring indictment, 181, 191
  imprisonment, false, 174
  incontrovertible proceedings, 185
  India, 176
  indictment
    copy of, 186
    defective, 183
    ignoring, 181, 191
    preferring, 178, 179
  indictor, 197
  judge, by, 212
  judge's functions, 188, 192
  judgment, conspiracy to defeat, 204
  judicial officer, 174
  juror, 197
  jury, functions of, 188, 192, 197
  Justice of Peace, 198, 218, 219
  law, mistake of, 195
  maintenance and, 5–6, 11, 91
  malice, 189, 196, 197
  matter of action, 199–204
  military officers, 198
  ministerial officer, 175
  mistaken belief, 193
  mistake of law, 195
  motive, 178, 190
  naval officers, 198
  nolle prosequi, 183
  nonsuit, 183
  officers
    judicial, 175

Malicious prosecution (*contd.*)
  officers (*contd.*)
    military, 198
    ministerial, 175
  oral charge, 176
  perjured statement, 178
  persons, 197–199
  petty offences, 179
  plea in bar, 183
  preferring indictment, 178
  probable cause, 187–196
  proceeding civil, 202
  proof, 194
    acquittal, of, 185
    lack of reasonable cause, of,
      191–193
  prosecution
    what is, 174–181
    withdrawing, 193
  rationale of, 179
  reasonable and probable cause,
    187–196
  registration of order, 204
  reversal of conviction, 185
  scope of, 197–204
  search warrant, 203
  sheriff, arrest by, 203
  ship, arrest of, 199
  soldiers, 198
  summary proceedings, 179
  suspicion, 187–196
  termination of proceedings, 181–
    187
  trustee in bankruptcy, 177
  unpopularity, 198
  withdrawing prosecution, 193
  witness, arrest of, 203
Manutenentia
  curialis, 114
  ruralis, 114
Married woman. *See* Wife
Master, defence to maintenance, 34–
  39
Medical Council, General, 211
Merchandise marks, 231
Mesne process, arrest on, 203
Military court, 198, 206, 209–210, 212
Ministerial officers, 175, 228
Misdemeanour, compounding, 153–
  154
Misprision, 122*n.*, 147, 152
Mortgage, 77
Motive in champerty and main-
  tenance, 13–15, 114, 115

Newspaper
  contempt by, 172
  maintenance by owner of, 81
Nolle prosequi, 154, 183

254 INDEX

Offences, compounding, 146–157. *See* Compounding Offences
Officers
  court, of, 211
  military, 198, 206, 209–210, 212
  ministerial, 228
  naval, 198
Offices in fee, 228
Official Receiver, 209
Officials
  champerty by, 94
  corrupt agreements by, 138
  maintenance by, 42, 94
Outlawry, 151

Palatine, County, 209
Parishioners, 73
Parliament, address by, 215
Payment into court, 243
Perjury, 230
Petition
  bankruptcy, 140, 199–201
  election, 143
Physicians, Royal College of, 209
Pleader, deceit by, 116
Pleading
  embarrassing, 242
  frivolous, 238–243
  inconsistent, 243
  prolix, 242
  scandalous, 239
  vexatious, 238–243
Policy, public, 53, 100, 128, 129
Poor, assistance to, 40
Poor rate, 220
Praemunire, 216
Preventive proceedings, 229–243
  affidavit, 240
  appeal, security for costs of, 243
  Attorney-General, 230, 232, 235, 236
  bail, 233
  bankruptcy offences, 231
  children, offences against, 231
  civil procedure, against abuse of, 236–243
  conspiracy, 230, 232
  corruption, 231
  costs, 235
    security for, 243
  counts, joining, 234
  County Court, 239
  Court, Rules of Supreme, 240–243
  courts, inferior, 243
  criminal procedure, against abuse of, 229–236
  debtors' offences, 231
  Defence of Realm offences, 231
  demurrer, 240

Preventive proceedings (*contd.*)
  dismissing action, 240
  disorderly house, 230
  embarrassing pleading, 242
  false pretences, 230
  fiat of Attorney-General, 232
  frivolous pleading, 238–243
  gambling house, 230
  grand jury, 235
  incest, 231
  inconsistent pleading, 243
  indecent assault, 230
  indictment, vexatious, 229
  inferior courts, 243
  inherent jurisdiction, 237, 238, 240
  judge, consent of, 230, 231
  jury, grand, 235
  Justice of Peace, 230, 231, 232, 234
  libels, 231
  magistrate, 230, 231, 232, 234
  merchandise marks offences, 231
  payment into court, 243
  perjury, 230
  prohibition, writ of, 243
  prolix pleading, 242
  recognizance, 229–236
  Rules of Supreme Court, 240–243
  scandalous pleading, 239
  security for costs, 243
  sexual offences, 231
  solicitor, 241
  Solicitor-General, 230, 235
  staying action, 240
  subornation of perjury, 230
  summary interference, 238–243
  Supreme Court, Rules of, 240–243
  trade union, 241
  trustee in bankruptcy, 241
  vexatious
    civil procedure, 236–243
    criminal procedure, 229–236
    pleading, 238–243
    prosecution, 229–236
  writ of prohibition, 243
Printer, 150
Private international law, 145
Prize Court, 8
Probate action, 144
Proceeding, malicious civil, 202
Proceedings, preventive of abuse, 229–243. *See* Preventive Proceedings
Procedure
  civil, contracts affecting, 140–145. *See also* Maintenance
  criminal, contracts affecting, 117–140. *See also* Maintenance

INDEX

255

Procedure (*contd.*)
  vexatious. *See* Preventive Proceedings
Prohibition, writ of, 243
Prosecute, duty to, 121. *See* Compounding Offences, Misprision, Stifling Prosecutions
Prosecution
  discontinuing, 154. *See* Compounding Offences, Stifling Prosecutions
  malicious, 174–204. *See* Malicious Prosecution
  stifling, 117–140. *See* Stifling Prosecutions, Compounding Offences
  vexatious, 229–236
  withdrawing, 154. *See* Stifling Prosecutions, Compounding Offences
Prosecutor, in malicious prosecution, 197
Public policy, 53, 100, 128, 129

Quarter Sessions, exemption of judges, 208
Quasi-judicial functions, 211

Rate, poor, 220
Ratification, 124
Recognizance to prosecute, 229–236
Record
  court of, 209, 210
  judge of, 217
  justice of, 206
Recorder, 208
Redoubbors, 147
Register in ecclesiastical court, 227
Release of goods, 144
Reporter, contempt by, 172
Returning officer, 210
Revising barrister, 211
Reward for stolen goods, 148–149
Royal College of Physicians, 209
Rules of Supreme Court, 240–243

Scandalous pleading, 239
Scots Law, 128, 212
Search warrant, procuring, 203
Security for costs, 99, 100, 243
Serjeant, deceit of, 116
Servant, defence to maintenance, 34–39
Sexual offences, 231
Sheriff
  arrest by, 203
  champerty, 95
  contempt by, 203
  corrupt agreements, 138–140

Sheriff (*contd.*)
  judge, as, 208
  maintenance, 95, 115
Ship, procuring arrest of, 199
Society, legal aid, 144
Soldiers, 198, 206, 210, 212
Solicitors, 23–27, 52, 56–57, 96–104
  agreements, 100, 143
  assignment to, 97 sqq.
  beneficial contracts with, 96–104
  champerty, 23–27, 52, 56–57, 96–104
  chose in action, 52, 56–57
  collusion, 116
  contract, 100, 143
  conveyance to, 96–104
  Coroner, as, 213
  costs, 97, 98, 100–104
  counsel's fees, 104–106
  deceit, 116
  disability, 96–104
  fiduciary position, 97
  foreign agreement, 104
  frivolous action against, 241
  gratuitous work, 101 sqq.
  history of, 23
  indemnity, 97, 99, 101–104
  lapse of time, 99
  maintenance, 23–27, 52, 56–57, 96–104
  mortgage, 103
  pendente lite, assignment to, 98 sqq.
  professional work, 98
  purchase by, 97
  remuneration. *See* Costs, *supra*
  sale to, 99
  security for costs, 99, 100
  share in proceeds of suit, 98
  third parties, 99
  undue influence, 103
  unprofessional work, 98 sqq.
Solicitor-General, 230, 235
"Speaking with" prosecutor, 154–155
Staying action, 240
Steward, 209, 212
Stifling prosecution, 117–154
  abstention, by, 119, 122
  agreement, 119
  apology, 136
  assault, 130, 131, 133–134, 135
  assistance, by, 119
  bail, 137, 139
  civil liability, where, 120
  civil remedy, 127
  civil rights, 134
  common formerly, 121
  compassion, 123
  compromise, lawful, 120*n.*
  conspiracy, 130

256 INDEX

Stifling prosecution (*contd.*)
  conviction, after, 137*n.*
  court, consent of, 123
  discovery, 122
  duty to prosecute, 121
  Equity, 125, 126, 128
  excise laws, 137*n.*
  false imprisonment, 131
  false pretences, 135
  felony, 117–128
  forgery, 124–125
  in pari delicto, 125
  indemnity, 137, 139
  judge, consent of, 123, 131–132, 133
  lawful compromise, 120*n.*
  maintenance order, 137
  misdemeanours
    for, 127, 128–140
    public, 131, 134–135
  no reference to, 118–119
  nuisance, 130–136
  offences, petty, 128 sqq.
  officials, 138
  pardon, soliciting, 122
  perjury, 129, 130, 143
  petty offences, 128 sqq.
  poaching, 129
  postponing prosecution, 122
  prevention, by, 122
  proof, 119, 127
  public policy, 128, 129
  ratification, 124–125
  recovery of money for, 127
  reparation, 120, 122, 123
  riot, 130, 133
  Scots Law, 128
  sentence, after, 122
  sheriff, 138–140
  stage of prosecution, 122
  stranger, 123–127, 133
  theft-bote, 128
  third party, 123–127, 133
  threat, 119, 120, 121, 126
  tort, felonious, 128
  trade-mark, infringement of, 136
  undue influence, 125
  what is, 119, 121 sqq.
  withdrawing, by, 123
  See also Compounding Offences
Stolen goods, reward for, 148–149
Stratton, Adam de, 214

Subornation of perjury, 230
Summary interference of court, 238–243
Superior courts, 208, 211
Supersedeas, 226
Supreme Court
  judges, 213
  Rules of, 240–243

Tenants, maintenance by, 73
Theft-bote, 117, 128, 146–148, 151, 152
  crimes akin to, 148–150
Thorpe, William de, 214
Tithe-payers, 73
Tort, felonious, 128
Trade union, 76, 109–111, 241
Treasurer. *See* Officials
Trust, 115
Trustee, 76, 157
Trustee in bankruptcy, 241

Ultra vires, 109, 111
Undue influence, 17*n.*, 28, 103, 125, 145
University court, 209

Vexatious
  indictment, 229–236, 237
  pleading, 238–243
  procedure
    civil, 236–243
    criminal, 154, 229–236, 228–243. *See also* Preventive Proceedings
Vice-Chancellor, 209

Warrant, search, 203
Weyland, Thomas de, 214
Wife and husband, conspiracy by, 159
Wild, Jonathan, 148, 149
Wite, 151
Witness
  arrest of, 203
  criminal conspiracy, 169
  exemption of, 41, 169, 206–207, 210
Writ of
  discharge, 226
  prohibition, 243
  supersedeas, 226

For EU product safety concerns, contact us at Calle de José Abascal, 56-1°, 28003 Madrid, Spain or eugpsr@cambridge.org.

www.ingramcontent.com/pod-product-compliance
Ingram Content Group UK Ltd.
Pitfield, Milton Keynes, MK11 3LW, UK
UKHW010859060825
461487UK00012B/1245